Socio-Economic Impact of Special Economic Zones in Gujarat

This book is part of the Peter Lang Political Science, Economics, and Law list.
Every volume is peer reviewed and meets
the highest quality standards for content and production.

PETER LANG
New York • Bern • Berlin
Brussels • Vienna • Oxford • Warsaw

Shashank Shende and Mehal Pandya

Socio-Economic Impact of Special Economic Zones in Gujarat

Edited by Assis Flaviano Sequeira

PETER LANG
New York • Bern • Berlin
Brussels • Vienna • Oxford • Warsaw

Library of Congress Cataloging-in-Publication Data

Names: Shende, Shashank, author. | Pandya, Mehal, author. |
Sequeira, Assis Flaviano, editor.
Title: Socio-economic impact of special economic zones in Gujarat |
Shashank Shende and Mehal Pandya; edited by Assis Flaviano Sequeira.
Description: New York: Peter Lang, 2021.
Includes bibliographical references and index.
Identifiers: LCCN 2020050351 (print) | LCCN 2020050352 (ebook)
ISBN 978-1-4331-8437-6 (hardback) | ISBN 978-1-4331-8438-3 (ebook pdf)
ISBN 978-1-4331-8439-0 (epub)
Subjects: LCSH: Gujarat (India)—Economic conditions. | Gujarat
(India)—Social conditions. | Economic development—India—Gujarat. |
Gujarat (India)—Economic policy.
Classification: LCC HC437.G85 S49 2021 (print) | LCC HC437.G85 (ebook) |
DDC 330.954/75—dc23
LC record available at https://lccn.loc.gov/2020050351
LC ebook record available at https://lccn.loc.gov/2020050352
DOI 10.3726/b18586

Bibliographic information published by **Die Deutsche Nationalbibliothek**.
Die Deutsche Nationalbibliothek lists this publication in the "Deutsche
Nationalbibliografie"; detailed bibliographic data are available
on the Internet at http://dnb.d-nb.de/.

Contents

List of Tables

List of Figures

List of Appendices

Acknowledgements

I am indeed indebted to the lovely people, who have held my hand and patted my back giving me the confidence to complete this book. The research leading to this book and my life bears the imprints of their friendship and comradeship. I shall remain forever grateful to each one of them.

I have to express my gratitude to my research guide and co-author of this book, Dr. Mehal Pandya, Associate Professor, B.K. School of Professional and Management Studies, Gujarat University, for mentoring and guiding me in this journey.

I am also grateful to the editor of this book, Mr. Assis F Sequeira, for his patience and perseverance in contributing to this research-based book.

I have to acknowledge and thank Prof. Dr. Sharad Gaikwad for his constant guidance in this journey. My friends Mr. Ankur Kumar Sharma and Dhiren Charania assisted in statistical methods and tools for Findings and Data Interpretation. Mr. Jitendra Bindal painstakingly assisted throughout my academic journey. Without their help, this book would not have been possible.

Shri Rajkumar IRS (Retd.), Head, Western Region Export Promotion Council for EOUs and SEZ (EPCES) has given me constant support during the period of my study. Dr. Amiya Chandra ITS and the then Zonal Development Commissioner KASEZ extended valuable assistance and guidance in collection of data. The inputs from the firm executives, developers and stakeholders in SEZs in the form of responses to the questionnaires are valuable indeed.

In a book of this nature, I am indebted to so many persons that a complete acknowledgement would be encyclopaedic. Some scholars are acknowledged through references in the text. I am specially indebted to my colleagues, particularly Satyadeep, Avinash, Jivendra, Tarun, Ashesh, Kundan, Neeraj and Bhavesh. I am very grateful to the team at Peter Lang especially Michelle Smith, Ashita Shah, Jacqueline Pavlovic and Malini Harikumar for their unstinted cooperation and patience. I am grateful to my daughter Sanya for taking the pain to create and design the cover page of this book.

Finally, my wife Dr. Anamika Shende, MBBS and my daughters Anoushkha and Sanya have been my pillars of strength in this sojourn!

Dr. Shashank Digamber Shende

Abbreviations

AD	Authorized Dealer
AGOA	African Growth and Opportunity Act
AHIDZs	Agricultural Hi-Tech Industrial Demonstration Zone
AI	Artificial Intelligence
AR	Augmented Reality
ASEAN	Association of South East Asian Nations
BECZs	Border/Cross Border Economic Cooperation Zone
BoA	Board of Approval
BOT	Board of Trade
BRI	Belt and Road Initiative
CAGR	Compound Annual Growth Rate
CEO	Chief Executive Officer
CHAID	Chi Square Automatic Interaction Detection
CPEC	China-Pakistan Economic Corridor
CSEZ	Cochin Special Economic Zone
CSR	Corporate Social Responsibility
DC	Development Commissioner
DCS	Distributed Control Systems
DDT	Dividend Distribution Tax

DGFT	Directorate General of Foreign Trade
DICA	Directorate of Investment and Company Administration
DIPP	Department of Promotion and Internal Trade
DSL	Dahej SEZ limited
DTA	Domestic Tariff Area
DTR	Daily Transaction Report
EC	Export Commissioner
EDF	Export Declaration Form
EOU	Export Oriented Unit
EPCES	Export Promotion Council for EOUs & SEZ Units
EPI	Export Preparedness Index
EPZ	Export Processing Zone
ETDZ	Economic and Technological Development Zone
EU	European Union
EXIM	Export Import Policy
EZ	Economic Zone
FCA	Foreign Controlled Affiliates
FDI	Foreign Direct Investment
FEMA	Foreign Exchange Management Act 1999
FETERS	Foreign Exchange Transactions Electronic Reporting System
FP	Free Ports
FSEZ	Falta Special Economic Zone
FTA	Free Trade Area
FTAs	Free Trade Agreements
FTWZ	Free Trade and Warehousing Zone
FTZ	Free Trade Zone
GCC	Gulf Cooperation Council
GDP	Gross Domestic Product
GIDC	Gujarat Industrial Development Corporation
GIFT	Gujarat International Finance Tech-City
GMS	Greater Mekong Sub-Region
GPS	Global Positioning System
GSDP	Gross State Domestic Product
GSP	Generalized System of Preferences
GVCs	Global Value Chains
HDPE	High Density Polyethylene
HIDZ	High-tech Industrial Development Zone
IFSCs	International Financial Services Centres

ILO	International Labour Organization
IoT	Internet of Things
IRDAI	Insurance Regulatory and Development Authority of India
IT/ITeS	Information Technology/Information Technology-Enabled Services
ITI	Industrial Training Institute
JICA	Japan International Cooperation Agency
KASEZ	Kandla Special Economic Zone
LDPE	Low-Density Polyethylene
LHE	Liquid Handling Equipment
LoA	Letter of Approval
LRT	Likelihood Ratio Test
MAT	Minimum Alternative Tax
MDG	Millennium Development Goals
MEPZ	Madras Export Processing Zone
MIHAN	Multi-Modal International Cargo Hub and Airport at Nagpur
MoC	Ministry of Commerce
MSEZ	Madras Special Economic Zone
MSME	Micro, Small and Medium Enterprise
NCR	National Capital Region
NEPZ	Noida Special Economic Zone
NFE	Net Foreign Exchange
NIP	National Industrial Policy
NVA	Net Value Added
ODA	Official Development Assistance
OFDI	Outward Foreign Direct Investment
OGL	Open General License
ONGC	Oil and Natural Gas Commission
PET	Polyethylene Terephthalate
PLC	Programmable Logic Control
PPP	Public-Private Partnership
PRC	People's Republic of China
PSP	Private Sector Participation
R&D	Research and Development
RBI	Reserve Bank of India
RCEP	Regional Comprehensive Economic Partnership
RTA	Regional Trade Agreement
SCZ	Special Customs Zone
SDGs	Sustainable Development Goals

SEBI	Securities and Exchange Board of India
SEEPZ	Santacruz Electronic Export Processing Zone
SEZ	Special Economic Zone
SIA	Socio-Economic Impact Assessment
SME	Small- and Medium-Sized Enterprise
SSEZ	Sustainable Special Economic Zone
SURSEZ	Surat Special Economic Zone
TAD	Territories of Advanced Development
TFP	Total Factor Productivity
THZs	National Tourist and Holiday Resorts
TIES	Trade Infrastructure for Export Scheme
TIZs	Taiwanese Investment Zone
TQM	Total Quality Management
UNCTAD	United Nation Conference on Trade and Development
UNIDO	United Nations Industrial Development Organization
USD	United States Dollar
VR	Virtual Reality
ZLD	Zero Liquid Discharge

1

Special Economic Zones: An Overview

Socio-economic development is measured by indicators like GDP, literacy, life expectancy and levels of employment. The transition from agrarian to industrial and post-industrial societies is marked by remarkable improvements in all the indicators of socio-economic development. Special Economic Zones (SEZs) called by other names (including free zones, export processing zones and industrial parks) play a pivotal role in socio-economic development. The main objectives of SEZs are to generate additional economic activities, create employment, promote investment from domestic and foreign sources and promote export of goods and services. Thus, socio-economic development is an unstated goal of SEZs. Presently, SEZs in some form or other are present in more than 147 economies around the world. This chapter covers the background on Special Economic Zones globally. The rationale and theory of socio-economic development and also its impact in SEZs are touched upon. It dwells briefly on the impact of Foreign Direct Investment (FDI) and Regional Trade Agreements. The chapter also covers general definition and objectives of SEZs in the context of the global and Indian scenario with an historical overview.

1.1 Background

It is a fact that socio-economic development is not uniform even in case of a small country or a state. Historical factors, cultural mores and natural resources all influence the pace of development. When there is variation even under a single legal set up, the chasm existing between different economies is vast. This was realised by the governments across the world. One way to address this problem is to provide a level playing field to the local entrepreneur by carving out land parcels and designating such parcels of land as Special Economic Zones (SEZs). These parcels of land are governed by fiscal and legal regulation on par with the foreign competition. Subsequently, SEZs also emerged as a favoured route to attract FDI (Foreign Direct Investment) given the investment crunch in the host country and the attraction of doing business, unencumbered by taxing fiscal regulations and laws, as applicable to the rest of the country.

Thus, the main characteristic of a SEZ is that it a geographically delimited area, within which government facilitates industrial activity through fiscal and regulatory incentives and infrastructure support. SEZs go by many names like Free Trade Area (FTA), Free Trade Zone (FTZ), and Economic Zone (EZ) and come in varieties and sizes. Within a defined perimeter, SEZs function under a regulatory regime for business and investors distinct from what normally applies in the broader national or sub-national economy, where they are established.

SEZs originated from Free Zones, which are essentially separate customs territories. Hence, most inputs for SEZs are exempted from custom duties and tariffs; the basic premise being that the manufactured goods would be exported to other countries. Governments not only sacrifice revenue by extending customs, fiscal and regulatory concessions, but also invest by providing support measures and physical structure. In return, the governments expect that SEZs create jobs, boost exports, diversify the economy and build productive capacity.

The historical trend in SEZs is shown in Figure 1.1. Though the SEZs were established in the 1960s, the widespread use of export-oriented industrial development strategy especially in Asia led to the mushrooming of SEZs in the 1980s. Many global manufacturers resorted to offshore production to leverage cost advantage in labour and transport. Subsequently, the rapid growth of Global Value Chains (GVCs), a highlight of the industrial growth in the 1990s and 2000s, led to a spurt in new SEZs. The growth has belied expectations that the new global trade order would curtail SEZs as most of the SEZs are export-based. In fact, the last financial crisis spurred more SEZs and new types of SEZs. There are nearly 5,400 SEZs at present, more than 1,000 of which were established in

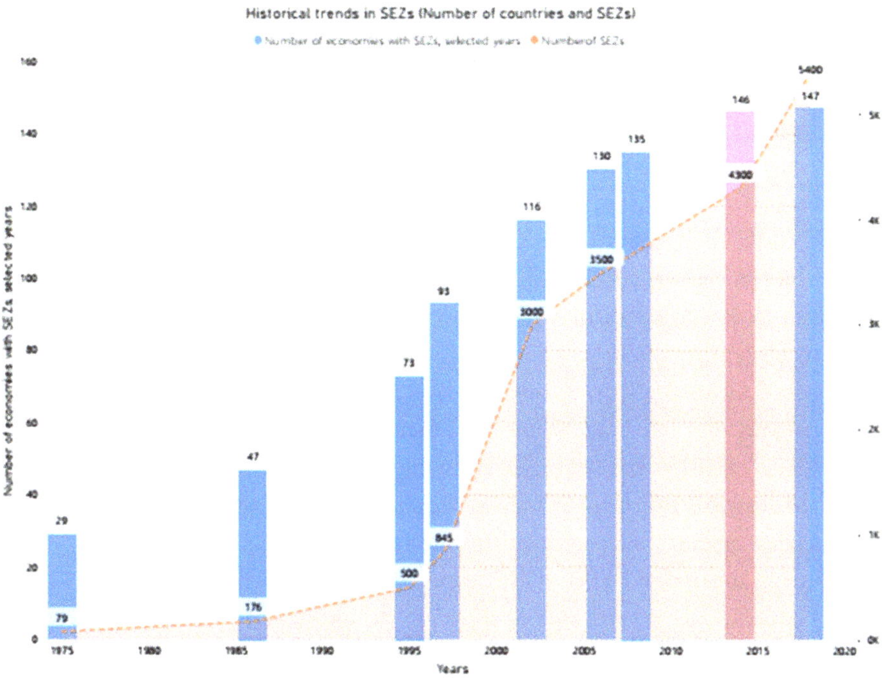

Figure 1.1: Historical Trend in SEZs
Source: UNCTAD: WORLD INVESTMENT REPORT 2019

the last five years. At least 500 more zones (approximately 10 per cent of the current total) have been announced and are expected to open in the coming years.

Notwithstanding the enthusiasm for SEZs by governments around the globe, the impact of these zones is often mixed. No doubt there are a few highly successful SEZs that have shaped the transformation of regions and people. At the same time, even in the same countries where some SEZs have been astounding successes, other SEZs have languished and failed to attract investor interest. There are cases where the zones are established and remain unutilised for decades together or are only partly utilised, thus locking precious land resource. Another criticism is that in some instances the SEZs may have created jobs through investments and generated exports, but the expectation that they would also have a pull effect on the broader economy remains unfulfilled and they remain islands of affluence in a sea of poverty.

In such a scenario, people grudge the special consideration given to the SEZs; the fact that SEZs are exempted from the tedious labour regulations as applicable to units outside SEZs rankles DTA (domestic tariff area) businessmen and others; it must be admitted, however, that the wages in SEZs are uniformly higher than those prevailing in industries surrounding the SEZs. Nonetheless, there is no significant difference in the rate of attrition between SEZ and outside SEZ.

In Asia, the first EPZ was set up in Kandla, India, as early as 1965. Currently, India as on 31.01.2021 has 378 SEZs notified, of which 265 SEZs are operational, engaged in manufacturing and services. The SEZ activity is not uniformly spread across the country but concentrated more in the south and west of India.

The total investment in SEZs in India up to 31.12.2020 is more than INR 6,077 billion. SEZs accounted for direct employment of over 2.28 million people as on 31.12.2020 and exports of over INR 5,534 billion in the period from April to December 2020.

According to the figures released by DIPP (Department for Promotion of Industry and Internal Trade), Foreign Direct Investment (FDI) in India totalled USD 49,977 million last year thus showing growth of 13 per cent over previous year. The impetus for the growth was the simplifying of the approval procedures in areas like defence, telecommunications and security equipment.

During the period FY06–FY12, exports from SEZs in India grew at a CAGR of 59 per cent. The growth rate declined in the subsequent years owing to withdrawal of tax incentives. Among the dark clouds visible in the horizon is the onset of income tax sunset in incentive regime and ongoing land acquisition protests resulting in idle land. Notwithstanding the above, SEZs are here to stay. The key is to revamp their "Special" parameter, transforming current zones into multi-activity zones by consolidation of manufacturing and service sectors.

1.2 Definition

In broad terms, SEZs can be termed as demarcated geographic areas (enclaves) contained within the country's boundaries; such enclaves are exempted from the laws as applicable to the rest of the country. The terminology used across countries varies widely, with the most common terms—Free Zones, SEZs, Free Trade Zones, Export Processing Zones, Free Economic Zones and Free ports—all used interchangeably.

The most common understanding of SEZs is centred on three exclusive criteria:

- A clearly demarcated geographical area,
- A regulatory regime distinct from the rest of the economy (most often customs and fiscal rules, but potentially covering other relevant regulations, such as foreign ownership rules, access to land or employment rules), and

- Benefits for units within the SEZ which are not available for those units outside the SEZ.

SEZs rules deal with:

- Investment conditions: covering, serviced land and flexible lease, purchasing option and provision of infrastructure,
- International trade and customs–duty-free imported inputs,
- Taxation: elimination of various taxes like corporate taxes, VAT, MAT, etc., and
- The regulatory environment—ONE-STOP SHOP arrangement, efficient processes for company formation, licensing and operations.

United Nations Industrial Development Organization (UNIDO, 2015) defines "SEZ" as the designated estate where trade laws such as tariffs, quotas, and duties differ from the rest of the country.

SEZ is also defined as the geographically delimited area, usually physically secured (fenced-in) with single management/administration and with eligibility for benefits based upon physical location, which is also benefited with separate customs area and streamlined procedures (FIAS, 2008).

Thus, on the above criteria, structural features incorporated in the model of Special Economic Zones include: (FIAS, 2008; Farole, 2011):

Delimited Area—SEZ is designated as a foreign territory within the customs territory of a nation; SEZ operates under a liberal legal framework.

Single Management/Administration—The administration of a SEZ consists of a dedicated governance structure, acting as a Single Window mechanism or One-Stop Shop for hassle-free operations in the interest of the investors.

High Quality Infrastructure—Zones are normally established at strategic locations having good connectivity, logistics and other basic infrastructure amenities necessary for economic activities, like barren land (real estate), potable water, hospital, educational facilities, roads and telecommunications.

Eligibility for Benefits (Duty-free benefits)—Zones are benefitted from various types of fiscal benefits and tax exemptions including duty-free import of raw and intermediate materials and capital equipment.

Flexible Labour Laws—Various economies provide flexible labour laws as compared to Domestic Tariff Area for hassle-free working and level playing field to compete globally as bulk of the output from the SEZs is exported.

Table 1.1: SEZs: General Definitions

General Definitions	EXAMPLES
Geographical location Special regulatory regime Economic activity	**Poland:** a separated, uninhabited part of the territory, on which a business activity may be conducted in accordance with the rules of the Act. **Pakistan:** a geographically defined and delimited area that has been notified and approved for economic, industrial and commercial activities. **Indonesia:** zones with certain boundaries within the territory that are designated to carry out an economic function and are granted certain facilities and incentives. **Gambia:** any area designated as a free zone where goods and services are deemed, insofar as import duties and taxes are concerned, as being outside the customs territory, where the benefits provided under the law apply.

Source: UNCTAD: WORLD INVESTMENT REPORT 2019

Presently, about 90 percent of SEZs laws incorporate general definition of a SEZ; some laws have specific definitions of SEZs. Table 1.1 depicts in brief examples of general definitions and types.

1.3 Objectives

Globally, almost 61 percent of SEZs laws define the objectives of the zones. Common goal of any economy is quantitative growth followed by dynamic growth objectives followed by socio-economic objectives.

Quantitative growth goals cover investments (FDI), promoting trade, increasing exports or generating employment. Dynamic growth objectives focus on industrial upgrading, economic diversification, skill development, innovation and structural changes as well as integration into value chains.

Socio-economic objectives include sustainable development, quality of employment, spillover effects, women empowerment, environmental protection and others.

In India, the SEZs policy was launched in April 2000. The Special Economic Zones Act, 2005, passed by the Parliament in May 2005 received presidential assent on 23 June 2005. The SEZs Rules, 2006, came into effect on 10 February 2006. The principal objectives behind setting up SEZs in the country include:

1. Generation of additional economic activities;
2. Promotion of exports of goods and services;
3. Promotion of investment from domestic and foreign sources;
4. Creation of employment opportunities; and
5. Development of infrastructure facilities

1.4 Features

Most economies have introduced incentives schemes in SEZs to attract Foreign Direct Investments (FDI). Incentives could be fiscal or non-fiscal in nature. Incentives help to overcome the constraints or barriers to investment. The incentive schemes are outlined in greater detail below.

1.4.1 Fiscal and Financial Incentives

Fiscal incentives relate to exemption or reduction of taxes or duties, lower customs tariffs, ease of profit repatriation and/or the provision of specific subsidies, for example, financial assistance for infrastructure development or land purchases.

Financial incentives consist of financial support to units to compensate for the disadvantages of the location and can often include investment in infrastructure to alleviate site challenges or contributions to meet training, relocation or land costs.

Typical fiscal and financial incentives observed in global SEZ development include:

- Income tax allowances;
- Exemption of exported products from export duties;
- Exemption of exported products from indirect taxes;
- Exemption of imported goods used in production processes from import duties;
- Exemption of waste generated by the production process from export duties;
- Exemption of goods stored in the SEZ from duties and indirect taxes; and
- Exemptions from other non-specific tax subsidies, including taxes imposed by national, regional and local authorities.

1.4.2 Non-Fiscal Incentives

Apart from the fiscal and financial incentives as stated above, many countries offer non-fiscal incentives to attract investors due to stiff competition. These incentives are mostly related to "Ease of Doing" business operations within the SEZs.

Typical non-fiscal incentives can include:

- Single-window fast track clearances;
- Simplified export-import procedures and customs clearances;
- Ease of restriction on foreign workers;
- Repatriation of profits;
- 100% foreign ownership; and
- Allowing sale of goods to the domestic tariff area.

1.4.3 The Regulatory and Institutional Framework for SEZs

SEZs can be characterised by three different attributes:

i) A dedicated regulatory regime,
ii) A dedicated physical infrastructure, and
iii) A dedicated governance structure.

1.4.3.1 Regulatory Framework

The establishment as well as dissolution of SEZs are regulated by legal framework enacted at different levels of governance. The SEZs regulatory framework deals with number of issues mainly concerned with investment, trade promotion and facilitation, taxation, land as well as labour and environmental issues. Thus, a country's specific industrial structures, growth opportunities and all such matters are covered separately under special regulatory regime for SEZs with a dedicated institutional set-up. Rules and regulations that apply in SEZs are framed in SEZ-specific legislation in the form of SEZ laws and decrees as shown in Figure 1.2.

1.4.3.2 Institutional Framework

1.4.3.2.1 Key Stakeholders The institutional set-up of SEZs varies from nation to nation and it depends upon the country-specific economic, regulatory, political and administrative systems. There is no uniform institutional model for SEZs. However, globally SEZs regimes have adopted some common features concerning the stakeholders as shown in Table 1.2.

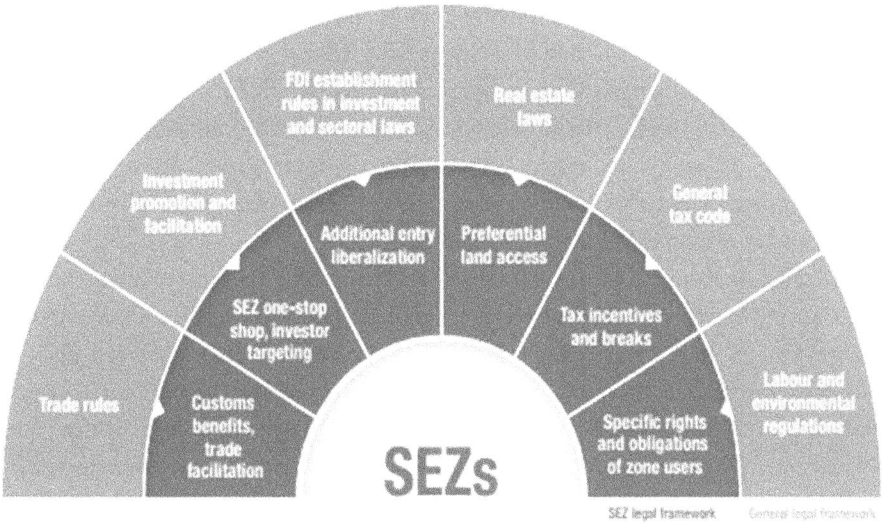

Figure 1.2: Main Elements of the Regulatory Framework of SEZs
Source: UNCTAD: WORLD INVESTMENT REPORT 2019

Table 1.2: Main Stakeholders in SEZ Regimes

Stakeholders	Main functions (selected)
Government	• Adopts SEZ-relevant policies and supervises its implementation. • Establishes specific SEZs through decrees.
SEZ Authority	• Conducts strategic planning and assessment. • Licenses private sector stakeholders.
Zone developer	• Provides essential infrastructure. • Makes land arrangements.
Zone operator	• Manages and administers a zone. • Promotes a zone and selects zone users.
Zone user	• Invests and undertakes business activities in a zone.

Source: UNCTAD: WORLD INVESTMENT REPORT 2019

i) Government: It plays a pivotal role in framing the SEZs policies in line with country's national mission of development, adopts favourable industrial policies and achieves the desired goals by establishing the SEZs. Government has to ensure coordination of national relevant policy and its international obligations; government allocates necessary support like budgetary allocation, personnel and assistance to the SEZs. Government can establish SEZs through individual decree and is responsible for overall administration.

ii) SEZ authority: Most countries have set up SEZ authority under the law. Such an authority is a specialised agency or state-owned agency supervised or manned by the host government officials. The authority coordinates zone policies and initiates related programmes and acts in responsible manner for strategic planning, zone-related issues and for overall developmental activities of the zone. The authority acts as the catalyst between the local economy and government by giving suggestions, and acting directly or indirectly for issuance of approvals and permits within the zones.

iii) Zone developers: They are responsible for establishment of SEZs by way of land purchase or public authorities can allot the land through them. Thus, land arrangements and provision of essential infrastructure are the main functions of zone developers. Economies have worked out different models of zone developer, for example, public model (government), private model (private) and hybrid model (public-private partnership) SEZs depending upon their strength and requirements. Zone developers are also responsible for the day-to-day operation of SEZs.

iv) Zone operators: Some countries have adopted a separate entity as zone operators. They are responsible for selling space and attracting FDI to the zone. They act in concert with investment promotion agencies of the government or others. Infrastructure assistance activities such as security, maintenance, water supply, telecommunication and electricity are other areas taken care of by the operators. They also provide additional specialised services like one-stop shops, training centres, consultancy desks, focal point of recruitment and provision for office space and conference facilities. They could undertake other welfare activity programme like health care, education, transport, housing and recreation facilities with the assistance of local administration.

v) Zone user: Finally, zone user is the ultimate and direct beneficiary of the special regulatory regime instituted in each zone. The zone user brings to the table his domain expertise, effective and efficient productivity, trading capacity and skill-upgradation. All of these are critical factors for a successful SEZ.

1.5 Theoretical Approaches to SEZs

Economists have postulated different theories in the search for an explanation of the SEZ phenomenon; some of the theories are outlined below to get a better understanding of SEZs.

1.5.1 The Neo-Classical Approach

The Neo-Classical Economic Approach (also referred to as Orthodox Approach) considers SEZ as a tool which enables Free Trade policies with the goal of promoting trade. The fundamental postulate of this theory is free trade, which is the best policy for any economy to adopt and to flourish. Since the policy of Free Trade may not be politically acceptable, it is best to carve out some areas for establishing SEZs.

The theory predicts that in a longer period of time, SEZs will have negative impact. SEZs result in unfair competition between domestic and SEZ units, distort trade patterns and loss of revenue to government. Hence SEZs are productive only when government of that country uses SEZs as the platform to usher in regime of nil or minimum trade restrictions to build the economy.

The role of SEZs should be of a catalyst in transforming the inward-looking economy based on import substitution to a healthy outward-looking free trade economy. SEZs loose significance as countries implement macroeconomic reforms in trade and exchange rate regime.

Studies have reported a considerable growth of SEZs across various economies which adopted trade and economic reforms in the rest of the economy. Thus, SEZs are not a vehicle to promote liberalization but are an outcome of liberalization (Madani, 1999; Aggarwal, 2010).

1.5.2 The Political Economy Approach

Buchanan and Tullock propounded the "Public Choice Theory" which focuses on people's decision-making process within the political realm. They used both the fields of Economics and Political Science to help develop public choice. It was argued that by examining the behaviour of the voters and the politicians, their actions would be predictable. This theory holds that individual behaviour within the political system is motivated by incentives similar to those motivating behavior in the private sector. Hence there is government intervention for promoting capitalist interest groups for rent seeking. According to this approach, the objective of the SEZ policy is to facilitate land acquisition and provide fiscal benefits to a few capitalists and to generate rent at the cost of the rest of the population, thus spending income collected through taxes on select groups rather than spending for overall welfare.

1.5.3 The Heterodox Approach

This approach views SEZs as a result of a mix of market-government interventions, in which the government plays an important role in contributing in investment, technology upgradation, human capital formation, and institutional and promotion of policy reforms (Chang, 2002).

SEZs are the best tools to attract FDI for obtaining new technology and managerial skills. They can bridge the gap between the host country and the international community in the fields of technology, management practices and human skills. The host country provides congenial business environment, excellent infrastructure and logistics, friendly business policies, good governance, skilled and unskilled manpower, strategic location, and fiscal and non-fiscal incentives to attract the foreign entrepreneurs. SEZs can thus become a One-Stop Shop that provides opportunity for learning, improvement and transformation through the flow of technology, knowledge and skills.

1.5.4 The Global Value Chain Approach

Many economies including India have embraced the concept of trade liberalization and globalization considering the world as Global Village. The slogan of "Local Touch, Global Brands" is in vogue and has led to Global Value Chain (GVC) process. The whole process from Mines to Market strategy has been sliced and every stage and process has been dissected at micro-level to obtain the competitive edge in raw material costs, resources used like power and labour, either through offshore outsourcing and/or offshoring. Sub-contracting partly/wholly production process to specialized firms abroad is a good example of offshore outsourcing; shifting production base to another country through affiliates (FDI) is offshoring.

However, in the longer run, it is necessary to integrate domestic firms in the GVC. The host country needs to adopt economic policies that are favourable to investment and to remove infrastructural bottlenecks. In addition, the host country should set rules, standards, regulations and processes that are in harmony with regional, domestic, regional, bilateral and international practices. Then only the domestic firms will be in a position to integrate within these networks.

In this context, SEZs are poised to facilitate the integration into global value chain through both offshoring and offshore-outsourcing. SEZs thus promote both domestic and foreign direct investment.

1.5.5 Agglomeration Economies Approach

SEZs are set up in industrial clusters to obtain the benefit of agglomeration. The units in the SEZs basically produce goods for exports and the units could be either foreign or local. Through the agglomeration approach, the optimum benefit is derived from Global Value Chains for enhancing the productivity through technology synchronization. It could also result in product innovation due to the deployment of hi-skilled talent combined with the support of academic and other related institutions.

Demand conditions and supporting industries, firm's structure, strategy and rivalry are drivers for success of clusters (ibid).

The process of globalization has given birth to global megacities that club resources at local, national and global scales. In this context, SEZs can be a catalyst for smooth integration of the domestic economy into the global economy and to enhance productivity of resources through knowledge spillovers, technology diffusion and demonstration effects by exploiting agglomeration economies (Aggarwal, 2007).

1.6 Socio-Economic Development

The way of understanding of the development concept in economics has metamorphosed from economic development to socio-economic development. Development has been defined in numerous ways and there is no consensus on this issue in economics (Piontek, 2010, p.117). Generally, development could be understood as a process of change or as an objective (Bellu, 2011, p. 2). The development concept in economic theory got updated with the changes in economic discipline by economists of different epochs: from economic growth, through economic development to socio-economic development.

The basic concepts of development economics are listed below:

1. **Economic growth:** It represents increase of volume of goods and services that are produced in real terms: this process involves quantitative changes.
2. **Economic development**: It is a broader term as it encompasses both quantitative and qualitative changes, for example, transformation of production structure, implementation of new methods of management of resources: economic development increases opportunities of economic growth as it allows to achieve higher trajectory of the latter (Fritz, 2004, p. 2; Kubiczek, 2014).
3. **Social development**: This phenomenon is associated with qualitative changes in social structure, including, among others, social integrity and social trust: it changes opportunities of individuals whose goal is to achieve higher social status (Fritz, 2004, p. 2).
4. **Socio-economic development:** It is a process of quantitative, qualitative and structural changes that are the result of actions of subjects taken within social (economic) practice. The changes influence life conditions in the field of:

> Material condition—to satisfy need associated with consumption of goods and services. It is related with the phenomena of economic growth, economic structure and entrepreneurship, access to public goods and services (that results in change of education level, a way of taking care of someone's health, etc.), relations within social systems (integration between individuals, trust, security, social conflicts), environment condition, and life satisfaction. (Stemplowski, 1987, p. 5; Chojnicki, 2010, pp. 7–9; UNDP, 2012; Bellu, 2011, pp. 5–6)

Presently, the preferred definition of development and factors influencing are drawn from mainly documents of international institutions (e.g. Development Agencies, UNDP, FAO, and International Monetary Fund, World Bank) and declaration of countries that cooperate in order to achieve development goals (Bellu, 2011, p. 7).

Millennium Development Goals (MDGs), proposed by UNDP (2000), encompass reduction of poverty, health, sustainable use of resources, education, food security and good governance.

The Sustainable Development Goals (SDGs), also known as the Global Goals, were adopted by the member states of United Nations in 2015 as a universal call to action to end poverty, protect the planet and ensure that all people enjoy peace and prosperity by 2030. The SDGs are based on a more holistic understanding of development than the Millennium Development Goals (MDGs). The seventeen SDGs are interlinked—that is, action in one area will affect outcomes in other areas, and development must balance social, economic and environmental sustainability.

Socio-economic development is associated not only with humanitarianism but also philosophical and sociological ideas concerning equality of possibilities. Obviously, taking care of environment and realizing of the role of social capital are significant factors too (Fritz, 2004, p. 2).

1.7 Socio-Economic Impacts: Concepts

The concept of Socio-Economic Impact Assessment (SIA) was developed in the 1970s and 1980s mainly in relation to the assessment of the impacts of major resource development projects such as nuclear power stations in the USA, hydro-electric schemes in Canada and UK's North Sea oil and gas–related developments. The growing interest in socio-economic impact was partly stimulated by the introduction of the US National Environmental Policy Act of 1969 and subsequent studies and publication including the works of Wolf (1974), Lang and Armour (1981), Carley and Bustelo (1984), and Finsterbusch (1980, 1985). Wolf (1974), one of the pioneers of SIA, adopted the definition of SIA as "the estimating and appraising of the conditions of a society organised and changed by the large scale application of high technology". Bowles (1981) has a similar definition: "the systematic advanced appraisal of the impacts on the day to day quality of life of people and communities when the environment is affected by development or policy change".

A recent study by Inter-organisational Committee on guidelines and principles for social assessment (1994) defines social impacts as "the consequence to human populations of any public or private actions that alter the ways which people live, work, play, relate to one another, organise to meet their needs and generally cope as members of society". Social impacts are the people impacts of development actions. Social impact assessments focus on the human dimension of environments, and seek to identify the impacts on people. An overview of what to include is outlined in Table 1.3.

Table 1.3: What to Include—Types of Socio-Economic Impacts

1. **Direct Economic**
    - Local and non-local employment
    - Characteristics of employment (e.g. skill group)
    - Labour supply and training
    - Wage levels
2. **Indirect/wider economic/expenditure**
    - Employee retail expenditure
    - Linked suppliers to main development
    - Labour market pressures
    - Wider multiplier effects
3. **Demographic**
    - Change in population size (temporary and permanent)
    - Change in other population characteristics (e.g. family size, income levels, and socio-economic groups)
    - Settlement patterns
4. **Housing**
    - Various housing tenure types
    - Public and private
    - House prices
    - Homelessness and other housing problems
5. **Other local services**
    - Public and private sector
    - Educational services
    - Health services: social support
    - Others (e.g. police, fire, recreation, transport)
6. **Socio-cultural**
    - Lifestyle/quality of life
    - Gender issues: family structures
    - Social problems (e.g. crime, illness, drunkenness, divorce)
    - Community stress and conflict: integration, cohesion and alienation

Source: Methods of Environmental Impact Assessment—Peter Morris & Riki Therivel (2001)

1.8 Foreign Direct Investment and SEZs

The transformation of a developing economy to a developed economy is accelerated by infusion of FDI on a large scale. Developing economies lack internal financial resources to build and develop their economies. FDI flows are however selective, since the investor seeks both higher return than that available in the country of origin and a reasonable level of security of the investment. It is in this context that SEZs provide a viable option for attracting FDI under the concept of cluster-specific industries. The prosperity of a location largely depends on the productivity of the units located there, what they manufacture and what competition they face among them. Units which are located in same geographical area and close to knowledge sources function in more productive and efficient manner leading to higher growth and profitability of units as compared to units in dispersed areas.

This is mainly attributed to the high level of clustering that drives knowledge creation through spillovers under the conditions that those firms are somehow near to their production frontier (Porter, 1990; Porter, 1998; Martin & Ottaviano; 1999).

Determinants of FDI depend on many factors like host country's rating, natural resources, skilled manpower availability, export/import policy, governance and so on.

Poor countries with low level of labour productivity may fail to attract FDI inflow, while the level of workforce skill and education is a major determinant of FDI to the host country (Lucas, 1990; Dunning et al.,1998; Zhang & Markusen, 1999).

The sophistication and productivity with which units compete in a location is strongly influenced by size of the unit itself in terms of revenue growth, initial capital invested, technology transfer and upgrading of manpower. Two important effects of multinational establishment or host economies cluster can be distinguished. First, they can trigger the emergence of new clusters, and second, they can stimulate development of existing clusters. Development can be seeded and reinforced by inward FDI where SEZs serve this purpose very well (Porter, 1998).

Economists tend to favour the free flow of capital across national borders because it allows investors to seek out the highest rate of return. Feldstein (2000) and Razin and Sadka (2007) note that:

- FDI facilitates the transfer of technology—particularly in the form of new varieties of capital inputs—that cannot be ordinarily achieved through financial investments or trade in goods and services.

- Recipients of FDI often gain employee training thus contributing to human capital development in the host country.
- Global integration of capital markets can contribute to the spread of best practices in corporate governance.

Though SEZs give a boost to investment, exports and jobs, they are neither a pre-condition nor a guarantee for an above-average performance on FDI and GVC participation. Some studies reveal that the overall impact on economic growth tends to be temporary and after a period, most zones grow at the same rate as the host economies.

Investment attraction. SEZs play an important role in attracting FDI and compensate to some extent for an adverse investment climate. Unfortunately, the impact of zones on FDI—and especially on additional FDI that would not have been attracted without SEZs—is hard to measure because of scarce data. Countries and international statistics (including UNCTAD's FDI data) do not track investment in zones separately from investment outside zones, and SEZs themselves mostly do not register foreign investment flows separately.

1.9 Regional Trade Agreements and SEZs

Bulk of the world trade is through the mechanism of trade agreements, which lay the framework for both bilateral and multilateral cooperation between countries and promote trade based on comparative advantage and other factors. Such trade agreements cover SEZs too. These agreements cover other areas like government procurement, investments, intellectual property, competition policy, labour, environment, state-owned enterprises and regulatory provisions. Sometimes SEZ-related policies are tweaked to align with the rules covering these areas. The details of bilateral Free Trade Agreements (FTA) and Preferential Trade Agreements (PTA) are annexed in Appendix 1.A.

India has a FTA with ASEAN that came into effect from mid-2015. India has Generalized System of Preferences (GSP) with major trading partners like the USA and the EU. Most Favored Nation status has been accorded to the neighbouring countries and major trading partners like China and Russia. In services sector too India has worked out bilateral trade with Japan, Malaysia, Singapore and South Korea. Some of the trade agreements signed by India with service chapters are compiled and shown in Appendix 1.B.

Two types of interests are at play when SEZs are considered in the Regional Trade Agreements (RTA) context.

(i) Countries that host SEZs typically seek to have as few constraints as possible to create and administer SEZs (e.g. by protecting policy space to provide incentives, introduce industrial policy requirements and transition SEZs to focus on sustainable development). Other RTA members, however, have an interest in preventing partner countries' SEZs from hampering their own competitiveness and economic performance (e.g. "free riders" from outside the RTA areas or products whose production process benefits from SEZ support). Countries' interests are not necessarily static, as new SEZs may appear while others are being phased out. Therefore, developing balanced rules benefits all RTA partners. The great majority of regular RTA provisions apply to SEZs in the same manner as they apply to the remainder of a party's territory.

(ii) Sometimes, however, RTAs include rules that explicitly refer to SEZs; such rules are normally rare. Such rules include definitions, reaffirmations of treaty obligations, exceptions or reservations from obligations, provisions on institutional cooperation, or rules setting out specific SEZ-focused content. Some rules specific to SEZs set out how products originating from partner countries' SEZs should be treated upon importation. Others modify general rules of origin for products originating from SEZs (by making them more stringent) (Koyama, 2011).

1.10 Synopsis

Social development is the desired result of economic growth. Developed as well as emerging economies are establishing various programmes and welfare schemes for overall development and better quality of life.

SEZs are growth engines for the socio-economic growth of the country. Although, India pioneered in establishment of EPZs in Asia almost half a century back, subsequent progress has been tardy. Globally, foreign direct investment has emerged as a driver for growth of SEZs; in India, however, SEZs have failed to attract foreign investors on the expected scale. This could be partly attributed to the lack of institutional authority and administrative procedures characterized by chaotic environment for industries to operate. India should view SEZs as integral component of country's economic basket. The SEZs should be re-engineered with various government initiatives, programmes and schemes with a holistic approach. There is the need to revamp the SEZ model from time to time with the global scenario and demand to make it more responsive to external changes. This calls for a paradigm shift by allowing flexibility for expanding scope of manufacturing and service exports activities. SEZs can help fulfill the government's socio-economic objectives of employment generation by contributing towards services, promoting Micro, Small and Medium Enterprises (MSME)/ Small- and Medium-sized Enterprises (SME) segment, Make in India and Start-up/Stand-up schemes, thus boosting socio-economic values of society.

Appendix (1.A)

A. Bilateral FTAs Already in Force

Sl. No.	Name of the Agreement	Date of Signing of the Agreement	Date of Implementation of the Agreement
1	India–Sri Lanka FTA	28 December 1998	1 March 2000
2	India–Nepal Treaty of Trade	27 October 2009	The treaty has been extended for a further period of seven years and is currently in force till 26 October 2023.
3	India–Bhutan Agreement on Trade Commerce and Transit	17 January 1972	Renewed periodically, with mutually agreed modifications. Agreement dated 29 July 2006 was valid for ten years. With mutual consent, the validity was extended for a period of one year or the period till the proposed new agreement comes into force. The renewed agreement has been signed on 12 November 2016 and came into force with effect from 29 July 2017.

Sl. No.	Name of the Agreement	Date of Signing of the Agreement	Date of Implementation of the Agreement
4	India–Thailand FTA–Early Harvest Scheme (EHS)	9 October 2003.	1 September 2004
5	India–Singapore CECA	29 June 2005	1 August 2005
6	India–South Korea CEPA	7 August 2009	1 January 2010
7	India–Japan CEPA	16 February 2011	1 August 2011
8	India–Malaysia CECA	18 February 2011	1 July 2011

Source: Lok Sabha Question No. 2284 of 24.12.18

B. Bilateral PTAs Already in Force

Sl. No.	Name of the Agreement	Date of Signing of the Agreement	Date of Implementation of the Agreement
1	India–Afghanistan	6 March 2003	13 May 2003
2	India–Chile	8 March 2006	11 September 2007. The agreement has been expanded on 6 September 2016 and came into force with effect from 16 May 2017.

Source: Lok Sabha Question No. 2284 of 24.12.18

Appendix (1.B) Trade Agreements Signed by India with Services Chapter

Agreement	Date Signed	Services provision	Targeted Sectors
SAFTA	2004	Article 8: Provisions for simplification of procedures for business visas	
India–Singapore CECA	2005	Market access for service providers	Telecom services
India–Korea CEPA	2009	Provisions on movement of natural persons, market access	Financial services and Telecommunication
Japan–India CEPA	2011	Provisions on movement of natural persons, market access	Financial services, Transport and Telecommunication
Malaysia–India CECA	2011	Provisions on movement of natural persons, market access	Financial services
SAARC Agreement on Trade in Services (SATIS)	2010	Market access, National Treatment and Mutual Recognition agreement to facilitate movement of peoples, special considerations for LDCs in the region (including Bhutan)	
India–ASEAN Services and Investment Agreement	2014	To be ratified	

Source: Author's compilation based on information presented in chapters on services in trade agreement texts

2 Research Methodology

Research by its very definition implies both extensive and intensive search for answers and solutions to the questions and problems that demand serious inquiry. It is imperative, therefore, that the approaches and methods to the enquiry are properly formatted and formulated for affording the study a logical as well as a practical base. In this effort and endeavour, the methodology adopted for research assumes far reaching importance.

This chapter has an overview of research methodology, followed by details of the research methodology used in the study; it codifies the methods selected, the rationale behind the choice and the correlation of the answers to the questions in the study of the socio-economic impact of SEZs in Gujarat.

The researcher seeks answers to the query whether SEZs in Gujarat are effective on development both on the economic and social front. The study seeks to make an impact assessment of the SEZs in Gujarat on economy both directly as well as indirectly. It also attempts to measure the social impact of SEZs in Gujarat. The study aims to draw a roadmap to achieve the outcomes of increased exports, job generation and socio-economic development through SEZ.

2.1 Aim of the Study

This study examines the contribution of SEZs in socio-economic development of Gujarat. The research focuses on the measurable socio-economic impact of SEZs in the state of Gujarat. Such a measurement will provide a valuable tool to the stakeholders and the decision makers to tailor policies that promote exports, employment generation, social growth and development of local human capital; these are the desired outcomes for all the SEZs stakeholders.

2.2 Statement of the Problem

Through this study, the researcher seeks answers to the following questions:

1) Whether SEZs in Gujarat are effective on the development front in the context of social and economic aspects?
2) Impact assessment of Gujarat SEZs by reckoning metrics based on direct economic impact, indirect/wider economic impact and social impact.
3) How vacant land in SEZ can be optimally utilized in Gujarat to fulfil the export promotion, employment generation and overall socio-economic development?

2.3 Objectives of the Study

In order to achieve the aim, the following objectives are set for the study:

To study the various type of SEZs in India and Gujarat
To study the socio impact of SEZs in Gujarat
To study the economic impact of SEZs in Gujarat
To study and investigate the drivers for development of SEZs in Gujarat

2.4 Hypothesis

The hypotheses of the research are stated as under:

- **Null Hypothesis (H_0):** There is no significant independent variable or input variables such as Direct Economic, Indirect Economic, Demographic,

Housing, Social Services, Socio-Cultural factors towards socio-economic growth of SEZs (Special Economic Zones) in the state of Gujarat.

- **Alternative Hypothesis (H_a):** There is at least one significant independent variable or input variables such as Direct Economic, Indirect Economic, Demographic, Housing, Social Services, Socio-Cultural factors affecting socio-economic growth of SEZs (Special Economic Zones) in the state of Gujarat.

2.5 Scope

SEZs have emerged as potent instruments in developing countries for pursuing not only export-led growth strategy but also as effective tools for promoting industrialization.

The purpose of this study is to investigate the impact of multi-product and sector-specific SEZs in Gujarat on social and economic development. The objective of the research is to be achieved by building a model (Research Concept) from the literature to understand what variables within the SEZs influence shaping the social and economic development. Then the research concept is to be validated through an exploratory study and case studies to come up with the research framework. The outcome of this research may be used by policy makers in the state of Gujarat as well as central government on how best SEZs can help in achieving social and economic objectives. It would be helpful to Units and Developers (stakeholders) in SEZs for various important aspects as highlighted below:

(1) With the help of this study, functioning of SEZs in Gujarat state will be highlighted.
(2) Direct economic benefits like FDI attraction, job creation and income generation, export growth and diversification and foreign exchange earnings will be measured with this study.
(3) This study will also assess the indirect economic benefits like supplier linkage beyond the zones, the indirect employment and induced income generated through the zone-based wages spent in the surrounding economy.
(4) This study will help in investigating the drivers for development of SEZ.

This study will explain the importance of social and economic factors, integral for growth and sustainability of some of the selected SEZs.

2.6 Research Gap

Though SEZs have been around for decades in India, there has been little systematic research on their performance or social and economic impact. Globally too, only a few studies have been conducted in the area of socio-economic impact of SEZs.

On a review of the various research papers, it was observed that very few research studies have been carried out in the field of socio-economic development in Gujarat.

Not a single study on this aspect has been done so far on the basis of primary data. A few research studies do cover this aspect on the basis of secondary data or research on a conceptual basis. The time is therefore ripe to fill the gap and hence this study.

2.7 Research Methodology

2.7.1 Primary Data

Primary data was collected through written responses to four different questionnaires; the questionnaire addressed to HR heads of units in all the six selected SEZs were in structured format; the questionnaire addressed to others were in semi-structured formats. Responses to these partly structured questionnaires were buttressed through interview in person or over the phone to explore or to build up case studies.

2.7.2 Tools for Data Collection

Table 2.1 shows the summary of the four questionnaires:

Socio-economic aspects were measured through questions with answers on five-point scale from strongly disagree to strongly agree (Likert scale).

2.7.3 Questionnaire

2.7.3.1 Question Design

Questions were designed in a manner to capture the key critical areas and framed in clear language with simple and short sentences. The objective was to encourage the participants to submit detailed responses objectively. The critical key areas include social impact, economic impact, development and growth of SEZs.

Table 2.1: Summary of Questionnaire for Data Collection

Questionnaire	Respondents	Purpose	Mode
Questionnaire No. 1	HR Heads (Units of Sample SEZs)	Exploration Phase (Phase1: Localization of Variables)	Survey
Questionnaire No. 2	CEO/Head (Developers/ Stakeholders of All Sample SEZs)	Exploration Phase (Phase1: Localization of Variables)	Survey
Questionnaire No. 3	CEO/Head/ Proprietor (One Unit Per SEZ)	Case Study Phase II	Personal Interview
Questionnaire No. 4	CEO/Head/ Proprietor (One Unit Per SEZ)	Validation of Research Framework (Phase III)	Personal Interview

The questions were sequenced logically in a general flow with the intent to have clarity and understanding. Each question was rechecked to ensure that it wasn't suggestive or likely to bias the respondent to a particular response. Questions of a redundant or repetitive nature were eliminated; other than a couple of questions to test for consistency of responses from the respondent.

Details obtained through the process of case study are sensitive. The units would be comfortable in divulging information once their anonymity is assured. Hence, the researcher assigned a letter of the alphabet to each respondent in the Case Study for confidentiality and anonymity. As a corollary, information that could pierce the veil was excluded or generalized. Furthermore, another stage was used as participants would see the layout and design of questionnaire. The format and plan on the page additionally served to determine whether the questions were reasonable and could be answered with ease by the participant.

Stages Involved in Question design are depicted in Figure 2.1

Further, different design concepts needed to be considered; crowded and unstructured question designs would be unappealing to the participants and were therefore eliminated. The questions were numbered and structured in a manner so that the page contained a lot of vacant space. The font type used was simple and easily legible.

Care was taken to make the participants aware by broaching about the interviews and at the same time not to lead the participants to react with a specific

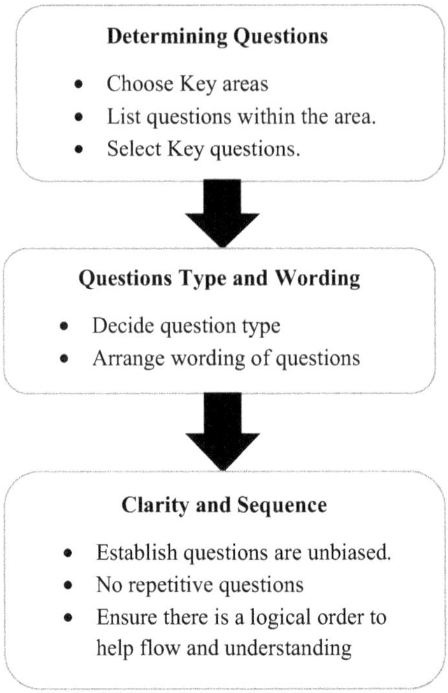

Figure 2.1: Question Design

answers or specific goals in their mind. In case of interviews, the language used was simple English. Where the interview responses were in the vernacular, they were translated to English as quickly as possible to avoid any translation loss. Answers from the questions could be easily compared due to the small number of participants.

2.7.3.2 Framing of Questions

The researcher developed four different types of questionnaires which were used for the study

a) For SEZs' Units

   The questionnaire is exhaustive in nature and framed after considerable deliberation by reckoning the variables as derived from literature review and discussions with some SEZ stakeholders. The findings of the research are based to a large extent on the responses submitted by the participants. To put the respondents at ease, the initial questions are open-ended. Progressively, the questions are narrowed down to obtain measures on a

Likert scale. Localization of the variables for the research framework was one desired outcome of this questionnaire (Appendix 2.A).

The universe for this structured questionnaire consisted of the 492 operational units in the 6 SEZs. Soft copies of the questionnaire were mailed to all the units. Additionally, hard copies were circulated through the SEZ associations, developers and the office of the Development Commissioner. The optimum target for response is 20 per cent of the universe, that is, around 99 units.

b) For SEZs Developers

SEZs developers by virtue of their position in the SEZ hierarchy are in position to provide a broader perspective of socio-economic dynamics as well as on sustainability of Special Economic Zones. The questionnaire addressed to SEZ developers was accordingly designed to get their valuable feedback. Though there are six SEZs, the number of developers is only five as two SEZs, namely Electronic Park and Apparel Park at Ahmedabad have a common developer, Gujarat Industrial Development Corporation (GIDC). This questionnaire is semi-structured in nature and addressed to each of the five developers. The researcher followed up the responses with personal interview or telephonic interview with the CEO/ authorized official of the developer (Appendix 2.B).

c) For Unit Case Study

Unit case study was conducted through this semi-structured questionnaire addressed to one selected unit in each SEZ that is total of six units. The questionnaire was followed up by personal or telephonic interview. The results were used to build a contrast cross case study (Appendix 2.C).

d) For Validation of Variables

A result is confirmed once it passes the confirmatory or validation test. The final questionnaire was designed for validity testing by choosing six units for validation of the variables and socio-economic indicators as derived from the questionnaire and case studies.

This questionnaire was similarly circulated and followed up with the units over phone and in person (Appendix 2.D).

As shown in Figure 2.1, the questions were organized in a number of different stages.

2.7.4 Secondary Data

Secondary sources are desk-based research from publicly available information sources. Literature review books, research papers and publications in journals, magazines, e-books, working paper series and news articles were considered for secondary data. Data was also gathered from various sources published and unpublished, documents and observations.

The researcher monitored during the course of research e-publishing specific sites on SEZs on daily basis and links like Google Alerts to relevant reports, articles and stories and press release.

In addition, media reports, press releases, answers to starred questions placed in either house of Parliament, Press Information Bureau, Ministry of Commerce trade bulletins and Annual reports, UNCTAD report on SEZs 2019, Union Budget 2019, Economic Survey 2019, past reports of Ministry of Commerce, reports prepared by consulting firms like Delloite, KPMG and SEZs reports submitted by Baba Kalyani Committee were accessed to get the inputs and data relevant to Special Economic Zones.

The data so accumulated was checked for validity and authenticity either by cross-checking from other sources, which additionally revealed it, or by legitimate access to the source it was cited from. The researcher consulted citation in archives: this gave demonstrably more depth on topics or helped to widen the search.

Thus, the exhaustive desk research based on various sources has provided a good platform to build the study upon; it also points the way for further research.

2.7.5 Training

The researcher was trained on the various research related aspects particularly research methodology in sessions totaling around 90 hours. Further, the research guide conducted one-to-one coaching in four sessions of an hour each. The researcher was thus equipped to seek answers from the target respondents to the questions in the questionnaire.

Some of the topics covered in the training were:

- Flow of questionnaire.
- Skills of conducting structured and semi-structured interviews.
- Framing of questionnaire with respect to objectives.
- Understanding the context and culture of each sector-specific SEZs.
- How to be quick and smart in getting information.
- Gathering of information through other sources.

2.8 Sample Selection

2.8.1 The Universe

For this research, the universe of the study consists of Special Economic Zones located all over Gujarat. As on 31 March 2019, there were 20 operational SEZs, 6 SEZs can be classified under multi-product category and the remaining 14 SEZs were grouped under sector-specific category covering areas like apparel, IT/ITeS, pharmaceuticals, chemicals, engineering, textiles, non-conventional energy and multi-service SEZs.

2.8.2 Sampling Unit

The functional unit based in multi-product and sector-specific special economic zones involved in manufacturing, services or both activities was defined as sampling unit for the purpose of the research.

The choice of a sample in a class can be at random or based on certain criteria. In the extant case, the researcher has used criteria of pedigree (in operation for at least five years), employment generated (substantial) and performance (exports) to filter and narrow the choice. At the same time, care has been taken that the sample selected is representative of the class. Figure 2.2 shows the sample set, while Figure 2.3 depicts the sample unit flow chart.

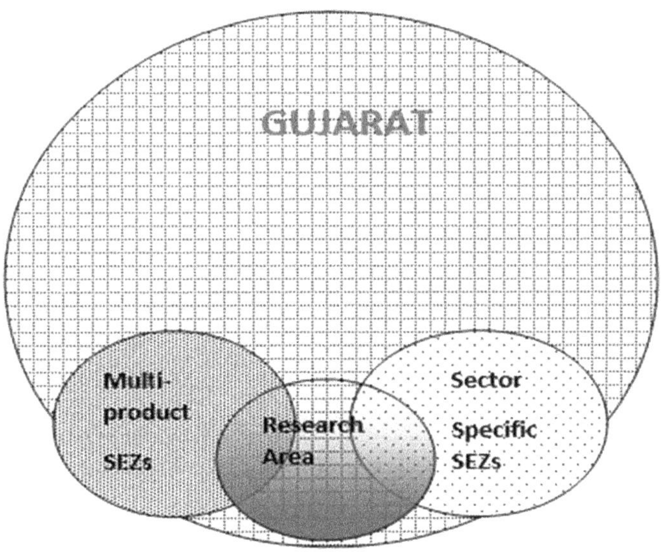

Figure 2.2: Sample Set

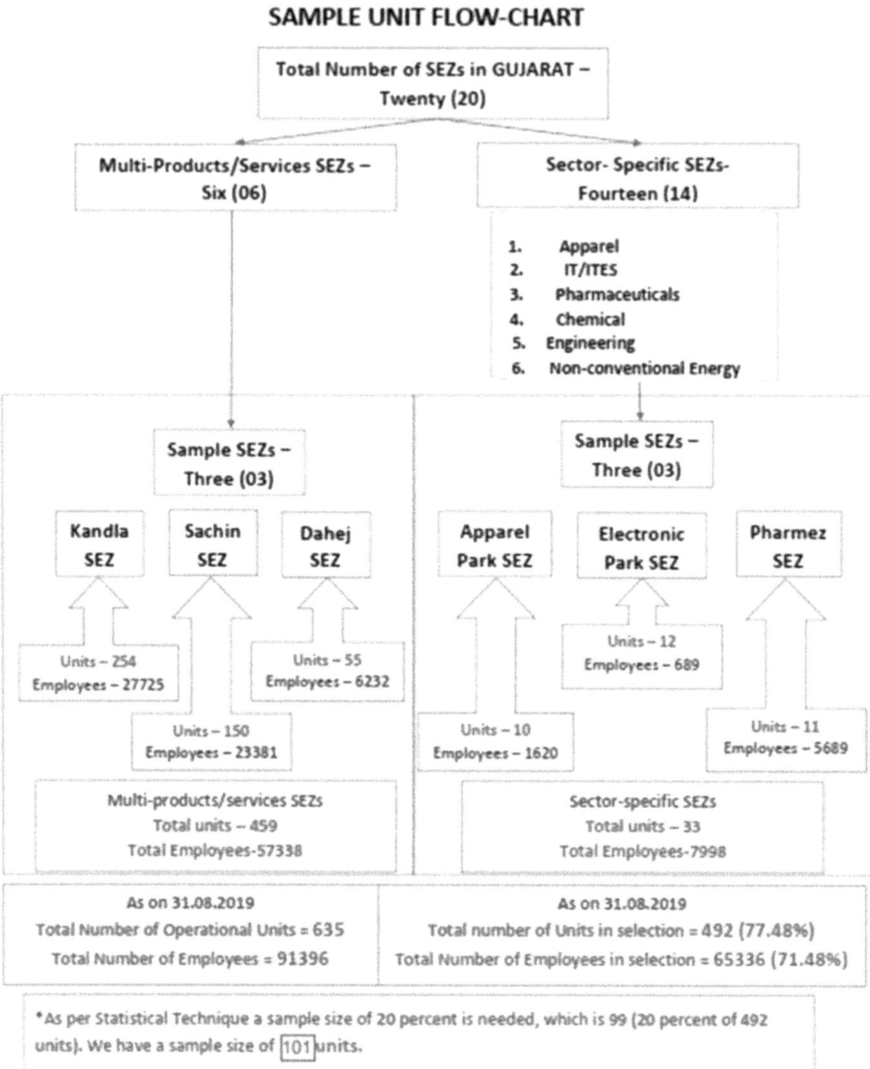

Figure 2.3: Selection of Sample Unit—Process Flow Chart

2.8.3 Target Sample SEZs

Three SEZs each in multi-product and sector-specific category respectively were chosen as samples; besides adherence to criteria as described above, care was taken to include class representative on variables like type of SEZ ownership (government/private), location, type of activity in SEZs, whether employee intensive and so on. As most of the extant employment is in manufacturing sector, units engaged in trading and services with limited number of employees were not reckoned for the purpose of selection. The 6 selected SEZs hosted about 492 operational units out of the 635 operational units in Gujarat and thus comprised 79 per cent of the operational units in the state. One unit each was selected from each of these six SEZs for Case Study. The six units were chosen on their fulfilling the following parameters, namely, history of operation of five years, relatively larger employee strength and significant exports.

Although the questionnaire was floated to all the 492 units in the 6 selected SEZs, only 187 units provided responses to the questionnaire. Scrutiny of the response sheets revealed that 86 of the 187 response sheets received were incomplete. The respondents had failed to answer or fill in important details and therefore these 86 responses were discarded. Thus, 101 response sheets (187–86), which had complete details were considered for the research. These 101 responses are more than the minimum optimal response number of 99, that is, 20 per cent of the universe. The number of responses is adequate for the data analysis, given that there are about eight major categories of variables.

Following SEZs were selected for the purpose of research:
SEZs in multi-product category, namely:

1. Kandla Special Economic Zone, Kutch District
2. Dahej SEZ Ltd., Bharuch District
3. Surat SEZ, Sachin-Surat District

SEZs in sector-specific category namely:

1. Textiles and Articles of Textiles SEZ, Ahmedabad District
2. Electronic SEZ, Gandhinagar District
3. Pharmez, Zydus Infrastructure SEZ, Ahmedabad District

2.8.4 Sampling Techniques

The sampling technique used is stratified sampling together with purposive sampling. The three steps for carrying out the sampling operation are:

Step 1: Selection of sample SEZs:

- SEZs, who have completed five years of operations after implementation of SEZs Act 2005
- SEZs in both categories, that is, multi-product and sector-specific categories

- SEZs representing all categories of developers (central government–owned/ state government–owned/private)
- Service SEZs were excluded from the research study
- Total six SEZs consisting of three SEZs under multi-product and three SEZs under sector-specific SEZs were selected as sample SEZs. The sample size was also tested statistically

(Minimum four SEZs using stratified sampling method)

Step 2: Selection of sample units (Exploratory study: Phase I)

- Units with large number of employees (direct/indirect), that is, labour-intensive manufacturing ones were selected.
- Unit sample size: 100 per cent functional units, that is, 492 nos. of working units in 6 sample SEZs were chosen representing approximately 77.50 per cent of 635 nos. of total working units (as on 31/08/2019) from 20 SEZs in Gujarat.
- These 492 units engaged about 65,336 persons out of total 91,396 people employed in SEZs of Gujarat thus representing 72 per cent of SEZ direct employees.

Table 2.2 shows the characteristics of SEZs selected for study.

Step 3: Selection of sample units for case study (Phase II)

One unit from each of the six SEZs was selected, that is, total six units were selected for the following phase (Case Studies: Validation of the proposed research framework). The six firms were characterized by different type, size and activities.

Following parameters were adopted for selection of unit for case study:

1. Type of activity: Manufacturing
2. Years of operation: Minimum five years
3. Export turnover: Positive growth for continuous three years
4. Number of employees in units: Substantial

2.8.5 Reference Period

The period of reference for the research and literature review was from 1980 till 2019. The policy framework for SEZ was laid down in 2000. Parliament passed the SEZ Act in 2005 followed by the framing of the SEZs rules in 2006. The state government of Gujarat was prompt in adopting a dedicated SEZs policy in

Table 2.2: Characteristics of SEZs Selected for Study

SEZs (Status and year)/ Date of Notification	Total Notified area (Ha)	Sector	Developer	Units as on 31/8/2019 (Nos.)	Employees as on 31/ 08/2019 (Nos.)
Kandla SEZ (FTZ-EPZ-SEZ) 1965–2019 (01.11.2000)	400	Multi-product	MoCI	254	27,725
Surat SEZ (01.11.2000)	49.99	Multi-product	DGDC	150	23,381
Dahej SEZ (20.12.06/ 07.04.10 / 23.04.10/ 14.11.11)	1682.65	Multi-product	GIDC JV	55	6,232
Pharmez SEZ (28.09.06 / 04.09.17)	179.25	Sector specific Pharmaceutical	ZYDUS	11	5,689
Textiles and Articles of Textiles SEZ (10.04.07)	20.41	Sector Specific Apparel	GIDC	10	1,620
Electronic Park SEZ (13.12.06)	28.00	Sector specific Electronic & IT/IteS	GIDC	12	689
TOTAL	2360.30			492	65,336

Source: www.kasez.gov.in

2004. The research covers the journey of the then existing EPZs to SEZs post the SEZ rules in 2006. It also covers all the SEZs which are in operation for more than 18 years since 2000. For reference purpose all the major SEZs have been considered. SEZs operational for at least five years after the SEZs rules, that is, 2006, are selected for thorough analysis to obtain comprehensive results. The findings of this study will be helpful to improve the understanding of the social and economic concept of the SEZs and its contribution in the development of SEZs.

2.8.6 Research Concept

The researcher could identify the research gap by analysis of desk-based data. The variables, which are not yet studied, were identified in the context of SEZs in India in general and in Gujarat in particular.

Figure 2.4 presents the preliminary research concept.

This research concept will be discussed in two stages.

- Socio-economic variables in SEZs
- Determination of drivers of socio-economic aspects in SEZs

2.8.6.1 Socio-Economic Variables

This research uses variables in measuring the socio-economic impact for the SEZs in Gujarat. The variables for the study are tabulated in Table 2.3.

An index would be built using these variables, by assigning qualitative and quantitative values to each variable. These would be validated in order to localize the research concept and work in the research framework.

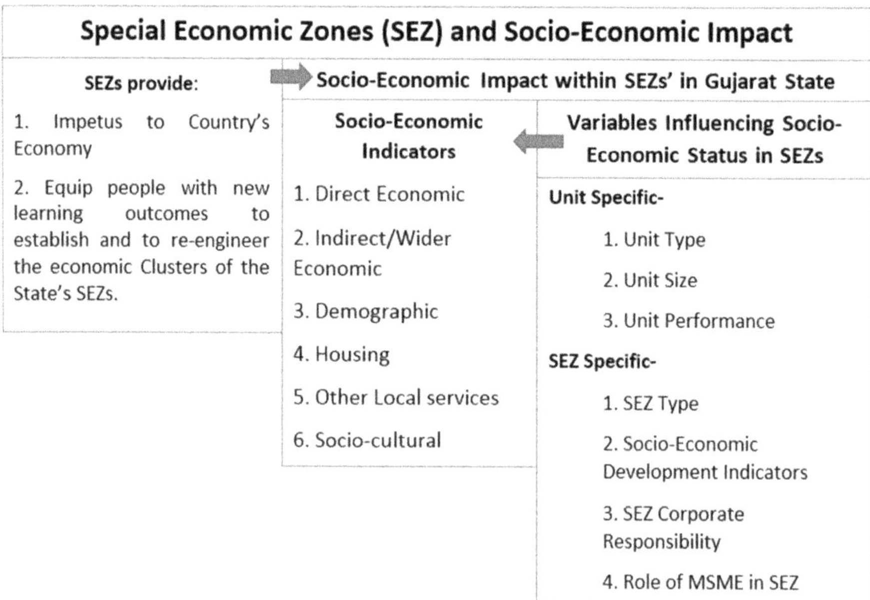

Figure 2.4: Research Concept

Table 2.3: Variables of the Study

Type of Variables	Main Variable	Sub Variable
Independent Variables	**1. Direct Economic**	Local and non-local employment
		Characteristics of employment (e.g. skill group)
		Labour supply and training
		Wage levels
	2. Indirect/ wider economic/ expenditure	Employees' retail expenditure
		Linked supplier to main development
		Labour market pressures
		Wider multiplier effects
	3. Demographic	Change in population (temporary and permanent)
		Change in other population characteristics (e.g. Family size, economic levels, socio-economic groups)
		Settlement patterns
	4. Housing	Various housing tenure type
		Public and private
		House prices
		Homelessness and other housing issues
	5. Other Local Services	Public and private sector
		Educational services
		Health services: social support
		Others (e.g. police, fire, recreation, transportation)
		Local finances
	6. Socio-cultural	Life styles/quality of life
		Gender issues, family structure
		Social problems (e.g. Crime, illness, divorce)
		Community stress and conflict: integration, cohesion and alienation.
Dependent Variables	**Socio-economic**	Based on the socio-economic questions asked to the respondent.

Source: Methods of Environmental Impact Assessment—Peter Morris & Riki Therivel (2001)

2.8.6.2 Determinants of Socio-Economic Allure in Gujarat's SEZs

The determinants of the socio-economic development in Gujarat's SEZs may be classified into two categories:

A. Unit-specific
B. SEZ-specific

I. Unit-Specific Determinants

These are the determinants which are related directly to the unit's operating within the Special Economic Zones.

a. Units Specification (Type and Size)

Type of activity (manufacturing/trading/services) is an important variable. So is the number of years of operations for determining the Socio-Economic Indicator. The volume of the capital invested would be another variable to judge how the units are willing to invest in their employees' welfare to maintain return on their capital invested.

Units Performance

Research studies reckon Units performance in terms of revenue generated per employee as a variable that would have positive impact on socio-economic aspects. The role of high caliber employees is significant to raise the productivity rate leading to unit's positive financial growth.

2.8.6.3 SEZs-Specific Determinants

These are the determinants related directly to the SEZs themselves.

a. SEZs: Level of Clustering/Type of SEZs

The level of clustering within the zones and type of SEZs (multi-product or sector specific) has significance in determining the socio-economic indicators.

b. SEZs: Corporate Responsibility

Corporate Social Responsibility (CSR) for any company/stakeholder is an important component for social development within the campus and nearby areas; this is true for SEZs too. Expenditure by SEZs on this account will have a positive impact on overall development of the society by way of promoting education, gender equality, women empowerment, health care services, generation of employment by enhancing skills and other welfare activities.

The sustainability of SEZs depends on protection of the environment; an important activity that could be covered under CSR.

c. SEZs: Role of Micro, Small and Medium Entrepreneur Sector (MSME)

SEZs play a very important role in development of micro, small and medium entrepreneur sector. SEZs develop long-term linkages with the domestic economy mainly in the MSME sector; hence progress of SEZ is beneficial to MSME.

2.8.7 Research Design

Figure 2.5 depicts the manner in which this study was structured to answer the research questions.

2.9 Sample Design

The first part of the study is exploratory in nature. The research design for this part uses qualitative techniques to determine the various factors affecting the social and economic aspect in SEZs.

The second part is a combination of single cross-sectional descriptive research design and empirical research. Here quantitative techniques like questionnaire and interview methods and other statistical tools are used to find out the most sought dimension of the research study. A questionnaire was formed with Funnel Study approach on the basis of components found in first part of the study. Results were obtained by getting these questionnaires filled and conducting the interviews in respect of Case Study. The second part of the study was concerned with the establishment of the hypothesis and testing of hypothesis.

The third part gives the statistical findings of the variables in hierarchy and also the drivers for the socio-economic impact of SEZs in Gujarat based on the empirical data for drawing conclusions.

Case study is used as an empirical inquiry to investigate the socio-economic impact of SEZs in Gujarat. The study aims to unearth the drivers by exploiting occurrence of social and economic goals adopted by the units with triangulation method within the multi-product SEZs (i.e. KASEZ, Dahej and SURSEZ, Sachin) as well as sector-specific SEZs (namely textiles and articles of textiles, electronics and pharmaceuticals). As each unit has a different strategy and outlook towards socio-economic factors, the selection of one unit from each of the zones (total six units) for case study was done to get a broad perspective for a

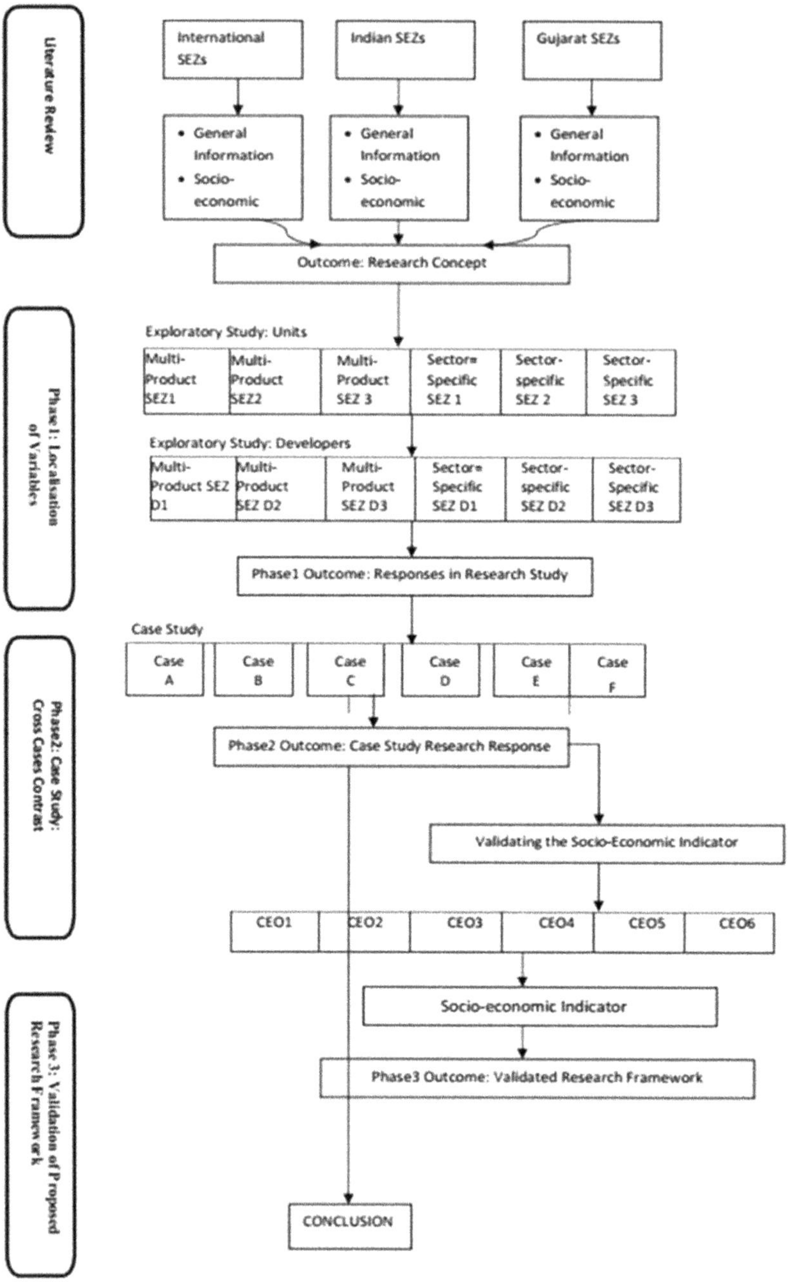

Figure 2.5: Research Design

Table 2.4: Research Methods and the Objectives

Research Method	Objective
Literature Review: Desk Research	**OBJECTIVE 1**: To study the various types of SEZs in Gujarat by review of the existing literature.
Socio Impact: Desk Research	**OBJECTIVE 2**: To study the socio impact of SEZs in Gujarat
Economic Impact: Desk Research	**OBJECTIVE 3**: To study the economic impact of SEZs in Gujarat
Exploratory Study: Questionnaire for all units	**OBJECTIVE 4:** To study and investigate the drivers of socio-economic impact for development of SEZs.
Exploratory Study: Questionnaire for Developers (Stakeholders)	**OBJECTIVE 5**: To investigate the drivers of socio-economic impact in relation to the SEZs and its stakeholders.
Case study: Interviews	**OBJECTIVE 6:** To study and investigate the drivers for development of Gujarat. To obtain information on their experiences, views and opinions on what challenges they perceive for SEZs.

multiple case design. The three phases of case study used to fulfill the research aim and objectives are summarized below:

Phase 1: Exploratory, Localization of Variables,
Phase 2: Case Studies: Validation of Research Proposed Framework, and
Phase 3: Cross Cases Contrast.

Table 2.4 depicts the research method with the objective in tabular form.

2.10 Statistical Techniques

Empirical data in the form of responses to the questionnaire addressed to all the operational units in the selected six SEZs was captured and coded in excel sheet of each questionnaire into columns. The first part covers statistical validation of responses from SEZs by using Cronbach's alpha item analysis. Cronbach's alpha is a convenient and simple way to measure whether or not a score is reliable. Rule of thumb says that score of 0.70 to 0.80 is good, between 0.80 and 0.90 is better and above 0.90 is the best. The Item-Adjusted Total Correlation and Squared Multiple Correlation are consistently high and the Cronbach's alpha test result of

0.8728 (which is better and tending towards the best score) suggests that all items measure the same construct.

The next part covers the analysis of questions as grouped in nine sections in the questionnaire. The responses received have been analysed with the use of statistical tools and the findings derived thereof narrated. Where needed the relationship between two variables, one independent and the other dependent variable was established by using Pearson Chi-Square and Likelihood Ratio Chi-Square statistical methods. Correspondence analysis was also used to group the variables in four quadrants; each quadrant populated by variables with associated properties. Models with predictor importance were validated by applying logistic regression method.

The statistical analysis is covered in two parts. The first part gives the working relationship of one dependent variable with other independent variables by building up six models to find out the various features, which contribute towards the Socio-economic Impact in SEZs. The models built are detailed as under:

Models

1. Economic Impact
2. Indirect Economic Impact
3. Housing Impact
4. Other Local Services Impact
5. Social Impact
6. Type of Drivers Impact on SEZs

These models were performed by using following methods:

1. *Likelihood Ratio Test*
2. *Decision Tree Analysis with Entropy Method and Information Gain*

The detailed methodology of Likelihood Ratio Test and Decision Tree Analysis with Entropy Method and Information Gain is covered in later chapters. The final part of this section covers the overall model summary showing various key features in the order of importance that contribute towards socio-economic impact of SEZs.

2.10.1 Statistical Tools for Data Analysis

The various statistical tools used for analysing the empirical data collected from the units (101 complete responses) with the objectives and the mathematical formulae are shown in Table 2.5.

Table 2.5: Statistical Tools for Data Analysis

Sr. No	Nomenclature	Objective/s	Formula and Assumptions
1	Regression Analysis	• To impute missing values Established Regression Model—To estimate annual revenue (dependent variable), number of employees, type of industry, SEZ as independent variable.	Maximum Likelihood Estimation for calculating regression parameters: **Y = Xb** where is Y is output variable vector, X is input variables matrix and b is vector for regression parameters $b = (X^TX)^{-1}(X^Ty)$ Where X^T and X^{-1} is transpose and inverse of input matrix X respectively
2	Statistical summary	• To derive statistical distribution in order to measure central tendency and variation of attribute.	$F(x) = \frac{1}{\sigma\sqrt{2\pi}} e^{-(x-\mu)^2/2\sigma^2}$
3	Correlation analysis	• To derive relationship between various variables.	$r = \frac{n(\Sigma xy) - (\Sigma x)(\Sigma y)}{\sqrt{[n\Sigma x^2 - (\Sigma x)^2][n\Sigma y^2 - (\Sigma y)^2]}}$
4	Variance Analysis	• To measure change in one variable because of other.	$\sigma^2 = \frac{\sum(x-\mu)^2}{N}$
5	Chi Square Analysis	• To check relationship among categorical variables.	$\chi_c^2 = \sum \frac{(O_i - E_i)^2}{E_i}$ Where $O_{i\ is}$ observed value while E_i is estimated value
6	Correspondence analysis	• To compute the proximity between the question of any section and measurement scale	Row and column distances calculated are as follows: $d_i = \sum_j \left(\frac{1}{p_j}\right)\left(\frac{p_{ij}}{p_i} - p_j\right)^2$ $d_j = \sum_i \left(\frac{1}{p_i}\right)\left(\frac{p_{ij}}{p_j} - p_i\right)^2$ Where P is the proportion matrix of input data matrix

Continued

Table 2.5: *Continued*

Sr. No	Nomenclature	Objective/s	Formula and Assumptions
7	Decision Tree Analysis	• Provide a framework to quantify the values of outcomes and the probabilities of achieving them. • Helps in arriving at the optimal decisions on the basis of existing information and best guesses.	Entrope of dependent variable: $E(S)=\sum_{i=1}^{c}-p_i \log_2 p_i$ Entropy using frequency table for two variables: $E(T,X)=\sum_{c\in X}P(c)E(c)$ Information Gain: $Gain(T,X)=Entropy(T)-Entropy(T,X)$
8	Logistic Regression	• To measure relationship between categorical dependent variable and independent variable (Likert scale)	Logistic regression uses maximum likelihood estimation to calculate model coefficients: $\beta^1=\beta^0+[X^TWX]^{-1}.X^T(y-\mu)$ Where *β is a vector of the logistic regression coefficients.* *W is a square matrix of order N* *μ is a vector of length N with elements $\mu_i=n_i\pi_i$* Likelihood Ratio Tests: $LL=\sum_{i=1}^{n}y_i ln(p_i)+(1-y_i)ln(1-p_i)$ Where p is the logistic regression, predicted probability
9	Coefficient of Variance (CoV)	• To benchmark parameters among different sections of questionnaire; it also helps in making different cohorts of respondents.	Coefficient of Variation Formula Below is the formula for how to calculate the coefficient of variation: $CV=\frac{\sigma}{\mu}$ where: σ = standard deviation μ = mean

Table 2.5: *Continued*

Sr. No	Nomenclature	Objective/s	Formula and Assumptions
10	Clustering	• It helps in making cohorts of respondents in order to group them. • It helps in the review of current policies by gauging whether they fulfil respondents' expectations or not. • It indicates areas of improvement in current system.	$J = \sum_{i=1}^{m} \sum_{k=1}^{K} w_{ik} \lVert x^i - \mu_k \rVert^2$ where $w_{ik}=1$ for data point X_i if it belongs to cluster *k*; otherwise, $w_{ik}=0$. Also, μ_k is the centroid of x_i's cluster
11	Likelihood method to extract features	• Maximum Likelihood helps to rank the parameters from a model in order to find the most important one from the perspective of policies.	Likelihood score L, for dependent variable Y, for all given inputs Xs $= \sum_{i=1}^{N} \log p(y^i \mid x_1^i, \ldots, x_d^i).$ L(Y!X) $I(X;Y \mid Z) = H(X \mid Z) - H(X \mid YZ)$ $= \sum_{z \in Z} p(z) \sum_{x \in X} \sum_{y \in Y} p(xy \mid z) \log \frac{p(xy \mid z)}{p(x \mid z) p(y \mid z)}.$
12	Neural Networks	• Neural network helps to develop predictive analytics from given input variables to optimize the output variable. • In this research it helped to determine important factors which matter most for SEZ success.	In matrix notation, we write neural network function as below: $Y = b + W^T X$ Where b is bias, W is weight vector and X is input varaibale matrix. We optimize neural network function by keeping Mean Square Error minimal with the help of gradient descent algorithm as follows: $\frac{\partial J}{\partial b} = \frac{2}{n} \sum_i (y_i - (mx_i + b))$

2.11 Pilot Study

2.11.1 Introduction

The concept of reconnaissance mission originates from military history. The success or failure of a military campaign hinges on how effectively the reconnaissance exercise has been conducted. In research, the reconnaissance mission is termed as pilot study. In a research study of this nature, based on quantitative as well as qualitative data, there was the need to conduct the pilot study. The goal of such study is to not only experiment on the research techniques and methods, but to also frame the questionnaires and interviews. Therefore, pilot study can be defined as both a feasibility study as well as a pre-testing of instruments, questionnaires and interviews.

The researcher compiled the independent variables and applied this to a pilot group of SEZs. Simultaneously, the researcher tested an open-ended questionnaire on the socio-economic aspects, cultural mores, quality of life, direct and indirect economic benefits and so on. Three important facets of the research technique considered in the pilot study are as follows:

- Detection of flaws in measurement procedures and in the Operationalization of Independent Variable
- Identification of unclear or ambiguous items in a questionnaire
- The non-verbal behaviour of participants may give information about any embarrassment or discomfort experienced concerning the content of wording of items in a questionnaire.

This is valuable to some extent in the current research, because this study is not using a pure quantitative method, but a combined qualitative–quantitative method. The pilot study was used to identify practical problems in the process, sessions and methods used. This study could thus indicate whether the proposed methods and/or instruments are appropriate and commensurate with the research objectives.

2.11.2 Goal

The researcher sees the goal of a pilot study in general as related to the aim of the research project of which it forms a part. The general goal of a pilot study is to provide information, which can contribute to the success of the research project as a whole. In the current study, the goal of the pilot study consists of the following:

1. To find out possible practical arrangements that might have a negative influence on success of research procedure.
2. To sort out all practicalities related to measurement instruments as well as applicability of these instruments to the potential outcomes of the study.

The pilot study is conducted by the researcher by following the same design as for the main Research; this is the research strategy as stated in 2.8.7 (Research Structure). As shown in the flow chart (Figure 2.5), the pilot study consisted of two phases:

a) Literature Review

The researcher carried out the exhaustive desk-based research by referring the published research papers, publications in research journal, working papers, e-journals and news articles. The researcher also gathered data from various sources published and unpublished, documents, observations.

Various reports were studied and reviewed to know the objectives of the study, various variables considered for the study, methodology adopted by various researchers, findings, conclusion and various statistical tools and techniques adopted for the study.

On the basis of desk-based research, the researcher analysed and could identify the research gap. The variables which are not yet studied were identified in the context of SEZs in India in general and in Gujarat in particular.

From the broad area of subjects related to SEZs, the researcher narrowed down on the basis of literature review to a few focus areas related to SEZs. Not much research has been conducted on these few areas. These areas were relevant to formulate the objectives and goal of the main study as well as that of the pilot study.

Based on the research work done, the researcher could present and publish five research papers covering the core areas related to the present study. The topics covered in the research papers and presentations were Service Sector SEZs, Global Outlook of SEZs, Sustainable Development and SEZs, Paper on Literature Review, Emerging Areas in SEZs in Gujarat. Through these research papers, the researcher could get clarity on the subject to formulate the pilot study.

b) Exploratory Phase

After the desk research and identification of SEZs and units to be visited, the field visits were done in the following sequence.

i) Breaking the Ice

- The selection of the SEZs for the study is based on the outcome of the desk research. Six SEZs were selected namely multi-sector SEZs of Dahej, Kandla and Surat and sector-specific SEZs namely Pharmez of Zydus, Textile Apparel Park at Ahmedabad and GIDC Electronic Park at Gandhinagar.
- The researcher held interactive meetings with the SEZ developers and the unit heads initially to broach on the subject of research and apprise the units of the purpose of the research. Thus, the ice between the units and the administration was broken.
- Certain documents were obtained from the unit's such as audited annual reports, news publication and articles. Such documents enabled the researcher to frame the questions and align the research with the ground realities.

ii) Selection of group members for the pilot study

During the course of the initial visit, the resource persons in each unit selected for pilot study and in each SEZ were shortlisted.

After further discussions with the stakeholders, the resource person for pilot study was identified. The researcher used the same selection criteria for the pilot study as for the final intervention. The following are the main selection criteria used for the members for the group of the pilot study:

1. The resource person identified was heading the HR division with thorough knowledge about the subject.
2. HR team members handle the employees welfare matters.
3. An ethical approach.

In the next visit to the units, the researcher held discussions with the resource person; briefed him/her in detail of the research topic and solicited their assistance in framing of the questionnaire. The objective was to frame the questionnaire in such a manner that the relevant data is captured and nothing is left out. In this manner, the variables were identified for further examination and interpretation.

An Ethical Approach

During the pilot study, the researcher used this resource group with the aim to identify possible practical difficulties, to find out which techniques are best suited to use in this intervention and to test the applicability of the tests and questionnaires used in the intervention.

Summary

The pilot study has proved valuable for both the assessment questionnaires and interviews done. With the help of pilot study, the researcher could identify possible difficulties related to this process. The study helped in removal of weaknesses which would probably have a negative influence. The researcher could also identify more factors and variables, which rendered the final study more fruitful.

Therefore, the pilot study had a definite contribution to the success of the main research study, its possibilities for further research, and also to the researcher's analytical approach towards carrying out the main research study.

2.12 Significance of the Study

This research study will contribute to the society adopting the Triple Helix Model of innovation which refers to a set of interactions between academia, industry and governments, to foster economic and social development.

- **Relevance to State/Central Government and Other Institutions/ Bodies**
    1. This study will help to identify the gaps and provide inputs for framing a robust policy for optimal usage of resources including the utilization of the vacant notified area for revamping the SEZs.
    2. This study will draw attention to the need for integration of SEZs as part of the country's industrial, trade and economic development policies.
    3. The need for framing SEZ policies in tune with the central government schemes and initiatives like Make in India, Start Up India and others is highlighted in this study.
    4. The concept of a sustainable SEZs model (SSEZ) to test different policies and new approaches in line with the United Nations Sustainable Development Goals (SDG) 2030 is introduced in this study.
    5. The Socio-Economic Model for SEZs in Gujarat proposed through this study would be useful for SEZs located outside Gujarat.
    6. This study focuses on the impact of SEZs on the social and economic development in Gujarat; it will, therefore, offer inputs to the policy makers on the roadmap for maximizing benefits of SEZ to the development of the state.

- **Relevance to Units/Developers/Stakeholders in SEZs**
  (1) This study will suggest to the SEZs units and stakeholders optimal use of land especially vacant land in notified SEZs.
  (2) Through this study the hierarchical importance of various parameters and factors will be established thus easing the task of internal interventions for achieving SEZs objectives of exports promotion, employment generation, investments and infrastructure.
  (3) Units/developer can use the work to formulate policies in areas of Product Mix, Business Development, New Markets, R&D, Training and Employee Welfare measures which will go a long way in improving the quality of life of the employees.

- **Relevance to Students/Academia/Research Institutions**

  (1) This study will bring into focus the role of SEZ in socio-economic development of the country.
  (2) The study will also be helpful for academia as a base to carry advanced research in these and related areas and also serve as a useful reference material.

Thus, this research study will contribute to the society adopting the Triple Helix Model of innovation which refers to a set of interactions between academia, industry and governments, to foster economic and social development.

2.13 Research Phases and Conclusion

The research phases are again detailed for reference.

Phase 1: Exploratory, localization of variables

Phase 1 is commissioned to come up with the Proposed Research Framework with localized variables. Discussions were held with the developers/stakeholders and unit's heads to pin down the variables. A detailed questionnaire was framed under nine subheadings and dispatched to all the operational units in the six selected SEZs. Incomplete responses were discarded and the complete 101 responses (this number of responses satisfies the condition of 20 per cent responses) were codified for analysis.

In this stage, questionnaire was also circulated to the five developers (though six SEZs were selected, developers were five only as two of the selected six SEZs had a common developer). The five SEZ developers were presented with the proposed socio-economic indicators in order to obtain feedback. During this stage, the views of the developers on the optimal use of the vacant land in SEZs were also solicited.

Phase 2: Case Studies: Contrasting the cases against the variables

In this phase, the formal interviews were held with the selected units and recorded.

As per the criteria designed, six units (each unit from every special economic zone) (case studies) were identified. A semi-structured questionnaire was developed and used extensively throughout an interview process to obtain data and information about each interviewed unit practices, their perspective and contribution towards social and economic factors individually, other factors like organizational change, green HR practices, opportunity identification, strategic reforms and other aspects.

This phase was utilized to contrast the case study against the research variables. In addition, this phase explains how units perform with respect to the main impetuses that affect such development.

Phase 3: Validation of research proposed framework

This last and final phase of validation process was carried out in this phase. The main purpose and outcome of this phase would be the validated research framework.

The research concludes with the hierarchy-wise listing of the parameters or factors impacting socio-economic development through SEZs. The final model with predictor value is unveiled. The contribution of the research findings to the knowledge bank, the research limitations and recommendations are outlined.

2.14 Synopsis

This chapter covers the research objectives and the research methodology utilized for this research. Thus, this chapter details the nuts and bolts of the research process in the context of the research objectives. In addition to the specific methods used, it also covers the various methods and techniques available with a brief on the different types of design, sample testing and techniques.

The researcher has at his disposal various research techniques. The aim was to choose a technique or method which is tested and gives reliable results with the kind of data collected. In this study, interviews and questionnaires were determined to be the most apt for the qualitative and quantitative information

Table 2.6: Skeleton of the Three Phases of Research

Technique	Phases	Objectives	Plan	Method	Outcome
Semi-structured Interview in addition to Data and Information gathered on each Variable (triangulation)	Phase 1: Exploratory Study Localization of Variables	Exploratory study to localize the variables and introduce adjustment Validate, verify and discuss variables obtained from literature review Present amendment of the research concept	Five developers and HR managers from units located in SEZs were selected carefully and interviewed on the following axis: A. Background to Multi-product and Sector-specific SEZ B. Components of social and economic indicators in SEZs C. SEZ's unit impact on socio-economic	Semi-structured Interview using Semi-structured/ structured Questionnaire	Proposed Research Framework with localized variables.

Phase 2: Case Studies: Cross Cases Contrast	To obtain data and information on each and every variable discussed in the literature review during Phase 1.	Six units to be interviewed to get data and information about the proposed research framework variables within each unit. Collect data to build up socio-economic indicators. In order to do that, interview of figureheads within SEZ' s units in order to get the following answers Are the Socio-economic indicators useful? Cross comparison among the six firms (three in multi-product and three in sector specific)	Six units to be interviewed to get data and information about the proposed research framework variables. Collect data to build up socio-economic indicators.	Data and information About each variable within the six cases. Validated the Socio –economic indicator and proposed this indicator for further specific research in the future.
Phase 3: Validation of socio-economic index	To compare the impact of special economic zones on socio-economic developments. Link the aggregate information and data to perform cross analysis with cases studies to reach the final results	In order to do that, interview figureheads within SEZ's units in order to get the following answers Are the Socio-economic indicators useful? Validation of the proposed indicators composed variables	Tabulation	Provide comments on what variables usually impact the socio-economic development with Special Economic Zones

required. The choice not only relies upon what method would deliver the best outcomes but also which would be the most practical and feasible method to implement.

Through a rigorous analysis of the empirical data collected, the research findings were derived and the research questions answered. The research concludes with a summary of the findings, the conclusions and recommendations, research limitations and directions for future research.

Table 2.6 condenses the skeleton of the three phases of research study.

Appendix (2.A) Interview Questionnaire for SEZs Unit

Name of Interviewee:
Email ID:
Contact No:
Note:

RATING SCALE GRADING: FROM 1 TO 5 (1–2–3–4–5)
(1 = poor: 2 = average; 3 = good; 4 = very good; 5 = outstanding)

1. General Information of SEZ Unit

1.1 Name of SEZ: ______________________Place: __________________

1.2 Year of Commencement: ____________________________________

1.3 No of Employees as on 31/08/2019: ___________________

1.4 Ownership Structure:

(a) 100 percent foreign owned ❏
(b) 100 percent locally owned ❏
(c) Joint venture ❏ Local equity ____________%
Foreign equity __________%

1.5 Activity type (Please √): Manufacturing/ Services/Trading/ Combined

1.6 What was the export turnover during last **THREE** fiscal years?

Year	USD (Millions)
2018–2019	
2017–2018	
2016–2017	

2. Direct Economic

2.1 What type of employment do you have in your unit? (Scale from 1–2–3–4–5)

Type Characteristics	Skill	Semi-skill	Unskilled
Permanent			
Temporary (contractual)			
Temporary (daily wages)			
Both			

2.2. Mention the percentage (%) (number of employees) of staff in your unit.

Nature Gender	Male	Female
Permanent		
Contactual		
Daily Wages		

2.3 Percentage (%) of local and non-local employment?

Type Characteristics	Skill	Semi-skill	Unskilled
Local			
Non-local			

2.4 Rate from strongly agree to strongly disagree the following statements?

	Strongly agree	Agree	Neutral	Disagree	Strongly disagree
2.4.1 We recruit temporary employee for bottom level.	❑	❑	❑	❑	❑
2.4.2 We recruit permanent employee at top and middle level.	❑	❑	❑	❑	❑
2.4.3 We recruit daily wagers for unskilled job.	❑	❑	❑	❑	❑
2.4.4 We recruit contractual employee for semi-skill job.	❑	❑	❑	❑	❑
2.4.5 We recruit skilled employee for middle and top level.	❑	❑	❑	❑	❑
2.4.6 We provide training to unskilled and semi-skilled worker on requirement basis	❑	❑	❑	❑	❑
2.4.7 We are providing regular training to middle and top management.	❑	❑	❑	❑	❑
2.4.8 We are paying employee wages/salary according to government norms.	❑	❑	❑	❑	❑

2.5 Human Resources factors considered at time of recruitment

	Strongly agree	Agree	Neutral	Disagree	Strongly disagree
2.5.1 Level of education	❑	❑	❑	❑	❑
2.5.2 Technical education background	❑	❑	❑	❑	❑
2.5.3 Type of skill	❑	❑	❑	❑	❑
2.5.4 Past experience	❑	❑	❑	❑	
2.5.5 Ability to skill up	❑	❑	❑	❑	

2.6 In your opinion, rate the level of importance by government policy to increase production activity leading to recruitment and retention of employees.

Policy area	**Scale from 1–2–3–4–5**
Procurement from domestic area	
Job-work from domestic market (DTA)	
Maintenance and services from local service providers	
Facility to carry out Research and Development etc.	
Labour-related issues	

Economic Impact

2.7 To what extent do you agree with the following statements?

	Strongly agree	Agree	Neutral	Disagree	Strongly disagree
2.7.1 SEZ increases the overall employment.	❑	❑	❑	❑	❑
2.7.2 Due to SEZ infrastructure facility is improved.	❑	❑	❑	❑	❑
2.7.3 Standard of living is increased due to SEZ.	❑	❑	❑	❑	❑

	Strongly agree	Agree	Neutral	Disagree	Strongly disagree
2.7.4 SEZs have affected the demographic pattern in rural and urban centres.	❑	❑	❑	❑	❑
2.7.5 SEZs generated limited employment as targeted, given the relative importance of capital intensive production.	❑	❑	❑	❑	❑
2.7.6 Increase of foreign exchange.	❑	❑	❑	❑	❑
2.7.8 Increase in exports.	❑	❑	❑	❑	❑
2.7.9 Easy Business Process.	❑	❑	❑	❑	❑

2.8 In your opinion, what is the level of importance of the following factor in human capital development?

	Of utmost Importance	Very Important	Of moderate Importance	Of little Importance	Of no Importance
2.8.1 Unit size	❑	❑	❑	❑	❑
2.8.2 Unit activity type	❑	❑	❑	❑	❑
2.8.3 Performance in terms of revenue growth percentage	❑	❑	❑	❑	❑
2.8.4 Clustering Level in SEZ (Similar firms within the same area)	❑	❑	❑	❑	❑

	Of utmost Importance	Very Important	Of moderate Importance	Of little Importance	Of no Importance
2.8.5 Research and development activities	❑	❑	❑	❑	❑
2.8.6 Organization Culture	❑	❑	❑	❑	❑

2.9 In your opinion, what is the impact of SEZ on the local economy? Please tick √

Very Low	1
Low	2
Moderate	3
High	4
Very High	5

3 Indirect Economic

3.1 (Rating Scale from 1–2–3–4–5)

Sr No	Particulars	Very High (>80)	High (60–80)	Moderate (40–60)	Low (20–40)	Very Low (0–20)
1	Average wage levels of workers in comparison to local market					
2	Average attrition rate (%) of workers staying for consecutive years					

3.2 In your opinion, rank the importance of the following **Human Capital Factors** which may facilitate technical know-how spillover?

	Not at all Important	Slightly Important	Important	Fairly Important	Very Important
3.2.1 Level of competitiveness	❑	❑	❑	❑	❑
3.2.2 Labour mobility	❑	❑	❑	❑	❑
3.2.3 Linkage to suppliers/clients	❑	❑	❑	❑	❑
3.2.4 Applying international quality standards	❑	❑	❑	❑	❑

3.3 How does your unit benefit from other units?

Sr No	Factors	**SCALE (1–2–3–4–5)**
1	Product development	
2	Process and quality control	
3	Policies and strategies	
4	Formal and Informal networking	

3.4 To what extent do you agree with the following statements?

	Strongly agree	Agree	Neutral	Disagree	Strongly disagree
3.4.1 Labour issues/laws are a challenge for unit development	❑	❑	❑	❑	❑
3.4.2 SEZs lead to multiplier effects.	❑	❑	❑	❑	❑

	Strongly agree	Agree	Neutral	Disagree	Strongly disagree
3.4.3 SEZs contribute to Indirect and induced jobs	❑	❑	❑	❑	❑
3.4.4 Retail expenditure by unit worker has increased	❑	❑	❑	❑	❑
3.4.5 Role of R&D in your unit is very important	❑	❑	❑	❑	❑

3.5 How well are you connected to local supply market (DTA), that is, Domestic Tariff Area?

Very Low 0–20	1
Low 20–40	2
Moderate 40–60	3
High 60–80	4
Very High >80	5

3.6 To what extent does your unit face competition with other units within the zones?

None (0) ❑ Low (1) ❑ Moderate (2) ❑ stiff (3) ❑ Very stiff (4) ❑

4.0 Demographics

4.1 What is the average age of workers in your unit?

<25	5
25–35	4
35–45	3
45–55	2
>55	1

4.2 What is the average number of dependants of your workers?

Upto 2	1
2–4	2
4–6	3
6–8	4
>8	5

4.3 How many cases, the worker is the only wage earner in the family?

Very High >80	5
High 60–80	4
Moderate 40–60	3
Low 20–40	2
Very Low 0–20	1

4.4 Location of employee's dwelling place? Rank 1 to 5

In the Zone
< 2 Kms
2 to 5 Kms
5 to 10 kms
>10 Kms

4.5 Whether the majority of population settled near is temporary/permanent residents?

1. Temporary　　　　2. Permanent

4.6 What is the majority income level of nearby families? (Scale 1–2–3–4–5)

Low income
Lower-middle income
Upper-middle income
Higher income

4.7 Education level of employees (%)

Upto Primary
Upto 8th Standard
Upto 10th Standard
Upto 12th standard
Graduate
Post-graduate

4.8 What is the composition of employees in your unit belonging to the following category (in percentage)?

Marginalized Category (e.g. SC/ST/ OBC)
Minorities
Female
Disabled persons/Divyangjan Category
Others (Ex-Service men etc.)

5. Housing

5.1 (Scale 1–2–3–4–5):

TYPE	>80%	60–80%	40–60%	20–40%	0–20%
OWN HOUSE					
KACCHA (TEMPORARY DWELLING)					

5.2 To what extent do you agree with the following statements?

	Strongly agree	Agree	Neutral	Disagree	Strongly disagree
5.2.1. Housing settlements nearby SEZs are become cosmopolitan	❑	❑	❑	❑	❑
5.2.2 Renting house nearby SEZs is difficult	❑	❑	❑	❑	❑
5.2.3. Non-processing area may be used to set up housing facility	❑	❑	❑	❑	❑
5.2.4 SEZ existence has created slum area near the zone	❑	❑	❑	❑	❑
5.2.5 SEZ has led to residential complex inside the zone	❑	❑	❑	❑	❑
5.2.6 SEZ has led to establishment of dormitory-type facility inside the zone	❑	❑	❑	❑	❑
5.2.7 SEZ has led to hostels /dormitory for women employees	❑	❑	❑	❑	❑

6. Other Local Services

6.1 To what extent do you agree with the following statements?

	Strongly agree	Agree	Neutral	Disagree	Strongly disagree
6.1.1 Does your unit believe in implementing the social schemes for employees	❑	❑	❑	❑	❑
6.1.2 Health Insurance Schemes must be mandatory for all employees working in SEZs	❑	❑	❑	❑	❑

	Strongly agree	Agree	Neutral	Disagree	Strongly disagree
6.1.3. Fire protection is an essential social measure in SEZ for employee's life security	❑	❑	❑	❑	❑
6.1.4 Canteen facility for workers and all type of employees.	❑	❑	❑	❑	❑
6.1.5 Provision of gymnasium and recreation club for employees	❑	❑	❑	❑	❑
6.1.6 Educational institution facility inside or nearby SEZ					
6.1.7 Educational loan or other educational schemes for employees and their family	❑	❑	❑	❑	❑
6.1.8. Providing pick-up and drop facility for employees (public transportation)	❑	❑	❑	❑	❑
6.1.9 Women safety measures for women employees	❑	❑	❑	❑	❑
6.1.10 Dedicated medical room and first aid facilities for employees	❑	❑	❑	❑	❑
6.1.11 Provision of in-house loan facilities for emergency needs or festival or other purposes	❑	❑	❑	❑	❑

6.2 Payment mode for employees (Please tick √)

TYPE	THROUGH BANK	CASH	ANY OTHER
PERMANENT			
TEMPORARY(CONTRACT)			
TEMPORARY(DAILYWAGES)			

6.3 Percentage (%) of workers having other essential documents for availing benefits under various government schemes

Voter Card
PAN card
Aadhaar
Passport
Ration card
Other (Pls specify)

7. Social Impact

7.1 How many employees are employed and out of total employees what is the ratio of female employees in the unit? ________________

7.2 Out of total employees how many women employees are the family head in your unit? ____

7.3 Total number of women and out of them how many women are subjected to regular domestic violence? __________________________

7.4 Ratio of female to male workers in the different scale jobs (scale 1–2–3–4–5 as above)

Administration/higher management
Middle management
Skilled workers
Unskilled workers

7.5 Frequency of labour audits/ compliances in firm

Bi-annual	5
Annually	4
Once in more than 2 years	3
Once in more than 3 years	2
Once in more than 4 years	1

7.6 Total number of women employees (marital status)

Unmarried
Married
Divorced/ Separated
Widow
Single mother

7.7 Percentage of employee's absenteeism

Less days 2 days a month
2–5 days
5–10 days
More than 10 days

7.8 Women-centric camps/meetings

Health check-up/ Breast Cancer awareness camp	Yes/No
Menstrual hygiene related	Yes/No
Education related	Yes/No
Knowledge of rights, laws, etc.	Yes/No
Sexual harassment committee meeting	Yes/No
Other issues-related meetings	Yes/No

7.9 To what extent do you agree with the following statements?

	Strongly agree	Agree	Neutral	Disagree	Strongly disagree
7.9.1 SEZs promote women employment and empowerment	❑	❑	❑	❑	❑
7.9.2 SEZ protect minimum wage, working hours and benefits and gender equality	❑	❑	❑	❑	❑
7.9.3 SEZs contribute substantially towards social objectives	❑	❑	❑	❑	❑
7.9.4 SEZs play positive role in tackling the social problems like crime rate, illness, divorce in and nearby areas	❑	❑	❑	❑	❑
7.9.5 SEZs promote women from marginalized community	❑	❑	❑	❑	❑
7.9.6 SEZs play crucial role in handling the community stress and conflict and promote integration and cohesion	❑	❑	❑	❑	❑
7.9.7 SEZ has impacted the lifestyle/ quality of life among workers	❑	❑	❑	❑	❑
7.9.8 Spatial concentration of SEZ around urban areas has created regional inequalities	❑	❑	❑	❑	❑

7.10 Do you have legal mechanism for protection of women sexual harassment like presence of sexual harassment committee/women cell **(Yes/No)**
7.11 Provision of maternity leave and wages for the duration of the leave **(Yes/No)**
7.12 Provision of creche facility/palnaghar for infants of working women **(Yes/No)**
7.13 Overtime facility for the women workers **(Yes/No)**
7.14 Transport facility (free/paid/subsidized) for women workers only **(Yes/No)**
7.15 Working women's hostel or dormitory facility for female workers **(Yes/No)**

8. Socio-Economic Impact

8.1 To what extent do you agree with the following statements?

	Strongly agree	Agree	Neutral	Disagree	Strongly disagree
8.1.1 Do you think that SEZ has impact on socio-economic status?	❑	❑	❑	❑	❑
8.2.2 Economic Drivers helped in overall Growth of SEZ?	❑	❑	❑	❑	❑

	Poor	Fair	Average	Good	Excellent
8.3.1 Which type of skills do your employees have?					
8.3.2 Analytical skills	❑	❑	❑	❑	❑
8.3.3 Conceptual skills	❑	❑	❑	❑	❑
8.3.4 Technical skills	❑	❑	❑	❑	❑

9. Type of Drivers—Impact on SEZ

	Strongly agree	Agree	Neutral	Disagree	Strongly disagree
9.1.1 Economic Drivers helped in overall growth of SEZ?	❑	❑	❑	❑	❑
9.1.2 SEZ policy has acted as major driver for investment and contribution for India's economy.	❑	❑	❑	❑	❑
9.1.3 Infrastructure facility inside SEZ is also important for growth of SEZs.	❑	❑	❑	❑	❑
9.1.4 Logistics facilities from SEZs to nearest port helped in boosting SEZ growth.	❑	❑	❑	❑	❑
9.1.5 Exports-incentives schemes like MEIS /SIES helped in growth of SEZs.	❑	❑	❑	❑	❑
9.1.6 Concept of SINGLE WINDOW MECHANISM acted as major driver for growth of exports from SEZs.	❑	❑	❑	❑	❑
9.1.7 Foreign Direct Investment (FDI) as driver for growth of SEZs.	❑	❑	❑	❑	❑
9.1.8 Private Investments as driver for growth, jobs, exports and demand from SEZs.	❑	❑	❑	❑	❑
9.1.9 Inflation and capacity utilization as driver for growth, jobs, exports and demand from SEZs.	❑	❑	❑	❑	❑
9.1.10 Monetary management and financial intermediation as drivers for growth of SEZs	❑	❑	❑	❑	❑

==

I am very much grateful for your efforts in filling out the questionnaire. Your feedback is so significant and will be managed with top confidentiality. Should you need any further information about the research, please free to contact the undersigned.

SHASHANK DIGAMBER SHENDE
GUJARAT UNIVERSITY
shende@rediffmail.com

==

Appendix (2.B) Questionnaire for SEZs' Developers

Note:

RATING SCALE GRADING: FROM 1 TO 5 (1–2–3–4–5)
(1= poor: 2= average; 3= good; 4= very good; 5 = outstanding)

1. General Information

1.1 Developer : ____

1.2 Year of Notification: _____________________________________

1.3 No of Employees as on 31/08/2019: _________________

1.4 Ownership Structure:

(a) 100 percent government-owned ❑
(b) 100 percent privately owned ❑
(c) Joint venture ❑ Local equity ___________%

Foreign equity _________%

1.5 Activity type: 1. Multi-product ❑
2. Sector Specific ❑

1.6 What was the export turnover during last THREE years?

Year	USD (Millions)
2018–2019	
2017–2018	
2016–2017	

2. SEZs—Business Model Analysis

2.1 In your opinion, please rate the following model in India? (Scale 1–2–3–4–5)

Private
Zones developed by foreign developers
Joint ventures with local company as private FDI
Zones developed through government–government partnership
Government (State/Central)
Public–Private Partnership (PPP) model
Others

2.2 In your opinion, please rate the contribution of SEZs units on the following parameters (Scale 1–2–3–4–5)

Employment
Bridging of Demand–Supply Gap
Socio-economic impact
Sustainable Development
Corporate Governance

3. Socio-economic Development Indicators

In your opinion, what are the factors that contribute to characterize socio-economic development in your SEZ? (Scale 1–2–3–4–5)

FACTORS	RATING
Direct economic (local and non-local employment/skill group and training)	
Indirect /wider economic/expenditure (employees' retail expenditure/linked suppliers to main development/labour market pressures/wider multiplier effects)	
Demographic (changes in population size (temporary and permanent)/changes in other population characteristics (e.g. family size, income levels, socio-economic groups))	
Housing (various housing tenure types—public and private/ house prices/homelessness and other housing problems)	
Other local service (public and private sector educational services/health services/social support /others (e.g. police, fire, recreation, transport)/local finances)	

4. Social Impact

4.1 To what extent do you agree with the following statements?

	Strongly agree	Agree	Neutral	Disagree	Strongly disagree
4.1.1 There is misuse of land in SEZs.	❑	❑	❑	❑	❑
4.1.2 SEZs has supported landless labourers in rural areas towards jobs/livelihood.	❑	❑	❑	❑	❑
4.1.3 SEZs have dedicated anti- corruption standards and polices.	❑	❑	❑	❑	❑
4.1.4 The oustees has been compensated while acquiring land for SEZ.	❑	❑	❑	❑	❑

	Strongly agree	Agree	Neutral	Disagree	Strongly disagree
4.1.5 Prices of neighbouring land/residential and commercial units have shown substantial rise after SEZ.	❑	❑	❑	❑	❑
4.1.6 Labour conditions and labour laws relevant to SEZs are favourable from the view of social aspects	❑	❑	❑	❑	❑

4.2 Impact on the livelihoods of landowners due to approriation on land (Scale 1–2–3–4–5)

Whether they have continued with traditional livelihood?
Whether they have secured employment?
Whether they have access to education and healthcare services?

4.3 Do you agree there is any effect on following due to development of SEZ? (Scale 1–2–3–4–5)

Whether as a result of SEZs they have motorable road to district/taluka headquarters?
Whether they have mobile connection facilities?
Whether the developer has taken any step to preserve and promote local traditional arts/culture?
Whether they are compelled to migrate to other places?
Whether any local person has been assisted in setting of unit in SEZ?

4.4 In your opinion, please rate the factors which are responsible for the slow growth of SEZ in the five year period 2013–2018 as compared to 2006–2012.

----

5. Economic Impact

5.1 In your assessment, what is the importance to the development of SEZs of the following factors on the various economic parameters as tabulated below? (Scale 1–2–3–4–5)

1. Export Promotion
1.1 Growth in Exports in terms of volume
1.2 New Products and Services
1.3 Ease of Import of Raw Materials
1.4 Export Norms like Value Addition, etc.
2. Performance Measures
2.1 Market Share of Exports
2.2 Accretion of new units
3. Geographic Concentration Indicators
3.1 Geographical distribution of export markets
3.2 Geographical distribution of import sources
3.3 Services trading partner (exports/imports)
3.4 Bilateral, Intra- and extra-regional trade intensity by region and partner country
4 FDI Indicators
4.1 FDI financial flows as percentage of GDP
4.2 FDI financial flow as percentage of gross capital formation
5. Foreign Controlled affiliates (FCA)
5.1 FCAs' share of the home country value added
5.2 FCAs' share of the host country value added
5.3 FCAs' share of the home country employment
5.4 FCAs' share of the host country employment
5.5 FCAs' sales as a percentage of the home country's total exports

5.2 To what extent do you agree with the following statements?

	Strongly agree	Agree	Neutral	Disagree	Strongly disagree
5.2.1 SEZs have contributed towards technology upgradation.	❏	❏	❏	❏	❏
5.2.2 Trade policy facilitators like WTO/MFN help SEZs economy.	❏	❏	❏	❏	❏
5.2.3 Impact of price indicators like term of trade, real effective exchange rate affected economy of SEZs.	❏	❏	❏	❏	❏
5.2.4 Trade intensity and specialization indicators like export specialization and net trade specialization indices affects SEZs.	❏	❏	❏	❏	❏

5.3 In your opinion, which economic indicators or factors will able to develop the economic growth from SEZs?

----

6. Corporate Responsibility

6.1 Whether CSR is applicable to your SEZ? (Yes/No)
6.2 If yes, please rate the following CSR activities in your SEZ: (Scale 1–2–3–4–5)

Promotion of education
Promoting gender equality and empowering women
Health care services
Ensuring environmental sustainability
Employment-enhancing vocational skills, social business projects

Sports/yoga/cultural activities, etc.
Welfare activities for Scheduled Castes, Scheduled Tribes, other backward classes, and minorities.

6.3 Please rate following environmental sustainability issues. (Scale: 1–2–3–4–5)
Water contamination/waste water disposal
Air pollution
Land degradation
Sound pollution
Conservation of Indigenous Fauna

6.4 To what extent do you agree with the following statements?

	Strongly agree	Agree	Neutral	Disagree	Strongly disagree
6.4.1 There are Government policies in place for environmental protection.	❑	❑	❑	❑	❑
6.4.2 The infrastructure and other assistance is provided by government for safeguarding the environment	❑	❑	❑	❑	❑

6.5 According to you, what are new opportunities for SEZs to utilize vacant land? (Rating 1–2–3–4–5)
Develop residential complex/malls /other infrastructure etc.
Divert to domestic industries
Change from single to multi-product
Dedicated service sector
Priority to MSME
Sectoral broad banding
Any other (please specify)

6.6 What methods should be used to identify, analyze and evaluate SEZs opportunities in India?

----

7. Micro-, Small-, and Medium-Size Business (MSME)

7.1 How far do SEZs help in government initiatives like Make in India Scheme, Start-up and Stand-up Scheme? (Scale 1 to 5)
7.2 How far MSME segment vendors and business are benefitted from SEZ? (Scale 1 to 5)
7.3 What promotional measures can be adopted by the government for protecting and promoting the interest of MSME? (Scale 1–2–3–4–5)

Special MSME SEZs

Special provisions for entry into existing SEZs

Relaxed norms for supply to/from MSME units

Incentives based on performance of MSME units in SEZs

Clustering of small and large enterprises

7.4 Any Suggestions

==

Appendix (2.C) Interview Questionnaire for Case Study of SEZs Unit

Note:

RATING SCALE GRADING: FROM 1 TO 5 (1–2–3–4–5)
(1= Poor: 2 = Average; 3 = Good; 4 = Very Good; 5 = Outstanding)

1. Organizational Change

1.1 Application of Management Principles

Adhering to Corporate policies and expectations	Yes/No
Complying with applicable regulatory requirements	Yes/No
Being consistent with universally recognized principles, assessing risks and acting on opportunities	Yes/No
Engaging with external stakeholders	Yes/No
Providing direct and indirect economic benefits such as local capacity development	Yes/No

1.2 To what extent does your firm believe in statement related to company's organization set up, working culture and management practises? Please give your ratings on the following statements

	Strongly agree	Agree	Neutral	Disagree	Strongly disagree
1.2.1 Management empowers employees to improve the processes and reduce failure rate	❑	❑	❑	❑	❑
1.2.2 There is more competition and less cooperation between the departments	❑	❑	❑	❑	❑
1.2.3 Official channels are used for communicating	❑	❑	❑	❑	❑

	Strongly agree	Agree	Neutral	Disagree	Strongly disagree
1.2.4 Company has an open communication culture. Transparent culture of flow of information between the departments and different levels of management.	❑	❑	❑	❑	❑
1.2.5 There is adaption of innovation at different levels	❑	❑	❑	❑	❑
1.2.6 Our employees strive to reduce any kind of waste (waste of time, waste of production space, etc.)	❑	❑	❑	❑	❑
1.2.7 Command and control is seen as the most effective leadership style rather than open culture.	❑	❑	❑	❑	❑
1.2.8 Our vision, mission and strategy is broadly communicated and followed by our employees	❑	❑	❑	❑	❑
1.2.9 Goal and objectives of the manufacturing units are closely linked with corporate objectives.	❑	❑	❑	❑	❑
1.2.10 Head of unit, site leader, etc have a good understanding of how the Corporate/Divisional strategy is formed.	❑	❑	❑	❑	❑

	Strongly agree	Agree	Neutral	Disagree	Strongly disagree
1.2.11 Managers of manufacturing unit know Which are the most important criteria for manufacturing jobs (i.e. low costs, delivery, quality).	❑	❑	❑	❑	❑
1.2.12 Managers and staff of the manufacturing unit have a site vision and strategy that is closely related to the corporate mission statement.	❑	❑	❑	❑	❑

1.3 In which ways will individuals need to adapt their work styles? (Please √)

Logical, analytical, linear and data-oriented	1
Organized, sequential, planned and detailed-oriented	2
Supportive, expressive and emotionally oriented	3
Big-picture, integrative and ideation-oriented	4

1.4 How far does the implementation of quality programmes help to increase employee morale and working efficiency? (Please√)

Five S	1
TQM	2
Six Sigma	3
Zero defect	4
Other (Pls specify)	5

2. Opportunity Identification

2.1 According to you, which industries and industry sectors are the most promising for SEZs? (Please√)

IT/ITeS	1
Textiles	2
Gems—Jewellery	3
Electronic	4
Pharma	5
Financial Services	6
Petrol, crude, etc.	7
Others (Please specify)	8

2.2 What parameters should be used to identify, analyse and evaluate SEZs opportunities in India? (Scale 1–2–3–4–5)

1) Location advantage
2) Macroeconomics of the country
3) Industrial investment support
4) Investment cost
5) Skilled labour
6) Management and service
7) Government policies
8) Laws and regulations
9) Stability and consistency of the government
10) Others (Please specify)

2.3 How can the for new digital technologies help in promotion of SEZs? (Scale 1–2–3–4–5)

Improved performance and flexibility	1
Increased productivity	2
A massive reorganization of the supply chain	3
Mass customization	4
Others (Please specify)	5

2.4 Scope of new technologies in SEZ? (Please√)

Block-chain Technology	1
Artificial Intelligence (AI)	2
Big Data analytics	3
Augmented Reality (AR)	4
Drones	5
Internet of Things (IoT)	6
Virtual Reality (VR)	7
3D Printing	8
Robots	9
Other (Pls specify)	10

2.5 At which level function of organization, technologies will be useful for manufacturing and service sector SEZs? (Please√)

Corporate Level	1
Research and Development	2
Manufacturing Department	3
Administration & HR Department	4
Sales and Marketing Department	5
Finance Department	6
Other (Pls Specify)	7

2.6 How can your unit be benefitted in redesigning value chain and use of new technologies? (Please√)

Increase of Flexibility	1
Increase Quality	2
Increase service level	3
Reduction of costs	4
Improved procurement and supplier structure	5
Sourcing by region	6
Innovation structure	7
Customer structure	8
Employment structure	9
Other (Please specify)	10

3. Strategic Reforms

3.1 How can units defend or build competitive advantage over other SEZs located outside India?

A change in govt. policies required in respect of procedures?	Yes/No
A stimulus package is required?	Yes/No
Any other	Yes/No

3.2 What strategic resources and competencies do you need? (Scale 1–2–3–4–5)

Location	1
Agglomeration with local suppliers	2
Govt. and institutional support	3
Factors of production	4
Infrastructure	5
Market	6
Any Other (Please specify)	7

3.3 In what way can SEZ units contribute to dynamic economics? (Please√)

Employment	1
Demand-supply	2
Socio-economic impact	3
Sustainability	4
Foreign exchange earner	5
Any other (Please specify)	6

3.4 Which methods or techniques are used by your unit which reduces net operating cost and generate more revenue from zones?

3.5 To what extent do you agree with the new approaches to strategic management?

	Strongly agree	Agree	Neutral	Disagree	Strongly disagree
3.5.1 The Internet of Things (IoT) strategy for your company	❏	❏	❏	❏	❏
3.5.2 Technologies that will impact everyone	❏	❏	❏	❏	❏
3.5.3 E-commerce strategy for your company	❏	❏	❏	❏	❏
3.5.4 People, talent and future of work	❏	❏	❏	❏	❏
3.5.5 Need for new organization structure	❏	❏	❏	❏	❏
3.5.6 HR—the weak spot in corporate transformation					
3.5.7 Roadmap for building corporate innovative capabilities	❏	❏	❏	❏	❏

3.6 Any other suggestions:

===

Appendix (2.D) Validation Questionnaire

Firm Code:

The following variables are used to build the proposed Socio-economic Index:

1. Direct economic
2. Indirect/wider economic/expenditure
3. Demographic
4. Housing
5. Other local services
6. Socio-cultural

To build an index, it is necessary to assign qualitative or quantitative values to each variable in the index. The following factors are reckoned in respect of each variable for this purpose:

1. Direct economic
    - Local and non-local employment
    - Characteristics of employment (e.g. skill group)
    - Labour supply and training
    - Wage levels

2. Indirect/wider economic/expenditure
    - Employees' retail expenditure
    - Vendor linkages to main development
    - Labour market dynamics
    - Wider multiplier effects

3. Demographic
   - Changes in population size (temporary and permanent)
   - Changes in other population characteristics (e.g. family size, income levels, socio-economic groups)
   - Settlement patterns

4. Housing
   - Various housing tenure types
   - Public and private
   - Housing costs, mortgage facility, municipal/panchayat services
   - Homelessness and other housing problems

5. Other local services
   - Public and private sector
   - Educational services, primary, secondary, technical and non-technical
   - Health services, primary, tertiary, emergency; social support systems
   - Others (e.g. police, fire, parks, recreation, transport)
   - Local finances

6. Socio-cultural
   - Lifestyles/quality of life
   - Gender issues; family structures
   - Social problems (e.g. crime, illness, divorce)
   - Community stress and conflict; integration, cohesion and alienation

1. In your opinion, are the above variables adequate components of socio-economic index?

----

2. Do you agree that the economic variables 1 and 2 are the driving factors and should be allotted heavy weights and the balance variables are light weight?

----

3. Is it justifiable to allot equal weights to each variable? In your opinion, what should be the weights given each variable in percentage terms?

4. The following threshold is used to classify the answers, what is your opinion on that?

1= Poor; 2 = Average; 3 = Good; 4 = Very Good; 5 = Outstanding

5. Does the proposed index measures what it should measure?

6. In your opinion, is there any other variable left out which needs to be considered within the index?

7. In your opinion, which variable relates most to your SEZ? Which variables are more related to SEZs in Gujarat?

8. How can the index be improved further?

3

Literature Review

The history of mankind is a chronicle of economic growth and prosperity attained through the ages. Economic history narrates the course of events either cataclysmic or evolutionary, which have impacted socio-economic development.

The deployment of SEZ as a tool for socio-economic progress by the governments is a relatively recent phenomenon. The Free Ports both of the bygone era and of modern times brought enormous wealth to city-states. SEZs, which are roughly modeled on the Free Ports, are driven by the need to get in FDI and technology and generate employment.

The socio-economic change, brought by the SEZs in the state of Gujarat, is the subject of this research study. It is, therefore, necessary to review the literature available on the socio-economic development and SEZs in general and in Gujarat in particular.

3.1 Introduction

Many studies have been conducted and papers written on Special Economic Zones (SEZs) both with International and Indian perspective. Such studies have covered many aspects of SEZs. There are published articles and series of working papers on SEZs as case studies. Most of these studies are based on using secondary sources. A few studies were carried out on socio-economic aspects of SEZs; however, no such evaluation study of SEZs appears to have been carried out in the context of SEZs in Gujarat.

After a brief overview of the theoretical background for economic development, the focus of this review is on the economic and social impacts of SEZs globally and in the Indian context covering the period broadly from 1980 to 2019. The literature is reviewed for each selected socio-economic parameter in two phases that are for the period from 1980 to 2004 and from 2005 to 2019. The second phase roughly corresponds to the period post the SEZ Act and related policies.

3.2 Theoretical Background for Economic Development

A bird's eye view of the various models of economic growth is necessary in order to gain an insight into the theoretical basis for the SEZs. A brief description of each of the three leading models is given below:

a. The Exogenous Economic Model
b. The Endogenous Growth Model
c. The Evolutionary Growth Theory

a. The Exogenous Economic Model

The increase in any input (labour, land, capital) at any specific point of the growth cycle will result in reduced output as compared to the output obtained by infusion of similar quantum of input at an earlier point. This is akin to the Law of Diminishing Returns; as the economy nears equilibrium, decreasing returns and rising marginal costs are experienced. This model was framed by Solow (1957). Technology is introduced as a factor in the growth model. Solow views technology and knowledge underlying the technology as forces that emanate from without the economic growth model and hence the term "Exogenous Economic Model".

b. The Endogenous Growth Model

In this model, technology and the underlying knowledge are not considered as external, but internal within the model. The technology and human capital

(Knowledge) generate increasing returns to drive the economy; unlike the diminishing returns of the physical capital in the exogenous model. In this scenario, it is very important that the policy makers focus on human capital growth. The basic steps are to facilitate and promote education and to invest in training and skill development through intervention directly or indirectly. Another important aspect is health care of the community and the individual which is necessary for sustained economic growth (Romer, 1986; Lucas, 1988). The rate of endogenous growth is determined by forces that are internal to the economic system, particularly those forces governing the opportunities and incentives to create technological knowledge. In the long term, the rate of economic growth, as measured by the growth rate of output per person, depends on the growth rate of total factor productivity (TFP), which is determined in turn by the rate of technological progress. It is silent on the determinants of technological progress. Endogenous growth theory as propounded by Lucas and Romer (1988; 1990) concentrates on technological progress and emphasizes the role of learning by doing knowledge spillover, Research and Development and education in driving economic growth. It starts from the observation that technological progress takes place through innovations, in the form of new products, processes and markets, many of which are the result of economic activities. For example, because firms learn from experience how to produce more efficiently, a higher pace of economic activity can raise the pace of process innovation by giving firms more production experience. Also, because many innovations result from R&D expenditures undertaken by profit-seeking firms, economic policies with respect to trade, competition, education, taxes and intellectual property can influence the rate of innovation by affecting the private costs and benefits of carrying out R&D.

c. The Evolutionary Growth Theory

The evolutionary growth, which is essentially in the biological domain, is applicable to economics. This approach is based on two distinct notions. The first notion is based on analogy and an appeal to the type of explanation common in biology: that forms of competition, innovation, variation and selection have analogues in the two fields and thus that similar reasoning can be extended to the non-biological domain. The second notion is even more universal in perspective. The argument is that, just as biological evolution has passed through distinct stages (prokaryotic and eukaryotic life, asexual and sexual reproduction, as well as a prebiotic stage), so too modern industrial society is just a distinct stage of this single process, subject to the same underlying laws if constrained by specific features of its current realization. Thus, economic evolution would be an intrinsic component of a larger evolutionary process, and not merely something accidentally amenable to certain forms of reasoning by analogy. The pioneers of the Evolutionary Theory were R. R. Nelson and S. G. Winter (1985) who proposed that both macro-economic behaviour, economic actors (firms, vendors and consumers) and the path of economic development can be depicted within the notion of economic evolution. This evolution is similar to biological evolution. Profit maximization is the objective of a firm; it is limited by the level of knowledge that the firm possesses to achieve this aim. Equipped with this limited knowledge, the firm selects paths to achieve the aim. Once a path fails than the firm chooses another path just like a biological species does. Hence economic growth is just like biological growth of species.

3.3 Phase I (1980–2004)

3.3.1 Economic Aspects

The canvas for the literature in this period consisted of matters of operations of SEZs or EPZs as they were then called on the economic front and issues relating to wages, livelihood, living conditions and others on the social front.

One aspect of operations that received a lot of attention in this period is the clustering of industries. The driving force behind cluster formation was cost reduction due to agglomeration.

Agglomeration Economies: Mass mechanized production of goods was the hallmark of the Industrial Revolution; this was a sea-change in the concept of space economy due to the transformation of industrial processes. The key enabler was technology that led firms to achieve constant returns to scale and fragment their production with minimum or nil cost implications. As more industrial processes were mechanized, there was the resultant increasing returns to scale, that is, the larger the quantity produced, the lower the average unit cost. Therefore, the industrialists increased the size of manufacturing units to derive benefit of the lower unit cost. Another development that was epochal in nature was the development of new transport systems by rail, road and sea which were quick and inexpensive. The reduction in transportation costs of goods was dramatic. Added to this was the increasing speed of transportation. According to Bairoch (1997), "... on the whole, between 1800 and 1910, it can be estimated that the lowering of the real (weighted) average prices of transportation was on the order of 10 to

1." Consequently, larger factories in central provinces could cater to the needs of markets in remote locations and cities. The idea of space economy was therefore propelled by the increasing returns to scale and non-prohibitive trade costs. This gave birth to a new economic field called economic geofigurey.

It is necessary to know the reason for firms to agglomerate instead of spreading evenly over space. Alfred Marshall was the first economist to furnish a theory and to build a model for agglomeration as early as in 1920. Marshall (1920) identified three categories of transport costs: moving goods, labour, and ideas. Reduced transport cost is the main driver for firms to form a cluster; this is called industrial agglomeration leading to "agglomeration economies." In the context of firms in a SEZ, the confines of the SEZ compel firms to be in close proximity to each other. The firms derive benefit from the presence of backward and forward linkages related to internal (firms located in SEZs) and external companies; the cost of moving final or intermediate goods is lowered.

There exist two key channels through which SEZs can develop networks of economic efficiency and interdependence (Martin, & Ottaviano, 1999). The first channel consists of the "backward linkages". Such linkages occur since suppliers and companies locate in close proximity, to minimize transport costs for raw materials and intermediate goods for SEZ-based firms. The second channel happens when the agglomeration externalities are reinforced via a demand channel, the "forward linkages" (ibid) (Farole, 2011).

The agglomeration of producers of final goods, intermediate suppliers, and consumers leads to a build-up of an ecosystem attracting more firms to SEZs or nearby locations; thereby creating a self-reinforcing agglomeration mechanism.

Core-Periphery Model and Agglomeration Mechanism: The economies of agglomeration have been further investigated by the economists. Krugman (1991) presented a model describing the phenomenon whereby firms tend to locate in areas where the transportation costs are the lowest. Such a location is also the larger market for the firm. The lower price of the manufacturing goods effectively means that the wages earned by the workers in real terms are higher. This single dynamic leads to migration of workers from the Periphery region to the Core region, which in turn enlarges the market of the Core region. As a result, more firms decide to locate closer to the Core market, which eventually leads to the agglomeration of all industrial activities in one region (the Core region). This Core–Periphery model has attracted the attention of economists, and its assumptions have been refined in many ways (Martin, & Ottaviano, 1999). Every variant attempts to simulate this agglomeration effect.

3.3.2 Social Aspects

Research in areas of labour rights or lack of the same, women-centric issues related to unequal wages, working hours and conditions like dormitory provision was conducted by scholars in different countries. Many researchers like Abeywardene, Alwis, Jayasena, Jayaveera, Sanmugam (1994), Bhattacharya (1998) and Smith (2003) made valuable contributions in these and other related areas both through empirical studies in the form of surveys and case history studies as well as through secondary research.

Remedio (1996) examined the situation with respect to employment, conditions of work and life and labour relations in four EPZs in Philippines. It was determined that the national and regional labour laws in the EPZs safeguarded worker's interests. Though the wage levels were higher, it also showed increase in the use of contract labour. The safety and health conditions were comparatively better. The labour was paid overtime for the extra hours worked and training programmes were in place. The working conditions, income levels, labour conditions, etc., are relatively well settled in EPZs.

One of the findings of Bhattacharya and Rahman A. (1999) is that local origin people including women secure employment in the EPZs in Bangladesh. EPZs became the vehicle for improving income levels of the local people and brought a transformation in their working conditions due to wage and non-wage benefits. EPZs may have failed in transfer of technology, but they are effective in diffusion of skills. It was further revealed that the female labour in Bangladesh's export-oriented apparel sector is concentrated mainly in the low-skills/low-wage segment of the production process limiting the prospects of future growth. There is, therefore, a strong case for a conscious public policy package which encourages skills development, facilitates technology transfer and raises productivity of female labour through training. Such a package will stimulate women's engagement in the apparel sector and will translate the comparative advantage of Bangladesh into competitive advantage. Such an approach will ultimately improve the quality of life in Bangladesh.

Smith (2003) in a study of Shenzhen SEZ compares the facility of dormitories provided by firms with housing facility provided earlier. One of the paternalistic management practices was provision of housing to workers. The dormitory facility for workers in SEZs is inherited from state-owned enterprises; the facility gives the employer control over the employees beyond the shop floor. Viewed in a larger perspective, common workers dormitories give individual employers access to labour like a tap which can be turned on and off as per the requirement of production and demand. The high labour mobility undermines the movement up the value chain as such movement is dependent upon retention of firm-specific skilled labour. The low cost to the employer acts as an incentive to persist with the system.

A few authors like Chen (1987) and Daniel Ding et al. (1997) made critical case studies. Approximate equal pay for men and women, limited difference between management and non-management salaries and widespread provision of housing and other benefits for employees seem to reflect the influence of the Chinese socialist ideology. These benefits are, however, conditional on employment and not guaranteed as a social right, thus modifying the previous institutionalized socialist view.

The rapid economic and demographic growth in Shenzhen makes a fascinating case study. Chen (1987) conducted a study titled "Magic and Myth of Migration in SEZ" to examine the sources and mechanisms of migration and characteristics of migrants to Shenzhen. It was determined that the labour force was young employed in new industries like electronics, textiles and precision instruments; while the age profile of workers in traditional industries like chemicals and construction materials was higher. Total income of Shenzhen workers varies widely across industries and is 2.0 to 2.5 times higher on average than that outside the zone. The educational level of the labour force is low. However, the living conditions of a growing temporary population in Shenzhen are a matter of concern. Shenzhen appears to have been built overnight. Higher wages are perhaps the strongest magnet, however, contractual employment structure which is becoming prevalent in Shenzhen offers limited security. The paper reviews on the rapid economic and demographic growth in Shenzhen especially on the concentration of various manufacturing units or clustering effect which had enormous benefits for women employment, growth in nominal and real wages and the best HRM practices.

3.4 Phase II (2005–2019)

There is a substantial body of literature covering this period on topics of socio-economic importance. The important aspects of SEZs are classified for a coherent review on the selected topics.

3.4.1 Infrastructure Boost

Governments across the globe desire for industrial development, which can be ushered in by the establishment of SEZs. Industrial development brings in its wake infrastructural development.

The feasibility of a SEZ depends on connectivity, distance from the factors of production and market. Devadas and Gupta in their treatise "Planning for SEZ: A Regional Perspective" (2011) proposed that land be identified by performing soft multi-criteria over land-suitability matrix. They further predict that SEZ will boost the infrastructure so that integrated development in a region can be achieved.

It is argued by Chandrachud and Gajalakshmi (2013) that development of infrastructure requires huge capital investment and the implementation of structural reforms is a time-consuming process. Thus, the establishment of SEZs would be the only realistic strategy governing the process of industrialization in India.

Hakami (2012) made a study of SEZ problems and prospects with special reference to Raigad and Pune Districts of Maharashtra and arrived at the conclusion that SEZ has led to infrastructural facilities in the study area.

SEZ pockets in landlocked areas particularly hubs like NOIDA and Gurgaon have emerged as key locations for IT, software and related areas. Palit (2009) found that SEZs in India are following specific locational patterns on account of discriminatory incentive structures that induce product-orientation in these zones. Coastal states are the favoured locations for SEZs probably due to existing infrastructure and low shipping costs. The new SEZs are being set up in favourable policy environments; giving SEZs a distinct service and specifically IT flavour.

On the other hand, S. N. Menon et al. (2009) in their paper "SEZ: The Rationale" postulated that the rationale of a SEZ is to increase exports and for this to happen the twin requirements are investment and infrastructure, while employment would be a consequence of the SEZ activity. Thus, the premise that SEZ leads to infrastructure boost may not hold true.

Another scholar Sampat (2010) also refuted that infrastructure development is a consequence of SEZ activity. He commented that SEZ are often interpreted as infrastructure or public facility whereas in reality they are enclaves for transnational capital to flourish in free market competition.

The establishment of SEZs has a profound impact on the local people's livelihoods, trade and tourism. The conundrum remains that while the people desire the benefits of development, they are wary of the evils that rapid development can bring like human and drug trafficking, traffic accidents and environmental degradation. Phyrum, Sothy, and Horn (2007) in their study on "Social and Economic Impacts of GMS Southern Economic Corridor on Cambodia" determined that infrastructure development along the corridors has improved the living conditions of the people in the corridor due to expanding business opportunities.

3.4.2 Foreign Direct Investment

International investors are wary of investing in foreign destinations due to barriers of regulation, local laws and so on. The SEZs which are outside the purview of local regulations and laws therefore serve as instruments of choice for investment.

Rzepka and Bujak in their seminal work "The Cross-sectional Analysis of SEZs in the Age of Globalisation, The Krakowska SEZ" postulated that FDI is growing at a pace faster than world trade or production and FDI minimizes the adverse effects of globalization. It was determined that investment decisions are conditioned by the possible benefits and SEZs have an advantageous position for the costs of conducting business activities in a zone are lower than the costs outside a zone, besides tax exemptions.

The quantum and quality of investment in a SEZ is determined by strategy, policy, service and control. The strategy and policy should be towards building brand image and business development in SEZ. How attractive a SEZ is for investment depends on the promotion measures like profile recognition, understanding of SEZ advantages, involvement of stakeholders. The values, volumes, kinds of business, benefits, profitability, procedures, character of SEZ should be disseminated to attract investment. The spatial location and other characteristics like uniqueness, size, zoning, magnitude, infrastructure all influence the investment decision. Rustidja et al. (2017) conducted case study for SEZ Mandalika and Bitung in Indonesia on investment promotion for community economic development. Bitung is into the manufacturing of agricultural implements and is close to the ocean, while Mandalika is a region that depends on tourism. The development of a positive image of the zone has emerged as the main driver for investments as it encourages growth and service centres. The positive image connects and promotes the intraregional and interregional activities. Findings of the study reveal that Mandalika SEZ emphasizes on promotion of competitiveness strategy, value chain and tourism network. On the other hand, Bitung SEZ focuses more on promotion strategy for increasing value-added logistics, profit, benefit and supply chain of industry.

FDI has accelerated the process of privatization of state enterprises in transition economies like Poland according to Jarosinski (2016). The economic development of areas, which remained undeveloped in the previous era and the qualitative changes in the lives of the people are clearly visible. In Poland, the establishment of SEZs was contemporaneous with the lifting of the iron curtain as mentioned in the work of Jarosinski titled "The Impact of SEZs on the Level of Socioeconomic Changes of Polish Regions".

On the other hand, a class of researchers, namely, Crane et al. (2018), suggest that the FDI should not be allowed freely as it may interfere with the policies of the local government. They therefore suggest that there has to be a balance between reforms that lead to a free market and the central plans for infrastructure development, provision of public goods and support to small-scale industries.

Mugobo and Mutize (2016) conducted a study by applying the Ordinary Least Squares (OLS) on SADC (South African Development Community) covering 15 of the 16 member countries' SEZs profit remittance data to draw a multi-regression model to establish the relationship between national income and FDI. Angola's GDP is driven by other variables and not FDI through SEZs. In Zimbabwe, there was no profit remittance despite $2.158 million FDI flowing into the country's SEZs in the most lucrative business segments. It is very difficult to quantify the costs of incentives and potential benefits lost in the creation of SEZs. SEZs are causing economic distortions due to preferential treatment to foreign investors, especially Chinese at the cost of local investors. The SEZs have also become a hub for graft and rent seeking by government officials and thus not yielding the desired benefits.

The existing theoretical literature is extended to explain the economic impact of SEZs and to assess the impact of newly notified SEZs by Aggarwal (2010). He also traces the economic philosophies to understand the rationale and benefits of SEZs. The heterodox school of thought suggests that the contribution of SEZ is that they serve as a platform to attract FDI; this is instrumental in the transfer of new technologies and generation of spillover effects which lead to the upgrade of the rest of the economy as well.

A study was conducted by Chakraborty, Gundimeda and Kathuria (2017) to investigate whether the enactment of the SEZ policies had any impact on the inflow of FDI for SEZs. It was determined that there is an increase in FDI; however, the fact remains that FDI flows continue to states with higher per capita income, states with better infrastructure and the coastal states. Thus, the issue of regional imbalance in development is not addressed and this may further widen the gap between the developed and less developed states. Deepak Shah (2012) states that the SEZ policy announced by the government of India in April 2000 aims at promoting exports of goods and services, investments from domestic and foreign sources, creation of employment opportunities, infrastructure facilities with emphasis on generating additional economic activity. There is, however, lack of a long-term strategy to counter the socio-economic consequences of the policy.

Anita Niraj (2016) in her work "Impact of SEZs on Indian Economy" published in the *International Journal of Social Science and Humanities Research* postulated that the first generation SEZs attracted a lot of FDI and exports; the second generation of SEZs is more into diversification of economic activities. Unlike Chinese SEZs, which have pivoted the development of the underdeveloped regions of the country, Indian SEZs have mushroomed near existing urban and industrial areas.

In a study of the SRI city SEZ, D. U. Kumar (2018) laments the fact that while the SEZ did act as a magnet for FDI, it did not address the issue of inequality and though the local people were provided employment and skills, the unequal setting of the village was replicated on to the SEZ.

Mukherjee et al. (2015) postulated that the government of India has permitted 100 per cent FDI to attract investment in SEZs and FTWZs. There is an apparent gap between the government and domestic private funding for infrastructural needs related to SEZs; this gap is best met by FDI.

The contribution of FDI in SEZs is to the tune of INR 4,331,420 million in 2017. The most important characteristic of SEZs in India is the 100 per cent FDI. Domestic as well as foreign and NRI investors are interested in investing their money in Indian SEZs. There has been constant rise in investment across all sectors because of change in policy after the SEZ Act, 2005 (Kumari, B., Tayyab, M., & Rahman, A. 2018).

Attracting foreign investment is the raison d'être of SEZs. K. L. Gupta (2016) conducted an empirical study on SEZs set up in Gujarat and found out that multi-product SEZs and IT/ITeS SEZs attract the largest amount of FDI. The investment in IT/ITeS increased four times in a limited period.

3.4.3 Exports

The rationale for setting up SEZs was to provide a level playing field for local industries to produce goods for exports. Thus, SEZs offer duty-free imports of inputs and encourage the flow of FDI all in an effort to promote exports from the host country through SEZs. The research scholars however draw mixed conclusions regarding the role of SEZs in export promotion. While some arrive at the conclusion that SEZs have led to additional exports, others do not subscribe to this view.

At the extensive margin, SEZ firms in open economies are 25 per cent more likely to export than their non-SEZ counterparts, with a large negative effect in closed economies. At the intensive margin, SEZs increase exports, but only in countries with barriers to imports where the estimate is 3.6 per cent. This suggests that SEZs may reduce the costs of intermediate inputs, encouraging both domestic and foreign sales. The estimated effect of introducing SEZ can be meaningful but is heavily contingent on the local economic environment. Difference in the probability of exporting seems to be the result of other differences across firms, not whether or not they are in a SEZ. R. B. Davies and A. Mazhikeyev (2019) arrived at the above conclusions through a detailed study on the firm's probability of exporting, export intensity and value of exports: The impact of SEZ on exporting behaviour.

S. Gopalkrishnan (2007) determines that the high level of imports both for production and for consumer durables affected the foreign exchange earnings in China; the net exports from SEZs were barely 16 per cent of their gross exports in 1990, approximately half of their already low figures for most Asian SEZs. This is a major negative aspect of SEZ.

SEZ led to a significant improvement in economic activity in the country, the most important contribution is making exports competitive. This is evident by the increase in India's share of exports globally. There is the need to make people socially and politically aware of the benefits of SEZs (Das, C. 2017).

A study was conducted by A. Shrivastava and M. Panga (2017) on export performance of India with reference to SEZ. The aim was to establish a causal relationship between exports from SEZs and total exports from India. The findings were: there is a decrease in total exports; however, the SEZ contribution to exports is on the increase; the increase in exports from SEZ will lead to increase in the value of total exports; SEZ performance in different states is not uniform, the export contribution to total goods and services exported from the states of Gujarat, Karnataka and Tamil Nadu is significantly greater.

An analysis of the efficiency of SEZs within the framework of stochastic production frontier technique was conducted by M. L. Tantri (2011). The analysis carried out in respect of the seven conventional SEZs indicates that foreign trade policy changes effected in the year 2000 have a significant impact on output/export efficiency of SEZs. As a result, the average TE score of these enclaves have increased by almost 25 per cent during the SEZ period as compared to the EPZ regime. During the EPZ period, there were very few exporting units operating in each SEZ. This resulted in underutilization of the area available and of government investment. Thus, the argument for large

SEZs as engine of growth and improvement of their efficiency is supported by this analysis.

S. N. Menon and S. K. Mitra (2009) in their study titled "SEZ the Rationale" state that the export-led growth strategy is beneficial and SEZs drive exports. The core objective of a SEZ would be to increase export-oriented economic activity. Investment and infrastructure would be prerequisites for this to happen, while employment would be a consequence of increased activity.

A study was conducted by Neelam Kumari and Kiran Dhanju (2017) on the export performance and efficiency of SEZ in Haryana. The specific tasks were to evaluate the export performance of SEZ during 2007–2013 and to calculate the efficiency of SEZs. It was revealed that these SEZs are highly inefficient at aggregate level as well as at individual level. With regard to exports, the picture for the reference period is a gloomy one as the trend is downward.

Deepak Shah (2012) in his paper on the effects of SEZs in India on the local people in terms of their accessibility to drinking water, release of effluents by industries into river systems thereby destroying the portability of the water, states that the SEZ policy of 2005 has noble objectives like promoting exports of goods and services, investments, employment, infrastructure facilities and general economic activity. He laments the lack of a long-term strategy to counter the socio-economic consequences, like loss of farming jobs and access to drinking water to the people living in the SEZ shadow area. In his view, the SEZs may have succeeded in promoting exports but they have not generated employment commensurate with the disruption of the lives of the displaced persons.

Kumari, B., Tayyab, M., and Rahman, A. (2018) report that the export output from SEZs in 2016 was INR 4,673,370 million which is 19.8 per cent of total exports from India.

Gujarat has undoubtedly a major role in total exports of SEZs in India; however, that can be attributed largely to one SEZ viz. Reliance (Parmar & Bhaiya, 2015).

3.4.4 Clusters/Agglomeration

Clustering is a phenomenon when firms producing similar products or complementary products tend to spout in proximity to each other. The savings on transportation costs are clearly visible; there are other benefits of ready market and of skill development. Thus, the benefits of clustering can be listed as follows: reduced transport costs, shared inputs and productivity spill overs due to learning and technology transfers. The clustering of firms in and around SEZs leads to formation of so-called thick skilled labour pools which would benefit SEZ-based firms (Neumark & Simpson, 2014). This availability of a big labour pool is particularly relevant for SEZs that focus on a specific industry or supply chain. Labour pooling improves the matching between firms and workforce (Combes & Duranton, 2006). SEZs can generate a large skilled labour pool, due to natural (workers being attracted by the higher wages or job opportunities) and intended (SEZ-specific policies or strategies to attract workers) forces. Firms can benefit from higher labour productivity, sustain lower search costs and obtain better labour matches for jobs (Combes & Duranton, 2006; Rodríguez-Pose & Crescenzi, 2008). In addition, employees can take advantage of a wider choice of employment opportunities.

These conclusions are based on the assumption that workers are able to move across firms and industries. The trade-off for employers is that easy job mobility leads to poaching (abid). As competition for skilled workers intensifies, employers raise the wages of these workers to avoid losing them or to attract the more productive ones. The agglomeration of firms in SEZs is expected to lead to technological spillovers. The agglomeration of firms in specialized SEZs promotes Marshall-Arrow-Romer (MAR) externalities (Hu 2007; Rodríguez-Pose and Crescenzi, 2008). Concentrating firms within a common industry facilitates industry-related knowledge spillovers among workers and promotes further specialization and industry-specific innovation, leading to firm growth (Henderson, 2004). Multi-sectoral SEZs create an environment for Jacobian externalities (Carlino et al., 2001; Rodríguez-Pose & Crescenzi, 2008). The diversity of firms and their activities in SEZs enable firms to take advantage of knowledge complementarities and cross-industry transfer of ideas.

The case for creating SEZs in Africa is considered in view of spatial industrial policies designed to facilitate clustering. Evidence from low-income countries suggests that such agglomeration economies may be substantial in endogenously formed clusters (Newman & Page, 2017). To date, Africa's experience with spatial industrial policy has been largely disappointing. Most African SEZs have failed to reach the levels of physical, institutional and human capital needed to attract global investors.

Walsh (2015) in a socio-economic study of SEZs in the Mekong region determined that clustering of related industries can provide benefits in the form of information spillovers, skill formation in the labour force and enhanced division of labour among involved enterprises. The proximity provides incentives for other stakeholders to locate within the same area, for firms to be able to exchange important resources and inputs and for intensified local knowledge of supply and demand conditions to reduce the risk of market failures.

Azhar and Adil (2019) in a study of the effects of agglomeration on socio-economic outcomes with reference to Punjab (Pakistan) determined that industries are agglomerated in Punjab and this agglomeration is positively associated with efficiency of firms. Both agglomeration and better infrastructure allows for more social inclusion. The firms and districts are benefitting from positive externalities of agglomeration economies.

An analysis by Aggarwal (2010) suggests that the economic contribution of SEZs in the Indian context can be explained within the framework of the agglomeration economies and global value chain theories.

3.4.5 Land Issues

The use of land for industrial development impacts the lives of not only the displaced people, their occupation and livelihood but also the country as a whole in terms of food security in case the acquired land is agricultural. In a broader perspective, the change in land use impacts global climate as is evidenced by the global warming and the increasing frequency of extreme weather events. This is brought home to us by the media and the activists including young children who have taken it upon them to save the planet. The literature on land as expected dwells on the ill-effects of land acquisition for the setting up of SEZs. It is seen that in the garb of setting up SEZs, huge chunks of land are acquired by the government; only small parcels of such land are used for setting up SEZs and the balance land remains unutilized or is used for the wrong purpose like real estate by the developers.

Many farmers lost their land due to SEZ development in the greater Mekong region. SEZs affect the nature of land not only within their confines but also have effects on the land around them. This is true whether their action might be considered in terms of a magnet which draws resources such as people and capital towards them or as black holes which destroy everything they consume (Walsh, 2015).

Thabchumpon et al. (2012) conducted a case study of the Dawei SEZ in Myanmar. The construction of a deep sea port, 160 kms eight-lane road and a large water reservoir will have a profound impact on the affected population. The resettlement plan is a threat to the livelihood security of the people who were mainly farmers and now have no food security as the paddy fields have all been acquired for the project. The decision makers in the government have focussed excessively on the economic benefits of the project giving scant attention to the environmental and social impacts on the affected local people who stand displaced.

The SEZ concept promoted land development in China without directly addressing impacts on cultivable land and the natural resource base (S. Gopalkrishnan, 2007).

SEZs can lead to some serious consequences. Struggles on the land issue are already surfacing in different parts of the country. Farmers are neither adequately compensated nor properly rehabilitated. Instead of firms competing with each other, we have the spectre of states competing with one another in a rush to the bottom by promising cheap land, tax incentives and other benefits to set up SEZs. N. K. Sharma (2009) concludes in the socio-economic study of SEZ that the SEZs are basically instruments of redistribution of wealth from numerous poor and marginal farmers to the private entrepreneurs.

It was revealed that no assessment study was conducted by the state government to study the impact of the proposed SEZs in Goa. The people successfully fought against the SEZs forcing the government to reject all the 15 SEZs including 3 notified ones. The land allocation was done in a hurry without following proper rules and regulations. S. Abreu (2014) reveals this in his work "The Struggle Against SEZ in Goa".

Although SEZs account for a quarter of India's exports, only 154 out of the 587 SEZs were operational as on March 2013. The major problems of SEZs are land acquisition without proper rehabilitation, sector-specific employment generation, revenue loss and so on. To be economically viable, SEZs should be approved over a particular land area (greater than 1,000 acres) for rapid economic growth in the area and for it to be profitable and self-sustainable (Prajapati, 2016).

Niraj Anita (2016) states that access to cultivable land, forest areas, grazing land, water resources gets restricted due to SEZs. Where the people could earlier freely avail of these resources, access is now blocked by the setting up of SEZs. These losses cause material, economic and social deprivations for the affected people. The acquisition of agricultural land for SEZs will create the problem of food security.

S. Parwez (2016) conducted a study of the dimensions of land acquisition with respect to establishment of SEZs across India. Large part of acquired land ends up in the hands of the real estate companies rather than intended productive sectors of industry and infrastructure. Forcible acquisition and transfer of land to corporates leads to large-scale unemployment and displacement especially when large part of tract remains unutilized.

There is no mention of the number of people to be displaced by these zones, let alone how the government intends to address the issue of displacement. The struggle of residents of the 22 villages against their inclusion in the MSEZ reveals the irregularities in the land allocation and acquisition process for the SEZ (Sampat, 2010).

Land dispossession is being used to facilitate projects that have, at best, limited prospects for improving the lives of the most historically oppressed groups in rural India; instead, relatively skilled and knowledge-intensive growth—IT/ITeS and pharmaceuticals—ensured that the bulk of secure employment went to better-educated city-dwellers (Agarwal, S. et al. 2019).

The land-affected people alleged that local politicians and brokers exploited them. Most of those who had legal documents evidencing title to the land agreed that the land fetched a fair price. Those who did not possess legal documents agreed that the land did not get a fair price. The awareness of state-level land acquisition norms and Land Acquisition Bill 2013 was very low (Nidheesh, 2018).

The resistance to land acquisition is related both to the acquisition processes and the relative costs and benefits of recent development initiatives of which SEZs are an integral part. The SEZs are not likely to create new infrastructure, rather they tend to be located in and around megacities; they may free-ride on pre-existing infrastructure. They are predominantly located in districts that already have high levels of non-farm activity. Indian SEZs are neither similar to China's manufacturing SEZs nor they are developing much social infrastructure (Jenkins et al. 2015).

A study by Paul and Sarma (2013) on the livelihood effects of industrialization on the displaced households with evidence from the Falta SEZ reveals that there is a need for a policy framework to address SEZ-related displacement, livelihood and gender issues. Many members of displaced households do get employment in the industrial zone. The wages are low due to lower level of education.

The acquisition of land for SEZs has impact on the livelihood of the communities located in the area surrounding the SEZs. It could at times destroy the livelihood sources of agrarian and landless households leading to their displacement. In Mundra, there was direct impact on livelihood of fishing communities; first, loss of access to the traditional transient fishing sites and second, an absence of entitlement to compensation. The impact of loss is severe in Reliance SEZ where about 80 per cent of the households fear a major decline in the livestock economy. Loss of gauchar land (grazing areas) is likely to have significant adverse effects for those mainly dependent on livestock for livelihood. With respect to economic benefits, the response was found to be somewhat positive in Dahej and Reliance

(Jamnagar) especially among farmers whose agricultural land could fetch handsome prices. Nonetheless in terms of direct employment gains, the impact is fairly low in Jamnagar followed by Mundra and then Dahej (Shah, A., Nandani, D., & Joshi, H. 2012).

A contrary view was propounded by Bhatnagar and A. Shrivastava (2009). There are so many benefits and exemptions available to the SEZ units and SEZ developers but politics is not allowing it to enjoy and contributing in economic growth. Farmers and land owners do not think about the future, they think that their land or motherland is being snatched by others, but they must be made to understand, that the development is only possible by the industrialization in rural area and political will.

3.4.6 Employment

The generation of employment is an important outcome of SEZs. Governments sacrifice revenue loss, for example, customs duties in SEZs with the belief that the employment generated will more than compensate for any such loss. The generation of direct and indirect employment aims at improving the quality of life for people especially those residing in or near the SEZ area. The quality of life including education levels, life expectancy, health care, housing and other indicators of prosperity have registered a dramatic rise in China, due to a large part to the huge employment generated by the SEZs. The experience in India is however mixed as most of the jobs are in IT/ITeS areas which may not benefit the local people (Kumari, B., Tayyab, M., & Rahman, A., 2018).

In the Pearl River Delta (PRD), specifically the Shenzhen SEZ, there is a new residence permit system for migrant rural workers with some access to social security benefits, for example, subsidized education and health services. Leong and Pratap (2011) conducted a study to understand the sufferings, challenges and opportunities confronting the Chinese working class in PRD. There is a new wage implementation with contract labour system. The working class has emerged as the single important factor with immense power to affect not only the economic growth but also the policies. It was concluded that the impact has been positive for labour.

Razzaque et al. (2018) in a study of the SEZs in Bangladesh concluded that SEZs have a strong impact on employment generation, including women employment. Export promotion from lagging regions triggers greater demand for labour from small farm, non-farm and lower-skilled households. Such households are otherwise vulnerable and tend to be excluded from governmental development schemes. Thus, SEZ-led industrialization strategy can facilitate the acceleration of economic growth, employment generation and poverty reduction in Bangladesh.

An and Kritchanchai (2018, December) conducted a case study in Kanchanaburi Province (Thailand) to propose hospital capacity planning in Kanchanaburi reckoning the upcoming SEZ. The key barriers to medical access in Kanchanaburi were the relatively poor socio-economic status, lack of health insurance, high mobility and real or perceived stigma of discrimination. Proper policy and legal frameworks are necessary to remove all barriers to health care access in respect of mobile and migrant population. Increasing the employment demand in a particular region has an impact on the health care system due to occupational diseases/injuries and number of workers.

Accessing labour and high energy costs are the key constraints to the cost competitiveness of SEZ firms. Kinyondo, Newman and Tarp (2015) suggest that the role and function of SEZs in Tanzania offer minimal benefits to the local economy.

Ebenstein (2012) examined the impact of entry of MNCs into local labour markets on employment, productivity and wages in the SEZs of China. Foreign MNCs raise employment levels in manufacturing and both foreign as well as domestic firms experience rising productivity as well as rising profitability levels. However, the record is not so good with generation of high-paying jobs for workers. No evidence was found suggesting that average wage rates have increased in SEZs relative to others, in spite of large increase in productivity of firms. The SEZs areas are characterized by rising prices, thus the welfare implications for the residents are ambiguous. While the SEZs have provided employment for millions of rural workers, these areas have yet to experience real wage growth.

The firms in the SEZs have positive effect on the regional labour market. SEZs are therefore the key tool of regional development in the Czech Republic (Damborsky, M., et al. 2012).

The Kigali SEZ has made significant contribution to permanent employment and domestic sales. Successful SEZs are those that generate spill-overs and foster institutional reforms in the broader economy. This SEZ has helped Rwanda steer away from its traditional export products (coffee, tea and minerals) into new sectors like food and agro processing, textiles and furniture (Steenburgen, V., et al. 2017).

SEZs are slightly above the national average in terms of employment and there has been no dynamic development in this impact factor over the policy horizon in Poland. Most of the effect comes from the FDI into the SEZ. The wage or income effect of the SEZ policy is absent (Jensen, C., & Winiarczyk, M. 2014).

In a study of the negative aspects of SEZs in China, S. Gopalkrishnan (2007) determined that labour abuse is accompanied, unsurprisingly, by crime.

Khan and Anwar (2017) in a study titled "SEZs Opportunities and Challenges for Pakistan" state that there is no clear labour policy for the protection of domestic labour. Enforcement of labour laws is patchy at best at federal level, the provinces do not have the muscle to implement at local level. Rent seeking, political interference and governance issues led to the failures of SEZs.

In the Indian context, SEZs are responsible for employment generation through industrial development along with other objectives of reviving ancillary industries, resolving housing problems, accelerating economic growth and infrastructure development, etc. (Devadas, V., & Gupta, V. 2011).

Employment generation, both direct and indirect, has thus far been the most important channel, through which SEZs have impacted on human development and poverty reduction in India. SEZs can therefore act as an initiator of human development and poverty reduction in India (Raheem, A., 2011, in Impact of SEZ on Human Development and Poverty Alleviation: An Indian Experience). Even though the contribution of SEZ to employment is rather limited, they have contributed significantly to employment at the regional level.

SEZs generate employment, attract FDI and promote exports from India (Kumari, B., Tayyab, M., & Rahman, A., 2018). Generation of employment is the main source of benefit of a SEZ. In India, SEZ provided employment to 13,470,000 people in 2006 and at present it is estimated that 2.2 million people work in SEZs at national level.

The performance of SEZs has been reasonably well for employment generation (Das, C., 2017).

Anuradha and Mahendra (2010) assert that the Mangalore SEZ will lead towards greater economic activity and development of the region. The multi-product SEZ would create 50,000 to 1,00,000 direct employment and 1,00,000 to 2,00,000 indirect employment by the end of Phase II.

Nearly 75 to 80 per cent of the proposed employment emanates from IT/ITeS and the traditional exporting sectors, viz., apparels, textiles, gems and jewellery, footwear and pharmaceuticals. Almost 90 per cent of the jobs are in the 20 districts of India which have higher than average ranking for urbanization, industrialization and education. The multi-product SEZs, which are the harbinger of manufacturing growth, contribute but a sixth of the projected employment growth. Thus, one cannot say that the SEZ policy is promoting manufacturing employment even by going with the official numbers (Partha, 2009). Apparently, it looks like the net foreign exchange earned is a bigger concern than employment generation.

Kadam (2012) observed that the current employment in SEZs is 1,13,426 persons. SEZs have potential for employment of software engineers and other skilled workers. The labour laws are stringent.

The direct employment gains by the land owners who lost land on account of setting up of SEZ is fairly low in Jamnagar, followed by Mundra and Dahej (Shah et al. 2012).

Aggarwal (2007) argues that while SEZs have been effective in generation of both direct and indirect employment, the human capital development is limited. SEZs have the potential to enhance human capabilities, but for this potential to be realized the government must devise strategies to strengthen the opportunities that are likely to arise, protect the interests of SEZ workers and forge linkages between the SEZs and the domestic economy.

Deepak Shah (2012) concludes that the SEZs do not have major impact on employment pattern in India. Therefore, one of the aims of the SEZ policy that is the creation of employment opportunities remains unfulfilled.

On analysing the effect of Indian SEZs on both the formal and the vast informal sector of the Indian economy, Hyun and Ravi (2017) determined as follows:

Positive effects on firm size and productivity are in the formal sector, whereas the informal manufacturing sector experiences the opposite effects.

The effect on workers' wages is non-uniform due largely to the opposite effects SEZs seem to have on the formal and informal sectors of the economy. Workers who are relatively more educated and employed in the formal sector experience positive wage increases. However, those workers who are less educated and employed in the informal sector do not positively gain.

Cirera and Lakshman (2017) on study of the impact of SEZs on employment, wages and labour conditions in developing countries conclude: there is no addition of employment, firms relocated from outside to inside; wages could be higher in some cases and lower in other cases, gender gap in wages also persists; long working hours as compared to outside the zone; evidence of health-related issues in some cases and unionization is banned which suggests absence of labour law.

There is little difference between the legal regime confronting labour within and outside the SEZs. The regime of labour governance in SEZs is oriented towards the non-implementation of the existing law. The act of shifting the implementation of labour laws from the Labour Commissioner to the Development Commissioner without doubt generates a conflict of interest in the office, generating costs to the extent there is an inducement with the office not to privilege labour interests in relation to those of employers. There is a definite case to reform the laws in a manner such that both labour and producer interests are adequately balanced; laws that enable producers to be more flexible backed by social security and labour standard legislation (Singh, 2012).

It was determined by More (2015) that SEZ developers and the units prefer capital rather than labour-intensive methods. Since labour laws are not followed, there is no protection to the labourers. He concluded that SEZs increase financial disequilibrium and lead to imbalance in the environment. However, SEZs are the best bet for export growth and development of the backward regions of the country.

Kumar (2018) postulated that SEZs are not much effective in reducing inequalities in society based on caste, gender, place of birth and so on.

Inequality is understood in this work as the state where the individuals and communities were disproportionately ranked in terms of social status, economic well-being, educational backwardness and the existence of unequal opportunities and rewards for different social positions or statuses within a group or society. Even though local people were employed and imparted skills, the inequality factor remained unchanged, it was replication of the unequal setting of the village on to the SEZ. Low caste persons continued to work in low paying jobs and promotion to higher levels was shunned. SEZs are not effective in improving inequality present in social settings based on sex, caste and so on.

Parwez (2015) did an analysis of labour law and practices followed in SEZs and their impact. Only a few firms in the SEZ abide by labour laws and recognize workers' basic rights and the importance of healthy industrial relations. Many workers face uncertainty regarding the tenure of their employment and live in constant fear. The proposed labour legislation framework in SEZ has been purposely structured to encourage the non-implementation of labour welfare laws and investment.

3.4.7 Women and SEZs

Johanna Rickne (2010), Prof. Rao and P. Usha (2018), and Esmaeilpour et al. (2016) in their studies proved that the SEZs had positive impact on women empowerment through equal wages to women.

Rickne (2010) conducted a study on gender, wages and social security in China's industrial sector. The study compared average earnings and productivities for men and women employed in roughly 0.20 million Chinese industrial enterprises. The results suggested that women's wages exceeded their contributions to firm productivity. There is no empirical evidence to suggest that there is earnings discrimination against female industrial workers. The under-representation of women in state-owned firms is balanced out by their over-representation in foreign-invested firms, which tend to comply with social insurance regulations. Equal average wages between men and women are found in firms located in Chinese SEZs.

Women, especially young women, get employment opportunities and improved status in family; however, women are prone to exploitation in the working environment (Aggarwal, 2007).

Women's share to total employment in SEZs is substantially higher. Most SEZs impart on-the-job training to their workers. Both direct and indirect employment are major spillover effects of SEZs (Mane & Salve, 2014).

SEZs have opened up opportunities for wage employment for women in the formal sector, thereby increasing their employability as well as improving their position in the household. Most SEZs impart on-the-job training to their employees; but training is focussed, employer-driven and lasts for a short duration. Women were employed in SEZs; however, their social status in family remained subordinate and they drew lower wages (Kumar, 2018). SEZs are not very effective in improving inequality present in social settings based on caste, gender and so on.

The emphasis on income and profits tended to overcome inhibition and discrimination against women entering into the labour market. Women's economic empowerment through workforce participation is highly connected with poverty reduction. The educational expansion has greatly improved women's skills to take up specialized jobs and ability to use improved technology efficiently. Improvements in techniques of production have contributed greatly in enhancing productivity and incomes of women. Urbanization has weakened the influence of joint families of social norms affecting women's role perpetuated by the system. The higher cost of living in cities offered strong motivation for increased female work anticipation to supplement family income (Prof. Rao & Usha P., 2018).

Women earn about 17 percentage points less compared to men after controlling for education and experience and this gap is 5–10 per cent higher for SEZ employees. This gap is narrowing over time likewise the gender education gap (Paul & Sarma, 2013).

3.4.8 Indirect Economy

SEZs cannot exist as enclaves for long. Backward linkages boost development of the area surrounding SEZs. They also provide employment for the skilled and semi-skilled people in the neighbourhood. A brief view of the literature on the indirect economy impact of SEZs is given.

A detailed study was conducted by Luthuli and Houghton (2015) on the role of Dube Trade Port in the development of the communities surrounding its area of operations. The Port allows for public participation as it holds briefing sessions with the members of the community, neighbouring municipalities as well as various government departments, especially the education department. The Port has worked with a number of schools from surrounding communities in its CSR&I programme. Thus, it was concluded that the Dube Port advanced human capital development through education and skill development programmes not only for its employees but also for communities around and beyond Dube Trade Port precincts.

Nallathiga (2007) made a critical evaluation of the performance of the Chinese SEZs to assess the potential for emulating the model for India to achieve industrial and regional economic development. The nearby areas would get economic stimulus as the input materials for the SEZs would be procured from these areas. The surpluses in idle capital, labour can be gainfully deployed. The SEZs would provide placements for students in the educational and technical institutions in the area, enhancing the growth of the knowledge economy. It was anticipated that the SEZs would provide an opportunity for the interface with the state of art production systems in the world through FDI and technology transfer. As in China, the SEZs could accelerate the development and industrialization of the hinterland in India.

Another study by Alkon (2018) was conducted to find if the SEZs induce developmental spillovers. It was concluded that SEZs do not have spillover effects on neighbouring sub-districts. Thus, there is a puzzling divergence of the effects of SEZs in India as compared to China. In China, the SEZs have accelerated the development of the sub-districts through spillover effect. Alkon offers the explanation that in India the extraction of rent and the absence of incentives to constrain such rent extraction could be largely responsible for the lack of developmental spillover.

By taking the life-cycle study approach to SEZs and their impact on the indirect economy, Omar and Stoever (2008) reached the conclusion that two crucial aspects of a successful EPZ is the development of backward linkages and gradual integration into the rest of the host economy. Hence, SEZs promote the structural transformation of the economy.

3.4.9 SEZs and Health Issues

Some research scholars have conducted studies on the direct impact of SEZs on the health of the people in the surrounding areas.

A study was conducted by Nair et al. (2011) on the respiratory health problems associated with development of infrastructure among residents living in the proximity of SEZs in India. The objective of the study was to obtain primary data on parameters of respiratory health so that guidelines may be framed on the health and safety implementation of the SEZ policy. It was determined that large-scale infrastructural development results in air pollution and high prevalence of respiratory diseases. When compared to other localities which aren't near SEZs, there was higher incidence of both obstructive as well as restrictive lung function among Bhangal residents. The lung function abnormalities and distance from NSEZ were seen to be inversely related. Infrastructure-related activities like house building, road construction, increase of heavy trucks and containers in the region lead to poor quality of air and increase in PM (particulate matter) concentrations. This leads to decrease in lung function.

A study by Nidheesh (2018) on the affected people in SEZs in India found that due to the working of the SEZs, air and sound had polluted, water level got reduced and various illnesses had affected the local people.

The residents of the district could be exposed to pollution generated by SEZ industries in non-residential localities such as places of work, education and shopping (Chakraboty and Basu 2019).

3.4.10 Impact of SEZs on Immediate Neighbourhood and Others

One important concern that bedevils governments across the globe is how to address the regional disparities in income and development. Traditionally, economic policies favour the development of urban centres while rural areas continue to lag on development parameters. Crane et al. (2018) on a study of "China's SEZs: Analysis of Policy to Reduce Regional Disparities" conclude that the one solution to reduce regional disparities is to extend the influence of SEZs. Every additional SEZ in China was used as a tool to attract FDI for economic activity. This led to convergence of economic development across regions and narrowing of the interregional gap.

An interesting approach to address the issue of regional disparities in a huge country like Russia was the application of Priority Development Area (PDA) plan. A study by Druzhinin (2019) on PDA for the Far Eastern Federal District reveals that the outcome of the PDA approach has been positive. It has resulted in 4.5 times increase in the volume of investments and doubling of the number of residents in the area.

Degtyareva et al. (2018) who also examined this approach, however, comments that the management companies of PDA are entrusted with almost unlimited powers and excessive centralized power. The danger is that the Federal Law No. 473 lacks the checks and balances necessary to avoid abuse of power by the management companies. Moreover, the legal regime is not available for small businesses.

The success of SEZs hinges on three factors namely low labour costs with high productivity, attractive FDI policy through tax and customs reliefs and trade preferences by the developed countries (Curran et al. 2009). These key factors were identified from the detailed studies of EPZs in Madagascar, Mauritius, Kenya and Maputo in Mozambique. This study concluded that the conditions obtained may not hold good for sub-Saharan Africa. It also concluded that the long-term costs and benefits for the SEZ units are unknown and that beyond providing employment there is little contribution of the SEZs to the local economy.

A 2009 benchmarking survey of the units in Batam, Bintam and Karimum SEZ (BBK SEZ) was conducted by Kam et al. (2009). The survey revealed that the units in BBK SEZ had strong linkages with Singapore on virtually all economic parameters. Singapore looms large as the source of revenue and purchase origin, technology licensing and R&D collaboration. The units were satisfied with infrastructure and business environment factors and relatively less satisfied with labour and governance factors.

When tax rates are generally high, that by itself is an encouragement for choosing SEZs as a location for business activities. In such a scenario, the main incentive for establishment of SEZs economic activity therein is the tax exemption. Rzepka and Bujak postulate that high tax rates outside is the driver for activities in the SEZs. The zone influences positively the development of the regions proximal to its location. This is supported by the fact that the land on which the zone is located is gradually expanded with increasing worksites and investment (Rzepka & Bujak, (2015).

Esmaeilpour and Ebrahimi (2015) conducted a study on the impact of Pars SEZ on the development of Kangan city. The impact was positive on many development parameters like exports, public education, government tax revenues, electrification and piped water supply to the neighbouring villages, road development, shrimp farming and employment generation. They concluded that the Pars SEZ had the most effect on economic indicators and the least on cultural ones.

In a study of hospital capacity planning for Kanchanaburi (Thailand), it was determined that increasing the employment demand in a particular region has an impact on the health care system due to types of occupational diseases/injuries and number of workers. The key barrier to a limited access to medical service in Kanchanaburi is the relatively poor socio-economic status, lack of health insurance, high mobility, language barrier and real or perceived stigma of discrimination. The barriers to access health care for migrant and mobile population would be removed with proper policy and legal framework (An & Kritchanchai, 2018, December).

Studies suggest that financially constrained firms may not be upgrading to more modern electricity-intensive technologies. On analysis of the electricity intensity of the firms in SEZs, it was determined that the sum of the financial variable and its SEZ interaction cancels out, in other words, for the firms in a SEZ, there is no difference in the electricity intensity of those firms that are financially constrained and those that are not (Davies et al., 2016).

In the Indian context, Sivaramakrishnan (2009) discussed on how to address the urbanization implications of SEZ development through laws or executive action. Of the sample of 154 SEZs selected, at least 127 SEZs are found to be in the vicinity of large towns or cities. The SEZs prefer to graft themselves onto existing urban centres in the economic sense.

A few studies go beyond and cover matters like social sustainability, social infrastructure and social health including measures like establishment of hospitals, vocational schools and even an academy for fisheries. Topics of this nature are covered in papers such as those by Deni and Husain; Abbas (2014); An and Kritchanchai (2018); Phyrum, Sothy and Horn (2007); Nair et al., (2011); and Singh and Sanjeev (2019).

3.5 SEZ Policy and Act

The blame for the poor performance of the EPZs in the pre-reform period can be squarely put on the loopholes in the policy structure of the country. The supply side of the Indian economy could not keep pace with the international requirement. Tantri (2013) commented that imitating the Chinese model of trade policy is an improvement on the conventional EPZs. However, decentralization is still lacking. The current SEZ policy is clear on the objectives, has a broader economic area to operate and recognizes the role of different actors in the promotion of SEZs. Tantri opines that despite the numerous credits in favour of the SEZ policy, the policy needs a pragmatic re-visit.

Kumar (2008) has similar views and argues that the SEZ policy was evolved gradually with relaxation of procedural and operational rigidities. The net value addition post the SEZ Act compares favourably with other Asian countries; however, it is not consistent. The trend growth rate in value addition is not statistically different from zero. SEZs failed to promote non-traditional exports; traditional export sectors like electronics, gems and jewellery dominate the zones. Kumar asserts that the SEZ scheme needs a total reorientation if the hype created on the SEZs is to be justified.

A detailed review of the SEZ Act was conducted by Sahoo (2015) with reference to economic policy, impact and land-related issues. The system of according extensions by the Board of Approvals devoid of an appropriate corrective measures or deterrent action resulted in de-notification and diversion of land for commercial purpose. The SEZ performance appraisal system had inadequacies; there is audit system or cross verification; the developers can get away by misrepresenting facts. The SEZ deal with different products like textiles, gems and so on; these product groups are under the domain of different government ministries. Thus, coordination with the multiple levels of government is necessary and crucial for the success. Sahoo suggested that policymaking should entail a series of steps, including evaluation and monitoring, with each cycle improving the policy and leading to higher achievement.

The SEZ policy is not creating a new manufacturing base, since the overwhelming focus is on IT/ITeS (67 per cent) and to some extent on existing strengths in exports, namely textiles, pharmaceuticals, gems and jewellery. The SEZ policy is not likely to create new infrastructure beyond buildings, since most are less than one square kilometre and are located in and around industrialized areas and close to metros; the SEZs free-ride on pre-existing infrastructure (Partha & Pradhan, 2019). The SEZ policy will add to regional imbalances, since they are disproportionately located in districts that already have high levels of industrialization.

Establishment of SEZs needs to be carefully designed as it depends on a number of sensitive issues. Prominent among them is the political decision-making power as it varies from state to state in India. Khan and Varshney (2012) further state that for the development of the industrial sector, there should be the right mix of factors such as large and skilled workforce, strong policy framework, intrinsic comparative advantage in several industries, availability of complementing and supporting ancillary industry, buoyant export sector and vast local markets. SEZs can combine these factors into a powerful alchemy to power investment creation.

Anwar (2014) reviewed the emerging geography of SEZs in India and the government's experiment with SEZ as the models of economic development. He affirmed that the current SEZ policy is designed along the lines of mainstream economic strategy for industrialization of Washington Consensus, that is, open economy with more market freedom coupled with minimal government intervention as this leads to rapid economic growth and rising income. It was determined that SEZs contribute to the disparity in development across regions with only some of the regions, sectors and classes deriving the benefits from the policy. The policy has given almost a free hand to private investors in terms of the nature of investment and performance indicators. It is apprehended that the policy will be beneficial to private capitalists for garnering huge profits by exemption of duties on exports and imports.

3.6 Literature Gap and Conclusion

Though there is a vast body of literature on different aspects of SEZs, very few studies have been conducted on the socio-economic impact of SEZs in India in general and in Gujarat in particular. The impact of SEZs on the society be it on employment, livelihood, education, women's empowerment in addition to the economic impact needs to be understood to frame policies for sustainable development. The literature review done with a high level of scholastic thoroughness is the appropriate lynchpin for further doctoral research.

There was no unanimity in the views among researchers on the advantages of SEZs. Some studies supported the hypothesis that SEZs have provided impetus to country's economy, while other studies highlighted on the lack of social benefits. They recommended better working conditions and provision of other social measures like employee health, safety, education and recreational facilities. The researchers derived that SEZs provided fillip for both economic and social growth; they, however, stressed on good governance, infrastructure, development, land laws and policy measures to be taken by the authorities.

One conclusion on review of the literature is that the SEZs promote social and economic development. This is theorized mainly by two sets of variables. The first set is firm-specific which are: type, size, performance and types of activity involved. The second set of variables is zone-specific which are having socio-economic impact like direct and indirect economic, demographic, housing, other local services and socio-cultural factors. For example, developed nations like China and Poland, which have robust infrastructure and structured policy, are successful in meeting the goals of promoting economic growth and employee welfare. On the other hand, developing nations like India have yet to put in place a systematic framework of land and labour law reforms. Other areas of concern are lack of social infrastructure and poor working conditions.

To conclude, some of the key areas are highlighted as under:

a. The Economic impact of SEZs

The growing numbers of SEZs globally are a testimony to the success achieved in fast-tracking regional economic development with welcome creation of both local and non-local employment. SEZs have also substantially contributed to the indirect economy by way of employees' retail expenditure and through vendors for products and services with multiplier effect.

b. The Growth and Development of SEZs

The researcher has identified this as the potential field with ample scope for research in areas like government policy, vacant land utilization, new product and new service development. Some of these areas have been mentioned only in passing by the authors.

c. The Social Impact in SEZs

The importance of social objectives is noted globally and the literature covers the positive impact especially in areas like employee skills enhancement, implementation of medical cover, extension of soft loans/finances for major expenditure like housing, to cope with natural disasters, in addition to the standard facilities like subsidised transportation, recreation centre, gymnasium, canteen facilities, crèche for kids and so on. The literature reveals that SEZs in India have, however, poorly performed in contributing towards social objectives on above benchmarks.

d. The Socio-cultural Impact in SEZs

Some authors have conducted studies in this field particularly for the Greater Mekong Region and for Africa. There is a need for examination and study of socio-cultural impact of SEZs in India.

e. Government and Ethics

SEZs have poorly performed in environmental aspects in India; there is also the need and scope to study areas like corporate social responsibility (CSR) and other government initiatives/schemes.

Issues such as environmental sustainability will become increasingly important in coming years in order to comply with SDGs goal Agenda 2030 of UNCTAD.

f. Micro-, Small- and Medium-Size Business (MSME)

SEZs route presents a golden opportunity for the MSMEs in India to make a global mark. This will help not only in generating more direct/indirect employment but also market Brand India. MSMEs can leverage on the much-vaunted characteristics of smaller firms, that is, focussed business strategies, flexibility.

g. Organisational Change and SEZs

The research in this area covers the management competencies required to develop good HR practices, working styles and various quality development programmes to enhance the productivity and efficiency of the employees. This essentially calls for a creative, collaborative and connected approach for collaborative working and principles for the designing of organizational structure in SEZs.

h. SEZs—Business Model Analysis

This theme is of prime importance and a major concern to developers, stakeholders, lawmakers and private institutions. Studies in this area attempt to work out a sustainable business model for SEZs on examination of the existing model and global practices.

i. Opportunity Identification

Some of the authors have done research studies to show the correlation of job creation with diversified product/market segmentation and adoption of latest technology in SEZs. However, there is scope to study new areas of IT/ITeS technology, IoT, and the new generation technologies like Block Chain, Artificial Intelligence and Big Data Analytics relevant both for manufacturing and service sector SEZs.

j. Strategic reforms in SEZs

Some of the topics covered by the studies in strategic reforms are technology dissemination, skill and know-how transfers, industrial diversification and upgrading and enhanced regional economic cooperation. There appears to be a research gap in studies on e-commerce and new strategic management strategy relevant to SEZs.

3.7 Synopsis

Foreign investment through SEZs has a positive impact on the local employment, productivity and wages as determined by Ebenstein (2011), Damborsky, Milan Wokoun, Rene Krejcova, and Bozena Nikola Kaderabkova (2012). Jensen C. & Winiarczyk, M. (2014) postulated that SEZ is an effective tool of regional economic development.

The Systematic Literature Review (SLR) reveals that some of the main issues faced by SEZs in India are land acquisition and loss of income consequent to withdrawal of tax benefits. The SLR also highlights the fact that the regional disparity in terms of economic progress is accentuated by SEZs in addition to the fact that they draw on scarce water resources and adversely impact food security due to shifting of land used from farming to non-farming use. These and matters related to discrimination of marginalized community are covered in the studies by Nidheesh (2018), Agarwal, S. and Leviena (2019), and Niraj Anita (2016).

Later literature addressed the need for dynamic economic contribution through skill and know-how transfer, human capital programme through technology-driven changes and dissemination. Such literature also added a social dimension to its economic development mandate (e.g. Luthuli, Nomkhosi Dr. Houghton, & Jennifer, 2015; Guang, Wang, Yongan, Yu, Qishui, 2018). Razzaque et al. (2018) recommended the SEZ route for acceleration of economic growth, employment generation and poverty reduction. Successful SEZs foster institutional reforms in the broader economy. This is supported by research of Steenburgen and Javorcik (2017), Jarosiński (2016), and Nallathiga (2007). Hyun and Ravi (2017) found that SEZs did not only benefit firms located within, but had spillover effects, that got reflected at the aggregate level of a district. The study also supported the idea that SEZs drive a structural transformation of the economy away from informal sector production towards greater formality.

Parwez (2015), Dr. More (2015), Cirera and Lakshman (2017) worked on the labour legislations stressing basic rights and healthy industrial relations of workers. Anuradha and Mahendra (2010) worked on close interrelationship between the policies, industry requirements, infrastructure-supporting facilities and urban and regional development.

Saumik and Vengadeshvaran (2013) identified and studied bridges (a significant knowledge gap) in the literature related to the welfare effect of industrialization especially for the less-privileged members of the society. Findings indicate the need for a policy framework to address SEZ-related displacement, livelihood and gender issues. There is also the need for affirmative implementation of the policy framework by local administrative units.

Most of the literature that has delved into the analysis of the impacts of SEZs has adopted a case study approach, mainly as a consequence of the limited availability of cross-country data to measure SEZ outcomes. Many of these cases are solid analyses of the economic dynamism and influence of individual zones and provide interesting insights about these zones' viability and the characteristics that make them successful. This fact raises questions about the validity of generalizing the factors behind the success of a specific SEZ, which is embedded in specific economic, social, political, and legal contexts. The positive effects of SEZs clearly are interrelated with the contexts in which they are implemented, that is, the capacities of non-SEZ-based firms and the supporting policies.

The literature suggests that (1) SEZs have the power to bring FDI and new businesses to regions and (2) to boost exports; and that (3) SEZ-based firms perform better than non-SEZ-based firms. However, regarding increasing employment and achieving spillovers in the larger region, the literature is inconclusive.

4

Special Economic Zones: An International Perspective

Almost 147 countries in the world host SEZs in some form or other. SEZs across the globe may have different avatars like Free Trade Zones, Export Processing Zones, Industrial Parks, Free Ports and so on. The international perspective of SEZs therefore merits a separate chapter.

The researcher traces the history and evolution of SEZs followed by brief sketches on Taxonomy of SEZs used by different economies, theoretical approaches for setting up zones, SEZs details across major economies and social and economic impact of SEZs globally.

4.1 SEZs: Taxonomy, Scope and Definitions

A common understanding of SEZs is based on three exclusive criteria:

- A clearly demarcated geographical area,
- A regulatory regime distinct from the rest of the economy (most often customs and fiscal rules, but potentially covering other relevant regulations, such as foreign ownership rules, access to land or employment rules), and
- Benefits for units within the SEZ which are not available for those units outside the SEZ.

One of the most comprehensive catalogues of Zones, used by the World Free Zone Organization and based on the "Atlas Mondial des Zones Franches" (Bost, 2010), uses the same criteria but focuses on customs-free zones only, excluding SEZs that provide other regulatory exemptions.

Some economic zones considered similar or equivalent to SEZs do not come within the ambit of the definition or can at best be regarded as border line candidates. For instance, common industrial parks, which are frequently found in urban agglomerations, especially in developed economies, have a clearly demarcated area and may even provide some publicly funded basic infrastructure, but they do not offer a special regulatory regime or incentives.

In the same manner, science parks, common in developed countries (European Union (EU), for instance, has more than 360 science parks), occupy a defined area and have infrastructure support. The public or semi-public sector establishes such parks to foster active clustering, attract businesses in high-tech industries and nurture start-ups linked to university research institutions. But like Industrial Parks, there are no exemptions from customs, fiscal or other regulatory obligations. Hence such Science Parks are not SEZs. At times the terminology and the names can be misleading. In some countries, the term "Free Zone" meaning Customs Relief is used for structure that is outside the purview of SEZs. France, for example, has "Urban Free Zones" that are essentially initiatives to support businesses by the urban poor and the underprivileged in inner-city areas.

Similar initiatives are taken especially in developed countries to revive local areas or regions with relatively high unemployment. Some such initiatives may include fiscal incentives, making them borderline SEZs. For example, in the United Kingdom, Enterprise Zones promoted by local governments provide discounts on local property taxes (but not on corporate income taxes, as is the norm in most SEZs). The target enterprises for such zones are small and medium-sized enterprises (SMEs); this activity is not part of National Industrial Policy (NIP) and does not promote clustering. The Opportunity Zones in the United States, for instance, provide succor in economically distressed areas by extending exemption from tax on capital gains.

A few countries extend the benefits of free zones to individual production sites. The maquiladoras in Mexico are the original examples of this approach. Such a free-point regime can be considered a form of free zone, without the demarcated geographical area. In some countries individual free points are counted as zones, resulting in reports of hundreds of SEZs. (For the purpose of computing the SEZs here, roughly 8,400 free points worldwide stand excluded from the count.)

At the other end of the spectrum, we have the province-sized SEZs, originally conceived in China. (The Chinese government reserves the term "SEZ" for its five original province-sized zones.) By and large, SEZs around the world range from less than a hundred to a few hundred hectares in area (about one square kilometer on average). Free zones, which are normally fenced to demarcate the separate customs territory, have limited area. Zones of the size of an entire province, established to pilot economic or business reforms, have distinct regulatory regimes. However, the infrastructure in such areas consists of existing urban or provincial infrastructure and is not dedicated to the zone.

Getting to define the exact parameters of SEZs is therefore a tough proposition; similar complexity is encountered in the process of distinguishing between different types of SEZs. The evolution of most of the SEZs can be traced to Free Zones or Free Trade Zones or Commercial Zones all of which have the defining characteristic of limited area with fencing (restricted access) and duty free.

Free zones are conventionally next to gateways like seaports, airports or border corridors and are host to firms that provide warehousing, logistics and other services. The free zone model stays true to this original concept in most developed economies. Adjacent to such zones, industrial parks have mushroomed and such parks rely on the services provided by the free zones and easy access to the international markets; but these adjacent areas generally do not fall under a distinct regulatory regime themselves. On the other hand, SEZs in developing countries are primarily established to attract investment in diversified industrial activity; they, therefore, tend to provide customs, fiscal and regulatory benefits to all businesses in larger, integrated areas.

To render it even more complex, there are numerous examples of zones within zones. The province-sized zones in China often contain various other types of SEZs. But even smaller SEZs that offer fiscal or regulatory incentives sometimes host a free zone (there by adding customs exemptions) within their perimeters. Table 4.1 summarizes a functional taxonomy of SEZs in various economies.

Table 4.2 gives an overview of the economic objectives with physical typology globally.

Table 4.1: A Functional Taxonomy of SEZs

Type	Description
	Organizing Principle: Specialization
Logistics Hubs (FTZs)	• Commercial warehousing and logistics service • Trade facilitation services for trans-shipping and re-exports, at airports, seaports, land borders • Fenced-in, duty-free areas relatively small in size can be located next to or within larger industrial estate.
EPZs	• Industrial estates with manufacturing exclusively for exports. • Offer special incentives and facilities for manufacturing. • Limited for export-oriented units under EPZ regime.
Hybrid Zones	• Zone divided for general industries with Separate EPZs reserved for only export-oriented, EPZ-registered enterprises.
Multi-activity SEZs	• General Industrial development, non-specialized. • Such SEZs have generally larger area, accommodating multi-manufacturing and service activities. • Broader set of incentives and benefits.
Specialized SEZs (Sector-specific)	• Sector-focused (e.g. Services, Resources based like Agro, Chemicals). • Industry-focused (e.g. Automotive, Electronics, Garments). • GVC activities-focused (e.g. Business Process Outsourcing, Call Centres, R&D Centres) • Configured to the needs of Specific Industries.
Innovative-driven SEZs	• Focused on industrial upgrading and New Industries (e.g. High-Tech Zones, Bio-Tech Zones, Ecotourism Zones). • Focused on promoting R&D activity, science-based industries.
Organizing Principle: Design and Governance	
Wide-area Zones	• Large Integrated Zones, mostly with a substantial administrative region or built as Townships with residential areas and amenities. • Main purpose of the large zones is to pilot economic reforms.

Table 4.1: *Continued*

	Organizing Principle: Specialization
OFDI/ODA-driven zones	• Result of collaboration between capital-exporting economies and lower-income economies. • Country-specific zones for attracting FDI, for example, Singapore SEZ in Indonesia; and Korean EPZ in Bangladesh.
Cross-border zones	• Transnational zones • Facilitated by cross-border infrastructure • Reduce border barriers
Regional development zones	• Transnational zones based on Regional Integration Agreements. • Mitigate effects of trade barriers and preferential investment policies. • Different forms of underlying agreements: Comprehensive Economic Agreement, Preferential Trade Agreement, Common Markets and Economic and Monetary Unions.
Enterprise-specific (single factory)	• Individual enterprise unit which could be set up anywhere. • Declaring Custom bonded area, for example, export-oriented unit (EOU) or Software Technology Parks of India (STPI).
Enterprise Zones	• Established to balance urban and rural economy. • Provision of tax incentives and financial grants.

Source: UNCTAD: World Investment Report 2019

FTZ = free trade zone, GVC = Global value chain, ODA = official development assistance, OFDI = outward foreign direct investment, R&D = Research and development,

4.2 SEZs: Global Distribution

SEZs have emerged as the instrument of choice to promote industrialization globally. The term "SEZ" is an omnibus term that includes Export Promotion Zones, Economic and Technology Development Zones, High-Tech Zones, Industrial Parks, Science and Innovation Parks, Free Ports, Enterprise Zones and others of similar nature. An increasing number of countries use this instrument for their industrialization process especially as a way of attracting foreign direct investment (FDI) mostly in the manufacturing sector; creating jobs, generating exports and foreign exchange and so on. So far, the results are quite mixed with

Table 4.2: Special Economic Zone Typologies

Parameters	Free Port	Industrial Free Zone/EPZ	Commercial Free Zone	Financial Services Zone	IT/Science Park	Tourism Zone	Special Economic Zone	Enterprise Zone
Physical Characteristics	Entire city or jurisdiction	Enclave or industrial park	Warehouse area, often adjacent to port or airport	Business park- adjacent to city	Business park – near university	Large Area jurisdiction	Entire province or municipality.	Part of city or entire city.
Economic Objectives	Development of trading centre and diversified economic base.	Development of export manufacturing / assembly industry	Facilitation of trade and imports	Development of offshore banking, insurance, securities hub.	Development of technology-intensive industry.	Integrated tourism development	Deregulation, private sector investment in restricted area.	Development of SMEs in depressed areas.
Typical Activities	Trade, service, industry, banking etc.	Light industry and manufacturing	Warehousing, packaging, distribution, transhipment	Financial services	Data processing, software development, computer graphics.	Resorts and other tourism-related activities.	All types of industry and services	All
Typical Examples	Hong Kong, Singapore, Batam.	Ireland, Korea, Malaysia, Dominican Republic, Kenya.	Jebel Ali, Colon, Mauritius, Iran.	Bahrain, Dubai, Mauritius, Uruguay.	India-Bangalore, China—Dalian, Poland-Krakow.	Colombia—Baru, Philippines-Cagayan de Oro, Jordan-Dead Sea DZ	China-Hainan and Shenzen, Jordan—Aqaba, Philippines—Subic Bay	US, Europe

Source: BuroHappold 2017

some countries such as China, Singapore, Malaysia, the Republic of Korea, and Mauritius showing spectacular results, as against the limited success in countries like India and Sri Lanka.

At present there are at least 5,400 SEZs in the world in over 147 countries, compared to 2,500 SEZs in 2005. Some SEZs like China's Shenzhen have turned into phenomenal success stories. Most of the developing and less developed nations attempt to emulate China's SEZ model as a tool for accelerating socio-economic growth with common objective of ushering prosperity. The SEZs numbers by region in 2019 are tabulated in Table 4.3.

Table 4.3: Number of SEZs, by Region, 2019

Particulars	Total Nos. of SEZs	. . .of which under development	Additional SEZs planned
WORLD	**5,383**	**474**	**507**
(A) DEVELOPED ECONOMIES	**374**	**5**	---
• EUROPE	105	5	---
• NORTH AMERICA	262	--	----
(B) DEVELOPING ECONOMIES	**4,772**	**451**	**502**
• ASIA	4,046	371	419
• EAST ASIA	2,645	13	---
• CHINA	2,543	13	---
• SOUTH EASTASIA	737	167	235
• SOUTH ASIA	456	167	184
• INDIA	373	142	61
• WEST ASIA	208	24	--
• AFRICA	237	51	53
• LATIN AMERICA & • CARRIBEAN	486	28	24
(C) TRANSITION ECONOMIES	**237**	**18**	**5**

Source: UNCTAD: World Investment Report 2019

Note: Zones are counted on basis of their establishment by law. They exclude 8,368 single-enterprise zones (free points) found in 18 economies. SEZs in other developed economies (Australia, Israel, Japan and New Zealand) and in Oceania were counted towards the respective economic group's aggregate and the global total.

4.3 History of Special Economic Zones

Phoenicia (modern-day Lebanon) was a great maritime power in ancient times. The model followed by them was safe passage guarantee to foreign traders at Tyre, then a leading port in the region. This can be construed as the genesis of free zones. Later this model was emulated by the Romans and Greeks to build their empires and dominate the political and economic landscape of the world.

The arrangement at Steelyard in London city, which was a special part of the port in London exclusively reserved for the businessmen from the North German cities, can be considered a rudimentary free zone. The businessmen were allowed to move goods in the Steelyard without paying customs duties on exports. The Gibraltar Export Processing Zone established in 1705 is the oldest among the operating zones in the world. The modern age special economic zones began with the United States of America, establishing its first export processing zone in the 1930s. Spain established first free zone in Barcelona, which became operational after the Second World War, the zone was sector-specific one for automobile plants. Ireland and Puerto Rico have also established zones in their late 1950s (FIAS, 2008; Hossain & Ali, 2015).

There was a spurt in the development of Special Economic Zones after the Second World War. The growth in the number of free zones is exponential from 1970 till date. In Asia, India established Export Processing Zone in Kandla in 1965; this was the first EPZ in Asia. Other early Export Processing Zones in Asia were the Kaohsiung EPZ in 1966 in Chinese Taipei, Masan EPZ in 1970 in South Korea and Bataan EPZ in 1972 in Philippines. Countries in the African continent like Liberia, Senegal, and Mauritius established EPZs in the 1970s. Latin America and the Caribbean Islands set up Export Processing Zones in the 1960s and 1970s. For example, Colombia established an EPZ in Barranquilla in 1958, Honduras in Puerto Cortés in 1973, El Salvador in San Bartolo in 1973 and Costa Rica in Santa Rosa/El Roble at the beginning of the 1990s.

4.3.1 Evolution of Special Economic Zones

Ancient countries/city-states made extraordinary arrangements and provided security to strategic areas like ports to promote their external trade; this type of arrangement resembles rudimentary form of free zone. Such special areas have progressed through numerous stages over the period, with significant changes in the perspective and objectives. How the concept of modern Special Economic Zones evolved is described below.

4.3.1.1 Trade-Based SEZs

The oldest SEZs were free ports, the origin of which can be traced back to the free port of Leghorn setup in 1547 in the Bay of Genoa in the north-west of Italy (Meng, 2005). In the early seveteenth century, free ports (FPs) emerged in some European cities, and gradually metamorphosed into Free Trade Zones (FTZs). FTZs are small, fenced-in, duty-free areas, offering warehousing and distribution facilities for trade, transshipment and re-export operations, located in most ports of entry around the world. The rationale of setting up these zones was to facilitate transiting trade. Foreign trade of superpower countries during that time was entrepot, basically transiting other countries' exports. The level of international trade was therefore not linked to domestic production but depended on expanding "transiting trade". Since the tax system was very elaborate, free trade areas (tax free areas) were set up to facilitate trade. Many countries have been upgrading/ setting up trade zones in recent years as "offshore warehouse and logistics hub" with world-class trade infrastructure, multi-modular transport facilities, barrier-free customs facilities and attractive incentives for transiting international trade.

4.3.1.2 Manufacturing-Based SEZs

In the late 1920s, a new variety of SEZs appeared in the Spanish city. These SEZs were set up with the intention of increasing exports by value addition to the raw materials available in that country. In 1950, the US Foreign Trade Zone Act 1934 was amended to allow manufacturing activities in free trade zones. The first manufacturing SEZ in a developing country was set up by the island of Puerto Rico in the Caribbean Sea during the period 1947–1951.

The genesis of SEZs with emphasis on manufacturing activity, however, lies in the Shannon EPZ (Export Processing Zone) in Ireland in 1958. It became instrumental in spreading EPZ knowledge around the world (Bolin, 2004). Thus, a new class of SEZs evolved. These SEZs are industrial estates offering special incentives and facilities for manufacturing and related activities aimed mostly at export markets with the entire area within the zone reserved exclusively for export-oriented enterprises licensed under a SEZ regime. Unlike FTZ, a SEZ of EPZ variety need not necessarily be located adjacent to a port. These can be set up at any location with good connectivity.

India was the first Asian country to set up its own EPZ in Kandla in 1965. This was followed by Kaohsiung EPZ in Taiwan in 1966. Soon the number increased to eleven in nine countries (five in Asia and Latin America each and one in Africa). By 1975, 29 countries had 79 SEZs across the world. Almost all of them were fenced-in industrial estates. Zones are not static in nature.

They evolve with economic growth of the domestic economy, in terms of the composition of economic activity and technological sophistication. They were dominated by low-cost labour-intensive industries in the earliest phase of development and known as first-generation SEZs. With skill upgradation in the economy, they began attracting technical consumer products such as radios, calculators, and wrist watches. As the economy further developed, they shifted to the production of skill-intensive chemical and engineering products and evolved into second-generation SEZs. Finally, they moved to third-generation high-technology industries. While the most important contribution of first-generation zones is the alleviation of unemployment and generation of foreign exchange, the second-generation zones contribute to human capital upgrading and export diversification.

The third-generation SEZs are important contributors to technology generation, transfers and technological spillovers. These are followed by service zones. In many countries (including the US), the scope of FTZs has been extended to include manufacturing along with entrepot functions.

4.3.1.3 Comprehensive SEZs

At the end of the 1970s, China designed its own model of "Special Economic Zones" (SEZs). Unlike export-processing zones, which are enclosed industrial estates, SEZs in China are mega-industrial towns spread over several square kilometers. Such SEZs generally encompass a broader concept and typically cover much larger areas. They accommodate all types of activities, including tourism and retail sales, permit people to reside onsite, and provide a much broader set of incentives and benefits. These are inspired by the Becattini (1990) concept of industrial district. It is defined as a socio-territorial entity which is characterized by the active presence of both a community of people and a cluster of firms in one bounded area. These zones have played an important role in attracting FDI, promoting exports, and creating global cities in China (Zheng, 1999; Li, 2001).

4.3.1.4 Newer Varieties of Zones

The concept of SEZs is further augmented by incorporating particularly innovative features to the basic design to tap their potential, and to gain competitive edge over international competitors. This has resulted in a new variety of zones. Some of these new varieties are High Technology (Science) Parks, Enterprise-Specific Zones, Service Zones, Country-Specific SEZs and Hybrid Zones.

4.3.1.5 Transnational Zones

In the 1990s, cross-border SEZs emerged as a growth strategy of transnational regions. Their objective is to exploit location advantages of border areas and boost the economic and trade cooperation and development in the region. These zones are an upgraded version of traditional border industries developed in Mexico and South Africa. Their objectives were more political and social than economic ones. In the early 1990s, growth triangles were conceptualized and proposed as a growth strategy of transnational regions (Kudo, 2009). Greater Mekong sub-region (GMS) countries like Cambodia, the People's Republic of China (PRC, specifically Yunnan Province and Guangxi Zhuang Autonomous Region), Laos People's Democratic Republic (Lao PDR), Myanmar, Thailand, and Vietnam have exploited this opportunity to develop industrial clusters in the border areas. These are termed "cross-border SEZs". These SEZs derive their competitiveness from complementary factor endowment, cross-border infrastructure services and reduced border barriers. China has promoted cross-border SEZs along the borders with Cambodia, Laos and Vietnam.

Cross-national regional integration which proliferated in the early 1990s is also a form of transnational SEZs. These economic arrangements aim at facilitating and enhancing economic integration at the regional level. Traditionally, they aim at addressing trade barriers. Over time, deeper regional initiatives have appeared. They contain not only trade-related provisions but also specific commitments on investment, services, intellectual property, domestic macro-policies, regulation of product and factor markets, movement of labour, technical barriers to trade, and dispute settlement with the objective of facilitating economic growth through increased trade and investment. Table 4.4 summarizes evolution of SEZs in selected countries.

4.4 SEZs Development Worldwide

Different countries and regions have differing rationale for SEZs policy, since the basic objectives and economic significance vary depending on the stage of economic development. It is observed that in developed countries, most SEZs are Free Trade Zones where no customs duty is payable. There is free movement of goods that are part of Global Value Chains. On the other hand, for SEZs in developing countries the main objective is to promote exports and to attract FDI.

Currently there are SEZs in more than 147 countries; however, the global distribution of SEZs is skewed. For instance, China by itself is host to more than

Table 4.4: Evolution of SEZs in Some Selected Countries

Country		First Stage		Second Stage		Third Stage	Current Status
China	Late 1970s	Large comprehensive SEZs developed by central government	Late 1980s	Economic and high tech zones at the state and provincial level	1990s	EPZ variety zones*: EPZs, FTZs, HIIZ BECZ, THZs TIZ, AHIDZ	All varieties of SEZs are operational
Korea	1970	Free export zones Of EPZ variety	2000	Duty-free Zones of FTZs variety	2003	Free economic zones of comprehensive SEZ variety	All varieties operational
Taiwan	1966–1997	EPZs: Labour intensive 1989–1997: capital intensive and technology intensive 2001: logistics	1980s	Science parks	2003	FTZs	All operational
Indonesia	1978	Bonded zones and warehouses equivalent to FTZs	2009	Special economic zones of EPZ variety			Large FTZs Converted into SEZs
Thailand	1979	EPZs and bonded Warehouses	2007	Free zones with enhanced package and better regional integration			EPZs are upgraded to free zones

Philippines	1969	EPZs	1995	Eco zones of SEZ variety			EPZs converted into SEZs SEZs
Vietnam	1991	Export processing Zones and industrial estates both treated at par in terms of incentives and administration	2003	Eco zones (Comprehensive SEZs)			All varieties are operational
Jordan	1973	Freeport	1983	Free zones of EPZ variety	2001	Special economic zone	All varieties are operational
UAE	1980	Free zones: all industrial estates with trading, manufacturing and service sector activities					Operational
Pakistan	1980	Traditional EPZ	2001	Project-based EPZs leased to foreign companies	Planned	Planned cities	All existing varieties are operational
Bangladesh	1972	Traditional EPZs	2007	Private SEZs	Planned	Eco zones of comprehensive SEZ variety	All existing varieties are operational
Sri Lanka	1978	EPZs in and around Colombo	Late 1990s	Country-wide Locations			

Continued

Table 4.4: *Continued*

Country	First Stage		Second Stage		Third Stage		Current Status
Egypt	Early 1970s	Free zones of EPZ Variety both public and private	2002	SEZs of comprehensive variety	2004	Quasi industrial zones (QIZ) for exports to US markets	All varieties are operational
Mauritius	1971	Traditional EPZ	1992	Free ports of FTZ variety			Both varieties operational
South Africa	2001	Industrial Development Zone					Operational
Russia	1991	Free economic Zones equivalent to free trade zone	2006	Industrial development zones, technology- innovative zones, tourist			All zones are upgraded to SEZs
Poland	1994	Special economic zones: Industrial clusters with special incentives. In addition, there are FTZs and bonded warehouses	-	-	-		Operational

Czech Republic	1991	Free zones : Equivalent to FTZs	1998	Industrial zones: Industrial clusters of EPZ variety			All varieties are operational
Brazil	1967	Free trade zone	1988	Free trade Zone with manufacturing	2007	SEZs of Export Processing zone variety	All varieties are operational
Mexico	1967	Maquiladoras of EPZ variety near US border	1994	Locational flexibility granted to Maquiladora	2006	An extended version of maquila: Maquiladoras and export services companies (IMMEX)	Maquila companies regulated by IMMEX

National Border and Economic Cooperation (BECZs), National Tourist and Holiday Resort (THZs), Taiwanese Investment Zone (TIZs); and National Agricultural Hi-Tech Industrial Demonstration Zone (AHIDZs).

Source: Economic impacts of SEZs: Theoretical approaches and analysis of newly notified SEZs in India (2010) By A. Aggarwal

50 per cent of the SEZs in the world. The United States and Philippines too host a larger number of SEZs. In terms of size, it is seen that smaller zones have attracted major investments and generated larger exports share as compared to very large zones (FIAS, 2008).

The development of SEZs has occurred in a series of regional waves (Bost, 2010). SEZs proliferated in 1970s and early 1980s in East and South East Asian countries. Latin America followed suit in late 1980s and early 1990s. SEZs became the preferred mode of reform for transition economies in 1990s, while Africa adopted SEZ model in the 1990s and 2000s.

The South East Asian nations made spectacular progress on development parameters through the successful implementation of SEZ program. SEZs were especially successful in attracting Foreign Direct Investment (FDI) on a large scale. This model of development was supported politically in these countries through strong leadership. That the political and socio-economic environment plays a big role on the development ladder of SEZs is evident from Table 4.5.

Most of the zones are multi-activity zones. The Industry-Specific Zones are predominant in transition economies, while there are more Innovation Zones in Asia. It would be seen that the free zones for facilitating trade logistics are mostly in the developed economies.

The desired outcomes of the zones differ in various classes of countries. Technology upgrade is the desired outcome for transition economies, whereas for advanced economies the outcome is industrial upgrade. Newer economies see the zones as a means to boost the fundamental activities of manufacture,

Table 4.5: Distribution of Zones Type, by Region or Grouping (in Percentage)

Particulars	Logistic Hub	Multi-Activity	Specialized	Innovation-driven
WORLD	**08**	**62**	**24**	**05**
Developed Economies	91	9	1	-
Africa	1	89	10	-
Asia	2	65	26	7
China	1	93	1	6
Latin America & Caribbean	9	77	13	1
Transition Economies	3	34	59	5

Source: UNCTAD: World Investment Report 2019

Table 4.6: The SEZ Development Ladder

Type of Economies	Zone policy objectives	Prevalent zone types
High-Income economies	• Focus on avoiding distortions in economy. • Platform for complex cross-border supply chain.	• Logistic hubs free zone only • Innovation and new industrial revolution objectives (science park).
Upper-middle-income economies	• Support transition to services economy. • Attract new high-tech industries, • Focus on upgrading innovation capabilities.	• Tech-based zones (e.g. R&D, high-tech, bio-tech) • Specialized zones • Services zones (e.g. financial services)
Middle-income economies	• Support Industrial upgrading • Promote GVC integration • Focus on technology dissemination and spillovers	• Specialized zones (e.g. Automotive, Electronic) • Service zones (e.g. BPO, Call Centres)
Low-income economies	• Industrial development and diversification • Offset weakness in investment climate • Pilot business reforms • Focus on direct employment and export benefits	• Multi-activity zones • Resource-based zones

Source: UNCTAD: World Investment Report 2019

industrialization and exports. Countries which are already on the middle rung of the development ladder have shifted focus of zones from manufacturing to services and vertical integration. Latin American countries have large farming areas and the zones were used initially for warehousing and logistics; now the zone activities are geared towards manufacturing and services. Thus, the outcomes of zones are dynamic in nature; the outcomes desired could be concurrent and many countries developed more than one type of zone, for example, FTZs and EPZs in Brazil and SEZs, single-enterprise free points and FTZs in Mexico. Table 4.6 shows the different objectives for adopting SEZ development ladder by some economies.

4.5 Regional Patterns and Innovations

The highest numbers of SEZs are found in China, the Philippines, India, the United States, Russia, Turkey, Thailand, the Dominican Republic, Kenya and Nicaragua in descending order.

Some of the new trends and concepts linked with SEZs are opening of economic corridors to bridge the gap and "Global Brand Local Touch" for that special local touch to a product/service.

4.5.1 Asia

Almost two-thirds of the world's SEZs are housed in Asia (Figure 4.1).

The nature and history vary greatly across the region's diverse economies; 35 economies in Asia have SEZs in some form.

Those economies that had a headstart in the early 1960s through focus on development based on exports have now moved to High-Tech Zones and Large Area Zones with in-built residential areas and amenities. The economies that are less developed are more into labour-intensive manufacturing activities.

Asian economic giants like Japan and China have invested in new areas in ASEAN member and associate countries. Thailand has invested in Myanmar SEZs, in addition to investments by Japan and China. The SEZs have diversified

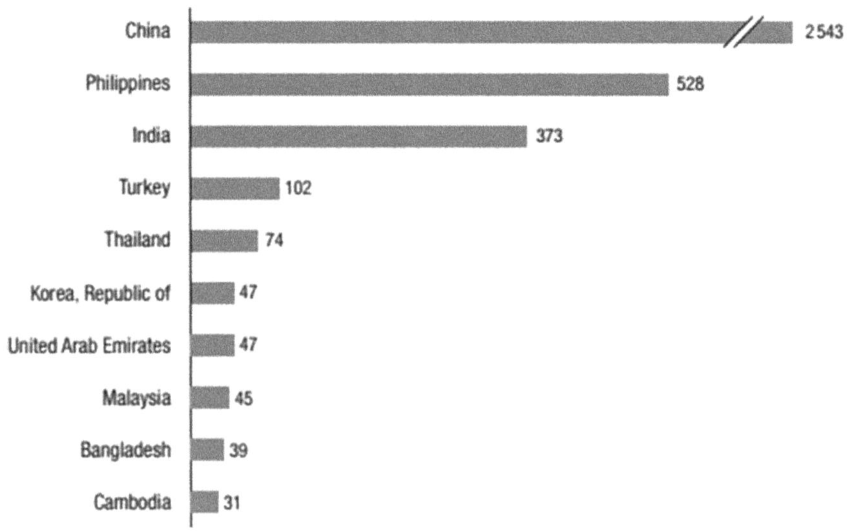

Figure 4.1: Developing Asia: Economies with Large Number of SEZs, 2019
Source: UNCTAD: World Investment Report 2019

in new areas and segments like entertainment industry (Casinos), logistics, tourism, health care, energy, petrochemicals, commerce, and education.

4.5.1.1 East and South East Asia/ASEAN Countries

The first EPZs were established in Taiwan (1966), Singapore (1969) and Republic of Korea (1970). The main focus of these EPZs was on production of labour-intensive goods for the purpose of export. EPZs policies as evolved in these countries were emulated by other economies in South East Asia in the 1970s. Table 4.7 gives brief of evolution of SEZs in major South East Asian countries.

These countries have benefited through the SEZs platform drawing the main benefits of increase in exports, FDI and employment. They have well-established administrative framework that promotes SEZ activities. There is the political will and push that is so necessary; now these countries are attempting for even more administrative reforms for expansion plans of the SEZs.

While ASEAN, one of the earliest and successful regional groupings, has propelled the economies on the quick road to development, SEZs close to the

Table 4.7: SEZ Evolution in South East Asia

Malaysia	Indonesia	Thailand	Philippines	Vietnam
1971: EPZs	1973: Bonded zones of EPZ variety in Batam and KBN	1977: EPZs and bonded warehouses (distinction between EPZ and industrial estate blurred)	1972: EPZs	1991: EPZs and Industrial parks (over 400 IZs: distinction blurred with only four EPZs)
1975: Enterprise-specific zone	1993: Enterprise zones	2007: Free trade zone with enhanced benefits	1995: Hybrid zones (Eco zones)	1998: High Tech Zones
1990: Trade-based zones	1992 The whole of Batam bonded zone	2018: SEZs on the border with Cambodia and Myanmar	More than 300 zones	2003: Eco Zones (large zones with hybrid features)
2006: Five Economic corridors	2007: Proliferation of bonded zones. Number increased from seven in 2007 to 1557 in 2012.			New generation zones under consideration

borders have further facilitated trade and exchange of resources, for instance, the common border of Laos, Cambodia (Kampuchea) and Thailand. Cambodia has set up SEZs in rural areas with links to urban areas making SEZs a tool for reduction of the disparity between rural and urban areas; Malaysia has set up Regional Economic Corridors, a new version of SEZs to promote development in rural areas.

Singapore, a small geographical entity and therefore not figuring in Table 4.7, started with multi-activity zones in the 1960s and moved on to specialized SEZs (e.g. petroleum refinery) in the 1970s. Now the focus area of SEZs is knowledge and innovation to promote R&D and other high-value activities.

The role of SEZs—which include industrial parks, special export processing zones, technology parks, and innovation areas—in development in ASEAN members is prominent. Regional Comprehensive Economic Partnership (RCEP) has, however, failed to take off due to the reluctance of India to join this regional grouping.

The ASEAN nations have introduced various fiscal benefits and tax sops for attracting FDI in SEZs. Fiscal incentives play a crucial role in motivating the investor mindset. Further, some of the local bodies, council and state implemented tax incentives for regional economic cooperation. Creating a trade and investor-friendly environment for SEZs functioning has been the guiding principle of ASEAN countries.

4.5.1.2 China

The People's Republic of China has done spectacularly well on the economic front to emerge as the fastest-growing economy and second only to USA in size. The SEZs established in four coastal cities (Shenzhen, Zhuhai, Shantou and Xiamen) in early 1980s through the "reform and opening up" process hastened the transition from a controlled economy to a market economy. Each of these locations was chosen due to proximity to the then economic powerhouses of Hong Kong, Macao, and Taiwan. Encouraged by the success of these SEZs, more were established in urban areas along the east coast to leverage on the geographical advantage of proximity to Japan and ASEAN countries. With the coastal regions turning prosperous, new SEZs were established in the subsequent period in inland areas and in western China. The 2018 official Zone Directory records 5 categories of 552 state-level zones and 1,991 provincial zones, together accounting for over half of all SEZs in the world (Table 4.8). This total excludes SEZs established at local levels.

Table 4.8: State-Level Zones in China

Five Categories in the Official Dictionary	Selected Type of Wide-Area Zones
Economic and technological development zone (ETDZ)	Special Economic Zone
High-tech Industrial development zone (HIDZ)	National new area
Special Customs Zone (SCZ)	National innovative demonstration zone
Border/Cross border economic cooperation zone (BECZ)	National key experimental zone for development and opening- up
Other types	Pilot FTZ
	Cross-border e-commerce pilot zone

Source: UNCTAD based on the Directory of Development Zones of China (Announcement No 4, 2018)

Post-2010, the wall of the Shenzhen SEZ was demolished and the entire city brought under SEZ regime. Similar process was followed in respect of other SEZs with the wide-area zones concept (FTZ) in vogue from 2013. This methodology could tackle developmental issues. In 2018, China adopted wide area zones concept as national policy.

China's Belt and Road Initiative (BRI) is the fulcrum of Chinese global intervention. Through BRI, China proposes to set up 56 economic and trade cooperation zones in more than 20 countries with a total investment of $18.5 billion and employment generation of approx. 1,800,0000 jobs. Tax revenue is estimated at $1.1 billion on this account. More than 70 countries have joined BRI connecting Asia with Europe and Africa along ancient silk road trade route for common prosperity covering areas of transportation, industrial parks, SEZs, financial services, digital cooperation, education and so on. India is one prominent country that chose not to join the BRI. China adopted millennium strategy and proposed dedicated SEZ focusing on non-government facilities, markets, universities, R&D, hospitals and planned investment for the next 15 years.

4.5.1.3 South Asia

India has the distinction of being the first country in Asia to establish EPZ at Kandla, Gujarat, in as early as 1965. The national economic policies were, however, not in sync with the SEZ programme resulting in stagnation of the EPZ in the 1960s and 1970s. The advent of the 1990s witnessed the adoption of strategy of economic liberalization and globalization in India. This ushered the era of an outward-looking economy with thrust on exports. The SEZ activities were galvanized with the introduction of SEZ policy in 2000. To protect interests of the investors and to lay a regulatory framework, the SEZ Act (2005) and SEZ rules (2006) were enacted.

As on 31 December 2020, there are 265 operational SEZs that provide direct employment to 2.28 million people. On 31 January 2021, the number of SEZs notified under the Act is 378; in addition, 7 central SEZs and 12 state/private sector SEZs were set up prior to the enactment of the SEZ Act 2005. Initiatives include new 14 SEZs under Coastal Economic Zone—SAGARMALA, coastal development project for JNPT and Kandla Port SEZs. In JNPT, Taiwanese investors have evinced interest in software and IT. Other SEZs like MIHAN are in greenfield areas of Defence and Aviation–manufacturing activities, health care, MRO, commodity exchanges, naphtha cracker plants and so on. India's prestigious GIFT SEZ—International Financial and other services, for example, legal services, are emerging as a new destination and job creation center projecting one million jobs in near future. A dedicated women SEZ is proposed in Karnataka with focus on women employment.

The number of SEZs in South Asia is set to increase substantially in coming years mostly in the field of manufacturing activities. Bangladesh has already emerged as apparel and textile hub with all the eight public and one private EPZ engaged in these activities. While Bangladesh has planned for a hundred SEZs, Nepal has targeted for 14 more SEZs; 2 of its SEZs in Bhairahawa and Simara SEZs mostly in garment sector are operational. India too has about 160 new zones in the pipeline.

Recently, Pakistan has extended business-friendly incentives under China-Pakistan Economic Corridor (CPEC) by allowing complete ownership for foreign firms investing in SEZs under CPEC. The proposed incentives for SEZs included income tax exemptions, no taxes on non-residents and income tax exemptions for expatriates till 2040. Fiscal benefits on imports and procurement from local sources are also exempted from duties.

4.5.1.4 West Asia

The tryst with SEZ by West Asia begun with the Jebel Ali Freeport set up in Dubai (United Arab Emirates) as early as in 1985. The Gulf Cooperation

Council (GCC, a regional economic grouping) pushed both inter-country trade and establishment of SEZs in the Gulf countries.

From a leading re-export hub in the world, UAE progressed to non-trade areas like technology, e-commerce and media. Today we have the thriving Dubai Internet City, Dubai Media City, Knowledge Village, Dubai Multi Commodities Centre and Dubai Health Care City.

China has invested in SEZs in Oman, Qatar and Egypt with activities related to automotive, refinery and petrochemicals, hotel industry and so on.

Turkey has some 18 active SEZs mostly based close to the coast and geared towards exports. Turkey passed the Free Zone Law in 1985.

Towards the beginning of millennium, Turkey has expanded to create a new type of SEZ—technology development zones—mainly to attract investments in R&D and high-tech industries.

4.5.2 Latin America and the Caribbean

Latin America has the distinction of setting up FTZs at Colonia and Nueva Palmira (Uruguay) as early as 1923. SEZs in Latin America are largely governed by SEZ laws enacted during 1990s. The SEZs were re-engineered during 2010 to generate more jobs.

The Central American and South American countries house almost 500 SEZs with more than 10,000 units and provide employment to about one million people.

Except for Suriname and Guyana, all the Central American countries have SEZs. On the other hand, only a few of the Caribbean countries host SEZs. Jamaica has undertaken reforms to make SEZs investor friendly, focusing on tourism, agriculture business and logistics hub. China is a major investor both in the Caribbean and in Mexico. Historically, Mexico's Maquiladoras which originated from the National Border Industrial Programme was launched in the 1960s; this encouraged local SMEs.

The Latin American countries face a number of challenges. United States looms like a giant and any changes in US fiscal policies impact them, rendering them less attractive destinations for investment. As in most middle-income and low-income countries sustaining fiscal incentives is a challenge. Brazil, Argentina, Mexico, Paraguay, Peru and Uruguay have all tweaked the FTZ strategies in the last five years to align them to economic development. In this manner, some 20–30 new SEZs are expected to set up by 2025.

4.5.3 Africa

The first EPZ in Africa was established in 1970 in Mauritius; it was governed under the EPZ Act which was enacted in the same year. Ghana, Liberia and Senegal followed suit in the next decade. By 1990s these countries and a few others emulated East Asian economies and SEZs proliferated but not with the same effectiveness as in East Asia. Thus, Africa is a latecomer in using SEZs as a tool to exploit resources for generation of business and employment.

It is only in 2017 that African nations took investor-friendly measures by changing policies to instill confidence. The focus is on employment of youth, rural development and accountability (government).

China has plans to invest $1 trillion under One Belt One Road Initiative in Africa; Japan has invested 171 billion yen in North Africa and 226 billion yen in the Middle East in 2017 under its Overseas Development Assistance Plan.

In many of the African SEZs like those engaged in multi-products manufacturing and sectors like logistics, tourism, financial services, energy, and fertilizers, China has emerged as the major trading partner. SEZs have thus become the tool of choice in 2017 for the socio-economic growth and prosperity.

The African continent has now approximately 237 established SEZs with some under construction and some new SEZs planned (see Table 4.1). In addition, there are about 200 single-enterprise zones (or free points). Some 38 of the 54 economies on the continent host SEZs, with the highest number in Kenya.

The three largest economies in the continent namely—Nigeria, Egypt and South Africa—have well-developed SEZs and policies in place.

African countries are endowed with natural resources; the exports basket consisted largely of unprocessed resources like metals and minerals; SEZs have emerged as the link in attracting investors and technology for downstream processing industries so that the value-added products are manufactured and exported. For example, Nigeria established a number of zones focused on oil refining. Morocco has oriented some of its free zones to high-tech activities and the automotive industry. Over 30 per cent of Chinese firms in Africa are manufacturing-oriented. Ethiopia, Rwanda, Uganda and Senegal are building new SEZ's. SEZs will be the catalysts for transformational development in these African nations.

4.5.4 Transition Economies

The fall of the Iron Curtain in the 1990s ushered in a sea change in the economies of the erstwhile USSR and East Europe. The concept of SEZ took on a totally different meaning when the economies opened up. Russia created Territories of Advanced Development (TAD also known as Advanced SEZs) in the period from 2015 to 2019. The rapid expansion was accompanied by a few failures; 11 SEZs were abolished between 2010 and 2015 (Kuznetsov & Kuznetsova, 2019). This period also witnessed SEZ expansion in ten other economies in the region; Russia continues to have supremacy in terms of numbers of SEZs in the region.

Recently 82 single-industry SEZs have been added in Russia, thus a majority of the SEZs in the region focus on a single industry. Some new areas where SEZs have ventured in Russia are Crypto currency mining, engineering and logistic sectors, and technology-oriented zones. Russia with its vast size and biodiversity is host to nine tourism zones.

Russia, which accounts for over 70 per cent of the regions GDP, hosts more than half of the 237 zones in region. It is having a complex network of different types of zones:

1. Two wide areas zones (Kaliningrad and Magadan)
2. 26 SEZs—under SEZ law 2005
3. Innovation Centre Skolkovo—under 2010 law
4. 100 TADs—Russian far east and in single industry (mono town)
5. Free port of Vladivostok—five sub-zones (ports)

Tiny North Macedonia and Serbia house 15 and 14 SEZs, respectively, while Kazakhstan larger in size but sparsely populated has ten SEZs. Belarus, Georgia and Armenia have welcomed foreign SEZ operators. It is estimated that some 18 SEZs are in various stages of construction chiefly in Russia and Turkmenistan.

4.5.5 Developed Economies

Traditional objectives drive the establishment of SEZs in a few cases in the developed countries. For instance, SEZs in Japan and Poland target the removal of barriers of regional inequality and tackle the issue of high unemployment. The urban free zones and enterprise zones in United Kingdom are set up on the same rationale.

However, by and large, SEZs in developed economies reduce the distortion effects of tariffs and regulatory "costs" associated with imports. Almost 70 per cent of SEZs and other zones in developed countries are custom-free zones. Thus, there are no SEZs or only customs-free zones in most of Europe. However, in addition to Poland, the republics of Bulgaria and Lithuania have both customs-free zones and SEZs offering other fiscal incentives.

The member states of the European Union can designate parts of the customs territory as free zones, where goods can be imported outside EU free of import duty and other charges.

Free ports in Monaco, Switzerland and Luxembourg are essentially warehousing areas to store valuable items like precious metals. Some governments assist in establishment of various forms of science and technology parks in the form of capital rather than extend fiscal or other regulatory incentives.

The SEZs in the United States termed as Foreign Trade Zones are Customs-Free Zones set up to encourage firms to undertake distribution or manufacturing operations at US facilities rather than elsewhere.

Administrative mechanisms have evolved differently in developed economies. SEZs in countries like Bulgaria, Czech and Poland are handled by state-owned/public company; foreign trade zones in USA are managed by local organization approved by Foreign Trade Zones Board and not by federal government.

Antwerp has grown to be the second-largest modern port in Europe with latest technology, multimodal logistics and value-added services (SEZ) in port areas acting as a single distribution centre for entire Europe.

Poland adopted a law in 2018 declaring whole country as SEZ by way of creating "Poland Investment Zone" to benefit the entire country.

There is a divergence in the trends emerging in developed countries; on one side there is rise in foreign trade zones in the United States, on the other hand, there is decline in usage of custom-free zones and SEZs in Europe.

4.6 International Cooperation and Regional Development Zones

Many economies are widening activities beyond the boundaries by way of development of border SEZs, and cross-border SEZs spanning two or more economies with joint ownership have emerged, fostering regional development and international cooperation.

4.6.1 Foreign Partnership Zones

China is investing heavily in most South Asian countries. Pakistan, Nepal, Sri Lanka and Myanmar are all beneficiaries of Chinese investment. Under the China Pakistan Economic Corridor (CPEC) Agreement, major investment of US$ 40 billion in 46 SEZs (p) is proposed. The total employment generation of

25 million in next ten years is anticipated. The flagship Hambantota SEZ in Sri Lanka envisages investment of US five billion in developing the port. Chinese companies, such as Holley Group and Yantian Port Group, are also increasingly visible in economic zone development, particularly in Asia and Africa. Under the Chinese Overseas Economic Cooperation Zone programme introduced in 2006, companies are encouraged to participate in overseas SEZ development for profit and competing through open tender system with support from the Chinese government (Farole, 2011; Farole & Akinci, 2011).

Besides China, the other economies to invest in South Asia SEZs are Japan, Thailand and India. In this manner they would like to tailor their respective global footprint policies. Large conglomerates and industrial estate developers are involved in economic zone development abroad. Example, Sembcorp Industries (Singapore), Ascendas—Singbridge (Singapore), Mitsubishi, Sojitz and Sumitomo (all Japan) are major international zone developers.

The various zone development models that host economies tend to label as "zones constructed with the cooperation of a foreign partner" are tabulated in Table 4.9.

Table 4.9: Types of SEZs Developed with Foreign Partners

Types of SEZs	Examples
Zones developed by foreign developers or through joint ventures with local companies as private FDI	• Pearl river SEZ (New south China) in Kenya (2017) through JV with African Economic Zones Ltd. • Techno Park Poipet, developed by Toyoto Tsusho (Japan) in Cambodia (2015) • Call Tech Park (Zonamerica, Uruguay) in Colombia (2016)
Zones developed through public-private partnerships with foreign developers	• Lekki FTZ, developed by Chinese consortium in Nigeria (2006) through a joint venture with Government. • Savan-seno SEZ Laos (003) developed through Malaysian private companies and the government.
Zones developed as Government-to-Government partnership projects	• Thilawa SEZs, Myanmar (2011) Myanmar and Japan Government. • Russian Industrial zones, developed in Egypt (2018) by Developer from Russian Federation.

Source: UNCTAD: World Investment Report 2019

MNCs have developed their economic zones to house the suppliers and leverage on logistics. For example, since 1998 Toyota has established an agglomeration of supply chain networks in its industrial parks in India. Samsung developed its own large industrial complex within a major industrial park in Vietnam in 2016. This shows that notwithstanding the attention that government-to-government partnership zones attract, the majority of such zones are developed by foreign private companies with no bilateral government agreements.

Japanese government unveiled in 2014 the Japan-India Investment Promotion Partnership with the objective of encouraging Japanese SMEs to invest in India by developing 12 Japan Industrial Township in India. One example is One Hub Chennai which was developed by Japan's Mizuho Bank and an Engineering company JGC, along with Ascendas, a business complex developer from Singapore.

India has emulated China to some extent in the Global Foot Print policy through investments and joint partnership; development of Chabahar port in Iran, Mattala airport in Srilanka, SEZs in Mombasa, Sittwe SEZ in Rakhine region of Myanmar. Plans are afoot for investment strategies on similar lines in other South Asian nations with the objective to set up SEZs which are into multi-products manufacture and labour intensive. In a few weak economies like Bangladesh and Nepal, non-tariff barriers like Certificate of Origin and quotas are the other factors responsible for growth of SEZs.

The Public-Private Partnership (PPP) model is in vogue for the development of some SEZs in host economies; the foreign developer undertakes these projects through joint-venture arrangements with both public and private local partners. The foreign developer usually assumes the role of the manager of the SEZ or a partner in the management company. Government-to-Government partnership SEZs have also become popular in recent years. Such partnerships are a result of bilateral agreement to jointly develop SEZs, setting up the cooperation framework, the division of responsibilities, and the development and management mechanism of the zones. Government partnership zones can be built and managed by host-economy developers, home-country developers, joint ventures or third-country developers, to benefit from their capital or expertise in zones development.

Table 4.10 shows the establishment of government partnership zones at the initiative of both the host country and the partners.

The Government Partnership Zones offer many benefits particularly for host economies. The prime advantage is that the development cost is shared. Limited budgets and the need for more economic zones have resulted in the

Table 4.10: Selected Government Partnership Zones

Zone	Home Economy	Host Economy	Bilateral Agreement	Development Model
Batamindo Industrial Park	Singapore	Indonesia	1989	JV (Singapore Govt.-linked companies & Salim group, Indonesia)
Suzhou Industrial Park	Singapore	China	1994	JV (Singapore and Chinese consortia)
Sittwe SEZ	India	Myanmar	2016	In planning stage
One Hub Chennai	Japan	India	2013	JV (India—Singapore and Japanese Consortia)
Russia Industrial Zone	Russia	Egypt	2018	To be developed by Russian Industrial developer.
Sihanoukville SEZ	China	Cambodia	2010	JV (Chinese and Cambodia International Investment Development Board)
Lekki Free Trade Zone	China	Nigeria	2006	JV (Chinese and Lagos state government)

Source: UNCTAD: World Investment Report 2019

mushrooming of SEZs under this model. Second, host countries benefit from the expertise and experience of foreign zone developers. Third, having foreign partners in SEZ development enhances the probability of attracting foreign investments into these SEZs.

A mixture of development assistance, economic cooperation and strategic considerations encourages the development of partnership zones initiated by investor home-country governments. Major ODA donors and multilateral development institutions have included development of SEZs as part of development assistance. The World Bank, along with the U.S. Agency for International Development and the European Investment Bank, supported the establishment of the Gaza Industrial Estate in 1999 to increase employment and GDP. Japan is known to extend assistance for industrial development and has included Industrial Park Development in this scheme in the early 2000s. The premier agency of the government of Japan, namely Japan International Cooperation

Agency (JICA) assisted in the setting up of SEZs in the Middle East and Africa. Since 2000, France, Germany, India, the Republic of Korea and Turkey have all engaged in the construction of FTZs in Palestine to promote economic development.

4.6.2 Border and Cross-Border SEZs

Some of the developing countries share land borders with their prosperous neighbours. Mexico is a leading example sharing its northern border with California, Texas, Arizona and New Mexico, all southern states of USA. Mexico, in fact, established its first SEZs (Maquiladoras) in Tijuana, Baja near California border and Ciudad Juarez in Chihuahua (Texas border) in the 1960s.

The concept of SEZs close to land borders has also been embraced by some economies for Regional Integration and Reduction of Regional Disparity. In course of time, the SEZs have promoted Regional Economic Corridors furthering regional development initiatives and cooperation programs. China established SEZs in its less developed regions near borders to boost local economic development. Thailand adopted a new SEZ programme in 2015 to establish ten SEZs at its border. Countries like Cambodia, China, Laos, Myanmar, Thailand and Vietnam have joined hands together and encouraged SEZs in border areas leveraging on the improved connectivity along the corridors. Improved technology in logistics has reduced costs for the participating economies. The travel time in the corridor has also significantly reduced, for example, pilot trial performed between Myanmar and Thailand corridor for semi-trailer swapping with bonded warehouse with strict control and monitoring of custom electronic seal within built GPS function to trace the trucks resulted in substantial saving in the travel time.

Similar strategy is being followed in the African continent though on a smaller scale. The objectives remain the same, that is, reduction of regional disparity through skill development and employment generation, for example, Musina/Makhado SEZ of South Africa is strategically located close to the border of South Africa and Zimbabwe.

Countries across the globe continue to be highly sensitive about land borders. Therefore, it is not surprising that cross-border SEZs are of relatively recent origin. The success depends on involvement and support from the governments concerned and local population. For example, on 1 March 2019, Ethopia and Kenya agreed to establish an FTZ for enhanced infrastructure development along the Moyle border region.

Summarizing, SEZ development in different continents/countries show that it is not a panacea and has to be implemented properly and carefully tailored into a country's specific situations. It is not necessarily the most suitable instrument for any country. Given the complex and heterogeneous environments in which zone programmes are implemented, it would be useful to establish a clear framework to guide the operations of SEZs in countries where they are found relevant.

To make this truly successful, the host governments and investors need more mutual understanding of the different developmental stages, legal and governance systems, institutions, social norms, cultures and even mindsets, and need to come out with a pragmatic approach which builds on the strengths of both sides and fits into the local context. Such an approach will eventually lead to a win-win situation.

4.7 Social Impact Assessment of Special Economic Zones

Since the formation of export processing zones especially in developing economies, lot of concern has been raised on social and environmental impacts. SEZs have always been in controversy in these economies and have been criticized for misappropriation of land or destroying agricultural land in the pursuit of industrialization, or for fraudulent private gains (Moberg, 2013).

International Labour Organization (ILO) carried a survey in 2017 and concluded that problems persist in the protection of fundamental principles and rights at work, in particular freedom of association and collective bargaining, and gender equality and that other violation of workers' rights are also common, especially concerning hours of work, safety and health.

Although most economies have ratified the ILO conventions, yet some nations still continue to pursue a low-wage strategy for EPZ development where labour law either does not apply or is not enforced (ILO, 2017). Survey was also conducted in respect to unpaid overtime, unremunerated work at night and lack of social security. Most of the countries lag in proper laws while some of the countries have developed mechanisms to monitor labour practices and avoid disputes, such as involving trade union representatives on SEZ boards (Farole & Akinci, 2011).

It is noteworthy that SEZs working conditions and environment impacts have directly/indirectly contributed to the surrounding economies of SEZs or within a specific industry than with the SEZ status per se.

Wage levels and occupational safety and health standards tend to be higher in SEZs-based foreign affiliates of MNE's than in domestic firm outside the zones. Wages and labour practices depend on the local context and on prevalent industries and economic activities in the zones.

SEZs have a significant impact on formal employment of women. Female workers are estimated to account for more than 60 per cent of zones workforces worldwide (FIAS, 2008). This share is higher in light manufacturing areas like footwear, garments and electronics and lower on heavy manufacturing or diversifies economic activities but average remains above 50 percent in SEZs.

Services provided by zones operating companies or shared services among zone investors are increasingly used to support higher social and environmental standards. Many EPZs assist companies operating within the zone with labour-related issues (UNCTAD, 2015b).

Services included inspection and management assistance. Some SEZs had clear labour standards for companies operating within their confines, addressing minimum wages, hours and conditions for the operation of unions.

SEZ in India polled as part of UNCTAD's survey actively encourages companies operating within the zone to become ISO 14001 certified. The use of these standards by SEZ management companies positively steers companies operating within their zones towards responsible business practices.

To sum SEZs can make a positive contribution to the environmental, social and governance (ESG) performance of countries' industrial base. SEZs can gain a competitive advantage by providing not only conventional benefits, but also cost-effective support for good environmental and social practices for firms operating within their boundaries.

4.8 Economic Impact Assessment of Special Economic Zones

4.8.1 Direct Economic

4.8.1.1 Investment Attraction

SEZs play an important role as key investment promotion tool in attracting FDI (Figure 4.2).

Through adequate infrastructure and best practices, zones can to an extent compensate for an adverse investment climate.

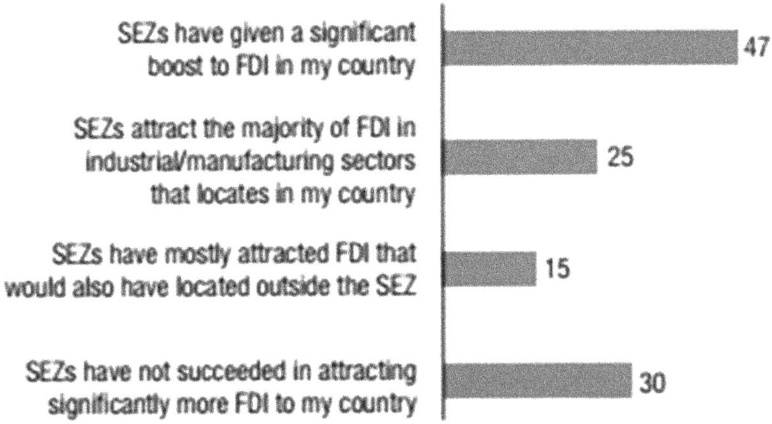

Figure 4.2: Contribution of SEZs to Investment Promotion (Percentage of Respondents)
Source: UNCTAD Survey of Investment Promotion Agencies (IPAs)

Implementation of SEZs programme has benefitted most of the economies by attracting FDI flows. China has demonstrated that there is a strong positive effect on FDI accounting for over 80 per cent of cumulative FDI, including on new green field investments. Importantly, SEZs do not seem to crowd out domestic investment (World Bank, 2017). Philippines has registered a positive growth of FDIs from 30 per cent in 1997 to over 81 per cent in 2000 (UNCTAD, 2002). In Malaysia, almost 90 percent of total investment found in SEZs originates from foreign investors. In Vietnam, 60–70 per cent of all FDI is located in SEZs, Cambodia and the Lao People's Democratic Republic, also attract foreign investment and account for significant share of total FDI.

In Myanmar, 80 per cent of investors in the Thilawa SEZ are foreign-owned, and another 15 per cent are joint ventures. The foreign investments by nine ASEAN countries in Myanmar totalled $38.155 billion for the period from 1988–1989 till September 2019, accounting for 46.6 per cent of the total FDI, according to the figures released by Directorate of Investment and Company Administration (DICA).

During last 31 years, 11 sectors which witnessed massive influxes of FDI are oil and gas sector, energy, production, transport and communications, real estate, housing, hotels and tourism, mining, livestock and fishery, agricultural and industrial zone sectors.

The FDI granted under the SEZ Law for Thilawa SEZ amounted to $1.861 billion. A total of 19 countries have invested in Thilawa SEZ. ASEAN countries that invested in the Thilawa SEZ are Singapore, Thailand, Malaysia and Vietnam. Myanmar is implementing the 20-year Myanmar Investment Promotion Plan to enable itself to become a middle-income country by 2030.

4.8.1.2 Export Generation and Diversification

SEZs in many economies account for the major share of exports, particularly manufactured exports. In Latin America and Caribbean, SEZs contribute more than 50 per cent of total exports in Costa Rica, the Dominican Republic and Nicaragua, 31 per cent in Mexico and 13 per cent in Colombia. In Asia, SEZs are credited with more than 60 per cent of the Philippines exports and close to 18 per cent of India's. In Bangladesh, just eight publicly owned zones account for about 20 per cent of the country's exports of goods.

The oil rich countries of West Asia and North Africa rely heavily on oil and gas exports; SEZs account for approximately 60 per cent of net non-oil exports in Morocco, 25 per cent in Egypt and 40 per cent in the United Arab Emirates.

Some African countries use SEZs as part of their export promotion strategies backed by trade preferences. For instance, Export Processing Zones play a pivotal role in Kenya's export strategy enabled by the African Growth and Opportunity Act (AGOA)—by attracting foreign investors in apparel industry with chief target of exports to the United States.

SEZs have also played an important role of diversification in export activities in many economies. For instance, in Costa Rica, the SEZs share of manufactured exports increased from less than 10 per cent in 1990 to 55 per cent in 2003 (FIAS, 2008; Gereffi, 2019). At the same time, SEZs have diversified production from apparel and textile to electronic components.

4.8.1.3 Direct and Indirect Employment Creation

Employment generation is a key takeaway of SEZ development. The role played by SEZs in job creation particularly for women entering the workforce is crucial. Worldwide, it is estimated that SEZs and Free Zones provide direct employment to 90–100 million people.

There is a substantial impact of indirect employment. The ratio of indirect to direct jobs created ranges from one-fourth to multiples of two depending upon the country's economy. This implies that the indirect employment effect of SEZs globally could range from 50 million to 200 million jobs.

Job creation by SEZs in individual countries is not uniform. For example, United States FTZ has created average 7 per cent growth in employment per year since 2013. There was an incremental growth in job creation in SEZs especially for women even in less developed economies like Tunisia, Ethiopia, Kenya, Colombia and Dominican Republic. The impact of these jobs in countries with high rates of unemployment and underemployment is significant. SEZs have emerged as an effective tool for formal employment even in the poorest of nations. It may be noted however that though SEZs could be effective tools to boost employment, such jobs could be relatively insecure.

4.8.1.4 Overall Economic Growth Impact

SEZs success can be measured directly by looking at FDI, exports and employment indicators and at overall production growth in the zones. A recent study (Frick et. al., 2019; World Bank, 2017a) based on sample of 346 SEZs across developing regions over the period 2007–2012, found that the average economic growth rate across SEZs was about 14.7 per cent over the period, with significant variation, and the median growth rate was only 2.8 per cent. Broadly, growth of SEZs was on average 2–5 per cent lower than national GDP growth.

Even in economies where SEZs growth was relatively high, for example, Kenya, Turkey and Ghana, it remained below overall national GDP growth. In countries like Vietnam and Russia, SEZs grew faster as compared to national growth. SEZs provide a temporary boost during the development phase. The additional growth effect gradually wanes as zones mature.

Further, it was observed that the SEZ growth stimulus mostly benefited workers at upper end of the income distribution. Those at the lower end of the wage and educational scale did not benefit significantly.

4.9 Synopsis

It can be deduced that SEZs are important instruments of industrial policy irrespective of status of economies because of the opportunity they provide for technology and skills development and upgrading in Global Value Chain (GVCs). Various economies have development strategies that incorporate SEZs for industrial development and upgrading. The driving factors are formal training and work experience which results in workforce upgrading and skills development. SEZ programmes have increased the domestic value added in exports over time, which indicates both higher value-added activities in the zones and greater linkages with the domestic economy. Linkages with local firms, spillover, crowding in and demonstration effects are the keys to maximizing the industrial development impact of SEZs. Linkages between zone-based investors and domestic suppliers are important to transmit technological and skills spillover that support broader industrial development. They are also important to ensure that zones become bridges to structural reform in the broader economy, as SEZ investors interact with the local business environment and local firms indirectly experience SEZs' business climate. This is the key rationale for the continued use of SEZs in the recent wave of new industrial policies.

Government-to-Government Partnership in SEZs, new generation cross-border SEZs and other innovations point to the continuing role of SEZs in economic transformation of participating nations.

5

Special Economic Zones: An Indian Perspective

Equipped with a global view of SEZs, the focus is now on the journey of SEZs in India. *This chapter begins with a brief overview on the evolution of the SEZ in India in the context of the regulatory framework.*

Within Asia, India is a pioneer with the first Asian Export Processing Zone (EPZ) established at Kandla as early as 1965. The term SEZ *came into vogue in 2000, although the EPZ and other earlier structures resembled modern SEZ. The central government while unveiling the Export Import Policy in April 2000 laid down the definition of a "Special Economic Zone" (SEZs). The then existing EPZs were renamed as SEZs. This was followed by the enactment of the SEZ Act in 2005 and SEZ Policy in 2006. The legislation and the policy framework accelerated the setting up of SEZs in the country. Of the total employment provided to 2.28 million people, the incremental employment after February 2006 is 2.15 million. The incremental investment in SEZs is to the tune of INR 6,036 billion after the SEZ Act 2005 to make a total of INR 6,077 billion. On the export front, the overall growth from 2005–2006 to 2019–2020 is a staggering 3,388 per cent.*

As on 31 January 2021, there are some 378 notified SEZs, out of which 265 are operational. Out of this, 164 are IT/ITeS, 25 multi-product, 2 multi-services and 74 other sector-specific SEZs. Almost 5,481 units have been set up in the SEZs till 31.12.2020.

This chapter covers briefly the history of SEZs in India, the phases of SEZ development in India, overview of operational SEZs, analysis of SEZ Act 2005 and policies enacted by the government and the socio-economic impact of SEZs.

It also covers topics related to land acquisition, de-notification and cancellation of SEZs and policy response to WTO.

5.1 Introduction

India is on the threshold of a high growth trajectory with a distinct possibility of achieving GDP of USD 5 trillion by 2024. A key driver for India to achieve the USD 5 trillion mark sooner would be boosting exports—both merchandise and services. SEZs provide the perfect launch pad for the rocketing growth of exports.

5.2 Special Economic Zones in India: The Journey

The first Export Processing Zone was established by the government of India on 7 March 1965, in Kandla, Gujarat, with the main objective of promoting exports to earn foreign exchange. This is the first EPZ in the Asian continent. This was followed by the Santacruz Electronic Export Processing Zone (SEEPZ) set up in 1973 in Mumbai, with focus on single product namely electronic goods. The objective was to facilitate technology transfer. Later on, gems and jewelry were added to the product profile of SEEPZ.

In 1986, four more multi-product zones were created to cover broadly the south, east and north of India. The Seventh EPZ was established at Vishakhapatnam in 1989. The details of EPZs from 1965 till 2000 are tabulated in Table 5.1.

The responsibility for establishing the zones initially rested solely with the central government. In 1994, by amendment of the policy, state governments and private sector were permitted to develop and operate EPZs. As per the Ministry of Commerce (MoC) Annual Report 2018–2019, EPZs could not emerge as effective instruments for export promotion on account of multiplicity of controls and clearances, the absence of world-class infrastructure and unstable fiscal regime.

Table 5.1: Evolution of SEZs in India—Early Days

Sl. No	SEZ (EPZ)	Host State	Year Set Up	Conversion From EPZ—SEZ	Product
1	Kandla SEZ	Gujarat	1965	2000	Multi-product
2	SEEPZ SEZ	Maharashtra	1973	2000	Electronics, Gems and Jewellery
3	Cochin SEZ	Kerala	1986	2000	Multi-product
4	Falta SEZ	West Bengal	1986	2003	Multi-product
5	Madras SEZ	Tamil Nadu	1986	2003	Multi-product
6	Noida SEZ	Uttar Pradesh	1986	2003	Multi-product
7	Vishakhapatnam	Andhra Pradesh	1989	2003	Multi-product

5.2.1 The Tryst with EPZs (1965–1980)

This was a period when the Indian economy was largely of the Command and Control type with government playing a dominant role in the economic development of the country. Industrialization, inputs and outputs were regulated on the basis of the Five Year Plans. It was an inward-looking economy and the emphasis was on Import Substitution. Therefore, it is commendable that in this environment, the government established the Kandla Free Trade Zone (KFTZ) at Kandla in 1965. This is the first such zone to be established in Asia. The government had the foresight to gauge the importance of electronics, when it was still a nascent industry globally and established the Santacruz Electronic Export Processing Zone (SEEPZ) in Mumbai in 1973. Notwithstanding the noble intentions of the government, clarity of long-term goals stymied the development of the EPZs. Added to this was the rigid policy framework, weak infrastructure and poor incentives to the developers, thus the EPZs never really took off. The exports as envisaged did not materialize and the government was concerned. In fact, the government appointed the Kaul Committee in 1978 to review Kandla EPZ; followed by Review Committee on Electronics for SEEPZ in 1979. Finally, the Tandon Committee was appointed by the government in 1981 to review both the EPZs.

The Committees were directed to suggest policies for the Free Trade Zones (FTZs) and 100 per cent Export-Oriented Units (EOU). The Committees diagnosed the shortcomings like the absence of a central monitoring and implementation authority, procedural constraints, inadequate infrastructural facilities, limited concessions, and limited powers of the zone authorities in the reports submitted to the government. The Committees made several recommendations to overcome these shortcomings and to improve the performance of the EPZs, FTZs and EOUs.

5.2.2 Growth Pangs (1981–1999)

With the acceptance by the government of the Tandon Committee recommendations, the stage was set for the transformation of the EPZs. Tandon Committee stressed on the importance of EPZs in export promotion; India needed badly to expand exports in value and volume terms for a favorable Balance of Trade. The government established four zones to cover the four corners of the country. The western part already had Kandla and Santacruz zones. The new zones were established in 1984 in Noida, Uttar Pradesh (NEPZ—North India), Falta, West Bengal (FEPZ—East India) Cochin, Kerala (CEPZ) and Madras (now Chennai), Tamil Nadu (MEPZ—South India). The Visakhapatnam EPZ in Andhra Pradesh was added in 1989.

There were now seven zones in total in the country, five new zones as listed above and two existing zones at Kandla and Santacruz (Mumbai). In this period, the government introduced as an export promotion measure, permission to open Export Oriented Units (EOU). Such EOUs were eligible for incentives and facilities on par with EPZs. These measures however did not elicit the desired outcome and the EPZs and EOUs did not flourish as expected.

The economic reforms of 1991–1992 ushered in major changes in the Export-Import Regime. Most of the goods were classified under OGL (Open General License) and could be freely imported or exported. A number of circulars were issued by the Reserve Bank of India and Central Board of Customs in connection with the operations of EPZs in the changed scenario. Activities like trading, agriculture, horticulture, re-engineering were brought within the ambit of EPZ operations. Another substantive change was the decentralization of the powers of the Board of Approvals.

5.2.3 Consolidation Phase Spurred by Legal Framework (2000–2007)

The dawn of the twentieth century was marked by two very important changes in the Foreign Trade Policy of the country. In April 2000, the Commerce Ministry brought out the document titled Export and Import Policy (EXIM Policy) with the twin objectives of facilitating globally competitive and hassle-free business environment for investors and simplifying the process of foreign trade. EPZs and other such structures were now termed as SEZs. The other important change was that SEZ merited an entire chapter in the EXIM policy. SEZs were positioned then as the launch pads for trade in general and export promotion in particular.

The policy announced in April 2000, intended to make SEZs an engine for economic growth supported by quality infrastructure and complemented by an attractive fiscal package, both at the centre and state level, with a user-friendly regulatory framework. It sought to correct the shortcomings of the EPZ model. All the EPZs were renamed as SEZs in 2000. For the first time, state governments as well as the private sector were empowered to set up SEZs.

SEZ is an umbrella term and subsumes a range of activities including exports, warehousing, manufacturing, and trading. Within SEZ, we have Free Trade and Warehousing Zone (FTWZ), manufacturing-based EPZs, services-based EPZs, SEZs of EOU (Export Oriented Units) and large comprehensive SEZs typical of the mainland China.

The minimum area of 1,000 hectares envisaged SEZs as townships by themselves with educational institutions, hospitals, public transport and so on. This minimum area requirement has been reduced to 500 hectares vide notification dated 12 August 2013 and further reduced to 50 hectares with effect from 17 December 2019.

The EXIM Policy outlined a few fiscal as well as non-fiscal incentive schemes for SEZs. The enactment of SEZ Act in 2005 and SEZ Rules in 2006 provided the regulatory framework for SEZ operations in the country.

5.2.4 Exponential Growth (2008–till Date)

Once the legal framework and the rules were in place, there was an exponential growth in SEZs across India; from 87 in 2008 to 170 numbers in 2012. As on 31 January 2021, the number of operational SEZs is 265. The pace of growth slackened subsequently due to implementation of Minimum Alternative Tax (MAT) and Dividend Distribution Tax (DDT); both these measures took off the sheen of investments in SEZs.

5.3 The Regulatory and Institutional Framework

5.3.1 Regulatory Framework

5.3.1.1 Special Economic Zone Act, 2005

This is the basic law for regulation of SEZs. Prior to the enactment of this Act, the central government not only developed the EPZs but also controlled operations in the EPZs. With the enactment of this legislation the central government is responsible only for the broad policy framework and monitoring of the SEZ programme.

5.3.1.2 SEZ Act, 2005: Objectives and Some Salient Features

The Act has guidelines for creation of SEZs from proposal stage to set up, including notification; the Act also has provisions for permitting exemption from taxes or duties; Constitution of Board of Approvals with the duties, powers and functions of the Board; Appointment and duties of Development Commissioner; Constitution, powers and functions of the Approvals Committee; procedures to set up a unit, setting up and operation of Offshore Banking Unit; Exemptions, Drawbacks and Concessions to the SEZ Developer and unit holder (SEZ Act 2005).

Prior to the enactment of the SEZ Act, 2005, a total of 19 SEZs were established/notified; of these 19 SEZs, the central government of India owned and operated seven SEZs and the remaining twelve were owned and operated by state governments and private sector, details as follows:

a. **Central Government SEZs:** SEEPZ-SEZ (Maharashtra), Kandla SEZ (Gujarat), Cochin SEZ (Kerala), Madras SEZ (Tamil Nadu), Visakhapatnam (AP), Falta SEZ (West Bengal) and Noida SEZ (UP),
b. **State Government & Private Sector SEZs**: Surat SEZ (Gujarat), Manickanchan SEZ (West Bengal), Indore SEZ (Madhya Pradesh), Jaipur SEZ (Gems and Jewellery) (Rajasthan), Mahindra City (Chennai, Tamil Nadu) (IT), Mahindra City (Chennai, Tamil Nadu) (apparel and fashion accessories), Mahindra City (Chennai, Tamil Nadu) (auto ancillary), Salt Lake Electronic City (Kolkata), Moradabad SEZ (Uttar Pradesh), Jodhpur SEZ (Rajasthan), Surat Apparel SEZ, Nokia SEZ (Chennai)

The Special Economic Zones Act, 2005, was passed by Parliament in May 2005 and received presidential assent on 23 June 2005. The main objectives of the SEZ Act are:

a. Generation of additional economic activity
b. Promotion of exports of goods and services
c. Promotion of investment from domestic and foreign sources
d. Creation of employment opportunities
e. Development of infrastructure facilities

5.3.1.3 SEZ Rules, 2006

The SEZ rules, 2006, came into effect on 10 February 2006. In terms of the SEZ Act 2005, a SEZ may be set up either jointly or severally by the central government, state government or any person for manufacture of goods or rendering services or for both or as a free trade warehousing zone. Such proposals duly recommended by the concerned state government are considered by the Board of Approval for SEZs. SEZs set up under the SEZ Act, 2005, and SEZ rules, 2006, are primarily private investment–driven initiatives.

The salient features of SEZ scheme as regulated by the SEZ Act 2005 and SEZ Rules 2006 are:

1. The SEZ area is a designated duty-free enclave, which is treated as a territory outside the customs territory of India for the purpose of authorized operations in the SEZs.
2. No license is required for import.
3. Manufacturing or service activities are allowed.
4. SEZ unit shall achieve Positive Net Foreign Exchange to be calculated cumulatively for a period of five years from the commencement of production.
5. Domestic sales are subject to full customs duty payment and in line with the import policy in force.
6. The SEZ unit can undertake some activities through sub-contracting.
7. No routine examination will be done by Customs Authorities for Export/Import cargo.
8. SEZ Developers/Co-developers and units enjoy Direct Tax and Indirect Tax benefits as prescribed in the SEZ Act, 2005.

Other Features of SEZs Act are:

- The central government is authorized to direct modified applicability of Central Acts (except labour matters) to SEZs and units therein.
- State governments are authorized to enact laws/notify policies for providing fiscal and other concessions.
- SEZ shall be deemed to be a port, airport, inland container depot, land station and land customs stations, as the case may be, under the Customs Act, 1962.

The SEZ Act is a progressive legislation aimed at reforming the old laws to the extent applicable to SEZ activities. Overall, the Act strives to usher a minimum regulatory regime and provide fiscal benefits to the SEZs so as to attract investment. This Act provides the stable long-term policy that is so necessary to promote investment in SEZs. For instance, the Act supersedes provisions of 21 earlier laws/Acts like, the Agricultural Produce Cess Act, 1940 (27 of 1940), The Coffee Act, 1942 (7 of 1942) and other laws.

(a) Incentives and Facilities Offered to SEZ Units and Developer The Directorate General of Foreign Trade (DGFT) and its regional offices, functioning under the Department of Commerce, Ministry of Commerce and Industry, Government of India regulates international trade in India. DGFT announces the policies and procedures required to be followed for exports from India from time to time.

As per the SEZs policy and its amendments, different types of incentives and facilities are provided for units in SEZs as well as to SEZs Developers/Co-developers. The major incentives offered in SEZ Act 2005 are briefed in Table 5.2.

Section 10AA of the Income tax Act, 1961, provides for deduction of profits and gains derived from the export of articles or things or from services in respect of newly established Units in Special Economic Zones referred to in clause (j) of Section 2 of SEZ Act 2005; exports from this unit, who begin to manufacture or produce articles or things or provide any services during the previous year relevant to any assessment year commencing on or after first day of April 2006, but before the first day of April 2021.

(b) Advantages on Export of Goods and Services for SEZ Units Export of goods and services from India is governed by clause (a) of sub-section (1) and sub-section (3) of Section 7 of the Foreign Exchange Management Act 1999 (42 of 1999), read with Notification No. G.S.R. 381(E) dated 3 May 2000 viz. Foreign Exchange Management (Current Account Transactions) Rules, 2000, further read with FEMA Notification No.23(R)/2015-RB dated 12 January 2016. These regulations are amended from time to time to incorporate the changes in the regulatory framework and published through amendment notifications. The key highlights for SEZs units as per the updated master directions dated 12 January 2018 are as under:

i) Realization and Repatriation of Exports Proceeds

a) The period of realization and repatriation of export proceeds shall be nine months from the date of export for all exporters including Units in SEZs.

Table 5.2: SEZ India Incentive Regime

Sl. No.	For SEZ Units	For SEZ Developers
1	**Duty Free Import and Domestic Procurement** • Applicable on goods for the development, operation and maintenance of SEZ units	**Exemption from Customs/ Excise Duties** • For the development of SEZs, on authorized operations, as approved by the Board of Approval.
2	**Benefit under Integrated Goods and Services Tax** • Exemption from Central Sales Tax, Service Tax and State Sales Tax, which have now subsumed into GST. • Supplies to SEZ are zero rated under the IGST Act 2017.	**Benefit on External Commercial Borrowing** • SEZ Developers may avail the ECB channel upon government approval, solely for the purposes of providing infrastructural facilities in the zone.
3	**Single Window Clearance** • Applicable for all Central and State-level approvals	**Exemption from Central Sales Tax (CST) and Service Tax** • Section 7, 26 and Schedule II of the SEZ Act.

Exemption Withdrawn

- *Exemption from the Minimum Alternate Tax (MAT) under section 115JB of Income Tax Act and Dividend Distribution Tax (DDT) with effect from 01/04/2012 and 01/06/2011 respectively.*
- *MAT is charged at 15% (W.E.F 20TH Sept 2019) + (Surcharge & CESS) and DDT at 15%*
- *Sunset* Clause for units is effective from 01/04/2020.

b) For goods exported to a warehouse established outside India, the proceeds shall be realized within 15 months from the date of shipment of goods.

ii) Exchange Earners' Foreign Currency Account (EEFC Account)

a) A unit located in a SEZ may open, hold and maintain a foreign currency account with bank (AD—Authorized Dealer) in India.

b) Payments received in foreign exchange by a 100 per cent Export Oriented Unit or a unit in Export Processing Zone, Software Technology Park or Electronic Hardware Technology Park for supply of goods to similar such unit or to a unit in Domestic Tariff Area and also payments received in foreign exchange by a unit in Domestic Tariff Area for supply of goods to a unit in SEZ.

iii) Export of Goods by SEZs

(i) Units in SEZs are permitted to undertake job work abroad and export goods from that country itself subject to the conditions that:
   a) Processing/manufacturing charges are suitably loaded in the export price and are borne by the ultimate buyer.
   b) The exporter has made satisfactory arrangements for realization of full export proceeds subject to the usual EDF procedure.

(ii) AD Category—I Banks may permit units in Domestic Tariff Area (DTAs) to purchase foreign exchange for making payment for goods supplied to them by units in SEZs. Authorised Dealer Banks are permitted to sell foreign exchange to a unit in the DTA for making payment in foreign exchange to a unit in the SEZ for the services rendered by it (i.e. a unit in SEZ) to a DTA unit. It must be ensured that in the Letter of Approval (LoA) issued to the SEZ unit by the Development Commissioner (DC) of the SEZ, the provisions pertaining to the goods/services supplied by the SEZ unit to the DTA unit and for payment in foreign exchange for the same should be mentioned.

(iii) Direct dispatch of documents by the exporter: Banks may permit units in SEZ to dispatch the export documents to the consignees outside India subject to the condition that export proceeds are repatriated through the AD banks.

iv) Netting-Off of Export Receivables against Import Payments

Units SEZs AD Category I banks may allow requests received from exporters for "netting off" of export receivables against import payments for units located in SEZs subject to the following:

(i) The netting-off of export receivables against import payments is in respect of the same Indian entity and the overseas buyer/supplier (bilateral netting) and the netting may be done as on the date of balance sheet of the unit in SEZ.

(ii) The details of export of goods are documented in EDF (O) forms/DTR as the case may be while details of import of goods/services are recorded through A1/A2 form as the case may be. The relative EDF will be treated as complete by the designated AD Category I banks only after the entire proceeds are adjusted/received.

(iii) Both the transactions of sale and purchase in R- Returns under FETERS are reported separately.

(iv) The export/import transactions with ACU countries are kept outside the arrangement.

(v) All the relevant documents are submitted to the concerned AD Category I banks that should comply with all the regulatory requirements relating to the transactions

5.3.1.4 The Special Economic Zones Rules, 2006, and Amendments Thereto

The central government notified the SEZ Rules 2006 on 10 February 2006, in exercise of the power conferred by section 55 of the SEZ Act, 2005 (28 of 2005). The Rules deal mainly with operational matters like procedure to be adopted for sub-contracting from outside, DTA sale, monitoring and compliances of units, de-bonding of units and others.

Some of the Salient features of the SEZ Rules are:

(i) Minimum area for establishing of SEZs

The requirement of land or built-up space for different categories of zone as specified in the Rules as per the third amendment of SEZ rules 2019 vide gazette notification dated 17 December 2019 is as under:

- All existing notified Special Economic Zones shall be deemed to be multi-sector Special Economic Zones. It means a special economic Zone for more than one sector where Units may be set up for manufacture of goods falling in two or more sectors or rendering of services falling in two or more sectors or any combination thereof including trading and warehousing.
- Special Economic Zone or Free Trade Warehousing Zone other than SEZ for Information Technology or Information Technology-enabled services, Biotech or Health (other than hospital) service, shall have a contiguous area of 50 Ha or more. However, for the states of Assam, Meghalaya, Nagaland, Arunachal Pradesh, Mizoram, Manipur, Tripura, Himachal Pradesh, Uttarakhand, Sikkim, Jammu and Kashmir, Goa or any union territory, the area shall be 25 Ha or more.

- Zones exclusively for Information Technology or IT-enabled services, Bio-Technology and health sector (excluding hospitals) will have no minimum area requirement but a minimum built-up processing area shall be applicable based on the category of cities as described in Table 5.3.

Table 5.3: Minimum Built up Area (Category of City-Wise)

Category of Cities	Minimum Built Up Area Requirement*
Category "A"	50,000 sq. metres
Category "B"	25,000 sq. metres
Category "C"	15,000 sq. metres

* with effect from 17/12/2019 SEZ (3rd Amendment) Rules 2019

Source: www.sezindia.nic.in

- In case of zones set up exclusively for electronic hardware and software (including IT-enabled services) the minimum area shall be 10 hectares and the norms for minimum built up processing area as tabulated (Table 5.3) above shall be applicable.
- Zone exclusively for handicrafts, the minimum area shall be 10 hectares.
- Zones exclusively for bio-technology, non-conventional energy, including solar energy equipment's or cell, agro-based food processing, the minimum area shall be 10 hectares or more with a minimum built-up area of 40,000 sq. metres.
- For zones exclusively for gems and jewellery, the minimum area requirement would be 10 hectares or more and minimum built-up area of 50,000 sq. metres.

5.3.1.5 Net Foreign Exchange (NFE) Criteria

The Unit shall achieve Positive Net Foreign Exchange to be calculated cumulatively for a period of five years from the commencement of production according to the following formula: Positive net foreign exchange = A-B>0

Where:

A: is Free on Board of Approval value of exports, including exports to Nepal and Bhutan against freely convertible currency, by the unit and the value of following supplies of their products namely

(a) Supply of goods against Advance Authorisation or Advance authorisation for annual requirement or Duty-Free Import Authorisation under the Duty Exemption or Remission scheme under the Foreign Trade Policy.

(b) Supply of capital goods to holders of licence under the Export Promotion Capital Good Scheme under the Foreign Trade Policy.

(c) Supply of goods to project financed by multilateral or bilateral agencies or Fund as notified by the Department of Economic Affairs from time to time under International Competitive Bidding in accordance with the procedures of those agencies or funds; where the legal agreements provide for tender evaluation without including the customs duty.

(d) Supply of goods to any project or for any purpose in respect of which the Ministry of Finance notifies from time to time, permitting import of such goods at zero customs duty.

(e) Supply of goods to United Nations-funded project approved by government.

(f) Supply of goods to nuclear power projects as per condition stipulated in Foreign Trade Policy.

(g) Supply against special entitlement of duty-free import of goods under the Foreign Trade policy:

(h) Export of services by service units including services rendered with the SEZ or such services rendered in Domestic Tariff Area and paid for in free foreign exchange or such services rendered in Indian Rupees which are otherwise considered as having been paid for in free foreign exchange by the Reserve Bank of India.

(i) Supply of Information Technology Agreement items and notified zero duty telecom or electronic items, namely, colour display tubes for monitors and deflection component for colour monitors or any other items as may be notified by central government.

(j) Supply to other units and developers in the same or other SEZ or EOU or Electronic Hardware Technology Park or Software Technology Park unit or Bio-Technology Park unit provided that such goods and services are permissible for import or procurement by such units and developers:

(k) Supply of goods against free foreign exchange by a Free Trade and Warehousing Zone unit.

Explanation: For removal of doubts, it is hereby clarified that the supplies under clause (j) shall be against procurement certificate, as applicable and the supplies under clause (d) to (g) shall be as per the terms and conditions of the respective duty exemption as notified by the central government through Ministry of Finance.

B: consists of sum of the following:

(a) Sum total of the Cost Insurance and freight value of all imported input used for authorised operations during the relevant period and the cost, Insurance and Freight value of all imported capital goods including goods purchased on high seas basis even though paid for in Indian rupees and the value of all payments made in foreign exchange by way of export commission, royalty, fees, dividends, interest on external commercial borrowings during the first five years period or any other charges:

(b) Value of goods obtained from other unit or EOU or Electronic Hardware Technology Park or Software Technology Park Unit or Bio-technology Park unit or from bonded warehouses or procured from international exhibitions held in India or precious metals procured from nominated agencies:

(c) The Cost Insurance Freight value of the goods and services, including pro-rata Cost Insurance Freight of capital goods, imported duty free or leased from a leasing company or received free of cost or on loan basis or on transfer for the period they remain with the unit.

Explanation: For the purpose (a), the expression "inputs" mean raw materials, intermediates, components, consumables parts and packing materials.

(d) For annual calculation of Net Foreign Exchange, value of imported capital goods and lump sum payment of foreign technical know-how fee shall be amortised at the rate of 10 per cent every year from the first year to the tenth year.

5.3.1.6 Monitoring of Performance

The Act and the Rules provide that the performance of the unit shall be monitored by the Approval Committee as per the guidelines. Units, which have not completed one year of operation from the date of commencement of production, will not be monitored. In case of completion of five years, it will be monitored for complete block year and in case of less than five years, it will be monitored on year-to-year basis. Units with negative net foreign Exchange in the first and second year shall be placed under the watch list.

In case the Approval Committee comes to the conclusion that the unit has not achieved positive Net Foreign Exchange earnings for five years, the unit shall be liable for penal action under the provisions of the Foreign Trade Development and Regulation Act, 1992.

5.3.2 Institutional Framework

5.3.2.1 Administrative Set-Up for Indian Special Economic Zones

The Special Economic Zones Acts 2005 provides for a three-tier administrative set-up for smooth functioning of SEZs and defines their roles and responsibilities of the authorities. Chapter 3 of SEZ Act deals with the constitution of Board of Approval and defines specific duties, power and roles. Chapter 4 of SEZ Act 2005 is focussed on appointment and functions of Development Commissioner. Chapter 5 details the constitution of approval committee and its function and power by reckoning the concept of single window clearance. Figure 5.1 gives in nutshell the three-tier system of administrative machinery as per the SEZ Act 2005. Figure 5.2 depicts the same in a pictorial form.

Board of Approval (BOA)

The BoA is the Apex Body constituted by the SEZ Act 2005 with the mandate to promote and develop in an orderly manner the SEZs in India. Section 9 of the Act lists the duties, powers and functions of BoA. The important ones are listed below:

[THREE TIER SYSTEM]

|
V

Board of Approval	Approval Committee	Development Commissioner
SECRETARY/ADDITIONAL SECRETARIES (*Chairperson*)	**SINGLE WINDOW CLEARANCE**	**OVER-ALL INCHARGE**
JOINT SECRETARY (2)-REVENUE (Members)	DEVELOPMENT COMMISSIONER (*Chairperson*)	ADMINSTRATIVE CONTROL
JOINT SECRETARY (1) – ECONOMIC AFFAIRS (*Member*)	OFFICERS CENTRAL GOVT (2) (*Members*)	SUPERVISORY ROLE
JOINT SECRETARIES (10) –DIFF MINISTRIES (*Members*)	OFFICER CENTRAL GOVT (2)-REVENUE (*Members*)	DISCHARGE FUNCTION AS PER THE ACT
STATE GOVERNMENT NOMINEE (*Member*)	OFFICER CENTRAL GOVT (1)-ECONOMIC (*Member*)	
DGFT (1) (*Member*)	STATE GOVERNMENT (2) (*Members*)	
DEVELOPMENT COMMISSIONER (*Member*)		
PROFESSOR/ACADEMIA (IIFT/IIM) (*Member*)		
DEPUTY SECRETARY (*Member Secretary*)		

Figure 5.1: Administrative Set Up for SEZs

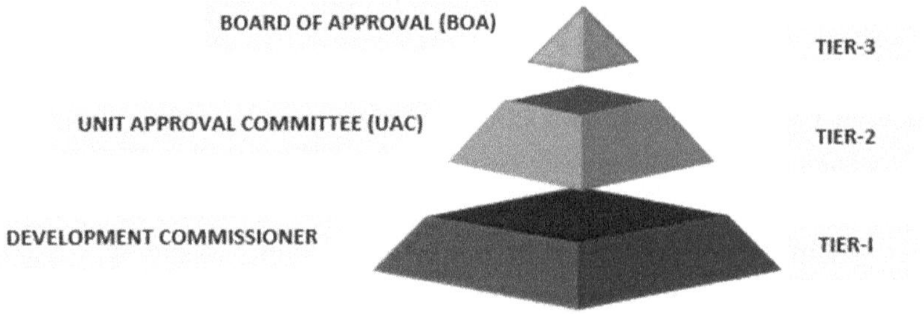

Figure 5.2: Pictorial Representation of the Administrative Set-up

- Granting, approval, modification or rejection of proposal for establishment of SEZ.
- Approving Authorised Operations to be carried out in SEZ by Developer/Co-Developer. For administrative convenience there is a default list of operations to be done by SEZ Developer/Co-Developer for which no permission is required from BoA. For all operations that are not enumerated in the default list, the approval is to be obtained from the BoA.
- The BoA grants approval in case of any foreign collaboration/FDI for both SEZ Developer and units. The BoA considers proposals related to FDI and foreign collaboration after seeking the comments of the concerned ministry depending on the sector in which the investment is proposed to be made.
- Suspension of LoA granted to developer and appointment of an administrator for the management of SEZ in case of default by the Developer/Co-Developer.
- **Matters related to Approval of Units.**
- Original power for renewal of letter of LOA for following sectors: Recycling of plastic scrap, reprocessing of used clothing, import of other goods for reconditioning, repair and re-engineering.
- The BoA has been vested with the power of approving the items which are prohibited for Import/Export under the DGFT Import/Export Policy. The proposals are to be approved on case-to-case basis.
- The BoA can approve the procurement of items from DTA which are restricted as per the DGFT import/Export policy.
- BoA can issue license to industries which are under the Industries (Development & Regulation) Act, 1951. For example, cigars and cigarettes of tobacco and manufactured tobacco substitutes, electronic aerospace and defence equipments, industrial explosives, hazardous chemicals like Hydrocyanic acid, Phosgene and so on.

- **Appellate Jurisdiction**
- The BoA acts as an appellate authority in case of appeal filed against the decision of UAC by the party.
- **Classifying any activity as a manufacturing activity**

The BoA is the authority that will decide whether a particular activity constitutes manufacture as defined in the SEZ Act.

- **Powers of clarification**

As the apex body, BoA is vested with the power for issuance of any clarification pertaining to any rule/circular/instruction.

Approval Committee: This committee is constituted to implement the Single Window Mechanism which is a major step in the "Ease of Doing Business". The approval committee may discharge the functions and exercise the powers in respect of import or procurement of goods from Domestic Tariff Area (DTA) in the SEZ, approving, rejecting or modifying the unit setting up proposal as well as the authorized services inside the zone. Other functions of the Approval Committee include monitoring, review of unit's performance and statutory compliance as per the Act.

Development Commissioner (DC): is the overall administrative in charge of the SEZ and exercises administrative control and supervision over all the officers, employees and units in the zone. He plays the role of catalyst between the trade community and government by way of guiding at every step of the journey right from setting up of units to taking suitable steps for effective promotion of exports from SEZs.

5.3.2.2 SEZs Policy: Ease of Doing Business

The changes in the legal framework, through amendments to the Act and the Rules to usher in a regime that is investor-friendly and to promote activities in SEZs are outlined below.

The SEZs (Amendment) Act 2019 was passed and came into force from 2 March 2019. Inclusion of "trusts" in the definition of a "person" is made in a bid to facilitate investments in these zones through the Amendment.

The Rules have been amended towards facilitating specifically "Ease of Doing Business" in the last few years.

- Zonal Development Commissioner is delegated on 1 November 2019 the power to transfer units from one SEZ to another SEZ within same zone.

- Revised guidelines have been issued on 16 February 2016 for power in respect of SEZ power plant in respect of power/captive power plants in SEZ, refunds, procedure for reimbursement of duty (RoD), offences, etc.
- Permission for dual use of facilities like Social & Commercial infrastructure by SEZs and non-SEZs entities in order to make SEZ operations more viable (Vide Ministry of Commerce, Government of India Gazette notification dated 02.01.2015).
- Legal and accounting services included vide notification of Ministry of Commerce, Government of India dated 03.01.2017 amending Rule 76 of SEZ Rules 2006.
- Amendment of time limit for filing of Annual Performance Reports by SEZ units.
- Allowing IT/ITeS units in SEZ to work from home or place outside the SEZ unit.
- Introduction of sectoral broad-banding to encompass similar/related areas under the same sector.
- A new sector "Agro-based food processing" sector has been introduced to encourage agro-based industries in SEZs.
- Amendments corresponding to GST law have been made in SEZ rules through the gazette notification issued by the government of India on 19.09.2018.
- Amendments related to sub-contracting period for studded gold jewellery, silver, the finishing goods requiring processing, etc., have been increased from 28 days to 45 days on 9 November 2018 and 31 January 2019.
- Revised norms of Net Foreign Exchange (NFE) introduced through amendment dated 7 March 2019.

SEZ rules were liberalized by way of further amendment (3rd Amendment) effective from 17 December 2019 for utilization of vacant space in SEZs by removing distinction between sector-specific and multi-sector requirement.

5.4 SEZs in India: Present Status

Equipped with an historical background of the SEZs evolution in India, their growth trajectory, challenges and opportunities, it is time to have a look at the current picture. The SEZ Act 2005 and SEZ rules 2006 gave an impetus to the development of SEZs; the changes in the regulatory framework to further the development and promote "Ease of Doing Business" have been covered above.

The current status is detailed in this part followed by the initiatives of the government of India for Ease of Doing Business. We then see the position specifically on the exports, employment and investment front.

Initially SEZs were perceived as tax free enclaves enjoying fiscal and non-fiscal benefits. The government did extend certain concessions with the objectives to attract FDI, facilitate the development of infrastructure facilities, promotion of exports of goods and services and employment and generation of additional economic activities. Both SEZs developers and the units were exempted from the purview of the Minimum Alternate Tax (MAT) for an indefinite period. They were also exempt from payment of the Dividend Distribution Tax (DDT) on dividends distributed making it attractive from the investment point of view.

In 2011, the central government withdrew DDT exemption followed by MAT exemption (April 2012), both these exemptions were withdrawn impacting SEZs operations and profitability. MAT was levied at the rate of 18.5 per cent on SEZ developers and units and DDT at the rate of 15 per cent. This measure enabled the government earn revenue, that it would have foregone with the continuation of the Exemption Scheme. However, it dented investor confidence, rendered SEZ operations unattractive overnight and business was left wondering, if government was really serious on export promotion.

Further, in 2017, the government brought in a sunset clause, whereby only units set up prior to 31 March 2020 would be eligible for income tax holiday. SEZs, which provided a major impetus to export activity in India, lost their allure consequent upon these changes.

The moot question remains whether the government is committed to the development route through SEZs. By the very nature, SEZs can flourish only in a regime, where they are given special treatment as against the industry in the general area. In view of the special treatment extended, government imposes conditions for SEZ activities like restricting output for exports only, minimum value addition norms and so on. Therefore, it is a fine balance between revenue loss and gain in exports and investment; in this scenario, the withdrawal of exemptions or introduction of sunset clause has disturbed the equilibrium. These measures have adversely impacted the SEZ model of development, stalling the further growth. A number of SEZ developers and units wish to be de-notified so as to be outside the ambit of the restrictive SEZ regulations.

5.4.1 Government Initiatives for State SEZs

As part of the initiatives for the promotion of exports, central government has come forward with certain initiatives for state SEZs.

a) Single Window Clearance System:

As per Rule 5 sub-rule 5(h) of the SEZ rules, 2006, the state government shall endeavour to provide a single window clearance system to the proposed SEZs Developers and Units, under their State Acts and Rules. The central government has advised state governments from time to time for implementation of effective Single Window Mechanism to ensure timely state government clearances for SEZs Developers and Units.

b) State SEZ Policy:

The central government has prodded the state governments to formulate and put in place SEZs policy at state level with the objective of promotion of exports through SEZs mechanism.

However, many states are yet to frame State SEZ Policy through legislative mechanism or otherwise.

The states that have enacted the State SEZ Acts are: (i) Madhya Pradesh in 2003 (ii) West Bengal in 2003 (iii) Gujarat in 2004 (iv) Tamil Nadu in 2005 (v) Haryana in 2006, and (vi) Punjab in 2009.

In all, total 15 states have formulated their export strategy: (i) Maharashtra in 2001, (ii) Jharkhand in 2003, (iii) Uttar Pradesh in 2007, (iv) Kerala in 2008, (v) Karnataka in 2009, (vi) Chhattisgarh, (vii) Jammu and Kashmir, (viii) Assam, (ix) Tripura, (x)Haryana, (xi) Manipur, (xii) Mizoram, (xiii) Nagaland, (xiv) Meghalaya and (xv) Odisha.

c) Appointment of State Export Commissioners:

To develop Export Strategy at state level, the state governments were directed to nominate a Senior Officer as the Export Commissioner (EC). The EC shall coordinate all export efforts, required from the different agencies of the state government. Presently, 26 states including Gujarat have nominated Export Commissioner.

d) Trade Infrastructure for Export Scheme (TIES):

The government of India has launched "Trade Infrastructure for export scheme (TIES)" effective from FY 2017–2018, to assist central and state government agencies for creation of appropriate infrastructure for growth of exports from the states. TIES covers export linkages like the Border Haats, Land Custom stations, quality testing and certification laboratories, cold chains, trade promotion centres, dry ports, export warehousing and packaging, SEZs and ports/airports cargo terminuses. Under TIES Scheme, a total of 28 export infrastructure projects covering 14 states were planned; a cumulative sum of INR 1,657.70 million was sanctioned on this account from the date of the scheme till 01.07.2019.

e) Advisory Boards: Government has put in place boards to handle export strategy, development activities to boost exports and other trade-related and policy matters. The central government conducts periodically export strategy meetings with the representatives of state governments for operational and policy issues.

The extant Advisory Boards constituted by government are as under:

(i) Board of Trade (BOT).
(ii) Interstate Trade Council.
(iii) Council for Trade Development and Promotion.

5.4.2 *Ease of Doing Business Measures and Initiatives*

Some of the measures taken for the Ease of Doing Business are highlighted below:

- The norms for renewal of letter of approval have been relaxed.
- The Ministry of Commerce holds regular review meeting with the Development Commissioners of SEZs.
- State governments have been advised to make their own Single Window Clearance mechanism more effective.
- Launch on 06.01.2017 of the Mobile app named "**SEZ India**" having four sections SEZ Information, SEZ Online Transaction, Trade Information, and Contact Details.
- Digitization and online processing of various activities relating to SEZ developers and units.
- SEZ online system to facilitate paperless transaction for movement of goods for imports and exports from SEZs.
- Periodical review of the policy and operational framework of SEZs by the government with follow-up measures for the removal of road blocks.
- Government is giving focussed attention to 12 identified Champion Services Sectors. Nodal Ministries/Departments have been identified to prepare sectoral action plans for their respective service sectors in consultation with stakeholders and DoC.
- Government has passed a bill to set up a unified authority for regulating all financial activities in International Financial Services Centres (IFSCs) in the country (11/12/2019) towards Ease of Doing Business. The first IFSC

in India was set up at Gujarat International Finance Tec-City (GIFT) in Gandhinagar, Gujarat.

5.4.3 Sector-Wise Special Economic Zones

The sector-wise analysis of the 265 SEZs that are operational as on 31.01.2021 provides interesting insights. Twenty-five SEZs can be classified as multi-product SEZs and two multi-services. The remaining 238 SEZs are sector-specific; within the sector-specific SEZs, it is seen that more than 61 per cent pertain to Information Technology and Information Technology Enabled Services (IT/ITeS) and the rest cover industries such as electronics, pharmaceuticals, engineering, gems and jewellery, and apparels. The state-wise break up of major categories of SEZs is summarized in Table 5.4.

The sectoral division of Operational SEZs is depicted in Figure 5.3.

It is apparent that SEZs dealing with IT/ITeS dominate the SEZ landscape in India. This can be explained by the fact that the policy permits for setting up of SEZ in IT/ITeS without any minimum area requirement. Consequently, many developers have set up such SEZs in and around metropolitan areas. It is gathered that the most important consideration is the commercial aspect in urban areas from tax incentive point of view. Hence the objectives of SEZ, like infrastructure development and employment generation, remain on the backburner when SEZs of this nature are set up. Moreover, such SEZs provide employment for the skilled people in urban areas and there is no scope of employment for the unskilled category people of nonurban background.

After an overview of the operational SEZs and the sectors concerned, we take a look on the categories of SEZs.

The terminology used is explained in brief:

1) **Formal Approvals**: The application with the recommendations of state government is forwarded to Board of Approval (BOA) of SEZs, central government, to consider the proposal. If the Board of Approval recommends "formal" approval; this is finally granted by Ministry of Commerce (MOC). The developer does not have the right (freehold/Leasehold/Developmental rights) over the land including possession.
2) **Notified SEZs**: After BOA gives formal approval, the concerned Development Commissioner certifies the contiguity and vacancy of the area and submits inspection report, the area is regarded as notified SEZ.

Table 5.4: Sector-Wise SEZs in India (As on 31.12.2019)

State/ UT	IT /ITeS	others	Elec +ITeS	Bio/ Pharma	Eng /Avia	Petro-Chem	Power/ NC/port	Tex/ Leather	Food	Gems Jwly	MP/ MS	Total
AP	5	1		4				3	1		6	20
CH	1		1									02
CG							1					01
GUJ	5		1	1	2	1	1	2			7	20
HR	7											07
KL	12	1	1				3		1		1	19
KN	24		2	2	2			1			1	32
MH	18	1	2	3	3		1				4	32
MP	04										1	05
ORS	2	2									1	05
PB	2		1									03
RJ										2	1	03
TN	19	3	5	1	5			5			3	41
TEL	21	1	2	3	2					1		30
UP	9	2					1				1	13
WB	5									1	1	07
Total	134	11	15	14	14	1	7	11	2	4	27	**240**
%	55.83	4.58	6.25	5.83	5.83	0.42	2.92	4.58	0.83	1.67	11.25	100

Source: www.sezindia.nic.in

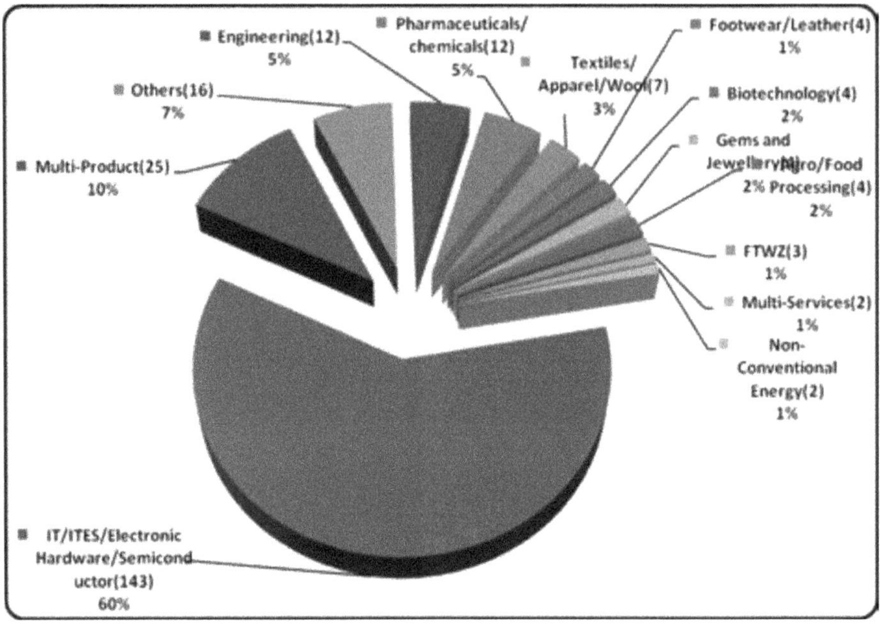

Figure 5.3: Operational SEZs in India—Sector-Wise Break-up
Source: www.sezindia.nic.in

3) **In-Principle Approval**: Implies that the developer does not have the right (freehold/Leasehold/developmental rights) over the land including possession and on the basis of the mandatory recommendation of the state to central government, Board of Approval considers the case in meeting and recommends "formal" approval; which is finally granted by Ministry of Commerce (MOC).
4) **Unit**: It means a unit set up by an entrepreneur in a SEZ and includes existing unit, an offshore banking unit and a unit in an International Financial Service Centre, whether established before or after the commencement of the Act.

Table 5.6 gives details categories of SEZs, that is, formal, in-principle, notified and operational SEZs as on 31 October 2020 in different sectors.

5.4.4 State-Wise Distribution of Special Economic Zones

Table 5.5 gives the state-wise distribution of SEZs. Depending on the number of SEZs in the respective state or Union Territories (UT), the host state or UT is

Table 5.5: SEZs in India-State Category-Wise (As on 29/02/2020)

Top-rung states/UTs				Middle-rung states/Uts				Low-rung states/UTs			
State	Formal	Notified	Operational	State	Formal	Notified	Operational	State	Formal	Notified	Operational
Maharashtra	50	44	32	WB	7	5	7	Chandigarh	2	2	2
Andhra	32	27	20	MP	12	7	5	Chattisgarh	2	1	1
Tamil Nadu	56	52	41	Odisha	7	5	5	Jharkhand	2	2	-
Telangana	63	56	30	Punjab	5	3	3	Manipur	1	1	
Karnataka	63	52	32	Rajasthan	5	4	3	Nagaland	2	2	
Gujarat	26	22	20					Puducherry	1	-	
Haryana	23	20	7					Goa	7	3	
Uttar Pradesh	23	20	13					Delhi	2	-	
Kerala	29	25	19					Tripura	1	1	-
Total	365	318	214		36	23	23		20	12	3
% of total	86.69	90.08	89.17		8.55	6.52	9.58		4.75	3.40	1.25

Source: www.sezindia.nic.in

Table 5.6: Sector-Wise Distribution of Approved SEZs (As on 31.10.2020)

Sectors	Formal approvals	In-principle approvals	Notified SEZs	Total Operational SEZs (Including prior to SEZs Act + under the SEZs Act) (as on 30.09.2020)
Agro-processing	5	2	5	2
Airport based multiproduct	2	0	0	0
Alumina/ Aluminium	2	0	2	1
Auto/Automobile Ancillary	2	1	2	2
Aviation/Aerospace/ Copper	5	1	4	3
Beach & mineral/ metals	2	0	2	1
Biotechnology	23	1	16	6
Building prod./ mal./ transport equipments / ceramic and glass	2	2	2	2
Electronic product/ Industries	2	0	2	2
Engineering/ Metallurgical Engineering	14	1	13	12
Footwear/Leather	5	0	5	4
Food Processing	3	0	2	2
FTWZ	10	5	6	3
Gems and Jewellery	4	3	1	4
Handicrafts & Carpets	2	0	1	1
IT/ITES/Electronic Hardware/ Semi-conductor/ Telecom equipments	280	1	239	161
Multi-Product	20	9	17	25

Table 5.6: *Continued*

Sectors	Formal approvals	In-principle approvals	Notified SEZs	Total Operational SEZs (Including prior to SEZs Act + under the SEZs Act) (as on 30.09.2020)
Multi-Services	4	1	4	2
Non-Conventional Energy	2	0	2	2
Petrochemicals & petro./oil and gas	2	1	0	0
Pharmaceuticals/ chemicals	17	2	17	14
Port-based multi-product	4	1	3	3
Power/solar	4	1	4	3
Textiles/Apparel/ Wool	7	1	7	7
Writing and printing paper mills	1	0	1	0
Granite processing Industries and other allied machinery/ manufacturing	2	0	1	0
GRAND TOTAL	**426**	**33**	**358**	**262**

Source: www.sezindia.nic.in

classified as top rung, middle rung and lower rung. India has a total of 36 states and UTs (28 states and 8 UTs). However, SEZs are present in only 22 state and UTs. This means that there is no SEZ in as many as 16 states/UTs.

The top-rung states which include some of the bigger states like Andhra Pradesh, Tamil Nadu, Telangana, Karnataka, Gujarat and Uttar Pradesh together account for more than 86 per cent of the total formal SEZs, more than 90 per cent notified SEZs and 89 per cent of operational SEZs in the country. Thus, it is apparent that the states, which are ahead in terms of industrial development, have garnered the lion's share of SEZs in the country.

In addition to 7 central government Special Economic Zones (SEZs) and 12 state/private sector SEZs set-up prior to the enactment of the SEZ Act, 2005, approvals have been accorded to 425 proposals for setting up of SEZs in the country. Presently, out of 378 notified SEZs a total of 265 SEZs are operational.

The SEZ policy does not lay any geographical restrictions on setting up SEZ nor does it extend any special incentives (except relaxation in land requirements) to set up in backward areas. Thus, the policy does not have any incentive or dis-incentive in regard to geographical location. This has resulted in concentration of SEZs in the more developed regions of the country with better developed infra-structure quality. In terms of space, SEZs currently account for over 22 per cent of the aggregate office stock in India spread amongst seven mega-cities. Within this, Bangalore, Chennai, Delhi-NCR and Hyderabad house almost 77 per cent of the lot and mostly connected with IT/ITeS sector.

The infrastructural development in the country is not uniform in the four cardinal directions, this is reflected in the distribution of SEZs in the four zones.

The distribution of SEZs in the four zones is shown in Figure 5.4.

The details of exports, employment and investments is shown in fact sheet as on 31.01.2021 on Special Economic Zones (SEZs) (Appendix 5.A).

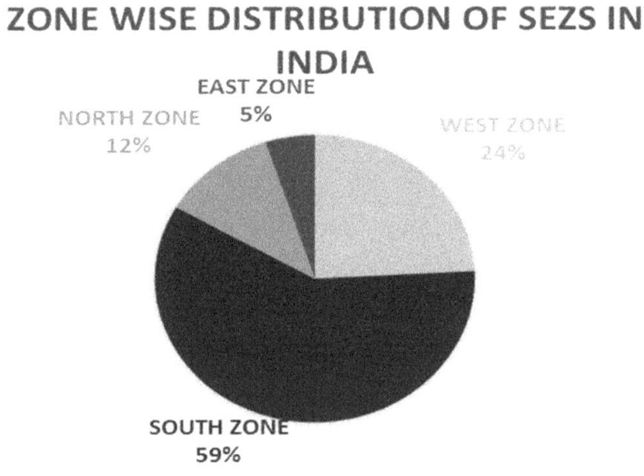

Figure 5.4: Zone-Wise Distribution of SEZs in India
** Notes; Zone-wise details are as below:
WEST ZONE: Maharashtra, Madhya Pradesh, Gujarat, Chattisgarh (58)
SOUTH ZONE: Telangana, Andhra Pradesh, Kerala, Karnataka, Tamil Nadu (142)
NORTH ZONE: Uttar Pradesh, Rajasthan, Punjab, Haryana, Chandigarh (28)
EAST ZONE: West Bengal, Odisha, (12)
Source: http://www.sezindia.nic.in

5.5 Economic Impact

The export basket of India has witnessed significant diversification over the last two decades. However, the export growth continues to be uneven and sluggish. Exports from SEZs have done exceptionally well during the period FY 06–FY 12, with a CAGR of 59 per cent. The exports from SEZs from FY 12 onwards have tapered probably due to sunset of tax incentives clicking in. Nevertheless, SEZ exports continue to constitute an important part of the overall exports.

5.5.1 Export Performance of SEZ Units

While India is reckoned to be one of the fastest-growing economy in the world today, its share in total global merchandise exports is still paltry; less than 2 per cent of the global export trade by value. Nevertheless, SEZs contribute a substantial part of the exports from India.

The details of SEZs exports performance since enactment of SEZ Act 2005 are summarised in Table 5.7.

Table 5.7: Exports from SEZs from 2005–2006 Onwards

Year	Value (In Rs. Millions)	Value in Billion USD	Growth over previous Year in % (INR)
2005–06	228400	5.08	
2006–07	346150	7.69	52
2007–08	666380	14.81	93
2008–09	996890	21.71	50
2009–10	2207110	46.54	121
2010–11	3158680	69.30	43
2011–12	3644780	76.01	15
2012–13	4761790	87.45	31
2013–14	4940770	81.67	4
2014–15	4637700	75.84	(-)6.13
2015–16	4673370	71.38	1
2016–17	5236370	78.07	12
2017–18	5810330	90.15	11
2018–19	7011790	100.28	21
2019–20	7966690	110.65	13.62
2020–21 (up to 31.12.2020)	5533960	75.34	---

The table shows that the growth has not been uniform but almost a roller-coaster ride with figures of 121 per cent, which go down to (– 6) per cent in 2014–2015 followed by recovery to 21 per cent in 2018–2019 over the previous year. For the year 2019–2020, the exports are INR 7,966,690 million which represent an increase of 13.62 per cent over the previous year. However, the export figures for the first three quarters of 2020–2021 are dismal with a reduction to the tune of 7.25 per cent for the corresponding period of last year (INR 5,533,960 million in April–December 2020 as against INR 5,935,172 million for corresponding period last year). The decline is mainly due to the lockdown for arresting the spread of Covid-19. While the authorities are optimistic of a V-shaped recovery and bounce back, the situation remains uncertain.

Details of development of SEZs, growth and unit details are captured in Table 5.8.

Table 5.8 shows that the number of operational SEZs witnessed an incremental growth from 110 to 265; the table also depicts the incremental growth in SEZs units from 2,850 to 5,481 during the last decade.

The 265 operational SEZs in India have generated an aggregate incremental investment of over INR 6,036 billion from 2006 till December 31, 2020, to make a total of over INR 6,077 billion and provided employment to over 2,284,948 persons. Exports from SEZs have registered decrease of more than 7.25 per cent over corresponding period of previous year, standing at INR 5,533,960 million in the first three quarters of 2020–2021. The decrease in exports can be mainly attributed to the pandemic.

Table 5.9 shows the performance of exports activities from respective zones classified under three categories, that is, manufacturing, IT and service exports and trading from various SEZs in the particular zone.

Exports can be broadly classified as Exports of Goods (Merchandise) and Exports of Services, mainly software. There is a discernible shift from the Goods sector to Services in Exports. This translates in a shift from labour-oriented manufacturing towards high-skilled technology-oriented processes. IT and services exports have emerged as high growth sectors with contribution of more than 52.71 per cent share in the total exports from all SEZs during 2018–2019. The share of manufacturing and trading sectors is 46.38 per cent and 0.91 per cent share, respectively.

Table 5.9 shows that the SEZs in Gujarat have registered maximum growth with 26.61 per cent share followed by COCHIN, MEPZ, SEEPZ; the share of Indore SEZ is a dismal 1.29 per cent during the year 2018–2019. Under IT (Service) Exports, Cochin SEZ tops and is followed by MEPZ, SEEPZ, VIZAG

Table 5.8: Details of SEZs and SEZs Unit and Its Growth

Sr. No	Year	Application for SEZs (Year wise)	Cum	SEZ (Operationalized)	Cum SEZ	No of Units	Cum units
1	2009–10	364	364	110	110	2,850	2,850
2	2010–11	16	380	23	133	440	3,290
3	2011–12	09	389	20	153	110	3,400
4	2012–13	05	394	17	170	189	3,589
5	2013–14	03	397	15	185	210	3,799
6	2014–15	06	403	17	202	260	4,059
7	2015–16	09	412	02	204	107	4,166
8	2016–17	35	447	14	218	290	4,456
9	2017–18	04	451	05	223	690	5,146
10	2018–19	02	453	09	232	-37	5,109
11	2019–20	01	454	16	248	415	5,524
12	2020–21 upto (31.12.2020)	----	---	17	265	-43	5,481

Source: Ministry of Commerce Annual report 2018–19 (Ref: 29)

Table 5.9: Zone-Wise SEZs Export Performance (2018–19) (INR in Million)

Zone Name	IT & Service Exports	Trading	Manufacturing	Total	% Share	Rank
COCHIN	965,797.70	2,581.6	519,271.9	1,487,650	21.21	II
DC SEEPZ	648,194.4	12,100	226,690	886,980	12.64	IV
FALTA	172,920.0	1,611.4	137,900	312,430	04.45	VII
INDORE	398.51	00.00	86,610.6	90,595.7	01.29	VIII
KANDLA	63,832.63	17,537.7	1,784,669.1	1,866,039.4	26.61	I
MEPZ	828,950.5	12,153.5	174,423.1	1,015,520	14.48	III
NOIDA	489,438.5	5,131.9	96,404.2	590,974.6	8.458	VI
VIZAG	523,161.9	11,754.08	226,684	761,600	10.86	V
TOTAL	3,696,300	62,870	3,252,620	7,011,790		
%TOTAL	52.71	0.91	46.38		100	
RANK	I	III	II			

Source: Compiled from EPCES (Export Promotion Council for EOUs & SEZ Units)

and NOIDA SEZ. In Manufacturing Exports SEZs in Gujarat ranked first and is followed by Cochin, Vishakhapatnam, SEEPZ and MEPZ. In Trading Exports, KANDLA SEZ emerged first and is followed by MEPZ, SEEPZ, and Vishakhapatnam; Indore SEZ has zero contribution in this category.

Table 5.10 shows the details of contribution from central government SEZs, all these SEZs predate the enactment of SEZs policy. The eight central SEZs are classified under multi-product segment and dominate the SEZs manufacturing exports with lion's share of 89.92 per cent; the share of IT Services Exports and Trading is 8.20 per cent and 1.98 per cent, respectively. Cochin SEZ has emerged as top export SEZ in 2018–2019 followed by SEEPZ, Vishakhapatnam, Indore and Kandla.

The contribution of the central government SEZs to all SEZs exports for the year 2018–2019 is outlined below:

Manufacturing 26.58 per cent

IT & Services 2.14 per cent

Trading 30.30 per cent

Overall, the central government SEZs (eight numbers) contributed to the tune of 13.72 per cent of total SEZs exports.

Table 5.10: Export Performance of Central Government SEZs (2018–2019) (INR in Million)

SEZ Name	IT & Service Exports	Trading	Manufacturing	Total	% Share	Rank
COCHIN	4,979.9	507	426,201.3	431,690	44.86	**I**
DC SEEPZ	18,251.2	2	162,550	180,810	18.79	**II**
FALTA	-	1,611.4	12,740	14,350	1.50	**VIII**
INDORE	-	-	86,610.6	86,610,6	9.00	**IV**
KANDLA	-	15,447.8	60,362.2	75,810	7.87	**V**
MEPZ	26,287.5	-	33,010	59,297.5	6.16	**VI**
NOIDA	29,099.3	362.1	64,155.9	93,617.3	9.73	**III**
VIZAG	329.2	1.100	18,730	20,170	2.09	**VII**
TOTAL	78,947.1	19,048.3	864,360	962,355.4		
%TOTAL	8.20	1.98	89.82		100	
RANK	**II**	**III**	**I**			

Each central government SEZ has its inherent strength. KANDLA SEZ dominates in the trading exports among other SEZs and the total contribution in trading exports is 30.30 per cent. NOIDA, MPEZ and SEEPZ dominate the IT and Service Segment Exports with total share of 2.14 per cent in all India SEZs. The share in manufacturing exports remains a substantial 26.58 per cent of Pan India SEZs exports in this sector.

5.5.2 Investment in SEZ Units Including FDI

The factors favourable for increase in investment are logistics, infrastructure development, multimodal systems and proximity to coastal belt. Hence extra effort may be necessary for boosting economic activities from various other SEZs/ locations. There is an urgent need to review the policies of incentives and other fiscal and non-fiscal measures to boost growth in traditional labour-intensive segments like textiles, leather and handicrafts. In some cases, it may be necessary to revive the processes for manufacture of niche products.

The Finance Ministry withdrew exemption from Minimum Alternate Tax (MAT) in the case of SEZ Developers and Units as well as the exemption on

Table 5.11: Investment in SEZs After MAT (01.04.2012)

Sl. No.	Financial Years	Investment * (INR Million)	Increase in Investment (INR Million)	Percentage %
1	2012–2013	2,367,170	-	-
2	2013–2014	2,966,630	599,460	25.32
3	2014–2015	3,387,940	421,310	14.20
4	2015–2016	3,764,940	377,000	11.12
5	2016–2017	4,231,890	466,950	12.40
6	2017–2018	4,749,170	517,280	12.22
7	2018–2019	5,146,370	397,200	8.36
8	2019–2020	5,717,350	570,980	11.09
9	As on 31.12.2020	6,076,798	359,448	6.29

*Calculated on cumulative basis.

Dividend Distribution Tax (DDT) for SEZ Developers under the Income Tax Act. This had an adverse impact on the investment growth rate.

Table 5.11 shows the details of Investment in SEZs post introduction of MAT.

The first year post SEZ Act (i.e. 2007–2008 to 2011–2012) witnessed 186 per cent increase in the new units in SEZs. Once MAT was imposed, in the next six years i.e. 2012–2013 to 2018–2019 (up to 30.08.2018) the increase in the new units in SEZs was 140 per cent.

Though investments in the SEZs registered growth over six times from INR 770,000 million in FY2008 to INR 6,076,798 in FY 2020–2021 upto December 2020, there was a significant negative trend in year-to-year percentage (YoY%) from 25.32 per cent to 6.29 per cent after implementation of MAT (01.04.2012).

5.5.3 Foreign Direct Investment (FDI) Inflows

Foreign Direct Investment (FDI) is a critical driver of economic growth of a middle-income economy like India. It plays a crucial role in development of SEZ. FDI has emerged as a major source of non-debt financial resource. Foreign investors are incentivized to invest in India through extension of privileges like tax exemption. The country is also benefited with technical know how and employment generation.

Government has put in place a liberal and transparent policy for FDI, wherein most of the sectors are open to FDI under the automatic route. The government reviews the FDI policy on an ongoing basis and makes necessary changes from time to time to ensure that India remains attractive and investor-friendly destination.

FDI in various sectors is allowed in a calibrated manner after having consultations with stakeholders, including concerned Ministries/Departments, state governments, Apex Industry Chambers, Associations and other organizations.

Government has now opened the doors for FDI in sectors like coal mining, single-brand retail, contract manufacturing and insurance. Over the years, the government eased the rules considerably; now there are only a handful of sectors where prior government approval is required for FDI. The nine sectors, where FDI is forbidden, include Gambling and Betting, Chit Funds and Nidhi Companies, Real Estate, Atomic Energy and Railway operations.

Table 5.12 gives the details of FDI inflows during last five years.

It is seen that FDI flows have shown significant growth in the years 2014–2015 and 2015–2016. In subsequent years, the flow has been reducing to the extent of negative growth in 2018–2019. However, there is recovery in 2019–2020 with an increase in FDI of 13 per cent over the previous year. The recovery is bolstered by an impressive increase of 19 per cent in 2020–2021 as compared to the previous year.

Table 5.12: Financial Year-Wise FDI Inflows Data (2015–2021)

Sr. No	Year	FDI Flow in India	Percentage growth in previous year terms (US$)
01	2015–16	40,001	(+) 35%
02	2016–17	43,478	(+) 9%
03	2017–18	44,857	(+) 3%
04	2018–19	44,366	(-) 1%
05	2019–20	49,977	(+) 13%
06	2020–21	59,636	(+) 19%
CUMULATIVE TOTAL (From April 2000 to March 2021)		763,576	-

(AS PER INTERNATIONAL BEST PRACTICES) (Amount US $ Million)

Source: www.dipp.gov.in

5.5.4 Employment

Generation of employment is one major objective of SEZ. There is both direct and indirect employment generated by SEZ. The data for direct employment is compiled and maintained. As far as indirect employment is concerned only estimates can be made. It may be noted that the indirect employment has a greater social impact by way of increasing income of the people nearby, their lifestyle, women empowerment and so on.

SEZs in India have generated total direct employment to the tune of 2,284,948 persons as on 31 December 2020.

While employment in central government SEZs constituted 90.81 per cent of aggregate employment in 2006 (headcount of 1, 22,236), the dynamics have now changed. Notified SEZs had 87.52 per cent of the share as on 31/12/2020 (1,999,871 heads), the contribution of central government SEZs reduced to 8.17 per cent (186,768 heads, despite the increase in absolute numbers) and 4.30 per cent by state/private-led SEZs (98,309 heads).

The incremental employment created by SEZs with an addition of 2,150,244 persons during the period after enactment of SEZ Act 2005 till 31/12/2020 is shown in Table 5.13.

Table 5.13: Year-Wise Employment in SEZs (As on 31.12.2020)

YEAR	Cumulative employment (All categories)	Additional employment generated	% Per cent Increase/decrease
31/03/2009	394,442	259,738	---
31/12/2009	490,000	95,558	19.50
31/12/2010	644,000	154,000	23.91
30/09/2011	815,308	171,308	21.01
31/12/2012	1,019,146	203,838	20.00
20/06/2014	1,283,309	264,163	20.58
31/03/2016	1,591,381	308,072	19.35
31/03/2017	1,731,641	140,260	08.01
31/03/2018	1,977,216	245,575	12.42
31/03/2019	2,061,055	83,839	4.06
31/03/2020	2,238,305	177,250	8.60
Upto 31.12.2020	2,284,948	46,643	2.09
TOTAL	**2,284,948**	**2,150,244**	

Table 5.14: Performance of SEZs in India (2016–2017 Till 2019–2020)

Financial Year	Investment* (INR in Million)	% Growth	Employment* (Persons)	% growth	Exports (INR in Million)	% growth
2016–17	4,231,890	---	17,31,641	---	5,236,370	-----
2017-18	4,749,170	12.22%	19,77,216	14.00%	5,810,330	11%
2018-19	5,076,440	6.90 %	20,61,055	4.25%	7,011,790	21%
2019–20	5,717,350	11.09 %	22,38,305	8.60%	7,966,690	13.62%

From Table 5.13, it is apparent that the incremental employment grew at a steady pace over the years (23 per cent in 2009–2010 to 20 per cent in 2013–2014). The decline in 2013–2014 can be attributed mainly to volatile market conditions across the globe. Overall SEZs have contributed to generate employment, but on a critical examination, it is observed that the jobs relate more to skilled/highly skilled workers as almost 54 per cent of the SEZs relate to IT/ITeS. Thus, the unskilled and semi-skilled category of labour force, which is vulnerable, did not derive much benefit.

SEZs also generate substantial indirect employment; contractual workers and outsourced jobs for various ancillary services to units in SEZs are covered in this category. The ratio of indirect to direct jobs ranges from one-fourth in countries, where SEZs function as relative enclaves, to multiples of two in countries, where SEZs have significant linkages to the domestic economy.

To sum the overview of the SEZs performance on the parameters of investments made, employment generated and exports, which are the quantifiable criteria for assessing economic development during the past three years have been presented in Table 5.14.

5.6 WTO and SEZs in India

In March 2018, USA challenged export subsidies provided by India under five sets of schemes—Export-Oriented Units, Special Economic Zones (SEZ) Scheme; Electronics Hardware Technology Park and Bio-Technology Park (EOU/EHTP/BTP) Schemes; Export Promotion Capital Goods (EPCG) Scheme; Duty-Free Imports for Exporters Scheme (DFIS); and Merchandise Exports from India Scheme (MEIS). The dispute DS541 was filed by USA in WTO and placed before a Dispute Settlement Panel of the trade body.

The thrust of the argument by USA was that these schemes were in violation of the SCM (Subsidies and Countervailing Measures Agreement) of WTO. Under SCM, a country is exempt from the provision that forbids subsidies contingent upon export performance till such time it achieves Gross National Product per capita per annum of $1,000.

The Dispute Settlement Panel in its report issued to members of WTO on 31 October 2019 found the US had "demonstrated the existence of prohibited export subsidies" that were inconsistent with provisions of the SCM Agreement. The Panel has ruled that the specified schemes violate Article 3 of the WTO Agreement on Subsidies & Countervailing Measures (ASCM), which prohibits the member countries, who have graduated out of the exemption provided under Annex-VII to ASCM, from providing subsidies that are contingent on export performance. It concluded that "no further transition period" was available to the country to stop these subsidies.

The panel recommended that India withdraw certain "prohibited subsidies" under the DFIS scheme within 90 days; under the EOU/EHTP/BTP, EPCG and MEIS schemes within 120 days and under the SEZ scheme within 180 days from the adoption of its report.

The response of the government was two pronged. On one hand, it filed an appeal against the ruling of the WTO panel and on the other hand, it moved to render some of the schemes WTO compliant. For instance, government of India announced the Remission of Duties or Taxes on Export Product to replace the MEIS as a more WTO-compliant scheme. The Rebate of State and Central Taxes and Levies (RoSCTL) scheme, which at present is available on export of garments and made-ups, will replace (MEIS).

India has appealed against the Panel Report on 19 November 2019 and the Panel ruling has been kept in suspension due to non-functioning of the Appellate Body. The dispute panel's appellate mechanism became dysfunctional after 11 December (when two of the three members of the body retired). India is not obligated to act on the ruling of the Dispute Settlement Panel till the appeal is heard and disposed of.

The government constituted a group of eminent persons under the Chairmanship of Baba Kalyani, Chairman M/s. Bharat Forge to study the Special Economic Zone (SEZ) Policy of India on 04.06.2018. One of the terms of reference for the Group was to make the SEZ Policy WTO compatible. The Group submitted its report to the government on 19.11.2018. A number of recommendations of the Group have already been implemented.

5.7 Social Impact

In the absence of SEZ-specific data on social parameters, it is difficult to assess the impact of SEZs in India. It was envisaged in the SEZ scheme that they would be mini-townships with facilities on par with the best in the world. Even the land allotted to the developers to establish SEZs is earmarked as land for operational and non-operational area. The developers were to build hospitals, crèches, institutions in the non-operational area for the benefit of the SEZ employees and the people in the locality adjunct to the SEZs.

However, by and large, most of the SEZ developers have not built this infrastructure and the non-operational area is largely vacant. In this connection, government (MOC) has issued guidelines in October 2010 and in June 2019 (further to rule 11(5)) for overall development of physical infrastructure and provision of facilities like transportation, housing, medical and food facilities, training and manpower. Some other social sustainability measures are setting up of cafeteria, crèche, gymnasium and similar facilities in the premises for the exclusive use of employees of such units.

The SEZs do contribute to local area development by direct and indirect jobs, ancillary support industries, road and rail network development, and so on. Employment of women in the SEZs leads to women empowerment.

Anecdotal evidence suggests that the units and the SEZ developers do take a keen interest in the welfare of their employees beyond what is mandated by the law. Ramesh Parmar (name changed to protect identity) was commuting to his unit (Sahajanand Laser Technology Ltd, Gandhinagar—SLTL) by bicycle in the early morning hours of 15 January 2015. He was momentarily distracted while cycling on the road adjoining Hillwoods School and landed directly under a bus ferrying the staff from SLTL resulting in his immediate death.

SLTL arranged immediate financial assistance of INR 1.50 million to the widow of Ramesh Parmar. His son was offered appointment in SLTL and he worked there for about four years. Road accident victims and their dependents are often denied of insurance benefits on flimsy grounds. The HR Department of SLTL assisted the family of Parmar and they could get the insurance claim of INR 1.50 million. Thus, the units do go out of their way to help their employees.

Economic development is often linked with environmental degradation. The world is facing global warming and extreme weather events, which are cataclysmic. Therefore, the impact of SEZs on sustainable development should be a matter of concern.

5.7.1 Impact of Environment Assessment on Sustainable Development

The environmental impact is reckoned both at the time of setting up of SEZs and as well as at the time of setting up of units for giving approvals. The concerned state government has to indicate whether the area proposed falls under reserved or ecologically fragile area. At unit level, Pollution Control clearance has to be obtained and registration with Central Pollution control board is mandatory.

Some of the aspects related to SEZs from the point of view of sustainable development are listed as under:

1. Site Identification, Land acquisition—Environmental sustainability.
2. Development Plan for SEZs—planned green areas, ground water recharging areas and disaster mitigation aspects.
3. Role of state government—Dedicated Committee for environmental provisions.
4. Proper water supply for industrial and domestic use, efficient use of water.
5. Drainage and sewerage facility.
6. Waste water treatment plant.
7. Solid waste management.
8. Provision for e-waste.
9. Guidelines for Energy Conservation in SEZs.
10. Use of renewable energy like wind and solar energy.
11. SEZ green guidelines and compliance certification.
12. Site preservation and restoration.
13. Power Guidelines in respect of SEZ Power as issued from time to time.
14. Air ambient quality, sound and noise regulation.

5.8 Land Acquisition and Land Issues

5.8.1 Overview of Land Acquisition

Land is the major resource for a SEZ. In India, land is under the jurisdiction of the state government and is procured as per the policy and procedures of the respective state governments. Therefore, no land is acquired by the central government under SEZ Act, 2005 and SEZ rules, 2006.

Entry no. 18 of the State List in the 7th Schedule of the Constitution of India deals with Land and Compensation to the Land Owners for the acquisition of land. Compensation to land owners for the land acquired for SEZs is covered by the provisions of Land Acquisition, Rehabilitation and Resettlement Act, 2013, which has replaced the earlier law, "Land Acquisition Act of 1894". The rehabilitation and relocation of the displaced persons including farmers is undertaken by state government agencies.

The states acquired bulk of the land for SEZs under the then prevailing law (Land Acquisition Act of 1894) which allowed forcible acquisition of land for "public purpose". This Act and public purpose gave unbridled power to the state governments to acquire land. Hence land acquisition for development of SEZ did lead to a loss of land and rural livelihoods especially for landless labourers in some instances. To add insult to injury, persons displaced in this manner could not get employment in the units in the SEZ created in such land as they lacked the skills.

Land acquired for SEZs and lying vacant is a major concern. As on 30 August 2017, 53.59 per cent of the Notified Special Economic Zones (SEZs) land is lying vacant. Out of total notified area of 45,629.43 hectares in respect of 375 notified SEZs, 21872.71 hectares of land have been utilized and 23779.19 hectares land are lying vacant in these SEZs. The land acquired for the 375 notified SEZs consists of waste/barren/dry/industrial (93.47 per cent), farming-single crop (5.28 per cent) and farming-double crop (1.25 per cent).

The Board of Approval (BoA) for SEZs only considers proposals for setting up of new SEZs which have been duly recommended by state government. This implies that only those proposals where land acquisition proceedings are in place are considered.

In terms of Rule 6(2)(a) of the Special Economic Zones Rules, 2006, the letter of approval granted to a Special Economic Zone (SEZ) developer is valid for a period of three years within which time effective steps are to be taken by the developer to implement the approved project. The Board of Approval may, on an application by the developer, grant more time by extending the validity period of the letter of approval. During the last six years, extension of time has been granted to 146 developers of SEZs across the country, for completion of their projects.

Table 5.15 gives the vacant land position as on 07.02.2019 in different SEZs.

It emerges that more than 50 per cent of the notified area is lying vacant in different zones more so in Western and Southern zones. This could be attributed to fundamental issues of property titles, acquisition proceedings and so on.

In West Zone, bulk of the vacant land is in the land-locked states of Chhattisgarh and Madhya Pradesh. Goa, a coastal state and therefore in a pole position for SEZ development, shows 100 per cent vacant land. In Maharashtra,

Table 5.15: Vacant Land Details in SEZs of Different Zones (As on 07.02.2019) Land Area in (Hectares)

Name of Zone	State/UTs under Jurisdiction	No of Notified SEZs	Total Notified Area	Total utilized Area	Total Vacant Area	% age
MEPZ SEZ	Tamil Nadu, Andaman & Nicobar Islands, Union Territory of Pondicherry excluding Mahe and Yanam	52	5,037.98	2,403.18	2,634.80	52.29
Cochin SEZ	Kerala, Karnataka, Lakshadweep and Mahe	76	2,997.24	1,790.36	1,206.88	40.26
Noida SEZ	Uttar Pradesh, Madhya Pradesh, Rajashtan, Delhi, Punjab, Haryana, Chandigarh, Uttarkhand, Himachal Pradesh, Jammu and Kashmir and Ladakh.	58	2,640.60	1,251.56	1,389.04	52.60
Kandla SEZ	Gujarat	27	14,333.72	7,763.83	6,569.89	45.84
VSEZ	Andhra Pradesh, Telangana, Chattisgarh and Yanam.	86	10,506.45	4,400.06	6,106.39	58.12
SEEPZ SEZ	Maharashtra, Goa, Daman and Diu, Dadra and Nagar Haveli.	52	6,975.28	2,177.17	4,798.11	68.78
Falta SEZ	West Bengal, Odisha, Jharkhand, Nagaland, Tripura, Manipur, Meghalaya, Sikkim and Arunachal Pradesh	17	1,614.61	683.85	930.76	57.65
	TOTAL	**368**	**44,105.88**	**20,470.01**	**23,635.87**	**53.59**

government recently de-notified seven SEZs of Navi Mumbai with approximately total area of 1,637.87 hectares due to local issues.

In Telangana and Andhra Pradesh, Farmers Associations agitated for relief and return of the acquired land on the ground that the land acquired for the purpose of SEZs is lying vacant and unutilized. This has defeated the purpose of acquisition as claimed by them in the suit filed in Supreme Court of India.

Some of the recent initiatives taken by the government under the "Ease of Doing Business" are listed below:

- Minimum Land Area requirement of 50 Ha for setting up of new SEZs for multi-product and sector-specific SEZs, which is a pragmatic solution given the mammoth task of land acquisition.
- No minimum land area for setting up an IT/ITeS SEZ. Only minimum built-up area criteria applicable to be met by the SEZ developers.
- Minimum built-up area criteria relaxed with requirement of 50,000 sq. metres to be applicable for seven major cities. For category B cities, 25,000 sq. metres and for remaining cities only 15,000 sq. metres built-up area will be applicable (17/12/2019).

The position of the land acquired for notified SEZs and the SEZs prior to the regulatory regime (earlier to SEZ Rules 2006) is encapsulated in Table 5.16. The percentage of land acquired for SEZ as a fraction/percentage of India's land area is also mentioned.

Table 5.16: Position of Land Acquired for SEZs

Sr. No.	SEZ Land Particulars	Area (in Ha)
1	Total Land Area related to 07 Central Govt.—12 State/ Private-notified SEZs	2245.33 Ha
2	Total Land Area related to 349 notified SEZs	40301.82 Ha
3	Total Land Area related to 68 Formally Approved SEZs	5506.38 Ha
4	Total Land Area related to notified SEZs & Formally Approved SEZs	48053.53 Ha
5	Land Area related to 33 in principle approved SEZs	20775 Ha
6	% of Area of notified SEZ to that of land area of India (328 MHa)	0.013%
7	% of Area of notified SEZ to that of agricultural land area of India (142 MHa)	0.026%

It is apparent from the table that the land acquired for SEZs is a tiny fraction of the land area in India.

5.8.2 De-Notification of SEZs

The concerned state government is responsible to ensure the full utilization of the land acquired for SEZs. The process of setting up of a SEZ is long drawn with a number of sequential steps involved. The Board of Approval (BoA) approves a proposal for establishment of a SEZ subject to the terms and conditions prescribed in the SEZ Act and Rules. The approval is granted only after the concerned state government recommends the setting up of the SEZ. After the approval, the implementation of SEZ projects by developers is monitored by the Development Commissioners as per SEZ Act and Rules on a regular basis.

Based on such monitoring, in case of violation of SEZ Act/Rules, action is initiated against the developers to recover any fiscal benefit availed by them as well as to penalize them for the violations. De-notification is done based on recommendation of concerned Development Commissioner and after obtaining the no-objection from the state government concerned as well as Department of Revenue and is also subject to refund of all duties and tax benefits availed by the SEZ private developer.

The reasons for violation of the SEZ Rules could be attributed to adverse business climate due to changed global economic situation, changes in fiscal incentives and so on. Some of the reasons why the notified SEZs failed to take off and become operational could be wrong location, change in investment climate, and economic outlook. Certain policy changes in 2011 like Introduction of Minimum Alternative Tax (MAT) and Dividend Distribution Tax (DDT) may be responsible for the failure to get operational. There are many studies conducted on land utilization where one view is that the SEZs developers have set up SEZs as real estate projects, which increases the value of land surrounding the SEZ that incidentally belongs to the developer.

Some of the reasons for the delay in commencement of commercial operations of the SEZs include time taken in obtaining approvals from statutory authorities and state government bodies. However, at times the promoters deliberately delay the process to tide over the adverse business climate due to changed global economic situation and changes in fiscal incentives regime for SEZs.

The promoters are at times compelled to proceed for de-notification due to business dynamics, global recession and other related economic parameters that impact the financial viability of SEZs. Board of Approval (BoA) on Special

Economic Zones (SEZs) has approved 101 cases of de-notification between 1 April 2008 and 29 February 2020 (information tabled by the Government in Parliament).

De-notification of SEZs has affected the regional economic development within and across the states in India.

5.9 Synopsis

In the Indian context, SEZs have contributed substantially in building nation's economy by way of generating investments and exports. In the last Financial Year 2020–2021 (for the period upto 31.12.2020), exports from SEZs of INR 5,533,960 million registered decline of 7.25 per cent over the exports in Financial Year 2019–2020 (corresponding period) of INR 5,935,172 million. The total investment in SEZs in India up to 31.12.2020 is more than INR 6,076,798 million. SEZs accounted for direct employment of over 2.28 million people as on 31 December 2020 (Fact Sheet at Appendix 5.A).

The growth in exports till 2019–2020 is commendable in midst of a volatile global economy and the trade war between the trading giants China and USA. While IT/ITeS contributed maximum to the growth with a share of 23.69 per cent, the performance of the Gems & Jewellery Sector and Leather and Footwear with 13.3 per cent and 15 per cent, respectively, is stellar. The decline of 7.25 per cent registered in the first three quarters of 2020–2021 can be attributed to the effects of Covid-19.

Growth in manufacturing, communication and financial Foreign Direct Investment (FDI) in India grew by 6 per cent to $42 billion last year, according to the UNCTAD. Impetus for FDIs came from the new development of India abolishing approval procedures for foreign companies in areas like defence, telecommunications, and private security.

The SEZ developers have kept social aspects on the backburner. There has been no effort made by them to set up residential complexes, hospitals, educational institutes, dormitories or any hostels for women/girl employees. Some units do have subsidized canteen facility, dedicated transport (pick and drop facility), thrift and credit societies, etc., which provide some social security to their employees, but the need to take social objectives in a holistic manner remains.

The overall experience of SEZs in India is therefore mixed. The SEZs have consistently performed well on exports front but have failed to generate employment on a big scale. There is immense scope for SEZs developers to create more job opportunities. The SEZ developers have also to pay attention to development of facilities like townships, dormitories for women, hospitals for employees and families and other social aspects. When benchmarked with the social aspects in SEZs globally, the SEZs in India are rated low.

To conclude, the past failings of SEZs do not have to be their future reality. There is the need for the government, SEZs and other stakeholders to make combined efforts to derive solutions for outcomes which will help both in sustaining the environment as well as long-term economic growth. The promotion of environment-friendly measures does have real economic benefits, for example, reduced energy costs, increased innovation and productivity, lower absenteeism on health grounds and an improved quality of life.

Further, to strengthen the SEZs Policy and make it WTO compliant, the government constituted a group headed by Baba Kalyani, Chairman M/s. Bharat Forge to study SEZs Policy of India on 4 June 2018. The group submitted its report to the government on 19 November 2018. The key recommendations of the group are at Appendix (5.B).

Appendix (5.A): Fact Sheet on SEZ in India as on 31 January 2021

Number of Formal approvals (As on *31.01.2021)*	425
Number of notified SEZs (As *on 31.01.2021)*	*378 (Including 7 Central Govt.+12 State Govt. I Private Sector SEZs set up prior to the enactment of SEZ Act, 20051*
Number of In-Principle Approvals (As *on 31.01.2021)*	33
Operational SEZs *(As on 31st December,* 2020)	265
Units approved in SEZs *(As on 31st December,* 2020)	5,481

Land for SEZs (As *on 31.01.2021)*	*7 Central Govt. + 12 State Govt. /Pvt. SEZs notified before SEZ Act, 2005.*	*Notified SEZs under the SEZ Act, 2005*	*Total Notified SEZsArea (1+2)*	*Formally Approved SEZs (425-359)*	*Total Area (3+4)*
	(1)	*(2)*	*(3)*	*(4)*	*(5)*
	2172.75 Ha	39869.76 Ha	42042.51 Ha	5453.71 Ha	47496.22 Ha
	Land is a *State subject. Land for SEZs is procured as per the policy and procedures of the respective State Governments.*				

INVESTMENT	Investment (As on February, 2006)	Incremental Investment	Total Investment (As on 31st December, 2020)
Central Government SEZs	Rs. 2,279.20 cr.	Rs. 18,943.04 cr.	Rs. 21,222.24 cr.
State/Pvt. SEZs set up before 2006	Rs. 1,756.31 cr.	Rs. 12,591.26 cr.	Rs. 14,347.57 cr.
SEZs Notified under the Act	-	Rs. 5,72,110.07 cr.	Rs. 5,72,110.07 cr.
Total	Rs. 4,035.51 cr.	Rs.6,03,644.37 cr.	Rs.6,07,679.88 cr.
EMPLOYMENT	Employment (As *on February, 2006)*	Incremental Employment	Total Employment *(As on 31st December, 2020)*
CentralGovernment SEZs	1,22,236 person	64,532_person	1,86,768 person
State/Pvt. SEZs set up before 2006	12,468 person	85,841 person	98,309 person
SEZs Notified under the Act	0 person	19,99,871 person	19,99,871 person
Total	1,34,704 person	21,50,244 person	22,84,948 person

Exports in 2018-19 *DTA* Sale *(Deemed exports)* *DTA* Sale *(Not counted for +ve NFE)*	Rs. 7,01,179 Crore (Growth of 21% over FY 2017-18) *Rs. 19,908 Crore (2% of total production)* *Rs. 1,01,866 Crore (12% of total production)*
Exports in 2019-20 *DTA* Sale *(Deemed exports)* *DTA Sale (Not counted for +ve NFE)*	Rs.7,96,669 Crore (Growth of 13.62% over FY 2018-19) *Rs.19,662 Crore (2% of total production)* *Rs.1,14,445 Crore (12% of total production)*
Exports in 2020-21 *(As on 31st December,* 2020) *DTA* Sale *(Deemed exports)* *DTA* Sale *(Not counted for +ve NFE)*	Rs. 5,53,396 Crore (Decrease of -7.25% over the exports of the corresponding period of FY 2019-20) *Rs.13,599 Crore (2% of total production)* *Rs.91,831Crore (14% of total production)*

Source: www.sezindia.nic.in

Appendix (5.B): Baba Kalyani Committee Suggestions

1. Framework shift from export growth to broad-based Employment and Economic Growth (Employment and Economic Enclaves-3Es).
2. Formulation of separate rules and procedures for manufacturing and service SEZs.
3. Shift from supply driven to demand driven approach for 3Es development to improve efficiency of investment-based on certain industries, current level of existing inventory in the region.
4. Enabling framework for Ease of Doing Business (EoDB) in 3Es in sync with State EoDB initiatives. One integrated online portal for new investments, operational requirements and exits-related matters.
5. Enhance competitiveness by enabling ecosystem development by funding high-speed multi-modal connectivity, business services and utility infrastructure. Critical to provide support to create high-quality infrastructure either within or linked to the zones, for example, high-speed rail, express roadways, passenger/cargo airports, shipping ports, warehouses and so on.

6. Promote integrated industrial and urban development—walk to work zones, states and centre to coordinate on the framework development to bring linkages between all initiatives.
7. Procedural relaxations for developers and tenants to improve operational and exit issues.
8. Extension of Sunset Clause and retaining tax or duty benefits.
9. Broad-banding definition of services/allowing multiple services to come together.
10. Additional enablers and procedural relaxations.
11. Unified regulator for IFSC.
12. Utilizing multi-services SEZ IFSC for all the inbound and outbound investment of the country.
13. Incentives for availing services from IFSC SEZ by domestic institutions.
14. Extension of benefit under services export incentives scheme.
15. Allowing alternate sectors to invest in sector-specific SEZs/3Es.
16. Flexibility of long-term lease for developers and tenants.
17. Facility of sub-contracting for customers outside 3Es/SEZs without any restriction or cap at any level.
18. Specified domestic supplies supporting "Make in India" to be considered in NFE computation.
19. Export duty should not be levied on goods supplied to developers and used in manufacture of goods exported.
20. Flexibility in usage of NPA by developers and sale space to investors/units.
21. Infrastructure status to improve access to finance and enable long-term borrowing.
22. Promote MSME participation in 3Es and enable manufacturing-enabling service players to locate in 3E.
23. Dispute resolution through arbitration and commercial courts.

Source: Rajya Sabha Unstarred Question No. 2288 for 2 January 2019.

6

Special Economic Zones: Gujarat

The state of Gujarat is host to 20 functional SEZs covering both multi-product and sector-specific SEZs in the sectors of Apparel, Information Technology/Information Technology-Enabled Services, Pharmaceuticals, Chemicals, Engineering, Textiles and Non-conventional Energy. Gujarat plays a pivotal role in the functioning of SEZs in India. Gujarat has the distinction of housing India's first and the only multi-services SEZ of International Financial Services, namely Gujarat International Finance Tec-City (GIFT) at Gandhinagar.

After an overview on the economy of the state, the evolution of SEZs is traced. The state government's policy initiatives that have propelled Gujarat to the pole position among the states of India in industrialization and urbanization are touched upon. The details of the SEZs spread geographically and the product profile mix is outlined in the context of the state SEZs policy. The contribution of SEZs towards the exports, investment and employment generation in the state is covered in great detail, to get an overview of the socio-economic impact.

6.1 Overview of Gujarat

6.1.1 Economic View

The state of Gujarat is home to about 5 per cent of India's population and covers roughly 6 per cent of the India's geographical area. The contribution of the state to the national industrial production is a healthy 17 per cent. The government of Gujarat state has launched the New Gujarat Industrial Policy 2020 with a focus on key thrust sectors, strengthening integrated value chains, innovation and research. The policy has provisions to promote industries adopting sustainable and cleaner manufacturing and innovative Industry 4.0 practices. The policy also seeks to encourage entrepreneurship and strengthen MSMEs and facilitate cluster development.

The pole position attained by the state in the Industrial Map of India can be partly explained by the strategies and policies in place for the last few decades. Gujarat has been consistently promoting industrial clusters, industrial parks and R&D activities. In fact, the state-owned Gujarat Industrial Development Corporation (GIDC) has pioneered setting up of industrial clusters across the state from as early as 1964.

Gujarat is located strategically on the west coast of India and offers world-class infrastructure as its main value proposition to the industries. The robust infrastructure includes road and rail connectivity till the last mile. The claim to world-class infrastructure is buttressed by the following:

- National Highways, State Highway and District Roads totalling 157,470 kilometres
- Power surplus state, with round-the-clock three phase power and more than 30 Giga Watt installed power generation capacity
- Forty-nine ports including one major port (Deendayal Port) and 48 non-major ports
- Seventeen airports/airstrips with two international airports (Sardar Vallabhai International Airport Ahmedabad and Vadodara International Airport—albeit international flights are yet to take off from Vadodara)

Equipped with this infrastructural advantage, Gujarat is poised for the next wave of growth through mega-industrial infrastructure projects, namely

- Dholera Special Investment Region (D-SIR) proposed as the largest Greenfield investment region in the country spread over 920 square kilometres. D-SIR will focus on Heavy Engineering, Automobiles & Auto ancillary, Defence, Hi-tech technologies, etc.

- Delhi–Mumbai Industrial Corridor (DMIC) is one of the largest infrastructure projects in the world with an estimated investment of $90 billion. Almost 36 per cent of the 1,500 kilometres length Western Dedicated Freight Corridor (DFC) will pass through the state of Gujarat. Twenty-four industrial nodes are proposed in the six states hosting DMIC. Gujarat will be hosting 6 of these 24 nodes, namely

  Ahmedabad—Dholera Investment Region
  Vadodara—Ankleshwar Industrial Area
  Palanpur—Mehsana Industrial Area
  Bharuch—Dahej PCPIR and Investment Region
  Surat—Hazira Industrial Area
  Valsad—Umbergaon Industrial Area

These six nodes cover twin cities implying industrial boost to twelve cities and the contiguous areas.

- Mandal Becharaji Special Investment Region (MBSIR) slated to be the largest Auto-Hub in the world. Auto companies such as Suzuki Motor Corp, Honda Motorcycles and Toyota Tsusho India have already established their units here.
- Gujarat International Finance Tec-City (GIFT) has world-class infrastructure for offshore and international transactions in banking, insurance and capital markets. Major institutions like Oracle, World Trade Centre, SBI, NSE, LIC, BSE, Bank of America are already operational here. GIFT City has committed investment of $1.57 billion and a workforce of 10,000 professionals across 225 companies.
- Diamond Research and Mercantile (DREAM) City is being developed close to Surat—the diamond capital of the country. DREAM city, spread over 2,000 acres will house an International Diamond Trading Hub and a Diamond Bourse.
- Petroleum, Chemicals and Petroleum Investment Region (PCPIR) to be located at Dahej will be India's first specially delineated investment region of 453 square kilometres for manufacturing of petroleum products, chemicals and petrochemicals.

- Mumbai Ahmedabad High Speed Rail will be the first high-speed rail project between the two cities at an investment of about $11.23 billion in association with Japan International Cooperation Agency (JICA).

The policy and legal framework laid by the government in the direction of Industrial Development of Gujarat are tabulated in Table 6.1.
Some of the drivers responsible for the emergence of Gujarat as one of the leading industrialized states in India are highlighted below:

- **Land Banks**
  The state earmarks land parcels for industrial use on online portal https://gujarat.ncog.gov.in/indextb. Details of Logistics Parks, Industrial Parks, SEZs, SIRs, GIDC land parcels and Private Industrial Parks are provided in the portal.
- **Policy Relocation Incentives**
  Special incentives will be offered to companies planning to relocate their operations and/or diversify supply chains in view of Covid-19 on case-to-case basis.
- **Promotion of MSMEs**
  Implementation of Gujarat Micro, Small and Medium Enterprises (Facilitation of Establishment and Operation) Act, 2019
  Institutionalization of MSME Commissionerate
  Online sanction of incentives
  Establishment of MSME facilitation desks in 11 districts
- **Market Development Assistance**
  Scheme for Market Development Assistance envisages financial support to MSMEs and start-ups for participation in national and international exhibitions. This is one of the outstanding schemes among the various schemes of the government of Gujarat.

6.1.2 Vision & Mission: Gujarat Industrial Policy 2020

Vision: To make Gujarat a Global Business Destination for next generation sustainable manufacturing and service industry driven by state-of-the-art infrastructure, employment generation, inclusive and balanced regional development and thereby contribute significantly to "Atmanirbhar Bharat".

Mission: To promote entrepreneurship and innovation in the state supported by:

Table 6.1: Gujarat State Acts/Policies and Objectives

Sr. No.	Policy/Act/Initiatives	Objectives/Highlights
01	Gujarat New Industrial Policy 2020	• To enable industries to set high quality standards and enable exports • To promote industries focusing to adopt sustainable, cleaner manufacturing and innovative Industry 4.0 practices • To facilitate growth of Service sector industries in the state
02	Investor Facilitation Agency (IFA)	• Nodal agency for supporting prospective investors; facility of Interactive Voice Response System (IVRS) and Dedicated "Relationship Managers" nominated by Industrial Extension Bureau (iNDEXTb) as single point of contact for all government-related queries and approvals.
03	Mega Online Permission and Centralized Inspection System	• In pursuance of "Ease of Doing Business" framework for mega permission with one form for 26 different state-related approvals and compliances for businesses. • Process for streamlining centralized inspection system to usher in transparency and ease.
04	Renewable Energy Target by 2022	• Renewable energy installed capacity to 30,000 MW by 2022. Work has commenced for a 700 MW park in Raghenesda and land identified for 5,000 MW in Dholera. A renewable energy park in Kutch district is planned for capacity of 30,000 MW to be built in stages.
05	Gujarat Micro, Small and Medium Enterprises (Facilitation of Establishment and Operation) Act, 2019	• MSME can start operation upon receipt of an acknowledgement certificate from the state nodal agency by submitting the "Declaration of Intent". This sector is exempted from taking various approvals for the first three years.

Continued

Table 6.1: *Continued*

Sr. No.	Policy/Act/Initiatives	Objectives/Highlights
06	Gujarat Single Window Clearance Act, 2017	• The Act aims to facilitate process for the speedy issuance of various licenses, clearances and certificates required for setting up a business unit. • It defines four levels of review committee and has a provision for submission of a combined application form for more than one approval with prescribed timelines for processing of applications.

- Inclusive and balanced regional development
- World-class infrastructure
- Competitive fiscal incentives
- Ease of doing business
- Strengthen Integrated Value Chains for an Atmanirbhar Bharat
- Employment generation: Direct and Indirect
- Export competitiveness: Vocal for Local to become Global
- Effective policy implementation

6.1.3 Primacy for Exports

Niti Aayog in partnership with the Institute of Competitiveness released the first Export Preparedness Index (EPI) 2020. The index ranked states on four key parameters namely—Policy, Business Ecosystem, Export Ecosystem and Export Performance. The index also took into account 11 sub-pillars namely Export Promotion Policy, Institutional Framework, Business Environment, Infrastructure, Transport Connectivity, Access to Finance, Export Infrastructure, Trade Support, R&D Infrastructure, Export Diversification and Growth Orientation.

As per the report released by Niti Aayog for the first ever EPI, Gujarat tops the index followed by Maharashtra and Tamil Nadu. This ranking validates the primacy for exports in Gujarat.

Just five states of India account for 70 per cent of exports of the country. Close to three-fourths of all exports from India are from the coastal states. The details of top five exporting states are shown in Table 6.2.

Table 6.2: Top Five Exporting States in 2018

Rank	State	Share of Total Exports	Cumulative
1	Maharashtra	22.30%	22.30%
2	Gujarat	17.20%	39.50%
3	Karnataka	12.70%	52.20%
4	Tamil Nadu	11.50%	63.70%
5	Telangana	6.40%	70.10%

Source: Economic Survey 2018

Maharashtra (22.3 per cent), Gujarat (17.2 per cent), Karnataka (12.7 per cent), Tamil Nadu (11.5 per cent) and Telangana (6.4 per cent), all coastal states except for Telangana, rank in the top five states, for exports. Haryana (4.9 per cent) follows, bringing up the cumulative to 75 per cent of total exports. The data also revealed that 16 of India's 30 states (29 states + Delhi) account for 97 per cent of exports.

- It can be inferred that the industrial base of Maharashtra and Gujarat has given them the kickstart to secure the two top ranks in the exporting states.
- Export numbers in the states of Karnataka and Telangana are driven by IT/ITeS, while Tamil Nadu has a bit of both industries and IT/ITeS.
- The share of Gujarat State in exports is likely to rise with India's trade.

Table 6.3: Gujarat Economic Performance Highlights

Parameter	Units	Value
GSDP—(Gross State Domestic Product)—at current prices (2020–21)	INR in Trillion	18.85
GSDP growth rate—CAGR 2015–16 to 2020–21	Percentage	12.87
State's contribution to India's Industrial Output 2020–21	Percentage	17
Contribution of Manufacturing Sector to State's GDP	Percentage	37
FDI from April 2000 to March 2020	USD in Billion	26.6

Gujarat contributes 8 per cent to the GDP of the country and is truly the economic engine of the country as evidenced by its stellar performance on various economic parameters as captured in Table 6.3.

6.2 Principal Characteristics: All Industries

Table 6.4 depicts the characteristics of the industrialization of the state of Gujarat and gives the Net Value Added (NVA) for three consecutive years (2014–2015 to 2016–2017). An increase in NVA is witnessed for 2015–2016 when compared to 2014–2015, but the increase is not secular, as it is followed by a decline of (–8.10 per cent) for the year 2016–2017 as compared to 2015–2016.

After Maharashtra which has first rank, Gujarat State has second rank in respect of percentage share in Net Value Added generated by manufacturing or factory sector in the country.

It is seen that there is an increase in number of factories annually on a consistent basis. Gujarat is ranked third at all India level in this respect.

The fixed capital increased by 18.58 per cent, that is, INR 6,869,330 million to INR 8,145,410 million in the state during 2015–2016 to 2016–2017. On this parameter, Gujarat continues to hold first rank in the country, with contribution of 19.84 per cent and 18.96 per cent for the two fiscal years respectively.

In terms of employment, Gujarat shows an incremental growth of 4.64 per cent for workers, that is, from 1,191,406 to 1,246,650. Gujarat maintained the third rank with contribution of 10.69 per cent and 10.96 per cent to India in the two years respectively.

Table 6.5 presents the status of Gujarat in 2016–2017 vis-à-vis India's with inter-state ranking and share.

It would be seen from the above that the state of Gujarat has consistently performed well on economic parameters securing the top ranks on many fronts. This success can be partly attributed to the following factors:

- The state has pioneered reforms in power sector, labour laws and other laws to usher in a productive work environment.
- When required, the state has stepped in to remove the bottlenecks in project implementation. Moreover, the state government has not only provided financial support for very large projects but also the guarantee of returns on investment to the private investor. This has helped the state to build infrastructure in a big way.

Table 6.4: Important Economic Characteristics—Gujarat

Sr. No.	Parameter	Unit	2014–15	2015–16	2016–17	Percentage Change in 2015–16 Over 2014–15	Percentage Change in 2016–17 Over 2015–16
1	2	3	4	5	6	7	8
1	Number of Factories	Number	23,433	24,426	25,966	4.24	6.30
2	Fixed Capital	INR in million	4,377,020	5,302,970	6,330,410	21.15	19.37
3	Invested Capital	INR in million	6,065,590	6,869,330	8,145,410	13.25	18.58
4	Workers	Number	1,103,204	1,191,406	1,246,650	8.00	4.64
5	Employees	Number	1,462,206	1,563,868	1,634,566	6.95	4.52
6	Emoluments	INR in million	336,120	390,780	432,110	16.26	10.58
7	Total Input	INR in million	10,736,740	9,430,840	10,229,900	-12.16	8.47
8	Gross Output	INR in million	12,701,250	11,540,400	12,222,010	-9.14	5.91
9	Depreciation	INR in million	267,830	309,520	337,770	15.56	9.13
10	Net Value Added	INR in million	1,696,680	1,800,050	1,654,330	6.09	-8.10

Source: Annual Survey of Industries 2016–17, Factory Sector report April 2019

Table 6.5: Share & All India Ranking of Gujarat—Economic Parameters (*Figures in INR Million and others in Numbers*)

Sr. No	Particulars	Gujarat	India	% share of Gujarat	All India Rank
01	Number of Factories	25,966	234,865	11.06	III
02	Fixed Capital	6,330,410	31,903,860	19.84	I
03	Invested Capital	814,541	4,296,100	18.96	I
04	Worker	1,246,650	11,661,833	10.69	III
05	Employees	1,634,566	14,911,189	10.96	III
06	Emoluments	432,110	3,750,950	11.52	III
07	Total Inputs	10,229,900	58,961,950	17.35	I
08	Gross output	12,222,010	72,655,140	16.82	I
09	Depreciation	337,770	2,220,710	15.21	I
10	Net Value Added	1,654,330	11,459,190	14.44	II

Source: Annual Survey of Industries 2016–17 Factory Report April 2019

- Enactment of Gujarat Infrastructure Development Act, which not only facilitated but also accelerated the process of setting up infrastructure projects with the help of private sector investment.

The majority of employees work in seven major industrial groups namely (i) Textiles (18.21%) (ii) Chemical and Chemical products (12.02%), (iii) Machinery and Equipment (8.65%) (iv) Other Non-metallic Mineral products (8.20%) (v) Other manufacturing (7.17%) (vi) Food products (7.13%) (vii) Others (38.62%).

The Annual Survey of Industries 2016–2017 identified and classified manufacturing activity into seven domains on the basis of factory data: (1) Coke & Refined Petroleum products [27.81%], (2) Chemicals & Chemical Products [21.53%], (3) Pharmaceuticals, Medicinal Chemical & Botanical [6.75%], (4) Textiles [6.50%], (5) Machinery and Equipment [6.14%], (6) Basic Metals [4.81%], (7) Non-metallic Mineral Products [26.46%].

These domains account for 52 per cent of total number of factories, 75 per cent of fixed capital, 65 per cent of total input, 67 per cent of total output and 76 per cent of Net Value Added (NVA) of Gujarat.

6.2.1 Thrust Sectors as per Industrial Policy 2020

With a view to retain and even improve upon the position in the industry among the states of India, the Industrial Policy 2020 has identified 15 thrust sectors. The selection of the thrust sectors is also in line with the mission of Atmanirbhar Bharat. The closest English translation of Atmanirbhar Bharat is self-reliant India, but the translation does not carry the full import of Atmanirbhar Bharat. The term incorporates much more than that; it signifies bigger and more important part of the global economy. The 15 thrust sectors have been categorized in 2 groups namely core sectors and sunrise sectors. Table 6.6 lists the core and sunrise sectors.

Core sectors are those where the state already has a strong base and the policies would be geared to draw on the inherent strengths to consolidate the position. Sunrise sectors are the sectors of the future, which are highly relevant in the Atmanirbhar Bharat mission.

6.3 Special Economic Zones in Gujarat

6.3.1 Overview

The state of Gujarat has the distinction of hosting the first SEZ in the Asian continent at Kandla. From this beginning in Kandla with one EPZ to a score of SEZs today, the journey of SEZs in the state is fascinating.

Gujarat now hosts 20 operational SEZs with formal approvals, excluding 10 SEZs approved by Board of Approvals (BoA) for cancellation/de-notification. The number of SEZs with notified approvals, as on 31 December 2020 is 29. The operational SEZs constitute roughly 7.55 per cent of 265 operational SEZs in India. Table 6.7 gives detail of SEZs status in Gujarat state as on 31 December 2020.

These 20 operational SEZs cover a wide range of products and services ranging from apparel, IT/ITeS, pharmaceuticals, chemicals, engineering, and textiles to non-conventional energy. The first Finance Technology Park in India under Multi-Services SEZs category (GIFT Tec-City) has been set up at Gandhinagar.

The functional SEZs in Gujarat are however not evenly spread in terms of geography but are restricted to eight districts of the state. In other words, 25 districts do not have any SEZs located within the district boundary. The main factors for the skewed distribution are complementary industrial development,

Table 6.6: Core Sectors and Sunrise Sectors

Sr. No	Core Sectors	Sunrise Sectors
1	Electrical machinery & equipment	Industry 4.0 manufacturing
2	Industrial machinery & equipment	Electric Vehicle and its components
3	Auto & Auto components	Waste management projects
4	Ceramics	Green Energy (Solar & Wind Equipments)
5	Technical Textiles	Eco-friendly compostable material (substitute to traditional plastics)
6	Agro & Food Processing	100% Export oriented units, irrespective of sector
7	Pharmaceuticals & Medical devices	
8	Gems & Jewellery	
9	Chemicals (in designated area)	

Table 6.7: Status-Wise Presence of SEZs in Gujarat

Status	Total SEZs as on 31.01.2021
Notified	29
Operational	20
Formal approval	29*

*Excluding 10 SEZs approved by BoA for cancellation/de-notification

Source: https://www.kasez.gov.in/

infrastructure in terms of logistics, availability of skilled manpower and proximity to ports/airports. Table 6.8 and Figure 6.1 give the location and activity profile of the SEZs.

The Central Zone has the most numbers of SEZs totaling six, followed by Southern Zone and Saurashtra/Kutch Region with five each and the Northern Zone with four SEZs.

Table 6.8: District-Wise Classification of Functional SEZs in Gujarat

Sr. No	District	No. of SEZs	SEZ Activity
01	Ahmedabad	4	Apparel and Textile, Pharmaceuticals and IT/ITeS
02	Amreli	1	Engineering goods
03	Bharuch	3	Multi-product, Chemicals
04	Gandhinagar	4	Electronics, IT/ITeS, Multi-Service
05	Jamnagar	1	Multi-product (Refinery)
06	Kutch	3	Port-based Multi-product, FTWZ, Non-Conventional Energy
07	Surat	2	Multi-product, Apparel
08	Vadodara	2	Engineering, IT/ITeS
Total		**20**	

Source: https://ic.gujarat.gov.in/

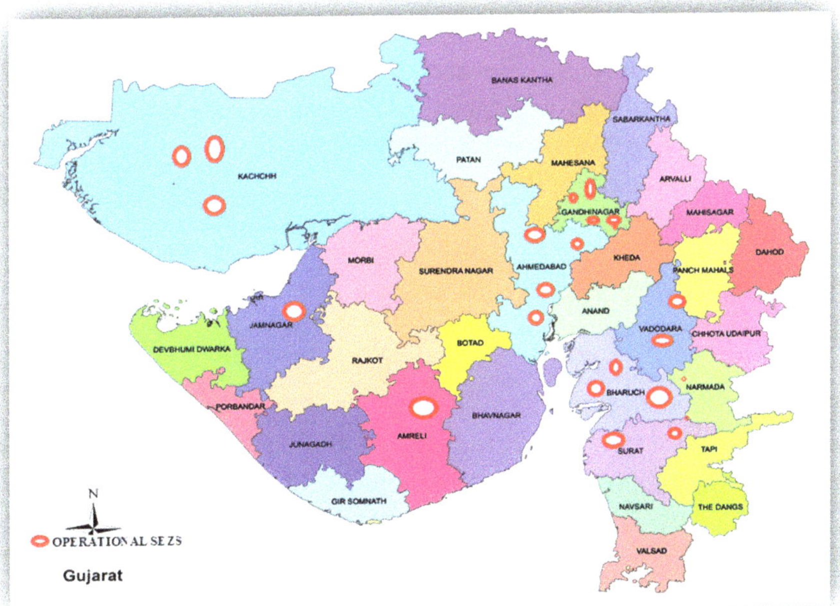

Figure 6.1: Locations of Operational SEZs in Gujarat
Source: Industrial Statistics 2018, Industries of Gujarat

6.4 Regulatory Framework

6.4.1 Gujarat Special Economic Zone Act, 2004

The state government of Gujarat has been proactive to provide the regulatory framework for SEZs in the state. It enacted the Gujarat SEZs Act which came into force from 10 February 2004. Under this Act, the state government constitutes an authority to look into the development of the SEZs. The main function of the authority is to secure planned development of the Special Economic Zone in the state and the authority shall be primarily responsible for the promotion, development and functioning of the zones in the state. Another important function of the authority is to acquire land in the zone, by consent agreement or through proceedings under the Land Acquisition Act, 1894.

Some salient features of the Gujarat Special Economic Zones Act 2004 with its amendment of 2007 coupled with the Gujarat State SEZ Rules 2006 are highlighted below.

6.4.1.1 Main Objectives

(a) Generation of additional economic activity;
(b) Promotion of exports of goods and services;
(c) Promotion of investment from domestic and foreign sources;
(d) Employment generation and
(e) Infrastructure.

Under the rules, every Special Economic Zone shall be under the administrative control of Development Commissioner.

6.4.1.2 Incentive Schemes

The Act and related rules provide fiscal as well as non-fiscal benefits to the developers and unit holders. Details of some Incentive Schemes are furnished below.

A. Fiscal Incentives - State Taxes and Levies—All sales and transactions within the processing area of the zone shall be exempt from all taxes, cess, duties, fees or any other levies under any state law to the extent specified below:

(a) Stamp duty and registration fees on transfer of land meant for approved units in the zone.

(b) Levy of stamp duty and registration fees on loan agreements, credit deeds and mortgages executed by the Unit, industry or establishment set up in the processing area of the zone.
(c) Inputs (goods and services) made to Zone Units from Domestic Tariff Area shall be exempted from sales tax and other taxes under the state laws.

B. Non-Fiscal Benefits

(i) **Single window clearance**—a common application for approval, clearance, license, and registration and no-objection certificate under one or more laws.
(ii) **Infrastructure facilities and services**—including generation and supply of electricity; water extraction, treatment, transmission and distribution; waste water treatment and solid waste management; provision of minor port and related services; provision of roads and bridges; provision for gas distribution network; provision for communication and data network transmission and any other services as may be prescribed by the regulations.
(iii) **Delegation of powers of Labour Commissioner to Development Commissioner** in which powers, duties and functions conferred on Labour Commissioner or any officer under those Acts shall be exercised by the Development Commissioner or any officer authorized by him in this behalf.

6.5 Land Utilization in SEZs

The Constitution of India demarcates the areas of legislation between the centre and the states. For the purpose of demarcation, there are three defined lists, namely Central List (List of areas where only the central government can legislate), State List (List of areas where the state government has exclusive right of legislation) and the Concurrent List (Covering areas where laws can be enacted by both the centre and the states). As per Entry No. 18 of the State List in the Seventh Schedule to the Constitution of India, "land" is a state subject. Land for setting up of Special Economic Zones (SEZs) is acquired by the state government as per the laws, policy and procedures of the respective state governments. The Board of Approval (BoA) for SEZs considers only those proposals for setting up of new SEZs, which have been duly recommended by the state government.

The development of land parcels and the allotment of land from such developed parcels to the units are done based on the demand and market conditions. Both the central and the state governments are concerned with the large unutilized parcels of land lying vacant from the land acquired for SEZ. The central government therefore was compelled to review the policy and operational framework of SEZs to ensure the maximum utilization of the land acquired for the

Table 6.9: Position of Utilization of Land as on 31.07.2020

Sr. No.	Name of SEZ	Total Allotted Area (hectares)	Total Utilized Area (hectares)	Total Vacant Land Area (hectares)
1	KASEZ	400.00	400.00	-
2	Adani Port & SEZ	8,434.59	3,587.2	4,847.39
3	Surat	49.99	49.99	0.05
4	Reliance	1,289.44	1,289.44	-
5	Dahej	1,682.65	1,349.21	173.56
6	Sterling	1,263.17	280.7	982.47
7	GIFT	105.44	57.71	47.73
8	Surat Apparel Park	56.64	54.58	2.03
9	Zydus	114.77	66.78	48.04
10	L&T	5.11	5.11	-
11	Ahmedabad Apparel Park	20.41	17.65	2.76
12	Aspen	51.17	37.70	13.47
13	Aqualine	27.83	7.66	20.18
14	TCS	10.32	10.32	-
15	Jubliant	125.72	75.09	50.63
16	Gandhinagar Electronic Park	28.00	23.40	4.60
17	Ganesh infrastructure	32.71	0.07	32.64
18	Calica	10.94	1.24	9.69
19	E-Complex	124.12	124.12	-
20	Euro Multivision	11.63	2.00	9.63
Total		**13,844.66**	**7,439.97**	**6,244.87**

Source: https://www.kasez.gov.in/

purpose of setting up SEZs and constituted a group of senior officials to look into the policy framework of SEZs.

As on 31 July 2020, approximately 6,244.87 hectares, that is, 45.11 per cent of 13,844.66 hectares of land allotted to SEZs (both functional and non-functional) in Gujarat is vacant. In terms of area, the Adani SEZ at Mundra tops with an estimated 57.47 percent of the 8,434.59 hectares of SEZ land lying unutilized. The GIFT City SEZ which houses the International Financial Service Centre (IFSC) located at Gandhinagar, is estimated to have 45.27 percent of the 105.44 hectares land lying unutilized. In case of GIFT Tec-City, it may be reckoned that the City is still 'work in progress' and this fact may explain the large quantum of unutilized land.

Apart from the vacant land issue, there are several SEZs units that have approached the state government asking their SEZs to be de-notified, for example, Apparel Park SEZ, Surat and Apparel Park, Ahmedabad set up by Gujarat Industrial Development Corporation (Developer) an undertaking of the state government of Gujarat.

Despite the various challenges, few SEZ Developers have done excellent job with regards to usage of land. Kandla SEZ, Reliance SEZ, TCS SEZ, and Larsen & Toubro Ltd SEZ are among seven SEZs in Gujarat where 100 percent of the land allotted has been utilized.

Zydus Infrastructure Pvt Ltd has already utilized land area of 48.83 hectares of Phase I, the Phase II activity has commenced with the notifying of additional land of 64.4823 hectares land to make total area of 114.77 hectares.

Dahej SEZ located at Bharuch in the category of multi-product SEZ is largely dominated by chemical industries and is now preened to expand by notifying additional land.

Table 6.9 gives the position of the utilization of land by the 20 operational SEZs in Gujarat.

6.6 Highlights of SEZs

While the highlights of all the 20 operational SEZs are tabulated in Table 6.14, it is preceded by the profile of some selected SEZs.

6.6.1 Kandla Special Economic Zone (KASEZ)

KASEZ has the distinction of being the first Export Processing Zone in Asia, established as early as 7 March 1965. KASEZ which is India's largest multi-product

SEZ is located some nine kilometers from the Deendayal Port on the Gulf of Kutch. The distance from KASEZ to the Mundra Port having deep draught and capable of handling supramax vessels at berth is some 55 kilometers.

In 1965, the region of Kutch was both industrially and economically backward and comprised the immediate hinterland of Deendayal Port (then known as Kandla Port). The objectives for establishing EPZ included attracting investment, generating employment and boosting exports. KASEZ could meet these goals to a large extent.

KASEZ provides direct employment to 27,725 persons (as on 31/12/2020), consisting of 18,524 men and 9,201 women. The indirect employment is estimated at 9,000 persons. As KASEZ handles merchandise exports, which involves voluminous work, the related employment on account of contractual labours, transportations, job work, outsourcing of various types of work and services, DTA procurement, others could be two-three times altogether of direct employment.

Table 6.10 gives the comparative figure of performance of KASEZ for the last five years.

The investments made by the developer and the units in KASEZ total INR 10,180 million till 31.03.2021. KASEZ registered exports of INR 70,590.60 million for the financial year 2020–2021. This represents an increase of 11 per cent when compared to the exports in the previous year. The increase may be attributed to the low base and would have been more spectacular but for the continuation of the pandemic.

KASEZ had originally an area of 700 acres. From this area of 700 acres, around 300 was acquired by the then Kandla Port for expansion of port activities. The area of around 400 acres with KASEZ is fully saturated showing 100 per cent utilization.

Table 6.10: Performance of KASEZ for the Period 2015–2021

Year	Exports (INR in million)	Investments (INR in million)	Employment (Direct) (Nos.)
2015–16	42,270.8	5,659.8	25,759
2016–17	43,967.7	9,352.2	25,433
2017–18	48,467.5	9,501.1	25,532
2018–19	75,810.0	10,060.0	27,725
2019–20	63,600.0	10,150.0	27,725
2020–21	70,595.6	10,180.0	27,725

Source: www.kasez.gov.in

6.6.2 GIFT (Gujarat International Finance Tec-City) SEZ

India's first and only International Financial Service Centre was commenced by the government of India, as International Financial Service Centre (IFSC) at Gandhinagar in April 2015. It is a vertical city with integrated development on 886 acres of land with 5.5 million square meters of built-up area. GIFT is also home to India's first International Exchange (India INX). Some big names like Singapore IAC, GERC, New India Assurance and LIC are currently operational. There are 154 operational units in this SEZ providing direct employment of 2,896 persons consisting of 2,200 males and 696 females. The regulators namely Reserve Bank of India (RBI), Securities and Exchange Board of India (SEBI), Insurance Regulatory and Development Authority of India (IRDAI) issue regulations from time to time allowing Indian and foreign institutions to open their office in the IFSC. The central government has enacted the Act for Establishment of Unified Regulator Authority to develop and regulate the financial services market in the International Financial Services Centres in India. Pursuant to this Act such an Authority has been set up at Gandhinagar.

A) Milestones for IFSC

- IFSC Regulations announced in April 2005;
- Competitive Tax regime introduced in June 2016;
- Company Law exemptions provided in January 2017;
- International Dispute Resolution Mechanism through Singapore International Arbitration Centre office at GIFT in August 2017;
- Unified Regulatory Authority Act in December 2019;
- Unified Regulator Authority established at Gandhinagar in April 2020.

Currently, major banks including largest Public Sector and Private Sector banks are operational at GIFT IFSC. The Bank of America, a US-based multinational investment bank and financial services company, has commenced operations in GIFT city. The IFSC banking units have crossed transaction of USD 24 billion, international stock exchanges have a daily volume of $4 billion (transactions) and the IFSC insurance units have crossed sum insured of $30 billion.

Comparative figures of GIFT SEZ from inception till date are depicted in Table 6.11.

This multi-service SEZ is the fastest-growing SEZ in Gujarat with an export growth of 12.50 per cent in 2019–2020 over that of the previous year. It has to be reckoned that the exports in 2018–2019 registered a spectacular increase of

Table 6.11: Exports from Gift SEZ (2015–2016 to 2020–2021)

Year	Export Figure (INR in million)	% Increase/Decrease
2015–16	70.5	705.0
2016–17	2,836.8	3,923.83
2017–18	16,725.1	489.58
2018–19	35,300.8	111.06
2019–20	39,713.1	12.50
2020–21	31,815.8	-19.89

Source: http://www.giftgujarat.in/

111.06 per cent over the previous year's exports turnover. Due to the global pandemic, the exports of INR 31,815.80 million for 2020–2021 registered a decline of 19.89 per cent as compared to the previous year.

6.6.3 *PHARMEZ: SEZ of Zydus Infrastructure Pvt Ltd*

Zydus Infrastructure Limited was notified as Sector-Specific SEZ for Pharmaceutical Formulations on 28/09/2006 and is now known as PHARMEZ. Under Phase I of PHARMEZ, 48.83 hectares of land was developed and made operational during 2009. This SEZ consists of 46.45 hectares of processing area and 2.38 hectares of non-processing area. PHARMEZ has 12 operational units each having area ranging from one hectare to five hectares. Now expansion in Phase II in 65 hectares is in progress; the total revised area of the SEZ will be 114.47 hectares.

PHARMEZ is located along the Sarkhej-Bawla Highway No. 8A, about 24 kilometers from Ahmedabad. It is strategically located in the pharmaceuticals corridor, also known as the golden pharmaceuticals corridor of Gujarat. PHARMEZ is not very far from Mundra and Deendayal sea ports (350 kilometers). Comparative figures of PHARMEZ for the last five years are shown in Table 6.12.

Zydus has delivered healthy increase in exports on a consistent basis. The increase of 38.06 per cent over the last year is especially commendable considering that the major markets for Zydus are the tough pharmaceutical markets of USA and European Union. Zydus was operational during the pandemic, rendering valuable service. This sector-specific SEZ provides direct employment to 5,852 persons as on 31.07.2020 comprising of 5,291 males and 561 females.

Table 6.12: Exports from PHARMEZ (2015–2016 Till 2020–2021)

Year	Exports (INR in million)	% Increase /Decrease
2015–16	27,484.4	15.63
2016–17	32,981.8	20.00
2017–18	40,890.2	23.98
2018–19	67,154.8	64.23
2019–20	65,095.8	–3.07
2020-21	82,004.8	25.98

Source: https://www.zyduscadila.com/

6.6.4 Dahej SEZ (DSL)

Dahej SEZ limited (DSL), a multi-product SEZ, is spread over 1,682 hectares area; DSL is developed by M/s Dahej SEZ limited, a joint venture company of GIDC and ONGC and located in Bharuch District of Gujarat state. DSL has emerged as a hub for chemicals and petrochemicals. On the social front, DSL has contributed to the environment by state-of-the-art Drainage and Effluent Disposal Facilities. The contribution to infrastructure is in the form of remarkably good internal roads and continuous water supply. Comparative figure of exports for the last five years is shown in Table 6.13.

Exports from Dahej in 2020–2021 of INR 82,004.80 million show an increase of 25.98 per cent over previous year, which is commendable considering the Covid-19 situation. As on 31 July 2020, the 55 units in the SEZ provide direct employment to 250 women and 6,041 men to make a total of 6,291 persons.

Table 6.14 gives the highlights of all the 20 operational SEZs in Gujarat.

Table 6.13: Exports from Dahej SEZ (2015–2016 Till 2020–2021)

Year	Exports (INR in million)	% Increase /Decrease
2015–16	15,081.1	36.69
2016–17	20,484.0	35.83
2017–18	25,759.0	25.75
2018–19	31,830.0	23.60
2019–20	41,040.0	28.93
2020–21	56,660.0	38.06

Source: http://www.dahejsez.com/

Table 6.14: Profile of Operational SEZs in Gujarat as on 31.07.2020

Name of Zone: Kandla SEZ (Gujarat)				
Parameters	Kandla SEZ	Sur SEZ (Sachin)	Surat Apparel Park	Reliance SEZ
Developers Name	Kandla Special Economic Zone Authority	Diamond & Gem Development Corporation	Gujarat Industrial Development Corporation	Reliance Jamnagar Infrastructure limited.
Website	http://kasez.gov.in	https://www.sursez.com	https://gidc.gujarat.gov.in	http://www.ril.com/html/aboutus/manufact_jamnagar
SEZs Sector	Multi-Product	Multi-Product	Apparel (sector specific)	Multi-product
Location	Gandhidham. Kutch	Sachin, Surat	Vanj, Surat	Jamnagar
Area (Hectares)/ Date of Notification	400(EPZ-07/03/65 SEZ-01/11–2000)	49.99(epz-1994: SEZ 01.11.2000)	56.64 (31.01.2005)	1,289.45(19.4.06/ 4.6.07/29.8.07)
No of units(operational)	265	153	03	01
Investments (In INR million)	10,150	3,830.8	1,665	776,430
Employment (Numbers)	27,725	24,756	1,425	2,219
Lease Rate	INR 16 per annum	INR 15,000 /Sq mtr	INR 2,420 /Sq mtr	Info upon request
Connectivity of SEZ (National Highway/ State Highway)	N H 8 A	Navsari –Surat SH; 3 kms, NH 8: 13 kms.	NH-8(8kms)	SH 25: 5KMS
Distance from nearest Port (Kms)	Kandla port: 9, Mundra Port: 55	JNPT: 260	Hazira: 30 Magdalla: 18	Sikka: 15

Distance from the nearest Airport (Kms)	Kandla: 15 Bhuj: 55	Surat: 15	Surat: 20	Jamnagar: 30
Nearest Railway Station and Distance (Kms)	Gandhidham: 17	Sachin: 1	Surat: 20	Mothikhavadi: 5 Kanalus Jn: 1
Major cities/towns in vicinity (in kms)	Gandhidham	Sachin:1, Surat 12	Surat:1	Jamnagar: 30
Effluent Treatment/ disposal plant	Available	Available	Available	Available
Industrial Presence	Hindustan Lever, Pharmaceuticals	Diamond, Cutting and polishing, Healthcare and Engineering	Safari Exports, Venus Garments, Benchmark	Reliance petroleum refinery and pp plant

PARAMETERS	PHARMEZ SEZ	DAHEJ SEZ	ADANI SEZ	L & T SEZ
Developers Name	Zydus Infrastructure Pvt LTD	M/s Dahej SEZ Ltd (JV of GIDC & ONGC)	Adani Port and Special Economic Zones Pvt Ltd (APSEZ)	Larsen and Toubro Ltd
Website	http://www.zyduscadila.com/	www.dahejsez.com	http://www.adaniports.com/	www.larsentoubro.com
SEZs Sector	Pharmaceuticals (Sector Specific)	Multi-Product	Multi-Product	IT / ITeS (Sector–specific)
Location	Sarkhej–Bavla NH, Ahmedabad	Vagra Taluka, Dahej, Dist: Bharuch	Mundra, kutch	Vadodara
Area (Hectares)/Date of Notification	114.77/(28.9.06/4.9.17)	1,682.65/(20.12.06/07.4.10/23.4.10/14.11.11)	8,434.59 (23.6.06/03.07.06/27.05.09/22.09.16)	5.11 (18/11/2008)

Continued

Table 6.14: *Continued*

No of units(operational)	12	55	42	05
Investments (In INR million)	37,690	405,401.2	590,833.4	4,590.4
Employment (Numbers)	5,852	6,291	5,481	2,989
Lease Rate	INR 9,000/Sq mtr	INR 1,650/Sq mtr	Info upon request	Info upon request
Connectivity of SEZ (National Highway/State Highway)	N H 8 A	NH -8.	SH 6 & 48 NH-8A	NH -8
Distance from nearest Port (Kms)	Deendayal: 360	GCPTCL for chemical cargo and Adani-Petro LNG for solid bulk cargo handling: 5	Mundra: 5	N.A.
Distance from the nearest Airport (Kms)	Sardar Vallahabhai International, Ahmedabad: 45	Surat: 120 Vadodara: 140	Mundra/Bhuj:60 Kandla: 50	Vadodara: 5
Distance from the nearest Railway (Kms)	Ahmedabad: 35	50 kms from Bharuch, Main Rail Head connecting Mumbai—Delhi.	Adipur—64kms	Vadodara station
Major cities/towns in vicinity and urban facilities and distance (in kms)	Ahmedabad:45	Bharuch: 45	Mundra: 60 Bhuj: 60 Gandhidham:58 Mandvi:45	Vadodara: 1
Effluent Treatment/ disposal plant	Available	Available	Available	N.A

Industrial Presence	Zydus Hospira, Intas Pharma etc.	ONGC, Godrej, ABG Shipyard Chemical and Petrochemicals set up	Multi-product set up	IT units
PARAMETERS	Textiles and Articles of Textiles SEZ	ASPEN SEZ	E-Complex SEZ	GIFT SEZ
Developers Name	Gujarat Industrial Development Corporation	Aspen Infrastructure Limited	E-complex Pvt Ltd	Gujarat International Finance Tec–city (GIFT)
Website	https://gidc.gujarat.gov.in	www.aspensez.com	www.pipavavdoc.com	http://www.giftgujarat.in/gift-sez
SEZs Sector	Apparel and Textiles (Sector-secific)	Engineering products & related services (Sector-specific)	Engineering (Sector –Specifc)	Multi Service SEZ with IFSC
Location	khokhara, Ahmedabad	Waghodia, Vadodara.	Rajula & Village Lunsapur Jafrabad, Amreli	Gandhinagar
Area(Hectares)/Date of Notification	20.41(10.04.2007)	51.17 /(03.7.07/11.07.08/27.5/09)	124.12/(02.01.2008)	105.44(18.08.2011)
No of units (operational)	09	04	01	140
Investments (In INR million)	1,372.33	5,812.35	14,641.7	52,428.2
Employment (Numbers)	1,337	345	44	1,233
Lease Rate	INR 5,370/Sq mtr	Information upon request	Info upon request	Info upon request

Continued

Table 6.14: *Continued*

Connectivity of SEZ (National Highway/State Highway)	N H 8	NH -8		
Distance from nearest Port (Kms)	Deendayal: 500 Hazira: 320	Hazira: 170	Pipavav: 5	Kandla: 500 Hazira: 320
Distance from the nearest Airport (Kms)	Sardar Vallahabhai International Ahmedabad: 7.4	Vadodara: 13	Surat: 131	Sardar Vallahabhai International Ahmedabad: 23
Nearest Railway Station and Distance (Kms)	Ahmedabad: 3	Vadodara: 15	Rajula: 15	Gandhinagar: 10
Major cities/towns in vicinity and urban facilities (in kms)	Ahmedabad	Vadodara	Rajula: 22	Gandhinagar, Ahmedabad
Effluent Treatment/disposal plant	Not Available	Not Available	Not available	Not applicable
Industrial Presence	Globe, Artex etc.	Engineering Products	Engineering Goods	Finance, Insurance, Banking and other IFSC units
PARAMETERS	AQUALINE SEZ	Tata Consultancy Services SEZ	JUBILIANT SEZ	STERLING SEZ
Developers Name	Aqualine Properties Private Limited	Tata Consultancy Services SEZs	Jubiliant Infrastructure Ltd	Sterling SEZ and Infrastructure Limited
Website	www.krahejacorp.com	https://www.tcs.com/	https://www.jubl.com/sez	https://www.sterlingsez.com/

SEZs Sector	IT/ITeS (Sector-specific)	IT/ITeS (Sector-specific)	Chemicals (sector-specific)	Multi-products
Location	Village: Koba, Gandhinagar	Gandhinagar	Vagra: Bharuch	Jambusar: Bharuch
Area (Hectares)/Date of Notification	27.834 (23/07/2008)	10.32 (30.09.2008)	125.72 (11.02.08/05/09/17)	1263.17 (09.01.2008)
No of units (Operational)	07	02	03	04
Investments (INR million)	2,201.2	6,472.1	9,531.8	41,299
Employment (Numbers)	926	7,680	422	908
Lease Rate	Information upon request	Information upon request	Info upon request	Info upon request
Connectivity of SEZ (National Highway/State Highway)	N H 8	NH 8		NH 8
Distance from nearest Port (Kms)	Deendayal: 500 Hazira: 320	. Deendayal: 500 Hazira port: 320	Dahej: 52	Dahej: 70
Distance from the nearest Airport (Kms)	Sardar Vallabhai International Ahmedabad: 23	Sardar Vallabhai International Ahmedabad: 23	Vadodara: 103	Vadodara airport: 65 Sardar Vallabhai International Ahmedabad: 170
Nearest Railway Station and distance (Kms)	Gandhinagar: 10	Gandhi Nagar: 10	Bharuch: 17	Jambusar: 13
Major cities/towns in vicinity and urban facilities (in kms)	Gandhinagar: 10 Ahmedabad: 15	Ahmedabad	Bharuch: 17	Bharuch: 15

Continued

Table 6.14: *Continued*

Effluent Treatment/disposal plant	Not Applicable	Not Applicable	Available	Not Applicable
Industrial Presence	IT units	IT units	Chemicals	IT units
PARAMETERS	ELECTRONIC PARK SEZ	EURO MULTIVISION SEZ	MILLION MIND SEZ	CALICA SEZ
Developers Name	Gujarat Industrial Development Corporation	Euro Multivision Limited SEZ	Ganesh Infrastructure Private Limited	Calica Construction & Impex Private Limited
Website	https://gidc.gujarat.gov.in	http://www.euromultivision.com	www.ganeshhousing.com/microsites	www.calicagroup.com
SEZs Sector	Electronic & IT/ITeS (Sector-specific)	Non-conventional energy including solar Energy equipment/cells (Sector-specific)	IT/ITeS (Sector –specific)	IT/ITeS (Sector–specific)
Location	khokhara, Ahmedabad	Village: Shikara, Taluka: Bachau, Kutch	Daskoi, Ahmedabad	Village: Ognaj, Dascroi, Ahmedabad
Area (Hectares)/Date of notification	28.00 (13.12.2006)	11.6347/(23.04.2009)	32.71/(22.06.07/ 19.09.07/26.07.07)	10.94 (08.05.09/ 12.1011)
No of units (operational)	10	01	01	03
Investments (INR million)	2,323.8	1,741.2	1,543.6	375.4
Employment (Numbers)	677	06	144	49
Lease Rate	INR 3,230 /Sq mtr	Information upon request	Information upon request	INR 269/ Sq mtr

Connectivity of SEZ (National Highway/State Highway)	N H 8	Bhachau-Bhuj Highway	NH 5: SP Ring Road	SG HIGWAY (NH-8 C) / SP Ring Road
Distance from nearest Port (Kms)	Deendayal: 500 Hazira port: 320	Deendayal: 55 Mundra: 120	Deendayal:380 Mundra: 450 Dholera: 60	Deendayal:500 Hazira: 320
Distance from the nearest Airport (Kms)	Sardar Vallabhai International Ahmedabad: 30	Bhuj: 75 Kandla: 52	Sardar Vallabhai International Ahmedabad: 20	Sardar Vallabhai International Ahmedabad: 25
Nearest Railway Station and distance (Kms)	Gandhinagar: 10 kms	Bhachau: 7	Ahmedabad: 18 Sabarmati: 12	Ahmedabad: 23
Major cities/towns in vicinity and urban facilities (in kms)	Ahmedabad	Kandla, Bhachau	Ahmedabad	Ahmedabad
Effluent Treatment/disposal plant	Not Available	Not applicable	Not Applicable	Not Applicable
Industrial Presence	Jagat, Euro circuit, PCB planet etc.	Euro Multivision Photovoltaic Cell unit	IT units	IT units, Pramukh web technologies

Source: websites of SEZs as mentioned above

6.7 Performance of SEZs

6.7.1 Overview

The contribution of the 20 operational SEZs in Gujarat is tabulated in Table 6.15 and Figure 6.2.

Gujarat has geographical area of 20,561.38 hectares under SEZ development which is 43 per cent of the total acreage for SEZs in India and thus is the leading state in terms of acreage under SEZs in India.

The SEZs of Gujarat were instrumental in contributing physical exports to the tune of 23.47 per cent during the year 2019–2020. A substantial contribution of 31.86 per cent in total investments as on March 2020 is another notable feature. Of the 20 operational SEZs, 6 SEZs can be classified under multi-product category and the remaining 14 SEZs grouped under sector-specific category covering areas like apparel, IT/ITeS, pharmaceuticals, chemical, engineering,

Table 6.15: SEZs in Gujarat in Nutshell

Sl. No.	Parameters	Gujarat SEZs	All India SEZs	Contribution (Percentage)
01	Exports (2019–20)	INR 1,869,600 million	INR 7,966,690 million	23.47%
02	Total investments (as on 31.03.2020)	INR 1,973,940 million	INR 5,717,350 million	34.53%
03	Employment (as on 31.07.2020)	90,535 Persons	2,238,305 Persons	4.04%
04	Total area for SEZ (Ha) (as on 31.07.2020)	20,561.38 (Ha)	47,563.20 (Ha)	43.23%
05	Units approved (as on 31.03.2020)	1,010 Nos	5,524 Nos	18.28%
06	No. of operational SEZs (as on 31.03.2020)	20 Nos	248 Nos	8.06%
07	Multi-product SEZs (as on 31.03.2020)	06 Nos	25 Nos	24%
08	Sector-specific SEZs (as on 31.03.2020)	14 Nos	223 Nos	6.28%

Source: http://kasez.gov.in/ and http://www.sezindia.nic.in/

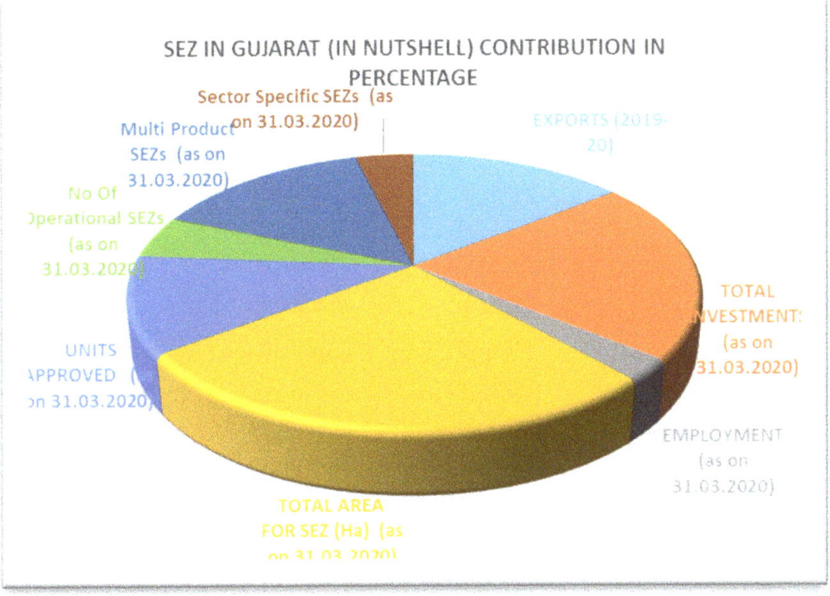

Figure 6.2: SEZs in Gujarat in Nutshell
Source: http://kasez.gov.in/ and http://www.sezindia.nic.in/

textiles, non-conventional energy and multi-service SEZs. Gujarat also has the privilege of hosting the International Financial Service Centre (GIFT), which comes under multiple services SEZ with a consistent growth of 12.50 per cent plus over previous year. As on 31 March 2020, there are total 1,010 approved units in all the state SEZs; 18.28 per cent share out of total 5,524 units in India. All 721 units are working and remaining 289 units are non-operational.

However, one major parameter, where Gujarat is a laggard is the employment generation, with a contribution of a measly 4.04 per cent of total employment in SEZ on pan India basis. This is a matter of concern.

The contribution of all SEZs in Gujarat towards the achievement of SEZs goals viz, investments, exports and employment generation is summarized in Table 6.16.

The figures as published for the period upto 31 July 2020 give an insight in the performance by business/trade sectors in SEZs. The same are tabulated in Table 6.17.

The table below shows that Chemicals & Pharmaceuticals (Crude Petroleum Refinery) dominate both for exports and investments to the extent of 75.47 per cent of the total SEZ exports and 60.48 per cent of the total investments. This

Table 6.16: Performance of SEZs in Gujarat

Name of SEZ (Operational)	Physical Export (2020–21)	Investment (as on 31.03.2021)	Employment (No) (as on 31.03.2021)
KASEZ	70,595.6	10,180	27,725
Surat SEZ	178,455.5	3,891.7	25,530
Reliance	871,228.7	829,460.0	2,014
Zydus	56,660.0	39,950.0	6,037
Dahej	82,004.8	437,992.6	7,660
Adani Port & SEZ	23,756.5	606,740.2	5,033
Surat Apparel Park	1,046.1	1,677.5	1,867
GIDC Apparel Park	1,546.2	1,405.9	1,316
ASPEN	2,394.0	5,861.0	326
E-Complex	-	14,641.7	23
Jubilant	5,824.7	9,750.1	421
Aqualine	1,095.6	2,201.2	914
TCS	24,360.3	6,527.0	8,671
Electronic Park, G'nagar	1,353.7	2,445.8	1,032
L&T	7,123.9	4,606.8	3,038
Sterling	18,967.9	42,603.5	971
Euro Multivision	-	1,741.2	05
Ganesh Infra	41.9	1,543.6	144
GIFT	31,815.8	52,735.2	2,896
Calica	1,81.9	1,096.3	1070
Total:	**1,378,450**	**2,077,050**	**96,663**

Source: www.kasez.nic.in

sector is also the biggest employer accounting for 21.23 per cent of the total direct employment in SEZs.

The exports pertain to the period from 01 April 2020 to 31 July 2020, which corresponds to the period when a large number of business operations and activities remain suspended under the locking guidelines of government of India to arrest the spread of Covid-19. It is therefore commendable that the gems and jewellery sector registered exports of INR 35,187.9 million which is nearly 10 per cent of the total exports.

Table 6.17: Exports, Employment and Investment in SEZs as on 31.07.2020 by Business Sectors

Sr No	Sector	Exports during 2020–2021 (upto 31.07.2020) (INR million)	Number of Direct employees as on 31.07.2020	Investment upto 31.07.2020 (INR million)
1	Biotech	-	-	39.1
2	Computer/ Electronic software	10,728.1	12,124	16,490
3	Electronics and Hardware	408.8	891	2,140
4	Electronics	-	353	30.3
5	Engineering	3,186.8	4,803	26,690
6	Gems and Jewellery	35,187.9	8,498	1,210
7	Chemicals & Pharmaceuticals (Crude Petroleum Refinery)	272,898.9	19,218	1,193,750
8	Handicrafts	-	11	1.4
9	Plastic and rubber	648.85	3,285	2,331.7
10	Leather, footwear and sports goods	9.4	1,517	39.8
11	Food and Agro Industry	4,123.7	1,560	12,580.8
12	Non-conventional and Solar Energy	734.1	1,608	25,698.5
13	Trading and service	17,170.2	6,306	123,719.2
14	Textiles and garments	3,979.8	12,145	17,230
15	Tobacco-related products	241.4	1,005	617.6
16	Miscellaneous	6,461.9	17,187	551,370
	Total	361,620	90,509	1,973,940

As per the Government Gazette for notification of SEZs, the 20 operational SEZs have been classified in 9 different categories: (1) multi-product, (2) multi-service-IFSC, (3) apparel, (4) pharmaceuticals, (5) IT/ITeS, (6) engineering products and related services, (7) engineering goods, (8) chemicals, and

Table 6.18: Exports from Gujarat SEZs (2015–2016 till 2020–2021)

Sr. No.	Financial Year	Exports (INR in million)	Growth Percentage vis-à -vis Last Financial Year
01	2015–16	1,356,330	Decrease of 20% (14–15)
02	2016–17	1,411,760	Growth of 4.1% (15–16)
03	2017–18	1,570,450	Growth of 11.24% (16–17)
04	2018–19	1,853,650	Growth of 18% (17–18)
05	2019–20	1,869,600	Growth of 1% (18–19)
06	2020–21	1,378,450	Decrease of 26% (19-20)

Source: Factsheet of KASEZ (http://kasez.gov.in/ Appendix VI A)

(9) non-conventional energy. IT/ITeS and multi-product SEZ account for about a third each of the total operational SEZs in the state. However, the state has representation of all nine categories of SEZs including the multi-service IFSC (GIFT Tec-City), which is one of its kind in India.

6.7.2 Exports

Gujarat leads in exports with a contribution of 16.39 per cent to the total exports of INR 5,533,960 million from SEZs. The exports from Gujarat SEZs for the last five years are shown in Table 6.18.

From the above table it can be observed that the exports performance from Gujarat SEZs exhibit a sinusoidal wave pattern with steep decrease of 20 per cent in 2015–2016 to gradual recovery with growth of 4.1 per cent in 2016–2017, followed by dramatic recovery of growth cascading to 18 per cent in 2018–2019 and a decline to 1 per cent growth over previous year in 2019–2020. The exports in 2020–2021 show a decline of 26 per cent over previous year. This can be attributed to the Covid-19 pandemic

The details of export performance for the last four years from all SEZs in Gujarat is exhibited in Table 6.19.

The Pandemic has impacted exports from the SEZs in Gujarat during 2020–2021 exhibiting a steep decline of 26 per cent as compared to the previous financial year 2019–2020.

Table 6.19: Details of Exports from SEZs (2017–2018 to 2020–2021)

Name of SEZ	2017–18 (INR in million)	2018–19 (INR in million)	2019–20 (INR in million)	2020–21 (INR in million)	Increase/ Decrease (INR in million)	% Inc/ Dec
KASEZ	48,467.5	75,810	63,600	70,595.6	6,995.6	11.00%
Surat SEZ	161,656.3	67,737	128,091.8	178,455.5	50,363.7	39.32%
Reliance	1,216,932.8	1,505,510.0	1,433,273.5	871,228.7	-562,044.8	-39.21%
Zydus	25,759.0	31,830.0	41,040	56,660.0	15,620	38.06%
Dahej	40,890.2	67,154.8	65,095.8	82,004.8	16,909	25.98%
Adani Port & SEZ	19,609.4	25,728.2	43,497.7	23,756.5	-19,741.2	-45.38%
Surat Apparel Park	1,125.6	1,333.5	1,196.5	1,046.1	-150.4	-12.55%
Apparel Park,	657.5	1,035.8	1,520.2	1,546.2	26	1.71%
Aspen	2,096.4	1,995.4	2,210.2	2,394.0	214.8	8.32%
E Complex	793.4	-	-	-	-	0.00%
Jubilant	5,376.8	3,185.2	4,676.6	5,824.7	1,148.1	24.55%
Aqualine	825.8	944.8	1,105.9	1,095.6	-10.3	-0.93%
TCS	16,307.8	19,248.7	24,225	24,360.3	137	0.57%
Electronic Park	759.5	966.5	935	1,353.7	418.7	44.80%
L&T	3,320.1	5,786.1	7,164.4	7,123.9	-40.5	-0.57%
Sterling	9,019.8	9,939.8	12,131.2	18,967.9	6,836.7	56.36%
Euro Multivision	-	-	-	-	-	0.00%
Ganesh Infra	123.8	126.8	71.5	41.9	-29.6	-41.40%
GIFT	16,725.1	35,300.8	39,713.1	31,815.8	-7897.3	-19.89%
Calica	3.7	18.6	51.2	1,81.9	130.7	255.27%
TOTAL:	**1,570,450**	**1,853,650**	**1,869,600**	**1,378,450**	**-491,150**	**-26%**

While Zydus Infrastructure Pvt Ltd and Surat SEZ continued with growth in 2020–2021, the quantum was not sufficient to offset the steep decline in two big contributors namely Reliance and Adani Port and SEZ. The spectacular recovery of exports from Surat SEZ appears to be in vain as it could not arrest the tapering of overall growth of exports from SEZs in Gujarat.

Zydus' Pharmez continues to put a stellar performance with 38.06 per cent growth in value of exports. In the course of three years, namely from FY-19 to FY-21, Zydus literally doubled its exports in value terms; from INR 31,830 million in 2018–2019 to INR 56,660 million in 2020–2021. Current trends indicate that Zydus is set to do spectacularly well this year with the focus on pharmaceuticals consequent upon the pandemic.

Surat SEZ reversed the declining trend of the past five years to record spectacular growth of 89.10 per cent growth in 2019–2020 over 2018–2019. In the current situation, where retail trade is subdued throughout the globe on account of the pandemic, Surat SEZ has recorded exports of INR 50,363.7 million for 2020–2021.

6.7.3 Units: Functional and Non-Functional

Table 6.20 furnishes the details of functional and non-functional units in the 20 operational SEZs in Gujarat as on 31 July 2020.

The percentage of non-functional units is 28.61 per cent which is substantial. In the case of the Surat SEZ housing the gems and jewellery units the percentage of non-functional units is as high as 40.69 per cent which is a matter of concern. The non-functional units in GIFT Tec-City numbering 69 are probably units which are work in progress and should be functional in the near future. One sector which has the largest number of non-functional units is the Surat Apparel SEZ where 39 non-functional units (92.87 per cent of the total units in the SEZ) outnumber the 3 functional units. Apparently, there could be some flaw either in the policy or procedure which needs to be identified and addressed.

KASEZ with 265 functional units (36.75 per cent of the total functional units in Gujarat) continues to have the most number of functional units showing the importance of the oldest SEZ in Gujarat.

6.7.4 Women Employment

The SEZs in Gujarat have women component of employees to the extent of 23.31 per cent of the total employees in SEZs. Women employment is a major enabler of social development. Women having access to job and a regular income

Table 6.20: Functional and Non-Functional Units in SEZs (as on 31.07.2020)

Sr. No.	Name of SEZ	No. of Functioning Units	No. of Non-Functioning Units	Total
1	Kandla SEZ	265	25	290
2	Adani Port & SEZ	42	6	48
3	Surat SEZ	153	105	258
4	Reliance SEZ	1	-	1
5	Dahej SEZ	55	32	87
6	Sterling SEZ	4	1	5
7	GIFT SEZ	140	69	209
8	Surat Apparel Park SEZ	3	39	42
9	Zydus SEZ	12	1	13
10	L&T SEZ	5	-	5
11	Ahmedabad Apparel Park SEZ	9	6	15
12	Aspen SEZ	4	-	4
13	Aqualine SEZ	7	-	7
14	TCS SEZ	2	-	2
15	Jubliant SEZ	3	-	3
16	Gandhinagar Electronic Park SEZ	10	5	15
17	Ganesh infrastructure SEZ	1	-	1
18	Calica SEZ	3	-	3
19	E-Complex SEZ	1	-	1
20	Euro Multivision Ltd. SEZ	1	-	1
Total		**721**	**289**	**1,010**

improves their social status and has many desirable outcomes like smaller family size, improved living standards and quality of life for the family unit. Table 6.21 gives the details of the direct employees in SEZs by gender and the percentage of women to total employees.

It is observed from the table above that the apparel sector is the only sector where both the genders have almost equal number of employees. In all other sectors, the percentage of women is very low. Among the SEZs, other than the apparel sector SEZs, KASEZ and TCS have a substantial representation of women to the extent of almost one-third of the total number of employees in these SEZs.

Table 6.21: Employment by Gender in SEZs in Gujarat (as on 31.07.2020)

Sr. No.	Name of SEZ	Men	Women	Total	Percentage of Women Employees
1	Kandla SEZ	18,524	9,201	27,725	33.19
2	Adani Port & SEZ	5,393	88	5,481	1.61
3	Surat SEZ	18,720	6,036	24,756	24.38
4	Reliance SEZ	2,176	43	2,219	1.94
5	Dahej SEZ	6,041	250	6,291	3.97
6	Sterling SEZ	902	6	908	0.66
7	GIFT SEZ	937	296	1,233	24.01
8	Surat Apparel Park SEZ	706	719	1,425	50.46
9	Zydus SEZ	5,291	561	5,852	9.59
10	L&T SEZ	2,654	335	2,989	11.21
11	Ahmedabad Apparel Park SEZ	544	793	1,337	59.31
12	Aspen SEZ	340	5	345	1.45
13	Aqualine SEZ	699	227	926	24.51
14	TCS SEZ	5,211	2,469	7,680	32.15
15	Jubliant SEZ	419	3	422	0.71
16	Gandhinagar Electronic Park SEZ	629	48	677	7.09
17	Ganesh infr. SEZ	132	12	144	8.33
18	Calica SEZ	41	8	49	16.33
19	E-Complex SEZ	44	-	44	-
20	Euro Multi. SEZ	6	-	6	-
Other SEZ		25	1	26	3.85
Total		**69,434**	**21,101**	**90,535**	**23.31**

6.8 Synopsis

The study of SEZs in Gujarat therefore presents a fascinating picture. Historically, Gujarat is home to the earliest SEZ in Asia, then named as EPZ Kandla. The Kandla SEZ named today as KASEZ continues to play a prominent role today with the highest number of units that are operational. About a third of the direct employees in KASEZ are women and therefore it serves as a model for the other SEZs in Gujarat.

The operational SEZs in Gujarat number 20 and their detailed statistics have been covered in terms of area allotted, utilized, financial performance in terms of investment and exports and direct employment provided. On the whole it is seen that the SEZs have a positive impact on the economy by way of growth in terms of exports and investments. GIFT is the first and only financial services SEZ at Gandhinagar and is slated to contribute substantially to exports and employment in the future.

As far as social aspects are concerned, there is no data directly attributable to SEZs other than women employment and indirect employment. On both these parameters, the SEZs have done better than the all India corresponding figures.

There are a few dampeners as in all India for the growth of SEZs like the withdrawal of fiscal benefits and the kicking in of the sunset clause. The WTO ruling and implications thereon are also a matter of concern.

On the other hand, the growth of GIFT, the successful completion of Phase I of Zydus and the commencement of Phase II as also the expansion Dahej SEZ are living examples that the SEZ route to development, growth and job generation is the right route for the state of Gujarat as well as for the nation.

Appendix (6.A): Fact Sheet on SEZs in Gujarat State as on 31 December 2020

Number of Formal Approvals	**29 (Excluding 10 SEZs approved by BoA for cancellation/ de-notification)**
Number of Notified SEZs (As on 31st December, 2020)	**29 SEZs (1SEZ Established by Central Govt.) + 2 Pvt. SEZ notified before SEZ Act, 2005 + 17 SEZs - established under SEZ Act, 2005)**
Number of In-Principle Approvals	**NIL**
Operational SEZs(As on 31st December, 2020)	**20 SEZs (Break up: Multi-product, remaining are Apparel, IT/ITeS, Pharma, Chemical, Engineering, Textiles, Non-conventional Energy, Multi-Service SEZ)**
Units approved in SEZs (As on 31st December, 2020)	**1019 (out of which 741 units are working and remaining 278 units non-operational)**

Land for SEZs	**1 Central Govt +2 Pvt. SEZs notified before SEZ Act, 2005**	**Notified SEZs under the SEZ Act, 2005**	**Total Notified SEZs Area (1) +(2)**	**Formally Approved SEZs**	**Total Area (3+4)**
	(1)	(2)	(3)	(4)	(5)
	506.63 Ha	**14128.50 Ha**	**14635.14**	**5926.24 Ha**	**20561.38**
INVESTMENT	**Total Investment (As on 31st December, 2020)**				
Central Govt. SEZs	1018				
State/Pvt. SEZs set up before 2006	554.52				
SEZs Notified under the Act	204780				
Total Investment	**206353**				
EMPLOYMENT	**Employment (As on February, 2006)**	**Incremental Employment**		**Total Employment (As on 31st December, 2020)**	
Central Govt. SEZs				27725	
State/Pvt. SEZs set up before 2006				26857	
SEZs Notified under the Act				39450	
Total Employment				**94032**	
Exports in 2013-14 (physical)	Rs.2,24,867 Crores (Decrease of 1% over 2012-13)				
Exports in 2014-15 (physical)	Rs. 179,792 Crores(Decrease of 20% over 2013-14)				
Exports in 2015-16(physical)	Rs. 135,633 Crores(Decrease of 20% over 2014-15)				
Exports in 2016-17(physical)	Rs. 141,176 Crores(Growth of 4.1% over 2015-16)				
Exports in 2017-18(physical)	Rs. 157,045 Crores(Growth of 11.24% over 2016-17)				
Exports in 2018-19(physical)	Rs. 185,365 Crores(Growth of 18% over 2017-18)				

Exports in 2019-20(physical)	Rs. 186,960 Crores(Growth of 1% over 2018-19)
Exports in 2019-20(physical) (upto 31st December, 2019)	Rs.142,706 Crores
Exports in 2020-21(physical) (upto 31st December, 2020)	Rs.90,720 Crores (Decrease of 36% over 2019-20)

Source: http://kasez.gov.in

7

Data Analysis and Findings

Meaningful and insightful findings could be derived from the field data gathered from the various units and the SEZ developers, through the extensive use of various statistical tools and method. The findings provided verifiable answers to some of the research questions. Through the findings, the contribution of SEZs to the socio-economic development of the community in Gujarat could be assessed and the drivers for such development identified and detailed.

This chapter comprises of three parts:

***Part I**: This consists of the comprehensive study carried out in two segments, first with responses to exhaustive questionnaire circulated to HR heads of the units in SEZs and next through personal/telephonic interview and written replies to questionnaire by the developers of the selected SEZs.*

***Part II:** Case Study—Cross-cases Contrast: A questionnaire featuring various factors like strategy, HR policy and management principles was circulated to the selected SEZ units followed by interview over phone/in person. The aggregate data/information collected were examined through cross-cases contrast methodology. Thus, the policies in the units for furthering the socio-economic impact could be determined.*

***Part III:** Validation of Research Proposal Framework: In order to validate the Research Proposal Framework used in this study, a questionnaire was circulated to six* *units engaged in different manufacturing activities from each of the six selected SEZs (both multi-product and sector-specific). The framework is validated through analysis of the responses from the units.*

Part I Socio-Economic Impact of SEZs in Gujarat: From Units

Segment I

7.1 Descriptive Statistical Analysis of Responses from SEZ Units

7.1.1 Data Collection

The designed questionnaire was circulated to the individual units in the six SEZs selected for research. The questions are grouped in nine sets/categories; the first set of questions elicits general information; the other eight sets elicit responses on socio-economic factors.

1. General Information (Q 1.1–Q 1.6)
2. Direct Economic (Q 2.1–Q 2.9)
3. Indirect Economic (Q 3.1—Q 3.6)
4. Demographic (Q 4.1–Q 4.7)
5. Housing (Q 5.2.1–Q 5.2.7)
6. Other Local Services (Q 6.1.1–Q 6.1.11)
7. Social Impact (Q 7.1–Q 7.15)
8. Socio-Economic Impact (Q 8.1.1–Q 8.3.4)
9. Type of Drivers—Impact on SEZ (Q 9.1.1–Q 9.1.10)

The questionnaire (Appendix 2.A) was addressed to the HR managers of approximately 492 operational units. One hundred and one complete responses were received during the period October–November 2019. (Please refer to the sample unit flowchart [Figure 2.3] in Chapter 2 and to the characteristics of the SEZs selected for the study Table 2.2 in Chapter 2.)

The three SEZs selected in the multi-product category are as follows:

1. Kandla Special Economic Zone (KASEZ), Kutch District
2. Dahej SEZ Ltd—Bharuch District
3. Surat SEZ, Sachin—Surat District

And the three sector-specific selected SEZs are:

1. Textiles and Articles of Textiles SEZ, Ahmedabad District
2. Electronic SEZ, Gandhinagar District
3. Pharmez, Zydus Infrastructure Pvt Ltd, Ahmedabad District

The responses were captured and coded in excel sheet of each questionnaire into columns. The data size consists of 176 columns (including Serial Number) and 101 rows (data).

The first part covers statistical validation of responses from SEZs by using Cronbach's alpha item analysis.

The second part covers the analysis of questions as grouped in nine sections. The findings derived on analysis of the responses with the use of statistical tools are detailed in this chapter.

7.1.2 Item Analysis Using Cronbach's Alpha

Cronbach's alpha is a convenient test used to estimate the reliability, or internal consistency, of a composite score. It gives us a simple way to measure whether or not a score is reliable.

Theoretically, Cronbach's alpha results should yield a number from 0 to 1, but one could get negative numbers as well. A negative number indicates that something is wrong with the data—perhaps one forgot to reverse score some items. The general rule of thumb is that a Cronbach's alpha of 0.70 and above is good, of 0.80 and more is better and alpha value of 0.90 and exceeding 0.90 is the best.

Cronbach's alpha is deployed to test the reliability and internal consistency of items used for eliciting responses from units located in sample SEZs of Gujarat.

The omitted item statistics table as depicted in Table 7.1 assesses whether removing an item from the analysis improves the internal consistency. The 49 questions in Part I covered under Section 1 to Section 9 of the questionnaire for the units were considered for analysis using Cronbach's alpha.

- Adjusted Total Mean—Mean of the total after omitting an item from the set.
- Adjusted Total Standard Deviation—Standard deviation after omitting an item from the set.

Table 7.1: Item Analysis—Cronbach's Alpha

Cronbach's Alpha = 0.8728

Omitted Item Statistics					
	Adj.			Squared	
Omitted	Adj. Total	Total	Item-Adj.	Multiple	Cronbach's
Variable	Mean	StDev	Total Corr	Corr	Alpha
Q_2_7_1	166.69	16.25	0.5747	0.8587	0.8665
Q_2_7_2	166.75	16.29	0.5692	0.8243	0.8669
Q_2_7_3	166.86	16.36	0.4627	0.8039	0.8684
Q_2_7_4	166.96	16.34	0.5145	0.8513	0.8677
Q_2_7_5	167.57	16.67	0.0860	0.6498	0.8744
Q_2_7_6	166.58	16.42	0.3927	0.9274	0.8695
Q_2_7_7	166.51	16.33	0.4518	0.9333	0.8684
Q_2_7_8	166.82	16.36	0.3985	0.7930	0.8692
Q_2_9	166.99	16.49	0.2887	0.6104	0.8711
Q_3_3_4_1	167.20	16.59	0.1606	0.7692	0.8735
Q_3_3_4_2	167.11	16.56	0.2678	0.6501	0.8714
Q_3_3_4_3	166.75	16.38	0.4418	0.6742	0.8687
Q_3_3_4_4	167.09	16.67	0.1267	0.7162	0.8732
Q_3_3_4_5	166.87	16.65	0.1043	0.6713	0.8743
Q_3_5	167.28	16.61	0.1256	0.6345	0.8744
Q_6_6_1_1	166.68	16.51	0.3792	0.7780	0.8701
Q_6_6_1_2	166.41	16.36	0.5341	0.8950	0.8678
Q_6_6_1_3	166.15	16.56	0.2983	0.8536	0.8710
Q_6_6_1_4	166.36	16.57	0.2764	0.5909	0.8713
Q_6_6_1_5	166.82	16.42	0.4056	0.7660	0.8693
Q_6_6_1_6	166.71	16.45	0.3686	0.8361	0.8699
Q_6_6_1_7	166.70	16.46	0.3986	0.8751	0.8696
Q_6_6_1_8	166.40	16.51	0.3114	0.8518	0.8708
Q_6_6_1_9	166.15	16.53	0.3420	0.8244	0.8705
Q_6_6_1_10	166.30	16.43	0.4143	0.7639	0.8693
Q_6_6_1_11	166.61	16.46	0.3855	0.8484	0.8697
Q_7_7_9_1	166.90	16.34	0.5452	0.8252	0.8675
Q_7_7_9_2	166.64	16.26	0.5803	0.8105	0.8665

Table 7.1: *Continued*

Omitted Item Statistics					
	Adj.			Squared	
Omitted	Adj. Total	Total	Item-Adj.	Multiple	Cronbach's
Variable	Mean	StDev	Total Corr	Corr	Alpha
Q_7_7_9_3	166.46	16.42	0.0239	0.6708	0.9028
Q_7_7_9_4	167.07	16.30	0.5047	0.8902	0.8675
Q_7_7_9_5	167.07	16.33	0.4979	0.8659	0.8678
Q_7_7_9_6	167.09	16.33	0.5408	0.9326	0.8674
Q_7_7_9_7	166.82	16.31	0.5390	0.8619	0.8673
Q_7_7_9_8	167.28	16.34	0.4406	0.8617	0.8686
Q_7_7_9_9	168.32	16.80	-0.0553	0.6308	0.8782
Q_7_7_9_10	169.30	16.69	0.2074	0.5950	0.8722
Q_7_7_9_11	169.08	16.76	0.0218	0.7913	0.8738
Q_7_7_9_12	169.05	16.73	0.0705	0.6700	0.8733
Q_7_7_9_13	168.88	16.75	0.0379	0.7536	0.8736
Q_7_7_9_14	168.66	16.77	0.0041	0.6771	0.8736
Q_9_9_1_1	166.83	16.38	0.5805	0.7548	0.8676
Q_9_9_1_2	166.73	16.26	0.6423	0.8463	0.8661
Q_9_9_1_3	166.39	16.39	0.5020	0.8019	0.8683
Q_9_9_1_4	166.45	16.32	0.5550	0.8416	0.8672
Q_9_9_1_5	166.56	16.26	0.5710	0.7778	0.8666
Q_9_9_1_6	166.65	16.32	0.5307	0.7372	0.8674
Q_9_9_1_7	166.78	16.31	0.5544	0.8103	0.8672
Q_9_9_1_8	166.78	16.32	0.5660	0.8168	0.8671
Q_9_9_1_9	166.67	16.37	0.5663	0.7859	0.8676

- Item-Adjusted Total Correlation—Correlation between the scores of one omitted item and the total scores of all other items. In practice, values range between 0 and 1. A higher value suggests that the omitted item measures the same construct as the other items.
- Squared Multiple Correlation—Coefficient of determination (R^2) when the omitted item is regressed on the remaining items. Values range between

0 and 1. A higher value suggests that the omitted item measures the same construct as the other items.

- Cronbach's alpha—Cronbach's alpha is calculated after an item is omitted from the analysis. Fairly constant values for all omitted items suggest that all items measure the same construct. An increase in Cronbach's alpha for a specific omitted item suggests that it does not measure the same construct.
- The results show that Cronbach's alpha is better: 0.8728, which is close to the best (0.90–1.0). With this score it is inferred that the 49 questions in the survey reliably assess the same construct.
- The questions framed were related to the relevant research topic chosen and respondents were able to understand the concept; this is statistically validated.
- The Item-Adjusted Total Correlation and Squared Multiple Correlation are consistently high and the Cronbach's alpha values do not differ significantly.
- Collectively, the evidence suggests that all items measure the same construct.

Section One: General Information of SEZ Units (Q 1.1–Q 1.6)

7.1.3 SEZs Units Details (Q 1.1)

- The bubble size in Figure 7.1 reflects the number of units that furnished response sheets from each of the six selected SEZs.
- SEZs in Gujarat are not evenly spread in all the districts; in fact, only eight districts in the state house SEZs. The balance 25 districts do not house any SEZs within their boundary, which implies that there is scope to cover these 25 districts with SEZs to generate employment and uniform development.

7.1.4 Unit Details: Year-Wise and Activity-Wise (Q 1.2 & 1.5)

- Figure 7.2 represents pictorially the establishment of units in SEZs on the basis of calendar year and activity.
- The enactment of SEZs Act 2005 and the framing of the SEZs rules 2006 resulted in the mushrooming of SEZs. In fact, most of the units in the SEZs were set up in the period between 2008 and 2018. However, the year 2015 is an outlier as only two SEZs were established.

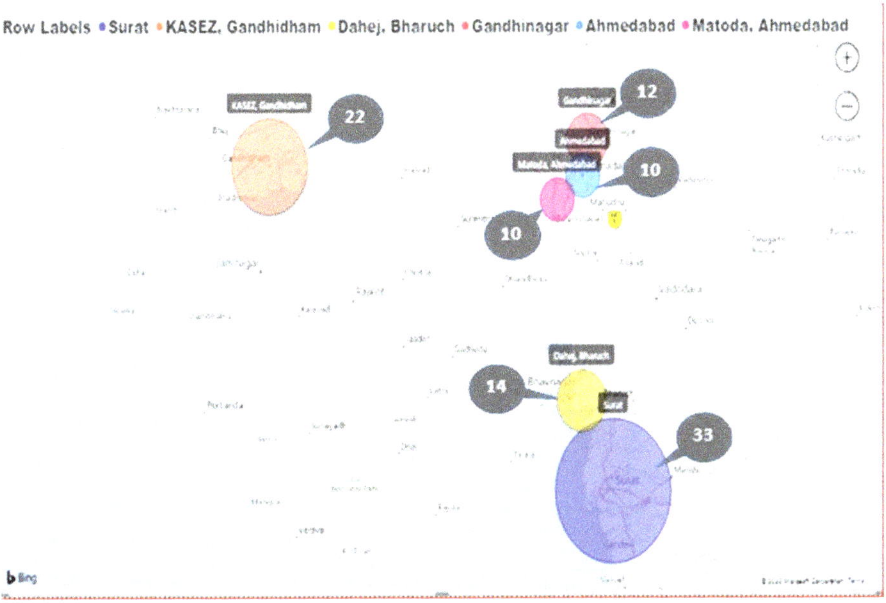

Figure 7.1: Respondent Units—SEZ Location-Wise

Figure 7.2: Year-Wise and Activity-Wise Establishment of Units in SEZs

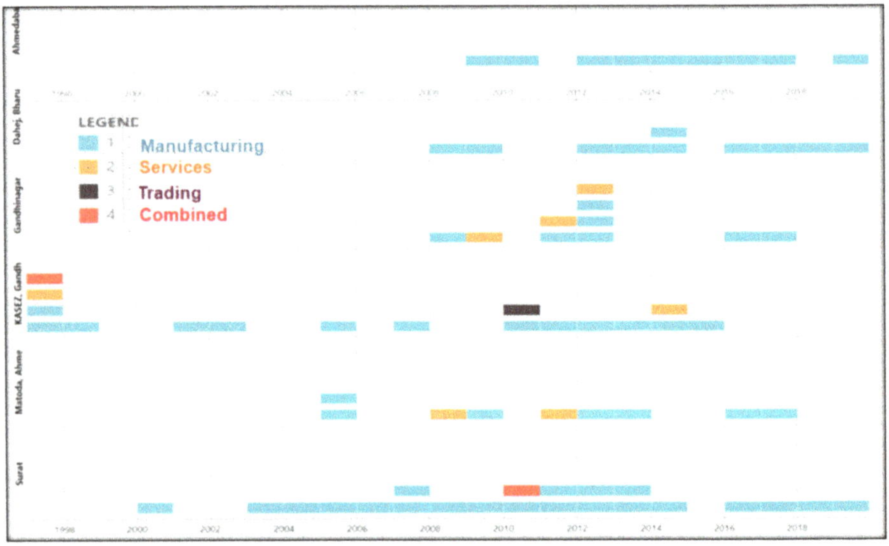

Figure 7.3: Year-Wise Commencement of Units in SEZs

- There is a healthy growth in the number of manufacturing units both in the multi-product and sector-specific categories; on the other hand, the number of SEZs and units engaged in services, trading and combined activities has not shown significant growth.
- The slackening of the pace in the establishment of new units post 2013 can be attributed partly to global recession and mainly on account of the withdrawal of exemption from MAT and DDT.

7.1.5 Commencement of Units (Q 1.2)

- Figure 7.3 depicts details of commencement of units in SEZs by the year.
- KASEZ is the oldest (1965) SEZ (formerly EPZ) established by the government of India; KASEZ is fully operational and occupied.
- Sector-specific SEZs (PHARMEZ, AAP and Electronic Park) started operation post-2008 only resulting in a spike in cumulative figures.
- Service units (like IT/ITeS) are concentrated mainly in Electronic Park Gandhinagar area and partly in PHARMEZ, Ahmedabad.
- There is a scope for more service sector SEZs in line with 12 Champion Services as identified and declared by the government of India in 2018.

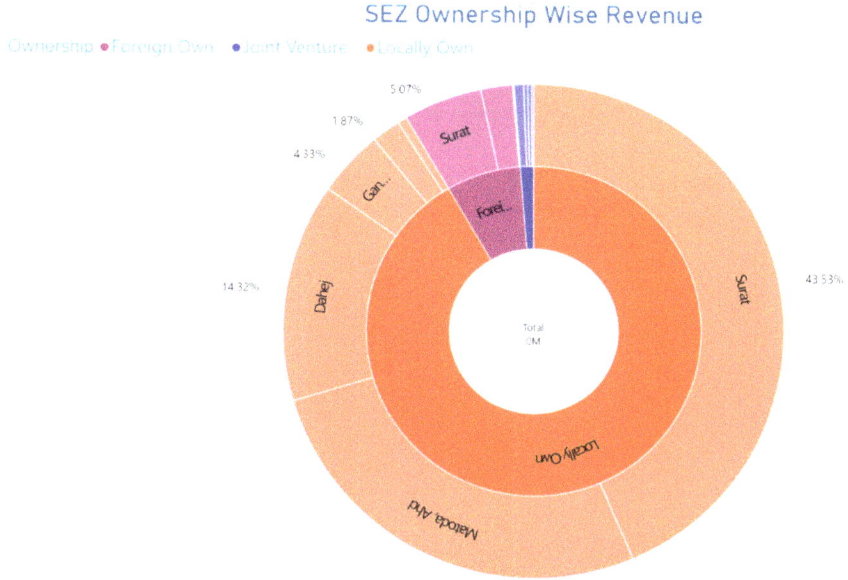

Figure 7.4: Revenue on Basis of SEZ Ownership

7.1.6 Ownership Structure (Q 1.4)

- Figure 7.4 depicts in a pictorial form, the revenue of SEZ units on the basis of the ownership structure.
- The ownership of the units is predominantly Indian.
- Only some units located in PHARMEZ and Electronic Park, Gandhinagar, have foreign ownership.
- This presents an opportunity to attract foreign investment on a bigger scale across other SEZs in Gujarat.

7.1.7 Turnover Analysis (Q 1.6)

- Bubble shadow and its size reflect the changes in revenue generation on year-to-year basis. The increment in revenue was significant from year 2016 to 2017 and peaked in 2018. Surat SEZ is an outlier registering dip in sales due to global reduced demand for diamonds.
- The male and female composition of the employees in percentage terms is represented by the green and blue lines, respectively, in the set of table

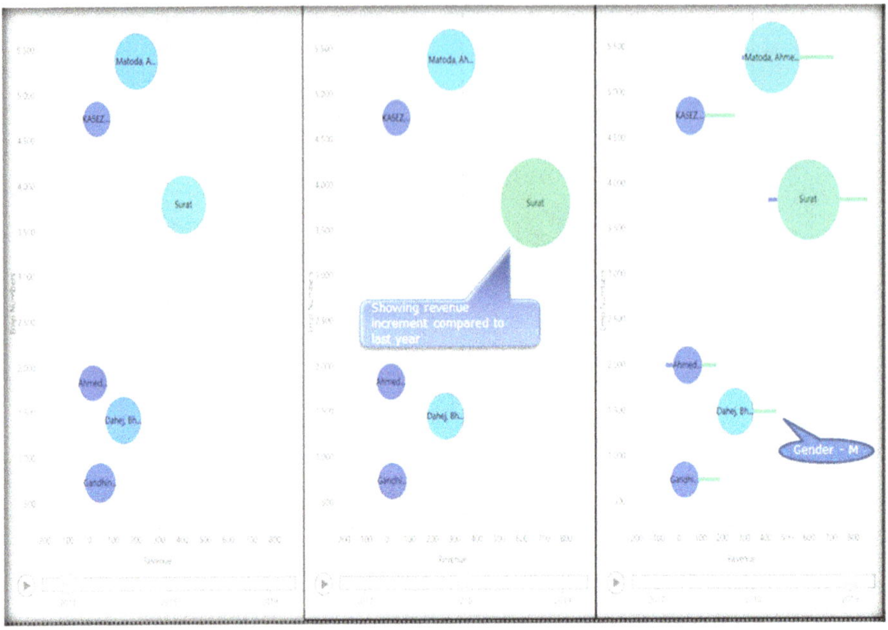

Figure 7.5: Revenue Comparison—Gender (FY16–FY18)

boxes above. It is observed that the SEZs are male-dominated, except for Apparel Park, Ahmedabad, which has a substantial female presence.

- Light industries like Apparel and Textiles (AAP SEZs) Ahmedabad, have a higher percentage of female employees, while heavy industries like chemicals and petrochemicals (Dahej), pharmaceuticals (PHARMEZ), plastics and other manufacturing industries (KASEZ) are dominated by male employees.
- More job opportunities need to be created for women employees so that their contribution can be increased; this will lead to women empowerment.

7.1.8 Comparison of Revenue Generated (Q 1.6)

- Revenue generation by units in different SEZs are compared for the FY 2016–2018 as shown in Figure 7.6.
- PHARMEZ SEZ has recorded maximum growth; next Ahmedabad Apparel Park has recorded higher growth followed by Sachin SEZ and Dahej SEZ.

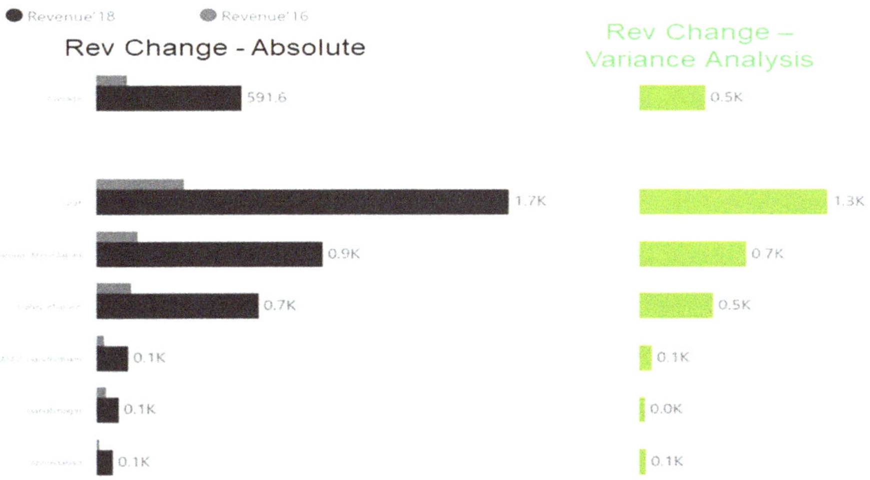

Figure 7.6: Comparision of Revenue Generated (FY16–FY18)

- Sectors like Pharmaceutical, Apparel and Chemical and Petrochemicals have shown positive growth from the SEZs

Section Two: Direct Economic (Q 2.1–Q 2.9)

7.1.9 Type of Employment (Q 2.1)

- Nature of employment at different skill levels is depicted pictorially in Figure 7.7. It is seen that all types of employees (permanent, contractual and daily wages) are employed in SEZs units.
- The largest count of employee numbers in permanent and temporary (contractual) under skilled and semi-skilled groups is recorded at Sachin, Surat SEZ; next highest count is observed at Apparel Park, Ahmedabad, and Dahej SEZ.
- The relationship between the type of employment and skill is established by using Pearson Chi-Square and Likelihood Ratio Chi-Square statistical methods as shown in Figure 7.8.

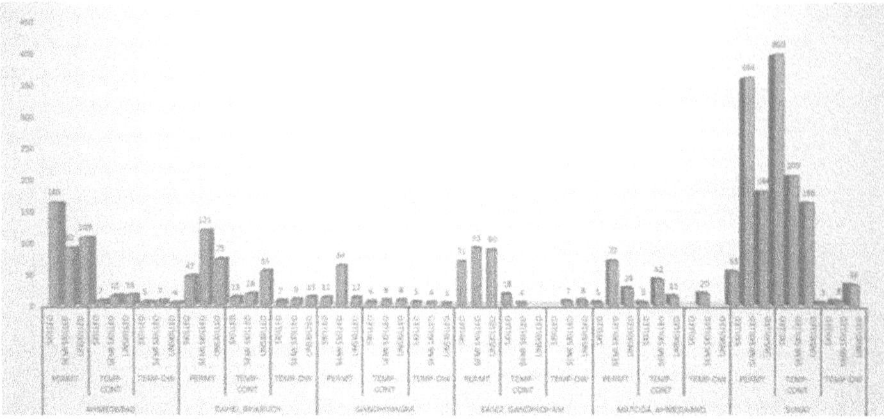

Figure 7.7: Employment Analysis: Type v/s Skill

Hypothesis:

H0: There is no relationship between Job Type and Skill Type

H1: There is significant relationship between Job Type and Skill Type

Rows: Job Type Columns: Worksheet columns

	Skilled	Semi-Skilled	Unskilled	All
Permanent	1,108	498	355	1,961
	1,108.0	474.6	378.4	
Contractual	852	296	260	1,408
	795.5	340.8	271.7	
Daily Wages	22	55	62	139
	78.5	33.6	26.8	
All	1,982	849	677	3,508

Cell Contents: Count

Expected count

Pearson Chi-Square = 113.386, DF = 4, P-Value = 0.000

Likelihood Ratio Chi-Square = 115.180, DF = 4, P-Value = 0.000

Figure 7.8: Chi-Square Test for Association: Job Type, Worksheet Columns

Take Away: P value is 0; thus, there is significant relationship between Job Type and Skills.

- As seen in Figure 7.7, the number of permanent employees in skilled group is higher; while the number of temporary (contractual and daily wages) employees is higher in semi-skilled and unskilled group.

7.1.10 Employment Analysis: Industry (Q 1.5 & Q 2.1)

Skill composition of employees is plotted on the basis of nature of the industry in Figure 7.9. Industries in the manufacturing sector provide employment for all categories of skill groups in larger numbers as compared to the industries in the services, trading and combined sectors.

7.1.11 Gender Analysis (Q 2.2)

- Employees across the three categories namely permanent, contractual and daily wages are predominantly male in all SEZs as depicted in Figure 7.10.
- Composition of employees (male or female) is a function of the type of activity, that is, manufacturing/trading/services/combined and nature of the industry, for example, heavy industries like chemical, petrochemicals (Dahej), pharmaceutical (PHARMEZ). The number of male and female employees in light industries like textiles and apparel (Apparel Park SEZ) is almost equal.

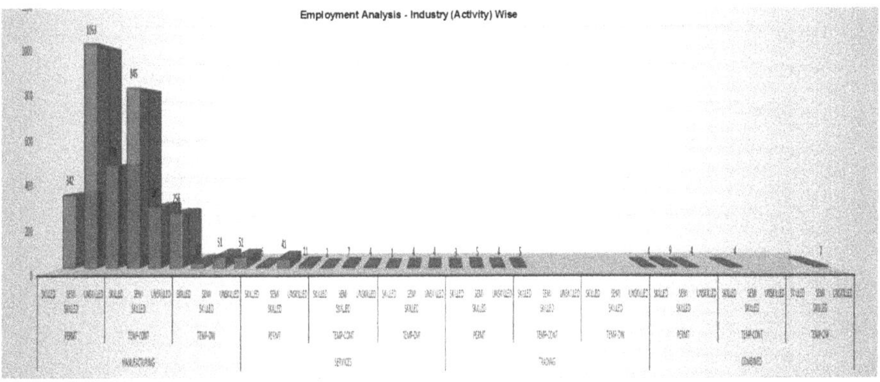

Figure 7.9: Employment Analysis—Industry (Activity)-Wise

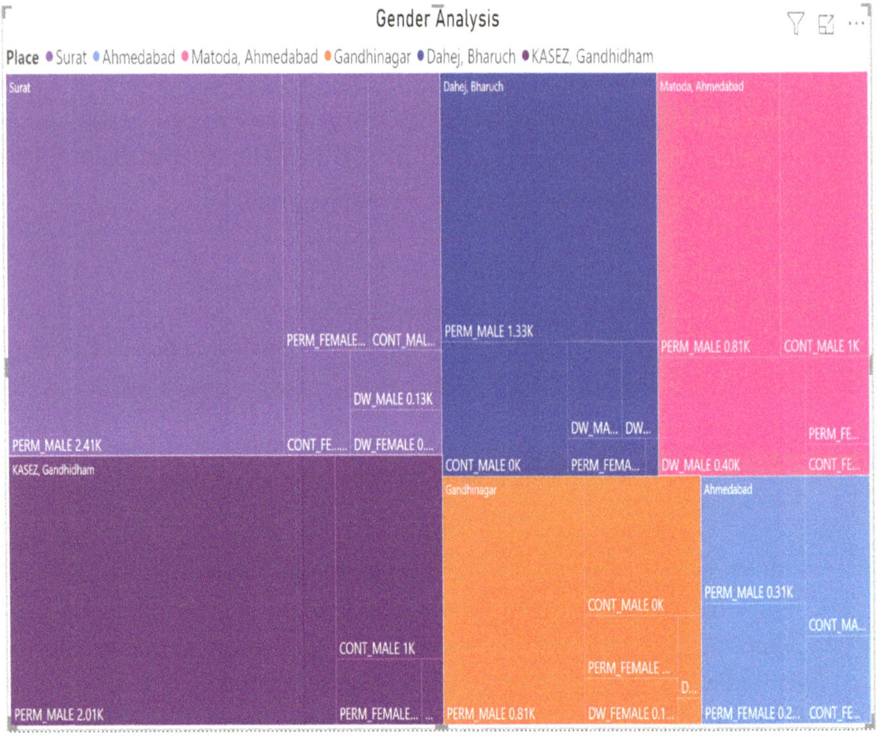

Figure 7.10: Gender Analysis

7.1.12 Local and Non-Local Employment (Q 2.3)

- Local residents (people residing in nearby areas) are more likely to be employed as seen in Figure 7.11. This is true for the category of skilled employees to a large extent; it is true in descending order for semi-skilled and unskilled employees respectively.
- The type of industries and nature of job dictates the deployment into different categories of jobs.
- SEZs have contributed towards the development of surrounding areas, improved quality of life and reduced migration, by providing employment to local residents. SEZs have thus contributed to the economy indirectly.
- Employment to local residents has protected the interest of locals, promoted socio-cultural values, social interest and security, reduced social conflict, thus meeting community goals.
- Non-local employees are less in number and mainly deployed under higher skills and specialist categories, possibly due to lack of local talent.

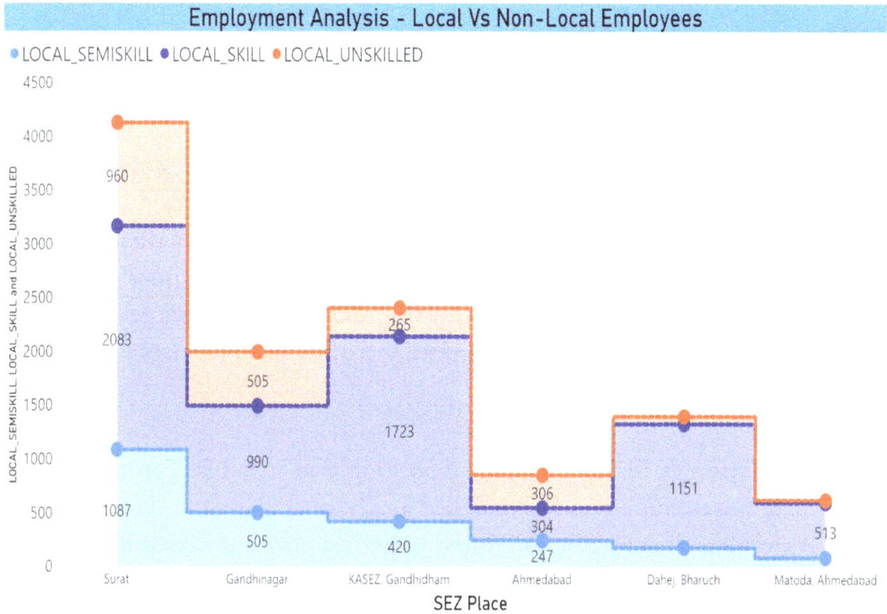

Figure 7.11: Employment Analysis—Local v/s Non-Local

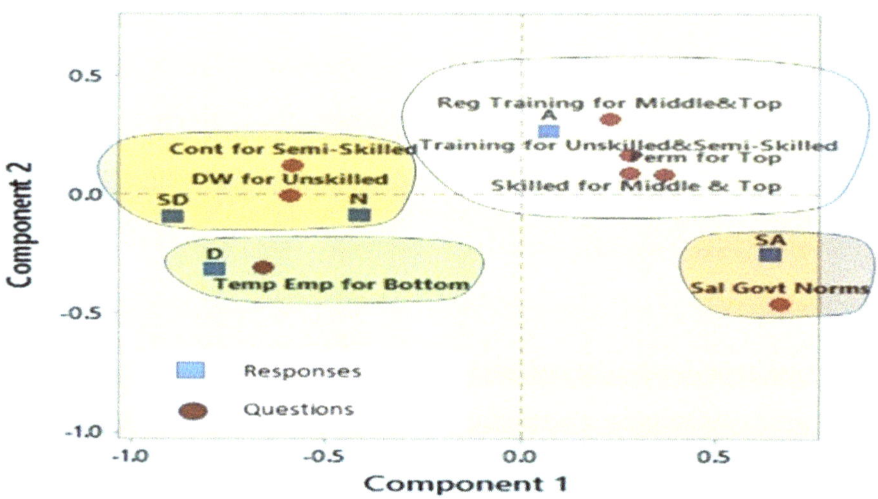

Figure 7.12: Correspondence Analysis—Symmetric Plot

7.1.13 Correspondence Analysis (Q 2.4.1–Q 2.4.8)

Quadrant 1

- Units agree that training on regular basis is provided to top and middle management as well as for unskilled and semi-skilled employees; this reveals focus on higher skills quotient in SEZ environment.
- Units also agreed that they hire skilled employees for manning positions at the top and middle rungs of management. There is, therefore, a premium on acquisition of skills through learning and training, which reinforces the professional approach in recruitment and other HR processes.

Quadrant 2

- Units strongly disagree to the proposition that they hire contractual and daily wages employees for unskilled and semi-skilled tasks; however, such response is in contradiction to the responses provided earlier for question 2.1 and 2.2. Some respondents opted to be neutral.

Quadrant 3

- Most of the units disagree with the proposition that temporary employees are hired for bottom level of jobs

Quadrant 4

- All firms strongly agreed that they pay salaries as per government norms, which means SEZs are compliant in matters of compensation. It is inferred that the SEZ employees are relatively well paid and the working environment is professional.

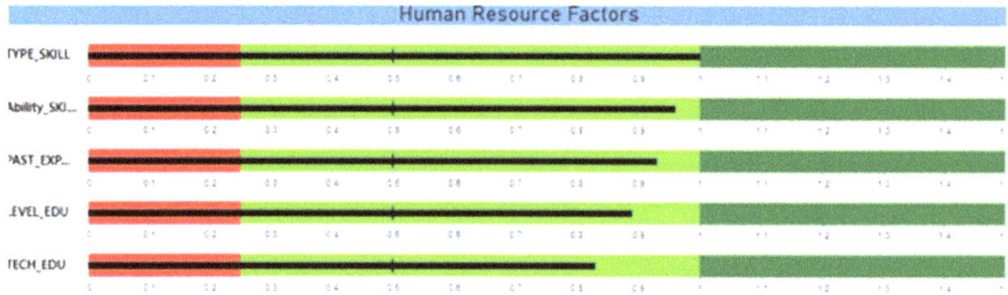

Legend: Not Important Important Very Important

Figure 7.13: Human Resources Factors

7.1.14 Human Resources Factors (Q 2.5.1–Q 2.5.5)

- "Type of Skill" is one of the most important parameters affecting Human Resources Factors.
- Other parameters are relatively important while recruiting workforce; there is an increasing trend towards hiring through professional agencies.
- In addition to conventional parameters for selecting a candidate, companies are giving priority to "Ability to Upskill". This shows their clear vision towards changing scenarios in corporate world as well as their preparedness to compete on international canvas.
- It can be inferred that units have assigned due importance to Human Resource Factors for continuous development of employees, this would ultimately help them to diversify their business model and make it more sustainable.

7.1.15 Government Policies Impact (Q 2.6)

- Research findings indicate that "Labour-Related Policies" play maximum role in the growth of SEZ, followed by "Facility to Carry out R&D" and "Job work from domestic area". Standard deviation is relatively very low, which shows consistency of response from different SEZs and sectors.

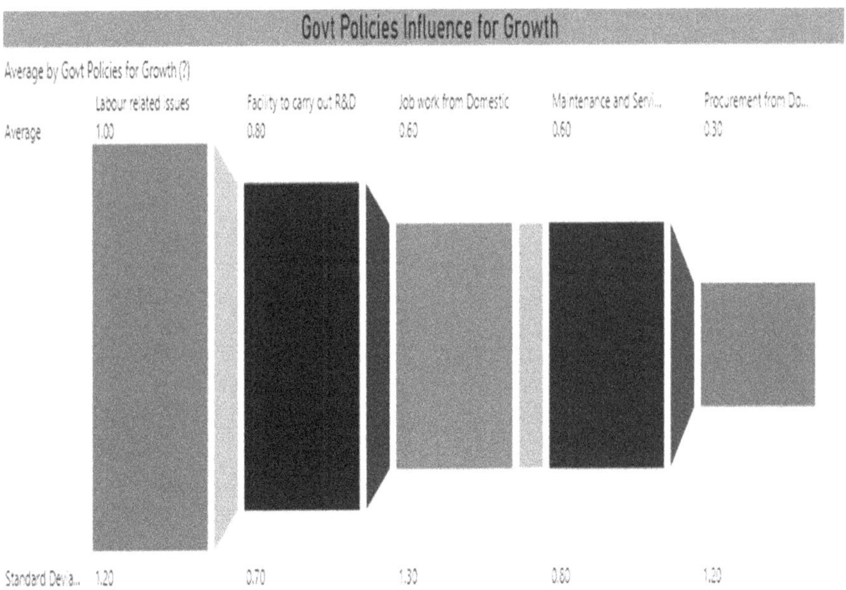

Figure 7.14: Government Policies Influence for Growth

- The results show that there is a need to make the labour laws more industry-friendly. Policy relaxations with respect to job work from DTA segment could be granted. These changes will help in improving employee productivity, retention of skilled labours, resolve labour issues and usher in cordial and healthy working environment.

7.1.16 Economic Impact (Q 2.7.1–Q 2.7.8)

- Respondents strongly agreed to "Increase Foreign Exchange" and "Increase export" propositions.
- There is agreement on a moderate level to "Easy Business Process", "Increase Employment", "Improved infrastructure facility" and "Enhanced Standard of living".
- Comparatively less number of participants agreed with the proposition, "affected demographic pattern in urban and rural areas".
- An even lesser number of participants agree with "Generated limited employment as targeted, given the relative importance to capital-intensive production".

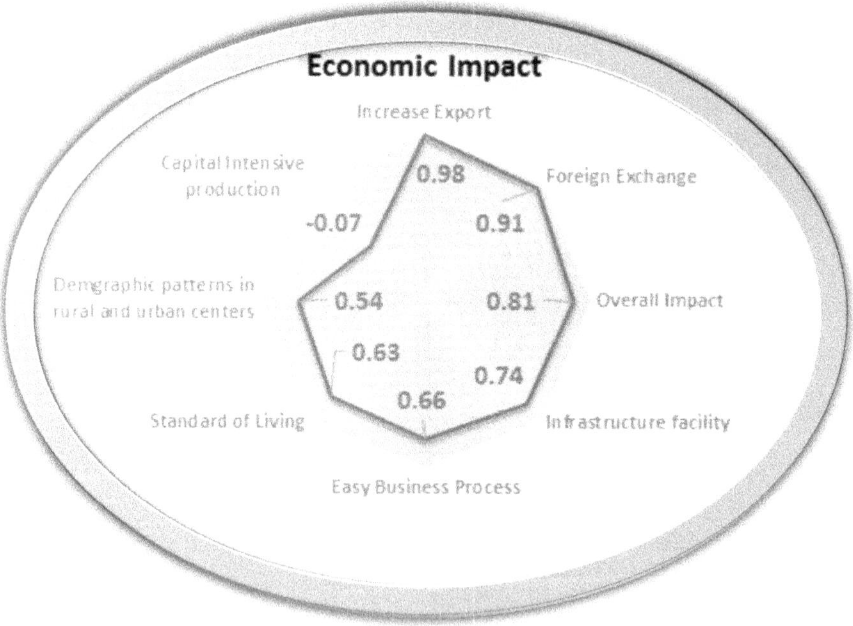

Figure 7.15: Economic Impact

- It can be inferred that out of the major objectives of SEZs, SEZs units have substantially contributed towards exports and generation of foreign exchange but have lagged in generating jobs and attracting foreign direct investments (FDI).
- There is a need to focus on improvement of "Standard of Living" of employees.
- Overall, there is a positive economic impact of SEZs.

7.1.17 Human Capital Development (Q 2.8.1–Q 2.8.6)

Decision Tree based on CHAID (Chi Square Automatic Interaction Detection) algorithms was run in order to identify the most important factors for Human Capital Development.

To run the model, "Performance in Revenue Growth" is taken as output variable while remaining five parameters as inputs as under:

- Organization Culture
- Unit Size
- Unit Activity Type
- Clustering Level in SEZ
- R&D Activities

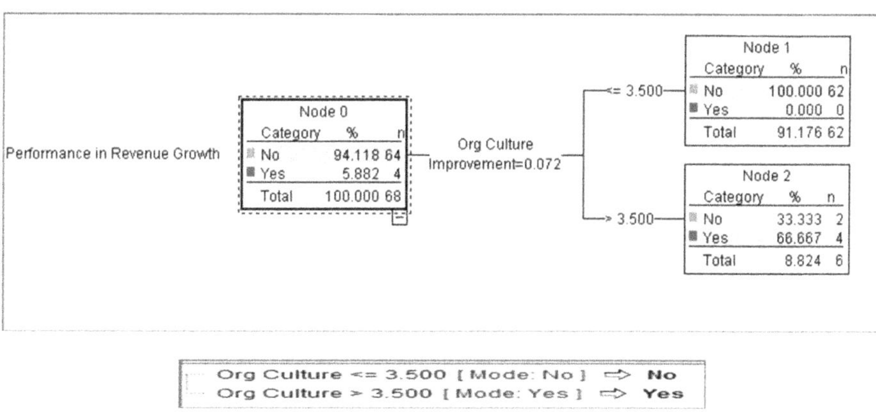

Figure 7.16: Performance in Revenue Growth

- It is established that there is direct linkage between the Organization Culture and Performance in Revenue Growth.
- Respondents who scored high on "Organization Culture" scored high on "Performance in Revenue Growth" with 67 per cent confidence level.
- It can be inferred that healthy organization culture promotes the confidence level in employee's working. It apparently helps in the discharge of responsibilities in an efficient and effective manner, which in turn contributes towards positive performance in revenue growth of the unit.

Figure 7.17 shows the analysis of importance of impact parameters as rated by the respondents, keeping the target of performance in terms of revenue growth percentage (output).

The hierarchy for inputs is as follows:

1. Organization Culture
2. R&D Activities
3. Unit Activity Type
4. Unit size
5. Clustering level in SEZ

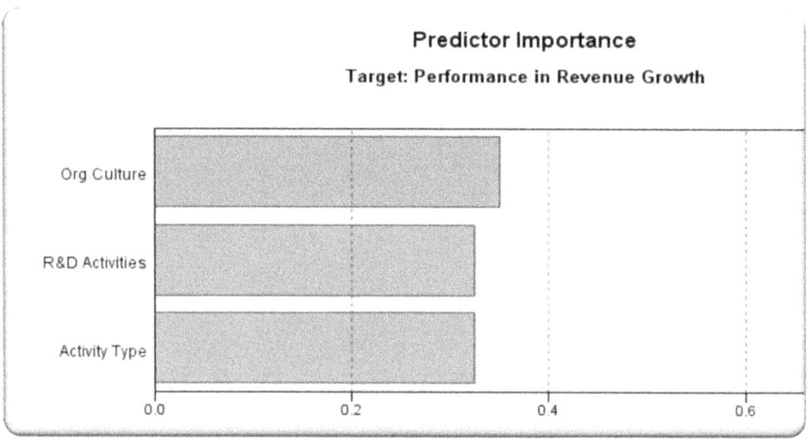

Figure 7.17: Predictor Importance

Parameter Estimates

Performance in Revenue Growth[a]		B	Std. Error	Wald	df	Sig.	Exp(B)	95% Confidence Interval for Exp (B)	
								Lower Bound	Upper Bound
Yes	Intercept	-178.359	4606.497	.001	1	.969			
	Unit Size	11.834	978.820	.000	1	.990	137915.728	.000	.[b]
	Activity Type	-2.792	1676.974	.000	1	.999	.061	.000	.[b]
	Clustering Level in SEZ	-14.960	798.768	.000	1	.985	3.184E-7	.000	.[b]
	R&D Activities	9.043	940.066	.000	1	.992	8456.101	.000	.[b]
	Org Culture	45.204	.000	.	1	.	4.286E+19	4.286E+19	4.286E+19

Figure 7.18: Parameter Estimates

The findings were validated by applying logistic regression method as shown in Figure 7.18.

- Logistic regression also shows high coefficient for "Organization Culture" followed by "R&D Activities" and "Unit Activity Type".
- It is inferred that irrespective of unit size, for firms within the same SEZ, Human Capital Development and Performance in terms of revenue growth percentage is dependent more upon organization culture, R&D activities and type of activities carried out by the units in SEZs.

7.1.18 Local Economy (Q 2.9)

- Around 50 per cent of the respondents consider impact of SEZ High or Very High; this is an indicator that the objectives of SEZs and government policies are in consonance.
- About 40 per cent participants consider impact of SEZ moderate.
- Only 10 per cent participants consider it is low/very low; there is a need to investigate their perspective further.
- Thus, it is derived that the SEZ model gives impetus to local economy and contributes towards nation's wealth.

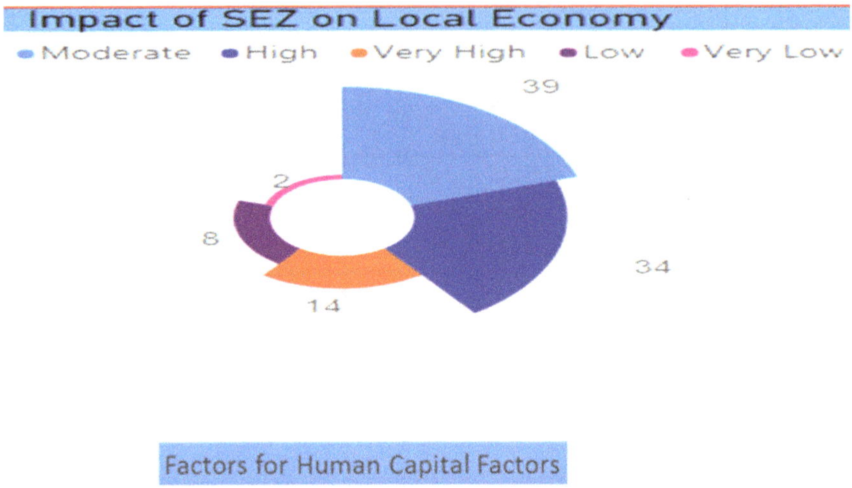

Figure 7.19: Impact of SEZ on Local Economy

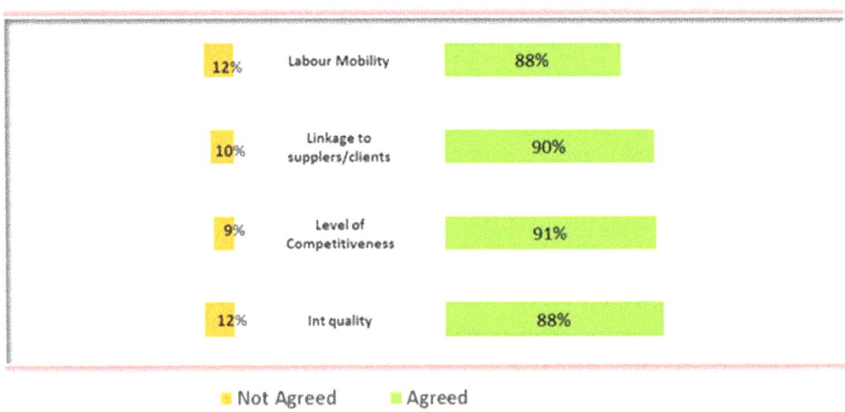

Figure 7.20: Human Capital Factors—Importance-Wise

Section Three: Indirect Economic (Q 3.1–Q 3.6)

7.1.19 Human Capital Factors (Q 3.2.1–Q 3.2.4)

- Figure 7.20 gives the rank analysis of the Human Capital Factors which may facilitate technical know-how spill over.
- From the figure, it is clear that roughly 90 per cent of the respondents agreed to the listed human capital factors with range from 91 per cent to 88 per cent.

- Level of competitiveness is the most important factor followed by linkage to supplier/client, labour mobility and application of international quality standards.
- Therefore, Human Capital factors play a crucial role in facilitating technical know-how spill over.

7.1.20 Benefit to Units (Q 3.3)

- On scale of -2 to +2, the highest benefit derived from other units within SEZ is "Formal & Informal Networking" followed by "Policies and Strategies". "Product Development" is ranked as moderately important while "Process & Quality Control" is not so important.
- It shows that there is no competition among the units in the same SEZs. Healthy working environment and common sharing of policies and strategies have resulted in overall positive growth.
- Units are engaged in different activities (manufacturing/trading/services) and catering to different export markets having different standards; hence product development and process and quality control standards differ and, therefore, units do not derive benefits from other units in this regard.

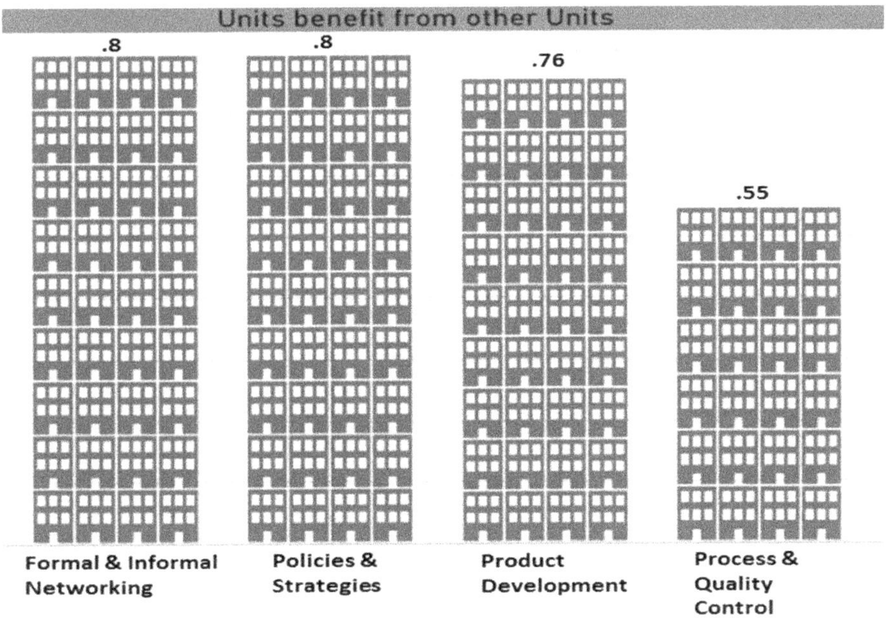

Figure 7.21: Units Benefit from Other Units

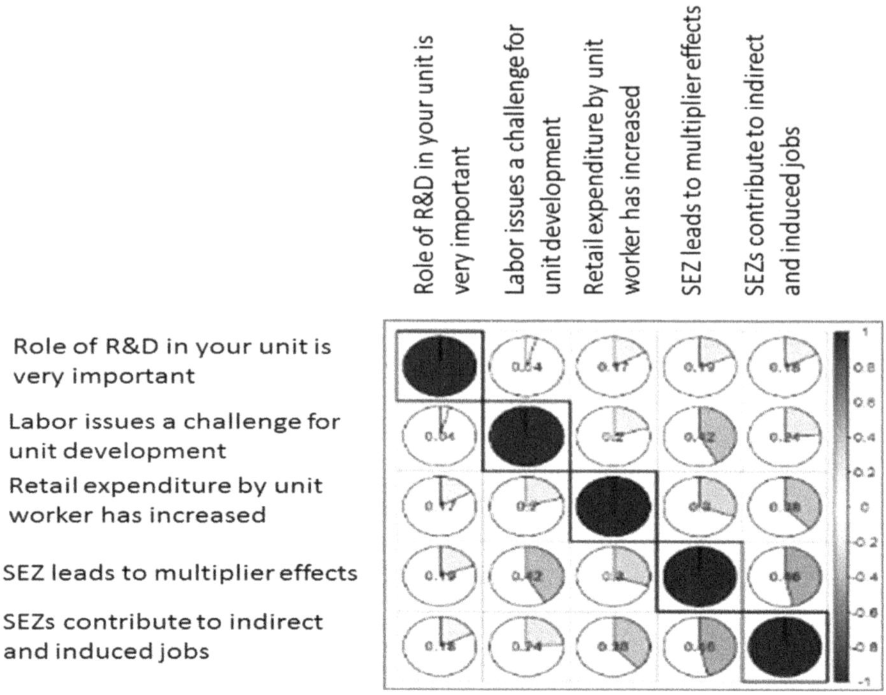

Figure 7.22: Parameters to Indirect Economy

7.1.21 SEZ: Multiplier Effects (Q 3.4.1–Q 3.4.5)

- Figure 7.22 shows the correlation of the five parameters and gives comparative measures on the effect on indirect economy.
- Moderate correlation is observed between "SEZ leads multiplier effects" and "SEZ contribute to indirect jobs".
- There is weak correlation between "SEZ as multiplier effect" and "labour issues".
- There is weak correlation between "SEZ-induced jobs" and "retail expenditure of unit".
- "Role of R&D in your unit is very important" does not exhibit significant correlation with any other factor.

7.1.22 SEZ Units: Connection with DTA (Q 3.5)

- Figure 7.23 maps the analysis of responses regarding connection of SEZ units with the Domestic Tariff Area (DTA).

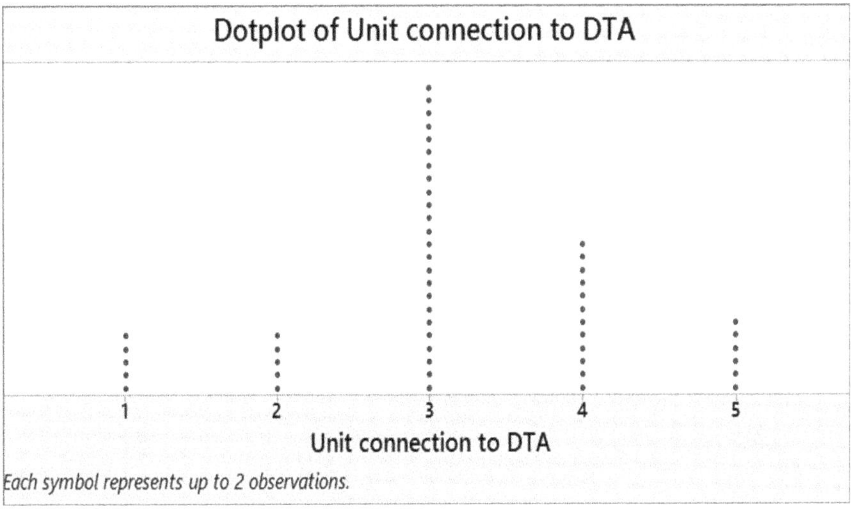

Figure 7.23: Dot Plot of Unit Connection to DTA

- About half of the participants selected moderate; they get 40–60 per cent work done from DTA.
- Around a quarter of the participants opted for High; they get 60–80 per cent work done from DTA.
- Only 10 per cent of the respondents chose Very High; they get more than 80 per cent work done from DTA.
- The balance 15 per cent selected Very Low; they get less than 40 per cent work done from DTA.
- It is inferred that SEZ units contribute to local economy by getting substantial work done from local DTA supplies and services.
- MSME segment located in DTA is also benefited from the SEZ units.

7.1.23 Competition with Other Units (Q 3.6)

- Roughly half (48 per cent) participants selected Low competition with other units within zone.
- Some 28 per cent selected Moderate competition with other units within zone.
- About 18 per cent selected Stiff while only 4 per cent selected Very Stiff competition with other units within zone.
- The findings supplement Figure 7.21 that low competition leads to healthy working environment, leading to a niche market and niche product. For

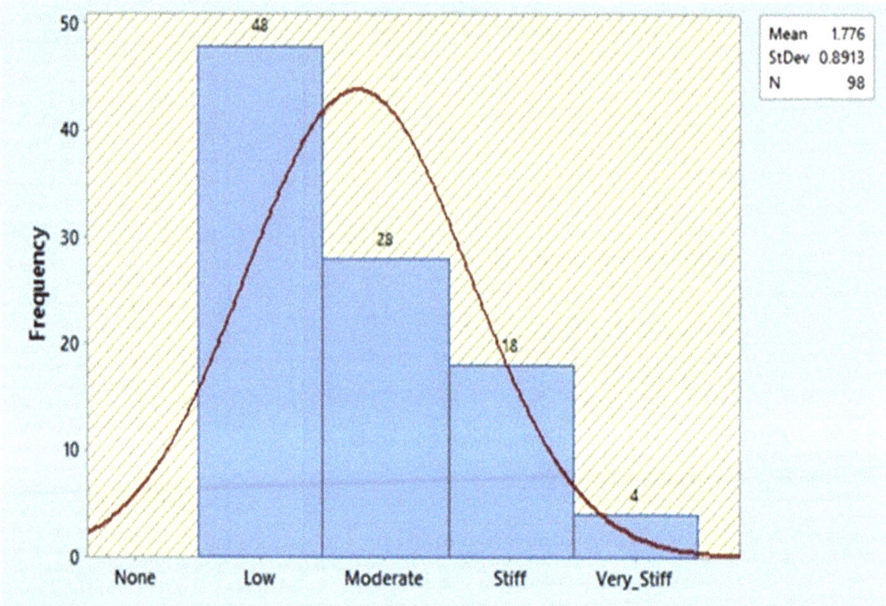

Figure 7.24: Competition with Other Units Within SEZ

example, units manufacturing industrial textiles or medical textiles product face low competition from the units manufacturing traditional textiles items.

Section Four: Demographic (Q 4.1–Q 4.7)

7.1.24 Average Age of Workers (Q 4.1)

- It is surmised from the responses, that the largest age group of workers in SEZs (almost 55 per cent of the total workers) consists of the 25–35 years age group.
- The next biggest group in size comprises of workers in the age group of 35–45 years, 35 per cent of the total workers in the SEZs belong to this age group.
- Workers in the age group 45–55 years account for approximately 7 per cent of the SEZ workers. The percentage of workers in the age group below 25 years, as well the percentage of workers above 55 years of age, is negligible. This shows that bulk of the workers employed in the units are in the

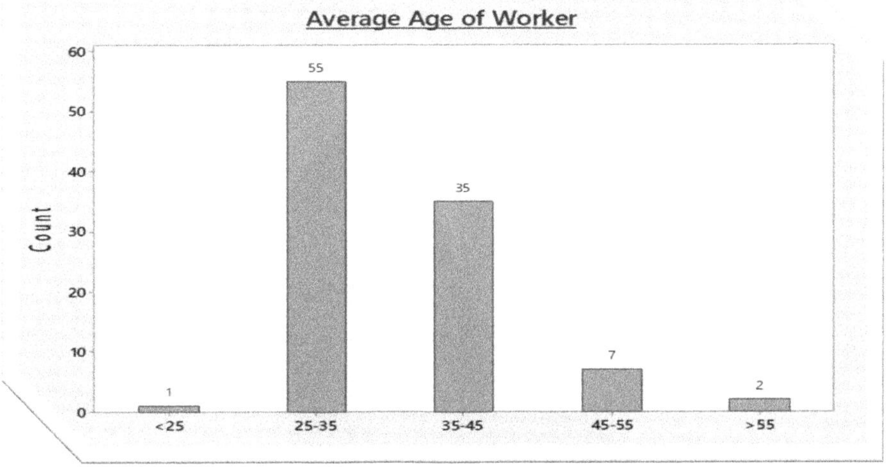

Figure 7.25: Average Age of Workers

prime age group; it also means that units are following government rules and there is no child employment in the units.

- It is inferred that maximum employment is from millennial generation; this generation consists 65 per cent of country's population.
- Youth employment should result in higher output in terms of per employee output of the units.

7.1.25 Average Number of Dependants (Q 4.2)

- About 57 per cent of the employees have two to four numbers of dependants; which suggests nuclear family structure.
- Some 20 per cent of the employees have four to six numbers of dependants; probably the parents are the additional dependants.
- Only about 9 per cent of the workers have more than eight numbers of dependants; this could be a pointer towards joint family structure.
- The percentage of workers with one to two dependants as well as the percentage of workers with six to eight dependants is around 7 per cent for either category.
- Hence, most of the workers live in nuclear families; this is reflective of the norm in current industrial society as compared to joint family structure prevalent earlier.

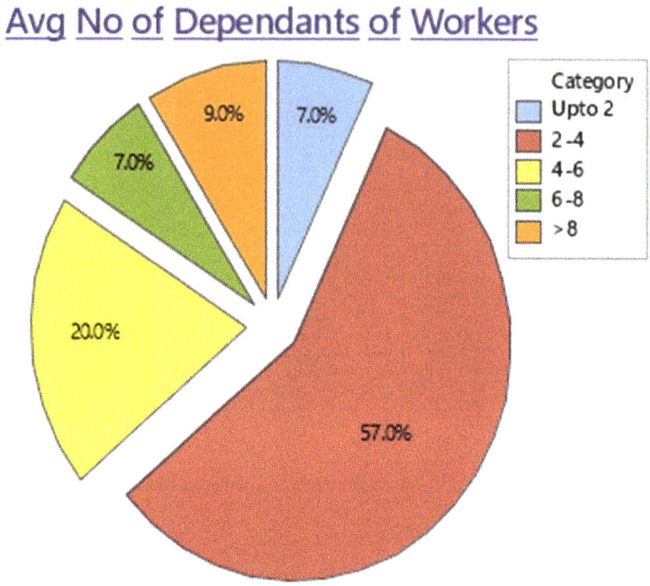

Figure 7.26: Average Number of Dependants of Workers

- Less number of dependants in family means that there are lesser claimants to the cake and should result in desirable outcomes of better education and health and better quality of life.

7.1.26 Single Wage Earner (Q 4.3)

- For only single wage earner about 46 per cent of the respondents agreed for moderate rank, while around 27 per cent opted for High rank.
- Some 16 per cent of the respondents chose low rank for only single wage earner; just 10 per cent of respondents gave Very High rank.
- Hence maximum number of workers comprise of single wage earner in the family.

7.1.27 Dwelling Place (Q 4.4)

- From the dot plot below, it is seen that the maximum number of employees have dwelling place within five to ten kilometres.
- The dwelling place of workers in lesser number of cases is within two kilometres; this is also true for workers having dwelling unit more than ten kilometres from the working place.

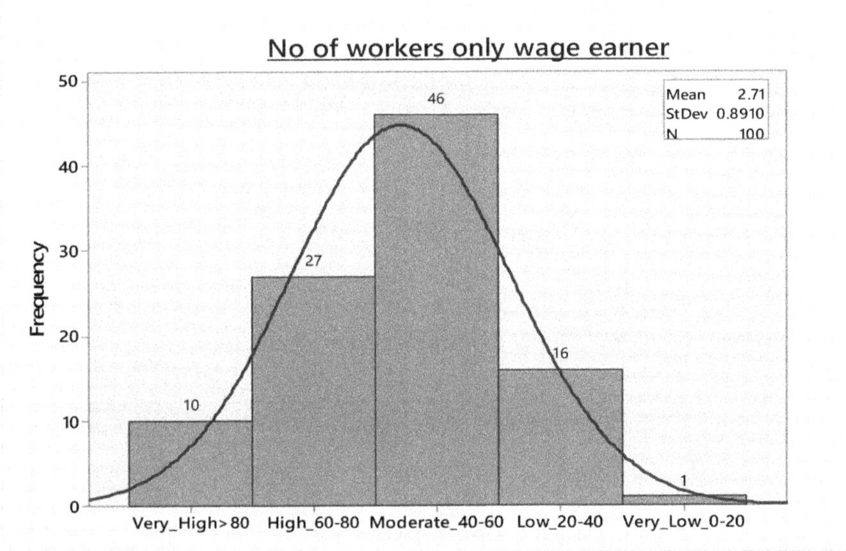

Figure 7.27: Number of Workers—Only Wage Earner

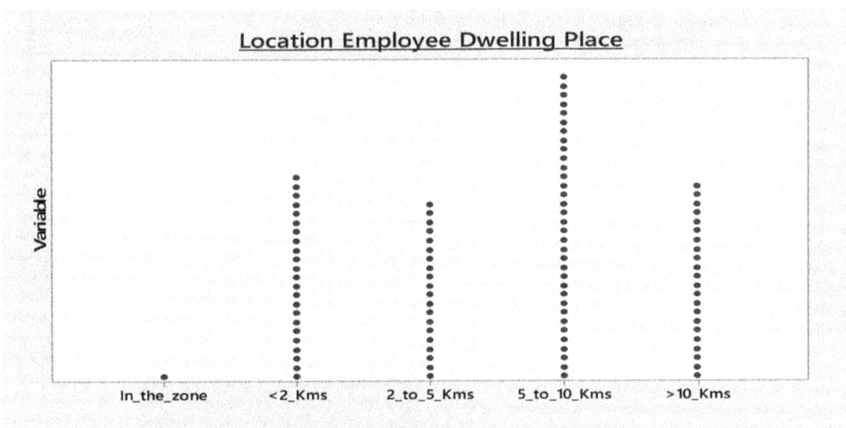

Figure 7.28: Location—Employee Dwelling Place

- In a negligible number of cases, the dwelling facility is provided within the zone.
- Therefore, the units and developer should provide the residential facility in the form of tenements, dormitory and dedicated women hostel inside the SEZs; such facilities will definitely improve working condition of the employees.

7.1.28 Population Type (Q 4.5)

- The ratio of permanent to temporary residents is 61:39. Thus, it is apparent that the units prefer to offer jobs to local residents. In this manner, they contribute to the development of local economy.

7.1.29 Income Level of Nearby Families (Q 4.6)

- The responses show that approx. 66 per cent (27 counts) of the nearby families belong to "Upper Middle Income" category.

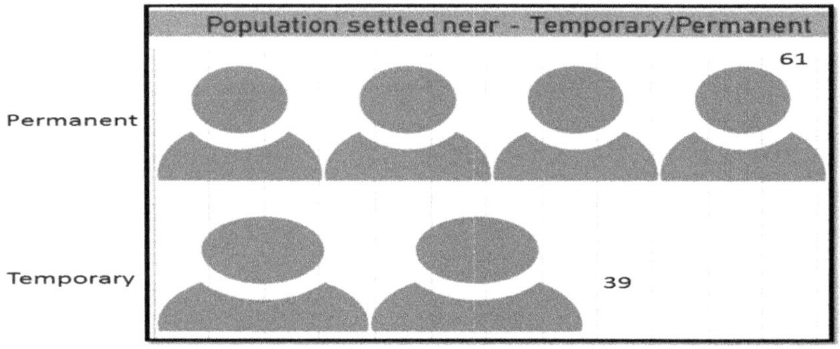

Figure 7.29: Population Settled Near—Temporary/Permanent

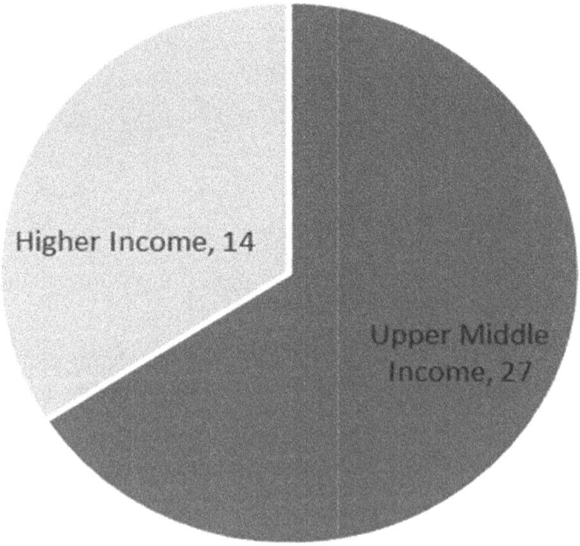

Figure 7.30: Income Level of Nearby Families

- About 34 per cent (14 counts) of the nearby families belong to "Higher Income" category.

Section Five: Housing (Q 5.2.1–Q 5.2.7)

7.1.30 Housing-Related Social Factors (Q 5.2.1–Q 5.2.7)

- Respondents agree with the proposition that "Housing settlements nearby SEZ are becoming cosmopolitan" and "Renting near SEZ is Difficult".
- Respondents disagree with the proposition that there exist "Resident complex inside SEZ" and "Hostel facilities for women".
- Many respondents have opted for Neutral option.
- Same findings are also depicted in Figure 7.32.

It is necessary that units and developer should provide residential facility in the form of tenements, dormitory and dedicated women hostel inside the SEZs for better working condition of the employees.

	Strongly Disagree	Disagree	Neutral	Agree	Strongly Agree	All
Housing settlement nearby SEZs	5	14	42	34	6	101
	11.30	23.18	39.20	22.46	4.86	
Renting near SEZ is difficult	5	24	33	34	5	101
	11.30	23.18	39.20	22.46	4.86	
Non processing area for housing	5	13	49	27	7	101
	11.30	23.18	39.20	22.46	4.86	
SEZ leads to slum area	22	23	32	22	1	100
	11.19	22.95	38.81	22.24	4.82	
SEZ leads to residense within c	13	31	41	11	5	101
	11.30	23.18	39.20	22.46	4.86	
Dormitory inside zone	15	26	40	14	5	100
	11.19	22.95	38.81	22.24	4.82	
Hostel for Women	14	31	37	15	5	102
	11.41	23.41	39.59	22.68	4.91	
All	79	162	274	157	34	706

Cell Contents: Count
Expected count

Pearson Chi-Square = 70.403, DF = 24, P-Value = 0.000
Likelihood Ratio Chi-Square = 73.451, DF = 24, P-Value = 0.000

Figure 7.31: Chi-Square Analysis for Housing-Related Social Factors

Labels	Strongly Disagree	Disagree	Neutral	Agree	Strongly Agree
Housing settlement nearby SEZs become Cosmopolitan	5	14	42	34	6
Renting near SEZ is difficult	5	24	33	34	5
Non processing area for housing facility	5	13	49	27	7
SEZ leads to slum area	22	23	32	22	1
SEZ leads to residense within complex	13	31	41	11	5
Dormitory inside zone	15	26	40	14	5
Hostel for Women	14	31	37	15	3

Figure 7.32: Housing-Related Social Factors

Section Six: Other Local Services (Q 6.1.1–Q 6.1.11)

7.1.31 Social Factors (Q 6.1.1–Q 6.1.11)

Quadrant 4: The high average rating and low standard deviation mean high importance is given to the services listed below by the respondents on a consistent basis:

- Life Security
- Women Safety
- Canteen Facility
- Health Insurance

Quadrant 3: The low average and low standard deviation imply that these facilities should be there for employees:

- Social Schemes
- Education Loans

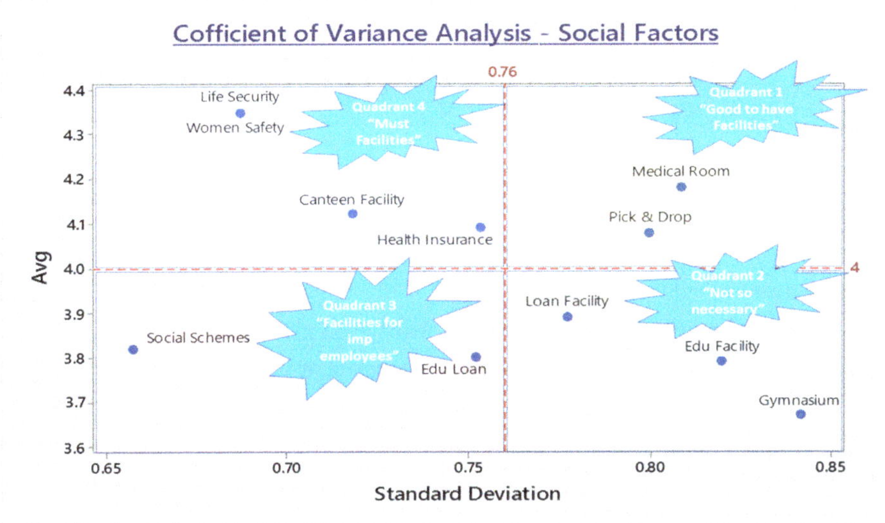

Figure 7.33: Co-Efficient of Variance Analysis—Social Factors

Quadrant 2: The low average combined with high standard deviation signifies the following facilities are not so important for employees:

- o Loan Facility
- o Education Facility
- o Gymnasium

Quadrant 1: The high average and high standard deviation would mean that the following services are "Good to Have".

- o Medical Room
- o Pick and drop facility

It can be inferred that SEZs should have proper infrastructure facilities inside the SEZs for employees working in units located in SEZs as listed below hierarchy-wise:

- o Transportation Services—Pick-up and drop-off facility
- o Medical Room—OPD Clinic
- o Health Insurance for employees
- o Canteen facilities

- o Life security—Fire station/Fire-fighting equipment
- o Women safety measures

Section Seven: Social Impact (Q 7.1–Q 7.15)

7.1.32 Female Employees: Family Head (Q 7.1–Q 7.3)

- A good number of respondents agreed that Women employees act as a Family Head.
- Figure 7.34 shows that 25 per cent units each give equal weights for 60 per cent or more: 25–60 per cent: 10–25 per cent and less than 10 per cent, respectively, for women employed in their units and acting as family head.
- 50 per cent of the units agreed that 20 per cent of the women head face domestic violence; 25 per cent of the units agreed that 50 per cent of the women family heads are the victims of domestic violence and the remaining 25 per cent of the units agree that women do not face domestic violence.
- The findings confirm that Indian society follows the patriarchal form of family system with the male as head of the family and always dominant. Hence, even if the woman is family head as the only earning member, she may continue to face domestic violence.

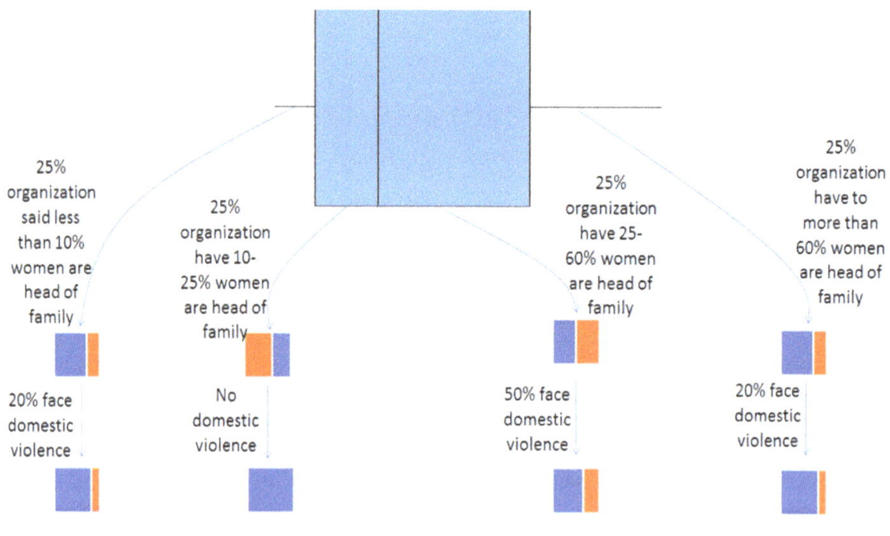

Legend: Yes ▢ No ▢

Figure 7.34: Female Employees—Family Head v/s Domestic Violence

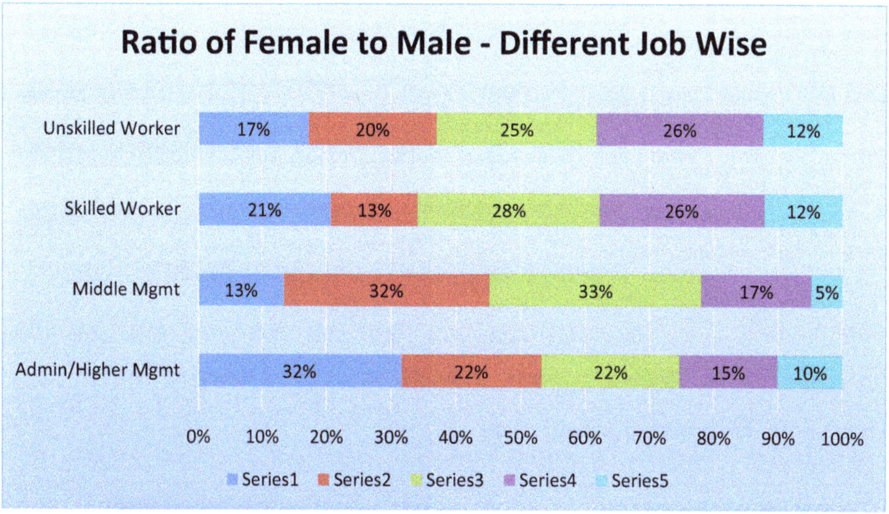

Figure 7.35: Ratio of Female to Male—Different Job Wise

7.1.33 Female to Male Worker Ratio (Q 7.4)

- Most units agreed with the proposition that women are equally distributed among different level of jobs.
- Preference is given to women to maintain gender diversity; but the recruitment and deployment of women employees is largely dependent upon the type of activity and nature of job deemed suitable for women.

7.1.34 Labour Audits/Compliance (Q 7.5)

- From the figure below, it is seen that approximately 93 per cent of the units comply with labour audits on yearly basis, follow government rules and directives from time to time.
- Some 52 per cent of the units follow bi-annual method of labour audits.
- Around 40 per cent units carry out labour audits once in more than three and four years.
- All units carry out labour audits and comply with labour laws at different intervals without any deviations.

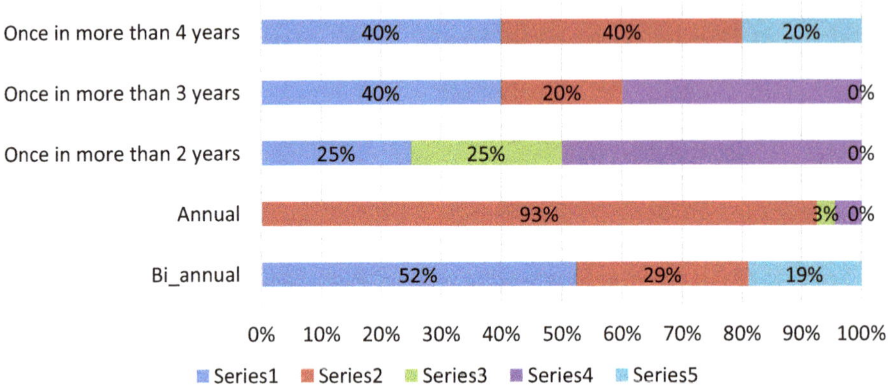

Figure 7.36: Frequency of Labour Audit

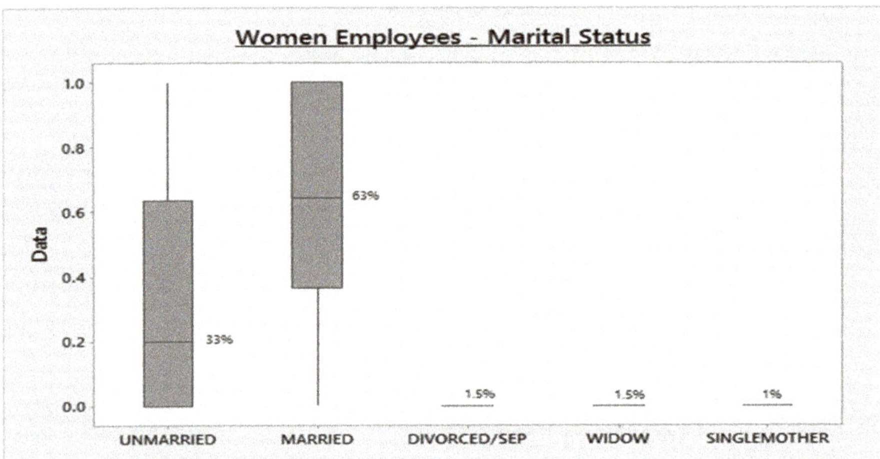

Figure 7.37: Women Employees—Marital Status

7.1.35 Women Employees (Marital Status) (Q 7.6)

- About 63 per cent of women employees are under married category, while 33 per cent are under unmarried category.
- The balance 4 per cent can be grouped under divorced/widow/single mother categories.
- Hence marital status does not affect the employability of women; SEZ units have supported women empowerment through employment.

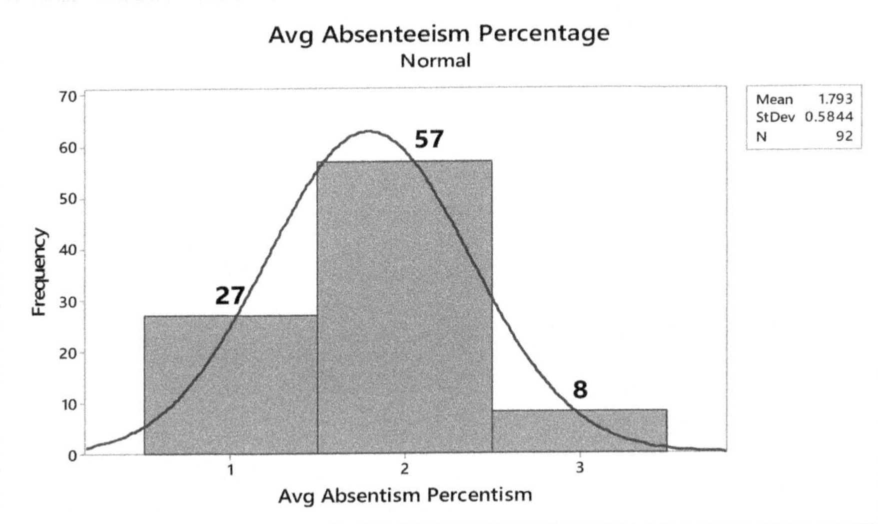

Figure 7.38: Average Absenteeism Percentage

7.1.36 Employees Absenteeism (Q 7.7)

- Close to 57 per cent of the employees remain unauthorized absent for two days in a month.
- Another 27 per cent of the employees remain unauthorized absent for one day in a month.
- Some 8 per cent of the employees remain unauthorized absent for three days in a month.
- It is seen that employees in all units have tendency towards absenteeism for maximum three days in a month.

7.1.37 Women-Centric Camps/Meetings (Q 7.8)

- From the figure below it can be seen that more than 50 per cent respondents replied in the affirmative for conduction of women centric camps/ meetings as per the hierarchical rating:
  a. Education related (54 per cent)
  b. Knowledge of rights/duties (53 per cent)
  c. Sexual Harassment (53 per cent)
  d. Other women issues/meetings (50 per cent)

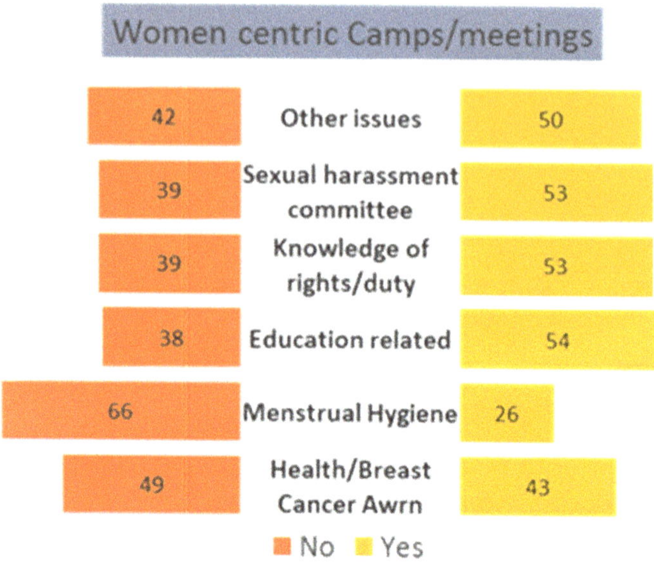

Figure 7.39: Women-Centric Camps/Meetings

- Some 43 per cent of the respondents agree to have health/breast awareness camps for women employees.
- However, around 66 per cent disagree to hold any camp related to menstrual hygiene.
- SEZ units should conduct such women-centric camps and meetings for general awareness; these activities will help to achieve social objectives.
- Indian society by large continues to have an orthodox outlook on menstruation.

7.1.38 SEZ Impact: Social Objectives (Q 7.9.1–Q 7.9.8)

Quadrant 1

- It can be observed from figure below that Units have Strongly Agreed the role of SEZs in:
  a. Contribution to Social Objectives
  b. Protection of Minimum Wages/Benefits.

Quadrant 2

- Respondents Disagree/Strongly Disagree in the area of Spatial concentration of SEZs around urban areas lead to regional inequalities.

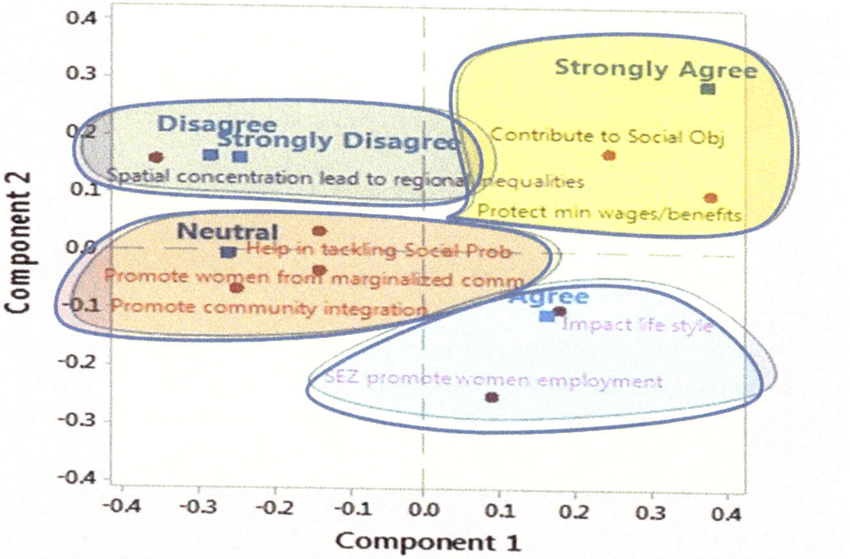

Figure 7.40: Correspondence Analysis—SEZ Impact

Quadrant 3

- Units have opted for Neutral response for the following areas:
  a. SEZs help in tackling social problems like crime rate, illness and divorce in nearby areas.
  b. SEZs promote women from marginalized community.
  c. Promote community integration.

Quadrant 4

- Units agreed for SEZs impact on:
  a. Life style/Quality of life among workers.
  b. Promotion of Women employment.

SEZs have a major Impact on social factors as stated above. The issue of regional disparity has not been addressed by SEZs.

7.1.39 Women Protection in SEZ (Q 7.10–Q 7.15)

- A high percentage of respondents, that is, almost 81 per cent confirmed there is legal mechanism in place in SEZs units for protection of women from sexual harassment.
- About 59 per cent respondents acknowledge provision of maternity paid leaves.
- Around 56 per cent respondents confirm the provision of creche facility in their units.
- A large number of about 84 per cent respondents confirm that women-only transport facility is not provided.
- About 62 per cent units do not provide overtime facility for women workers.
- None of the units have any working women hostels or dormitory facility for women employees.
- The units follow the Vishaka Guidelines as laid down in Sexual Harassment of Women at Workplace (Prevention, Prohibition and Redressal) Act, 2013 for women protection.
- Crèche facility as per the said Act is provided in most of the units. Maternity benefits are extended as per the extant laws.
- Dedicated transport facility may be provided to women employees for pick up and drop facility.
- Normally, women work in day shift only as per the provisions of Factory Act 1948, therefore, overtime for women is very rare.

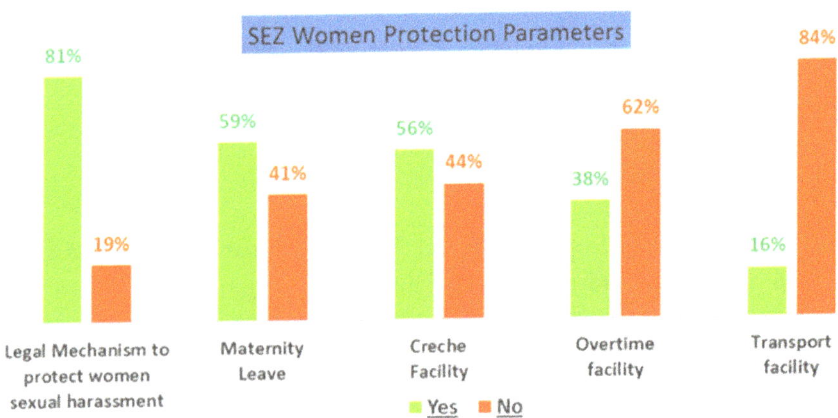

Figure 7.41: SEZ—Women Protection Parameters

Section Eight: Socio-Economic Impact (Q 8.1.1–Q 8.3.4)

7.1.40 Impact on Socio-Economic Status (Q 8.1.1)

- There is overwhelming support for the proposition that SEZs have an impact on socio-economic status; 60 per cent of the respondents voted Agree and 8 per cent selected Strongly Agree; this means a total 68 per cent of the respondents agree with the proposition.
- Around 26 per cent of the respondents opted for Neutral option.
- Only 5 per cent of the respondents selected Disagree and 1 per cent chose Strongly Disagree with the proposition.
- Therefore, the proposition that SEZs impact Socio-Economic status with positive contribution is well accepted.

7.1.41 Economic Drivers (Q 8.2.2)

- About 57 per cent of the respondents Agree and 11 per cent Strongly Agree with the proposition that Economic Drivers have positive impact on SEZs.
- Around 27 per cent of the respondents opted for Neutral on this aspect.

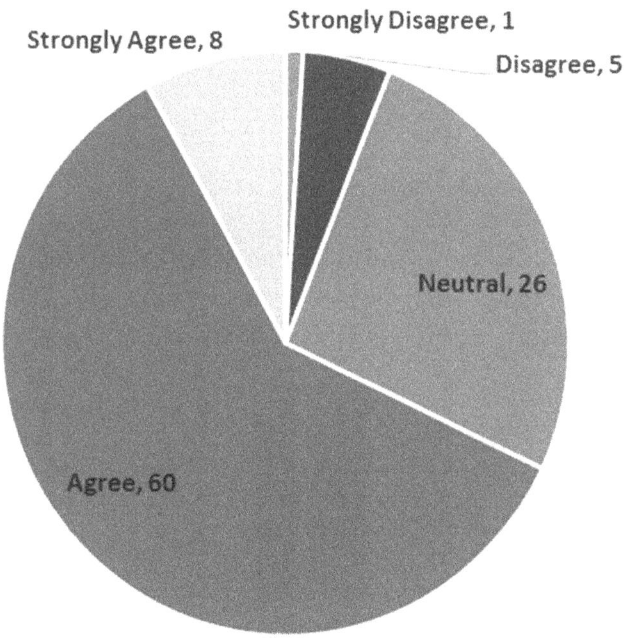

Figure 7.42: SEZ—Impact on Socio-Economic Status

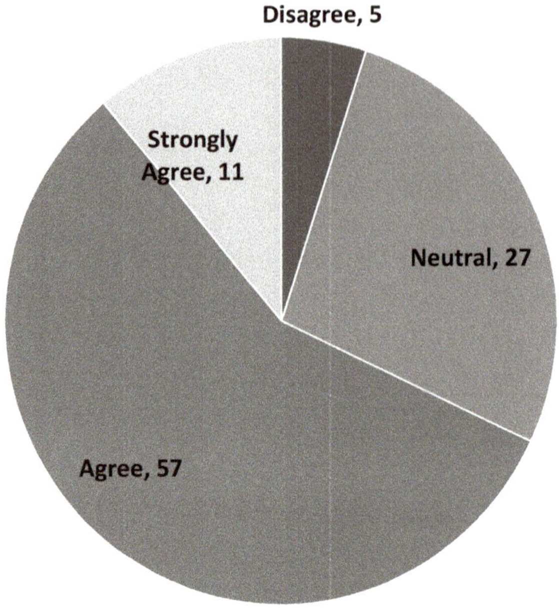

Figure 7.43: Impact of Economic Drivers—SEZ

- Only 5 per cent of the respondents Disagree with the proposition that Economic Divers have positive impact on SEZs.
- Therefore, the evidence is overwhelming that Economic Drivers help in overall growth of SEZs.

7.1.42 Industry-Type Skill Mapping (Q 8.3.1–Q 8.3.4)

- The Service Industry considers that analytical, conceptual and technical skills are very important; the manufacturing and trading industries assign considerably less importance to these skills.

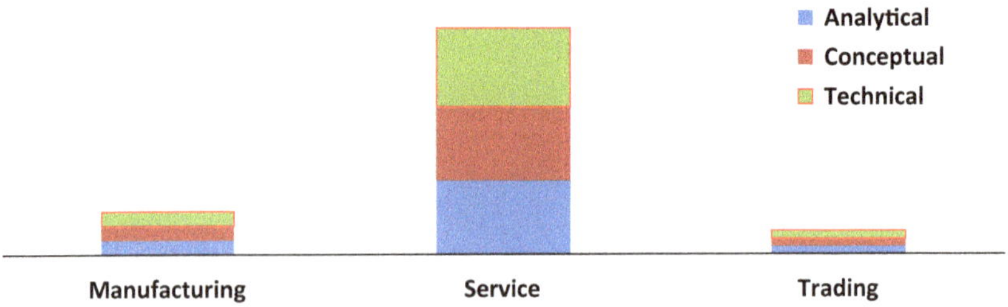

Figure 7.44: Industry Type Skill Mapping

- IT/ITeS services have the major share among service sectors from SEZs. This industry requires employees having high analytical, conceptual and technical skills as per their job assignments.
- Manufacturing and trading industry are mostly labour-intensive industries with most employees in the semi-skilled and unskilled category. Deployment of manpower is largely dependent upon the nature of activity and role to be performed.

Section Nine: Type of Drivers (Q 9.1.1–Q 9.1.10)

7.1.43 Drivers: Impact on SEZs (Q 9.1.1–Q 9.1.10)

- Units Strongly Agree that following Drivers have Impact on SEZs:
  a. Single Window Mechanism
  b. Exports
  c. Infrastructure facility inside SEZs

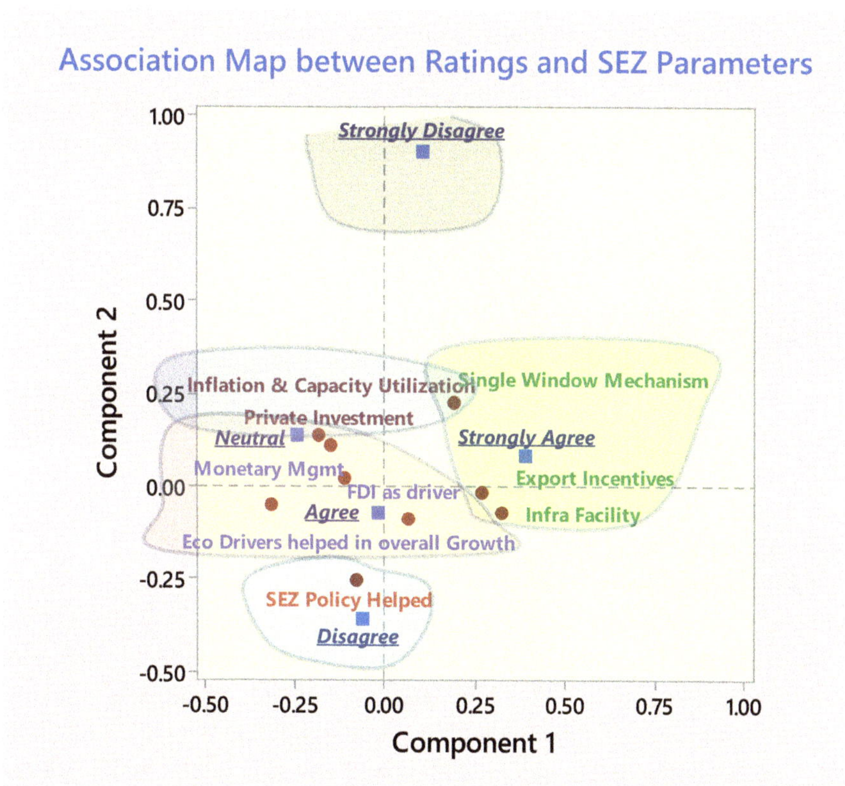

Figure 7.45: Type of Driver—Impact on SEZ

- Units Agree that Economic Drivers helped in overall growth of SEZs.
- Units Disagree that SEZs policy has acted as major driver for Investment and Contribution for India's Economy.
- The units remain neutral on commenting on below drivers:
  a. Monetary Management and Financial Intermediation
  b. Foreign Direct Investment (FDI)
  c. Private Investment
  d. Inflation and Capacity utilization

- There is, therefore, need to make SEZs policy more industry-friendly so that FDI is attracted; this will help in further growth, fill the vacant unused SEZ land and generate more employment.
- The exemption from MAT and DDT may be restored.

7.2 Statistical Analysis of Responses from SEZs Units

7.2.1 Introduction

The statistical analysis is covered in two parts. The first part gives the working of relationship of One Dependent variable with other Independent variables by building up six models to find out the various features, which contribute toward the Socio-Economic Impact in SEZs. The models built are detailed as under:
Models

1. Economic Impact
2. Indirect Economic Impact
3. Housing Impact
4. Other Local Services Impact
5. Social Impact
6. Type of Drivers—Impact on SEZs

These models were tested by following methods:
1. Likelihood Ratio Test

The likelihood ratio method provides a straightforward way to calculate confidence intervals, but could lead to an asymptotic result that may not hold for all situations. Often, likelihood ratio tests are done to decide whether one model fits the data substantially better than another; this is suggested if the ratio between the likelihoods of two models is much larger than one. If the likelihood ratio is significantly larger than one, the larger model is said to be significantly better than the smaller one. From such a result, it is concluded that the parameter, or the group of parameters, that are missing in the smaller model significantly increase the likelihood when they are added to the model, and thus these parameters are declared to be important in explaining the variance of the outcome variable. Likelihood ratio method is more amenable to the non-numerical responses as compared to Pearson analysis which is suitable for the numerical data analysis.

The likelihood ratio test statistic (LRT) is two times the difference in the logarithms of the likelihoods of the two models. Given the null hypothesis that the two models fit the data equally well, and given that the observations are independent, this test statistic follows a χ^2 distribution. However, for testing fixed effects, and when sample size is large, the approximate likelihood ratio test is reliable in practice.

2. Decision Tree Analysis with Entropy Method and Information Gain

Entropy method measures disorder or uncertainty (or measure of purity). The goal of any statistical model is to reduce uncertainty.

Entropy is measured between 0 and 1. (Depending on the number of classes in the dataset, entropy can be greater than 1 but it means the same thing, a very high level of disorder.)

The value of level of disorder is obtained by calculation of entropy through the mathematical equations.

Information Gain

The next step is to find a metric to measure the reduction of this disorder in our target variable/class given additional information (features/independent variables) about it. This is performed through method known as Information Gain by using mathematical equation.

Knowing the value helps to reduce the uncertainty around our target variable.

Decision Tree Analysis

Entropy and Information gain are the two pillars of decision tree analysis. These are used to determine which feature to split their nodes on to get closer to predicting the target variable with each split and also to determine when to stop splitting the tree! (This is in addition to hyper-parameters like maximum depth of course.)

In short, Decision Trees provide an effective method of decision making as they:

- Lay out clearly the problems so that all options can be challenged.
- Permit full analysis of the possible consequences of a decision.

- Provide a framework to quantify the values of outcomes and the probabilities of achieving them.
- Help to make the best decisions on the basis of existing information and best guesses.

The rating of various features arrived from these models importance-wise are also interpreted.

The second and last part of this section covers the Overall model summary showing in order of importance various key features, which contribute towards Socio-Economic Impact of SEZs. The detailed study of above two parts is elaborated later.

7.2.2 Analysis of Different Models

7.2.2.1 **Economic Impact (Q 2.7)**

- The economic impact analysis was carried out on the basis of responses on the important features (Q 2.7.1–Q 2.7.8) by using Likelihood Ratio Method.
- From Table 7.2, eight parameters are ranked in fashion of Important (0.998 to 0.965), Marginal (0.931) and Un-Important (< than 0.3).
- Important (0.998–0.965)
  1. Increase Exports
  2. Increase overall employment
  3. Increase foreign exchange
  4. Improve Infrastructure
  5. Improved demographic pattern

	Rank	Field	...	Importance	
✓	1	Increase Export		Important	0.998
✓	2	Overall Employment		Important	0.998
✓	3	Inc Foreign Exh		Important	0.994
✓	4	Improve Infrastructure		Important	0.971
✓	5	Imp Demographic pattern		Important	0.965
✓	6	Ease Business		Marginal	0.931
	7	Improved Living Std		Unimportant	0.3
	8	Imp Capital Intensive Proj		Unimportant	0.168

Table 7.2: Economic Impact—Important Parameters (Using Likelihood Ratio Analysis)

- Marginal (0.931):
  1. Ease of Business Process
- Unimportant (0.3 and less)
  1. Improved living standards
  2. Improved Capital Intensive projects

- These key parameters ranked "Important" acted as drivers and had a positive Economic Impact in SEZs. These drivers are also in line with the broader objectives of SEZs consisting of contribution to Exports, Investments, Employment and Infrastructure.
- India improved position in the last four years to attain 63rd rank globally as an attractive destination for doing business. Ahmedabad is ranked in the fifth position among Indian cities. There is apparently a gap to be filled in SEZs policy and foreign trade policy; the focus on Ease of Doing Business and Quality of life standards is needed. A greater thrust on non-fiscal benefits for SEZs units may help.

```
Rules for 2 - contains 1 rule(s)
    Rule 1 for 2.0 (8; 0.7)
Rules for 3 - contains 3 rule(s)
    Rule 1 for 3.0 (4; 0.833)
    Rule 2 for 3.0 (6; 0.75)
        if      Inc Foreign Exh in [ 1.000 2.000 3.000 ]
        and     Increase Export in [ 4.000 5.000 ]
        then    3.000
    Rule 3 for 3.0 (30; 0.656)
        if      Improve Infrastructure in [ 1.000 2.000 3.000 ]
        then    3.000
Rules for 4 - contains 3 rule(s)
    Rule 1 for 4.0 (3; 0.8)
        if      Improve Infrastructure in [ 1.000 2.000 3.000 ]
        and     Increase Export in [ 4.000 5.000 ]
        and     Ease Business = 5.000
        then    4.000
    Rule 2 for 4.0 (2; 0.75)
        if      Improve Infrastructure in [ 4.000 5.000 ]
        and     Imp Demographic pattern in [ 4.000 5.000 ]
        and     Increase Export in [ 1.000 2.000 3.000 ]
        then    4.000
    Rule 3 for 4.0 (72; 0.446)
        if      Inc Foreign Exh in [ 4.000 5.000 ]
        then    4.000
```

Figure 7.46: Combination of Inputs for Higher SEZ Impact on Local Economy

- Figure 7.46 represents the logic with mathematical equations (entropy method) using combination of Inputs for Higher Impact of SEZs on local economy.
- Figure 7.47 depicts the Decision Tree analysis of combination of Inputs for higher SEZ impact on local economy.

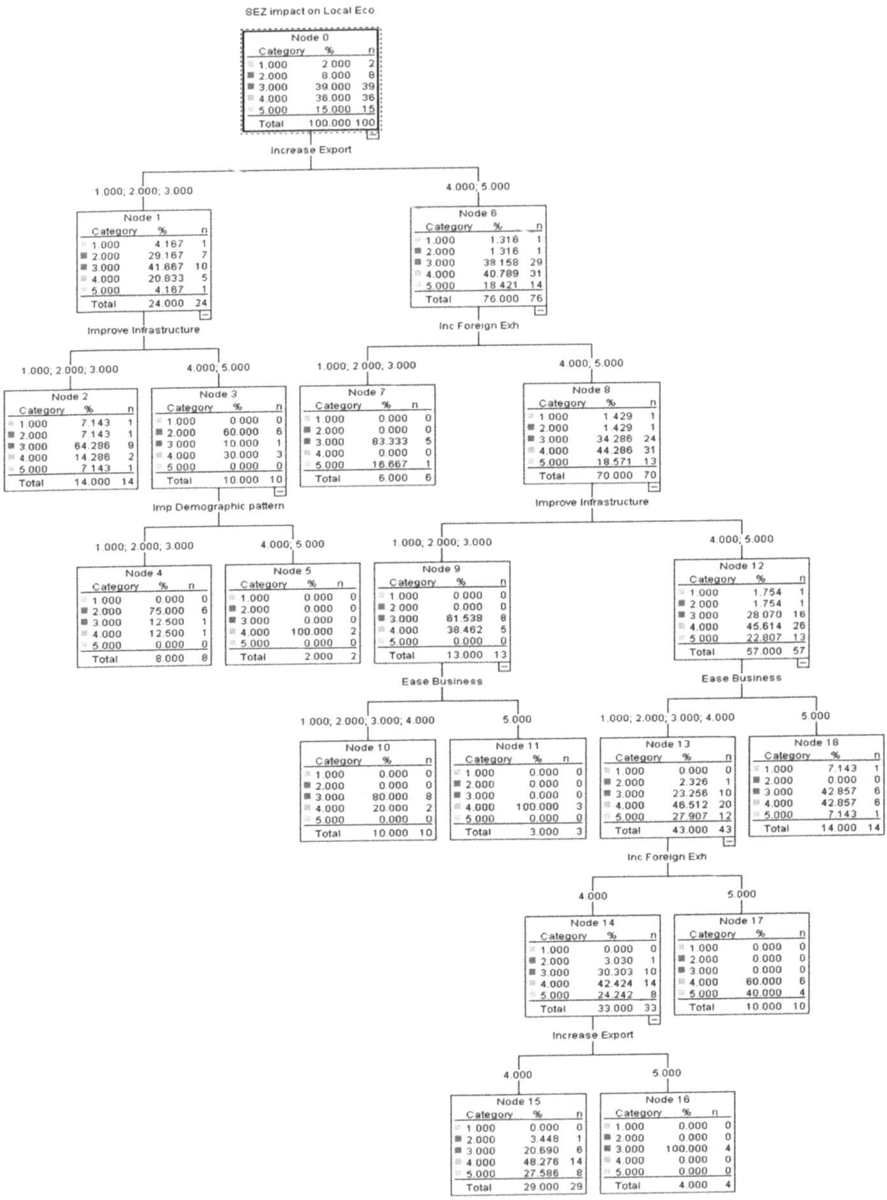

Figure 7.47: Combination of Inputs for Higher SEZ Impact on Local Economy

- The conclusion is that the following inputs have boosted the local economy from SEZs:
  1. Increased exports
  2. Increased overall employment
  3. Increased foreign exchange
  4. Improved infrastructure
  5. Improved demographic pattern
  6. Ease of doing business

7.2.2.2 **Indirect Economic Impact (Q 3.4.–Q 3.6)**

- Table 7.3 reveals that the establishment of SEZs leads to multiplier effects with other parameters by using the Likelihood Ratio analysis.
- The Figure 7.48 gives the pictorial representation of select important features with colour fill corresponding to the percentage.

	Rank	Field	Measurement	Importance	Value
✓	1	Q_3_3_4_5	Ordinal	Import...	1.0
✓	2	Q_3_3_4_1	Ordinal	Import...	0.999
✓	3	Q_3_3_4_3	Ordinal	Import...	0.995
✓	4	Q_3_3_4_4	Ordinal	Import...	0.986
	5	Q_3_6	Ordinal	Unimp...	0.844
	6	Q_3_5	Ordinal	Unimp...	0.664

Table 7.3: Likelihood Ratio Method to Select Important Features (Indirect Economic)

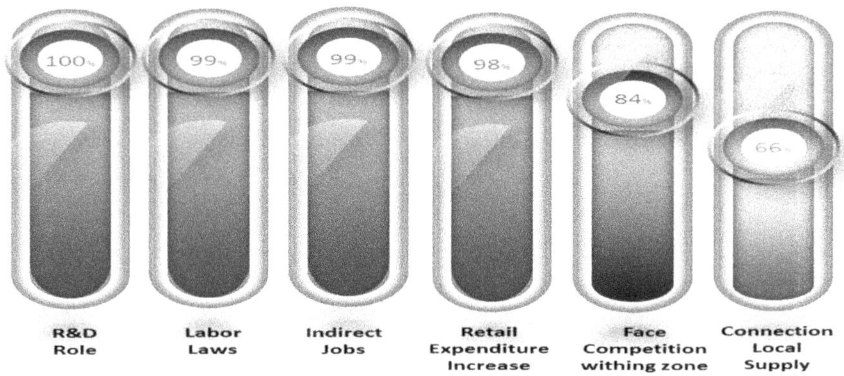

Figure 7.48: Indirect Economic Impact—Important Features

- The Important (1–0.98) four features impacting Indirect economic are ranked as under:
  1. Role of R&D
  2. Labour issues/Laws
  3. Indirect and induced jobs
  4. Increase in retail expenditure
- These four features are very important for Indirect Economic Impact, while competition within the zone (0.84) and connected local supplies (DTA) (0.664) have comparatively less important or unimportant role to play.
- Units agree that improving the role of R&D activities is important. Mandatory common R&D facility may be set up in each SEZ. Labour reforms may be ushered in through changes to existing labour laws.
- Indirect and induced jobs and increase in retail expenditure by unit workers are some of the other contributions to indirect economy.
- SEZs policies may be modified to mandate supplies of goods and services from DTA to protect domestic industry and also to promote the growth of MSME segment.
- Figure 7.49 represents the logic with mathematical equations (entropy method) with combination of inputs for higher indirect economic impact.

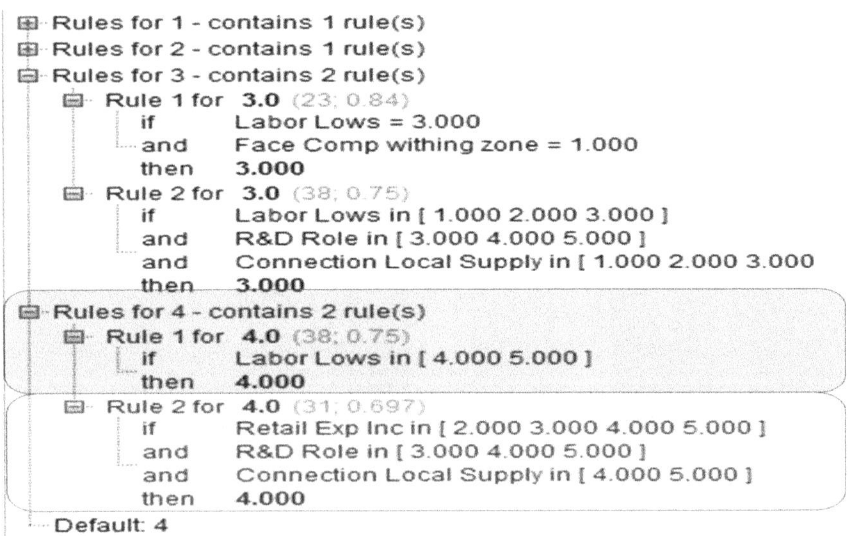

Figure 7.49: Combination of Inputs for Indirect Economic Impact

- Figure 7.50 gives the Decision Tree analysis of combination of Inputs for Higher Indirect economic impact.
- It supplements the interpretation as mentioned in Figure 7.49.

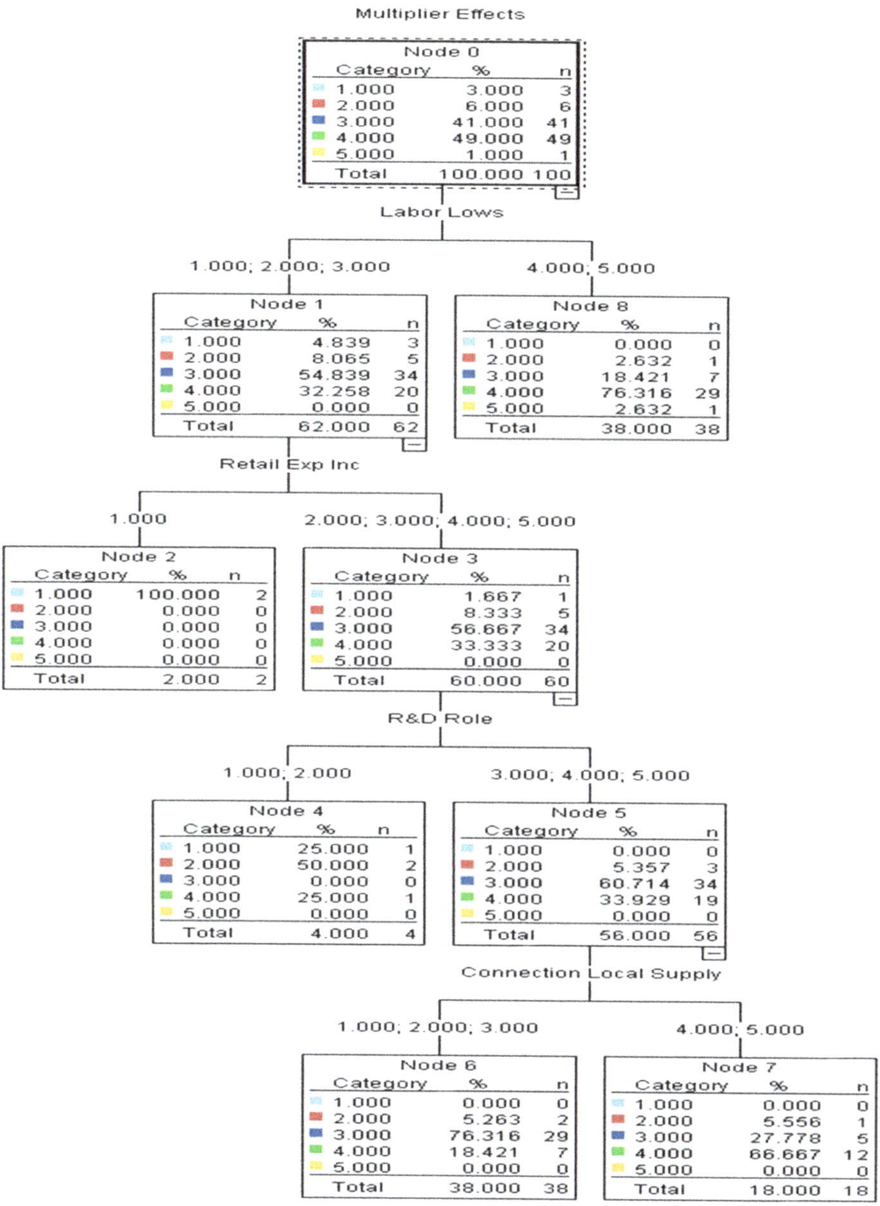

Figure 7.50: Combination of Inputs for Indirect Economic Impact

7.2.2.3 **Housing Impact (Q 5.2.1–Q 5.2.7)**

- Table 7.4 reflects the relation of Housing settlement nearby SEZs are cosmopolitan with other parameters by using the Likelihood Ratio analysis for the Housing impact.
- The important (1–0.98) three **features** impacting Housing Impact are ranked as under:
  1. Non-processing area for housing purpose
  2. Dedicated Hostel for women
  3. Separate dormitory for employees

- These three features are very important, while Residence within the zone (0.91) has marginal impact and Renting House nearby SEZs is difficult (0.80) and Slum area near the zone (0.681) are comparatively less important or unimportant.
- The SEZ policy permits dual usage of non-processing area for administrative (office) use or for non-administrative uses like educational institutions, residential complexes, hospitals; the developer (stakeholder) should compulsorily make use of the non-processing areas for such activities especially dedicated hostel for women and dormitory, for boosting social growth.
- Figure 7.51 represents the logic with mathematical equations (entropy method) for combination of Inputs for Housing.
- Figure 7.52 shows the Decision Tree analysis of combination of Inputs for Housing.

		Field	...	Importance	
✔	1	Non Processing Area for Housing		Important	0.997
✔	2	Hostel for Women		Important	0.99
✔	3	Dormitory		Important	0.987
☐	4	Res Comp Inside		Marginal	0.911
☐	5	Renting Difficult		Unimportant	0.803
☐	6	Slum Area		Unimportant	0.681

Table 7.4: Likelihood Ratio Method to Select Important Features (Housing)

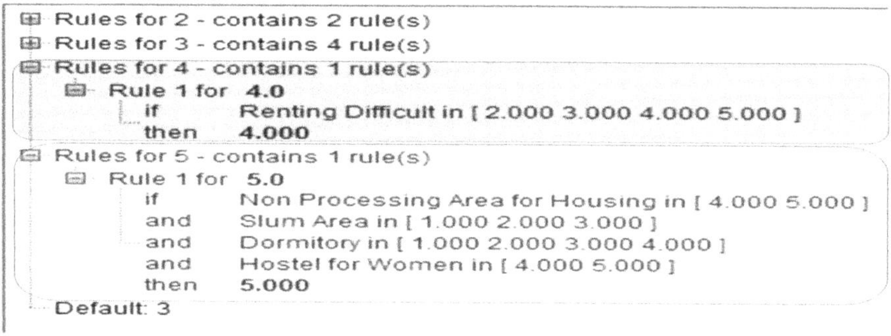

Figure 7.51: Combination of Inputs for Housing

7.2.2.4 **Other Local Services Impact (Q 6)**

- Table 7.5 reflects the relation of social schemes for employees of SEZs with other parameters by using the Likelihood Ratio analysis to select the important features for Other Local Services Impact.
- Seven important (1–0.95) features impacting Other Local Services Impact are ranked as under:
  1. Health Insurance Schemes
  2. Pick-up and drop facility
  3. Fire protection for life security
  4. Provision of in-house loan
  5. Dedicated medical room—OPD Clinic
  6. Women employees safety measures
  7. Educational loan or other education schemes
- While the features of Other Local Services Impact listed above are important, canteen facility (0.91) has marginal impact and gymnasium (0.89) and education institutional facility (0.778) have comparatively less importance or no importance.
- Though SEZs support some of the above features as a matter of policy, government could mandate certain requirements and facilities such as dedicated fire brigade stations, group health insurance schemes for all categories of workers, transportation facilities for employees, medical room/clinic, educational schemes, women safety measures and common canteen facilities. This will not only protect life and security of employees but also help to fulfil the social objectives and improve the quality of life.

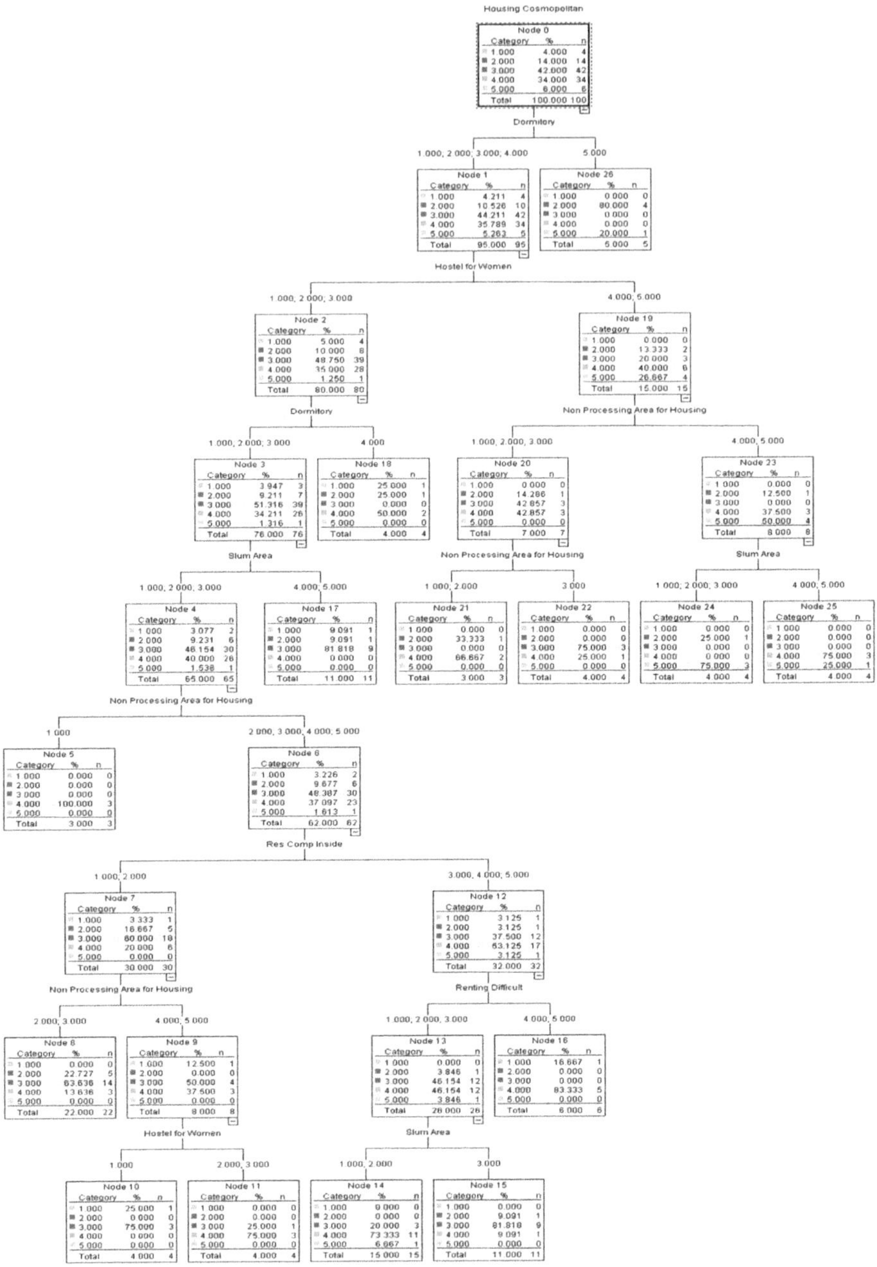

Figure 7.52: Combination of Inputs for Housing

	...	Field	...	Importance	
✓	1	Health Ins		Important	1.0
✓	2	Pick-up		Important	0.994
✓	3	Fire Protection		Important	0.983
✓	4	In-house loan		Important	0.978
✓	5	Medical Room		Important	0.972
✓	6	Women Safety		Important	0.968
✓	7	Edu Loan		Important	0.951
	8	Canteen Facility		Marginal	0.919
	9	Gymnasium		Unimportant	0.89
	...	Edu Institution		Unimportant	0.778

Table 7.5: Important Features—Other Local Services Impact (Using Likelihood Ratio Method)

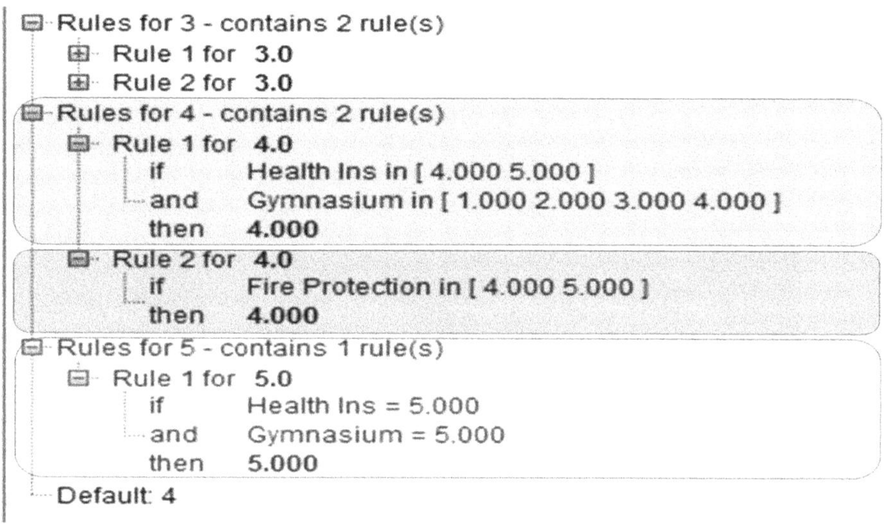

Figure 7.53: Combination of Inputs for Other Local Services

- Figure 7.53 represents the logic with mathematical equations (entropy method) with combination of Inputs for Other Local Services.
- Figure 7.54 shows the Decision Tree analysis of combination of Inputs for Other Local Services.

7.2.2.5 **Social Impact (Q 7)**

- Table 7.6 reflects the correlation of SEZs contribution towards social objectives with other parameters by using the Likelihood Ratio analysis to select the important features for Social Impact.

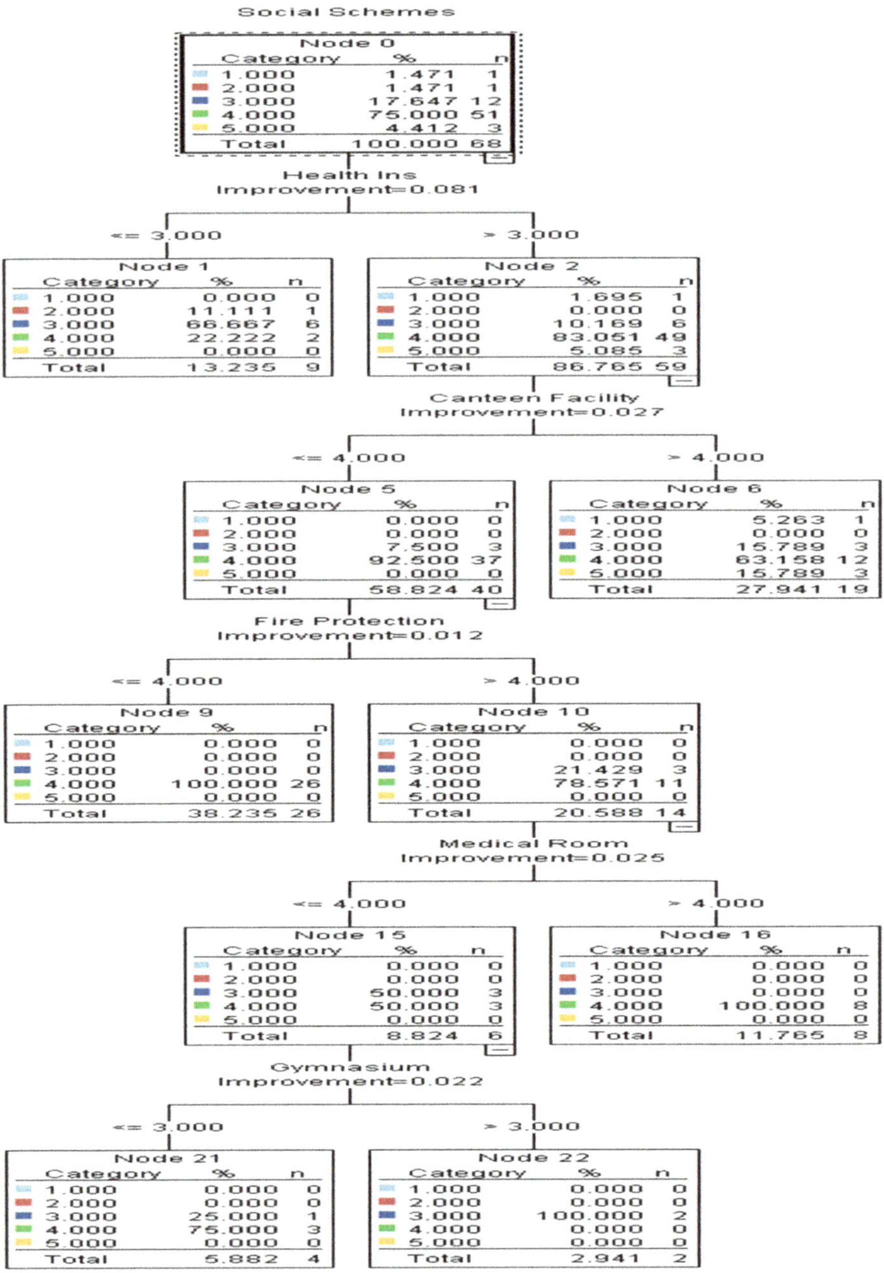

Figure 7.54: Combination of Inputs for Other Local Services

	.	Field	...	Importance	
✓	1	Min Wages		Important	1.0
✓	2	Tackling Social Problems		Important	1.0
✓	3	Promote Marginalized Comm		Important	1.0
✓	4	Reduce Comm Stress		Important	1.0
✓	5	Quality of Life		Important	1.0
✓	6	Women Empowerment		Important	1.0
✓	7	Regional Inequalities		Important	1.0

Table 7.6: Important Features- Social Impact (Using Likelihood Ratio Method)

- The selected features have been found to be statistically important showing value of maximum 1 and in percentage (100 per cent) seven features impacting Social Impact. They are ranked as under:
  1. Protection of Minimum wage, working hours and gender equality
  2. SEZ's positive role in tackling social problems
  3. Promoting women from marginalized community
  4. Reduced community stress
  5. Impact quality of life positively
  6. Promote women employment and empowerment
  7. Reduce regional inequalities
- Thus, SEZs have social impact and contribute substantially towards social objectives.
- SEZs have helped in promoting women employment and empowerment and currently roughly 50 per cent of employees in SEZs units are female globally.
- Government of India may promote dedicated SEZs for only women and MSME and for the members of marginalized community at par with South Africa policy for black economic empowerment (BEE). This will further boost women empowerment through employment and will also help in improving the quality of life.
- SEZs have contributed to some extent in tackling social problems and reducing regional inequalities.
- Figure 7.55 represents the logic with mathematical equations (entropy method) with combination of Inputs for Social Impacts.

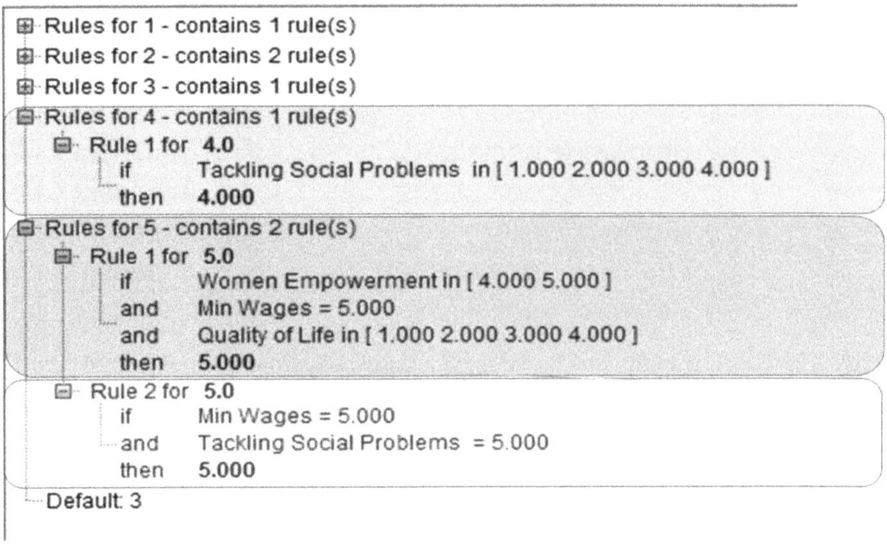

Figure 7.55: Combination of Inputs for Social Impact

- Figure 7.56 shows the Decision Tree analysis of combination of Inputs for Social Impact.

7.2.2.6 **Type of Drivers: Impact on SEZs (Q 9)**

- Table 7.7 reflects the relationship of Role of Economic drivers in overall growth of SEZs (dependent variable) with other parameters (Independent variables) by using the Likelihood Ratio analysis to select the important features for Type of Drivers and their Impact on SEZs.
- The selected features found to be statistically important showing value of (1.0–0.968) drivers impacting SEZs are ranked as under:
  1. Investment and contribution for India's economy
  2. Logistics facilities
  3. Export-incentives scheme
  4. Improved infrastructure facility
  5. Single Window Mechanism
  6. Foreign Direct Investment (FDI)
  7. Private Investments
  8. Inflation and Capacity Utilization

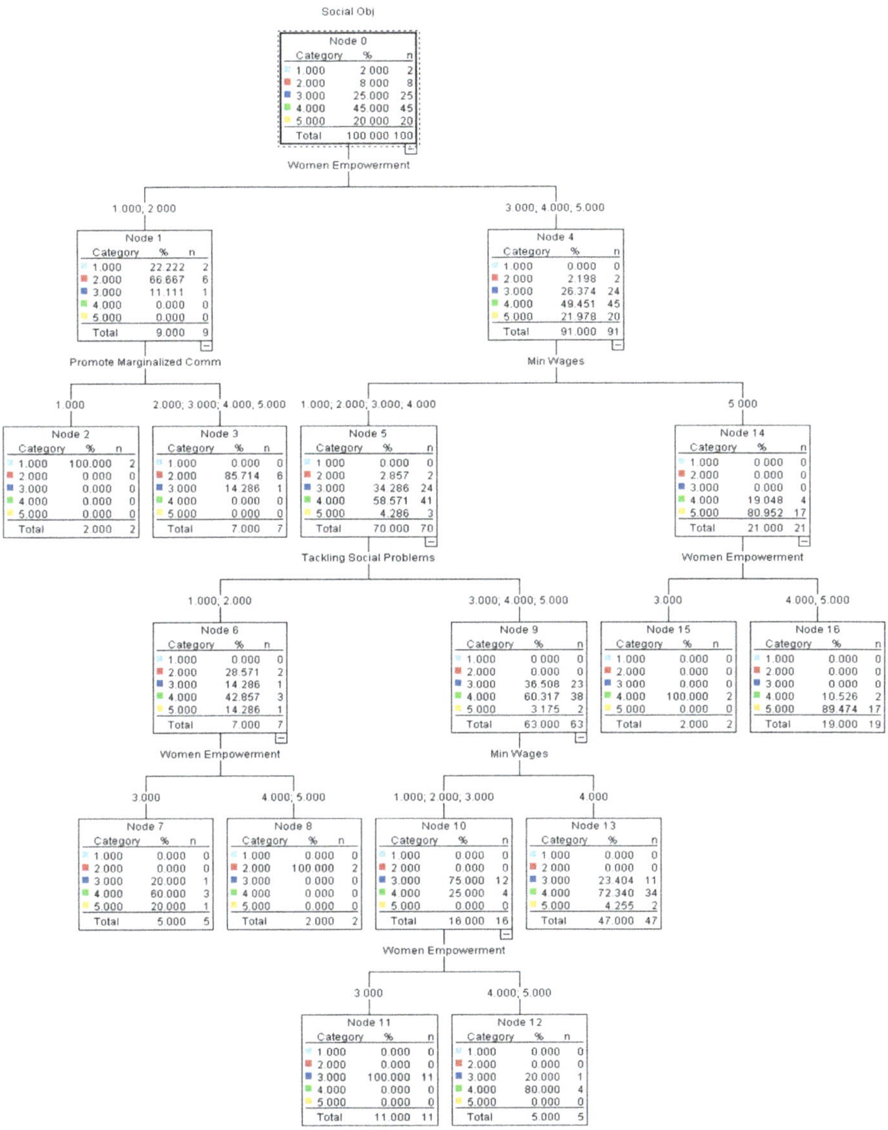

Figure 7.56: Combination of Inputs for Social Impact

- The drivers ranked (Nos. 1–8) are very important; they have positive impact on SEZs growth and development. Monetary management feature (0.831) is unimportant.
- SEZ policy does support the above features strongly. Monetary Management policy may need to be designed for SEZs.

	...	Field	...	Importance	
✓	1	Investment to India Eco		Important	1.0
✓	2	Logistics		Important	1.0
✓	3	Export Incentives		Important	1.0
✓	4	Improved Infrastructure		Important	1.0
✓	5	Single Window		Important	0.994
✓	6	FDI		Important	0.991
✓	7	Private Investment		Important	0.973
✓	8	Inflation & Capacity Uti		Important	0.968
	9	Monetary Management		Unimportant	0.831

Table 7.7: Type of Drivers—Impact on SEZs (Using Likelihood Ratio Method)

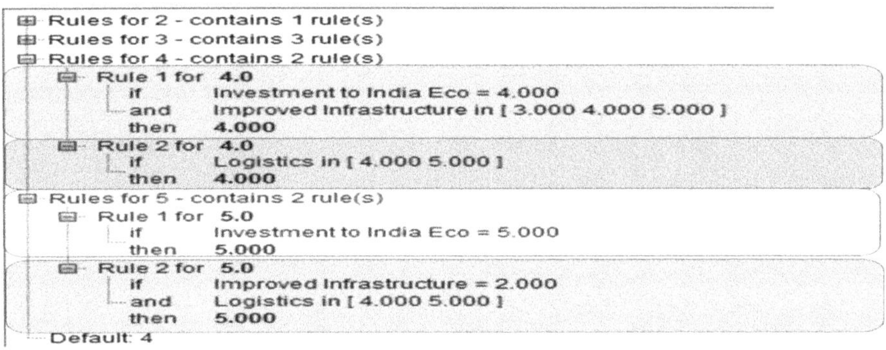

Figure 7.57: Combination of Inputs for Type of Drivers—Impact on SEZ

- Figure 7.57 represents the logic with mathematical equations (entropy method) with combination of Inputs for Type of Drivers—Impact on SEZs.
- Figure 7.58 shows the Decision Tree analysis of combination of Inputs for Type of Drivers—Impact on SEZs.

7.2.3 Models Summary

- From Table 7.8, the model reveals 87 per cent accuracy; this is relatively good for data largely compiled on Likert scale.

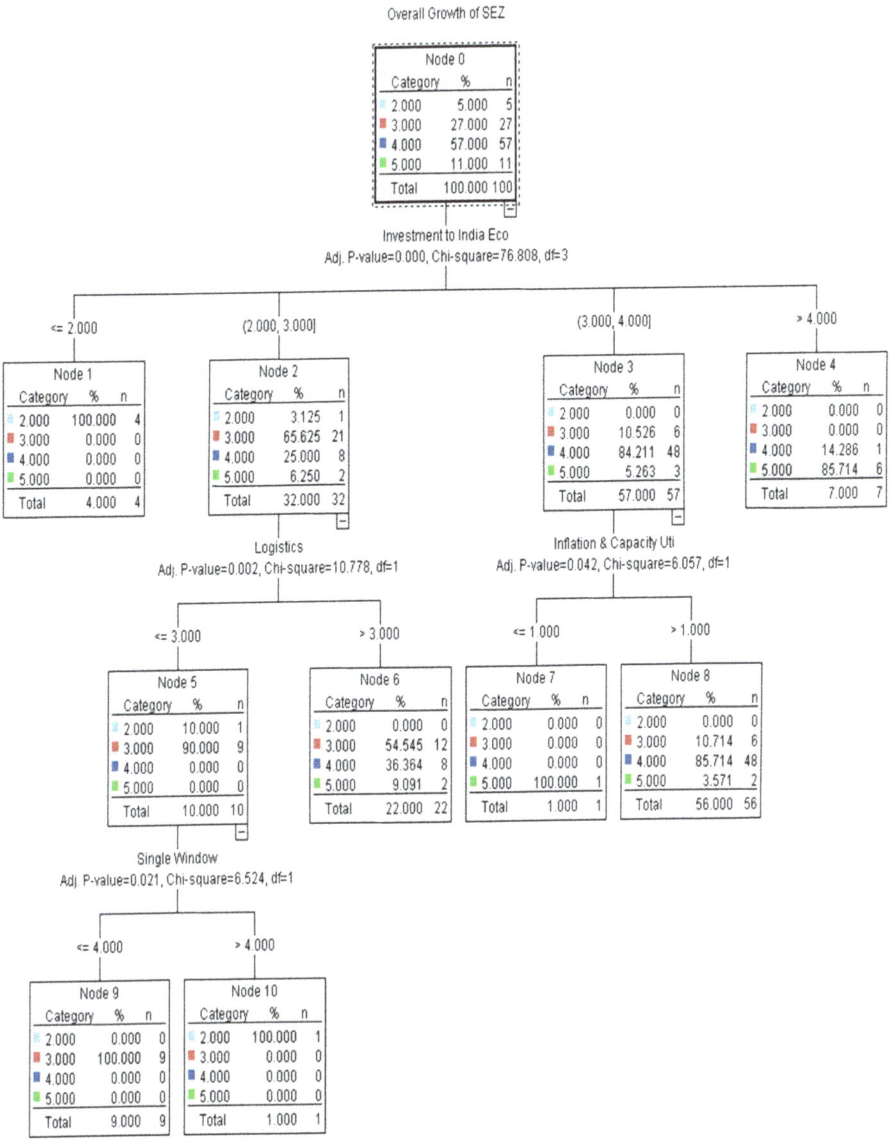

Figure 7.58: Combination of Inputs for Type of Drivers—Impact on SEZ

- With the help of neural network-based model, the important factors could be identified. The "Socio-Economic question" is considered as output variable, while all other questions as input variables.

Model Summary

Target	SEZ Impact on Socio-Economic
Model	Multilayer Perceptron
Stopping Rule Used	Error cannot be further decreased
Hidden Layer 1 Neurons	13

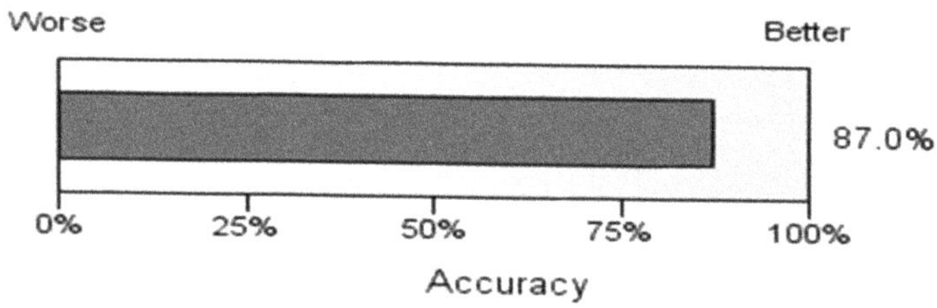

Table 7.8: Models Summary

- The "Sum of square errors" is sought to be minimized by arranging different weights to input variables and perceptron's on hidden layers during numerous iterations.
- Through this model, important factors can be determined. A prediction model can be developed where if the answers are supplied to all input variables, then the model will predict the response to output variable.

7.2.4 Network

- The multilayer Perceptron Neuron Network graph is shown in Figure 7.59.

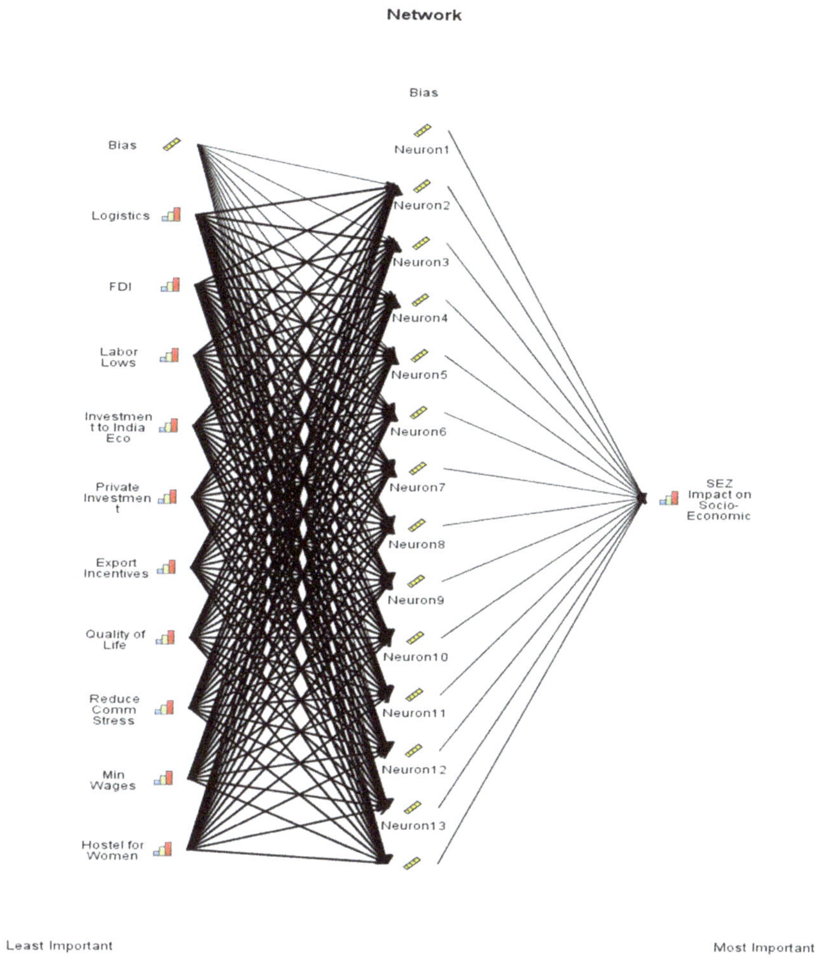

Figure 7.59: Graph of the Multilayer Perceptron Network

7.2.5 Importance of Socio-Economic Factors

- Figure 7.60 shows the Importance of Socio-Economic factors. These 22 factors are categorized in 6 groups and listed in the later chapter.
- The SEZs policy, as well as the policies of the state government, supports the factors depicted in Figure 7.60.
- Figure 7.61 represents the logic with mathematical equations (entropy method) with combination of Inputs for Overall Model—Impact of SEZ on socio-economic factors.
- Figure 7.62 shows the Decision Tree analysis of combination of Inputs for Overall Model—Impact of SEZ on socio-economic factors.

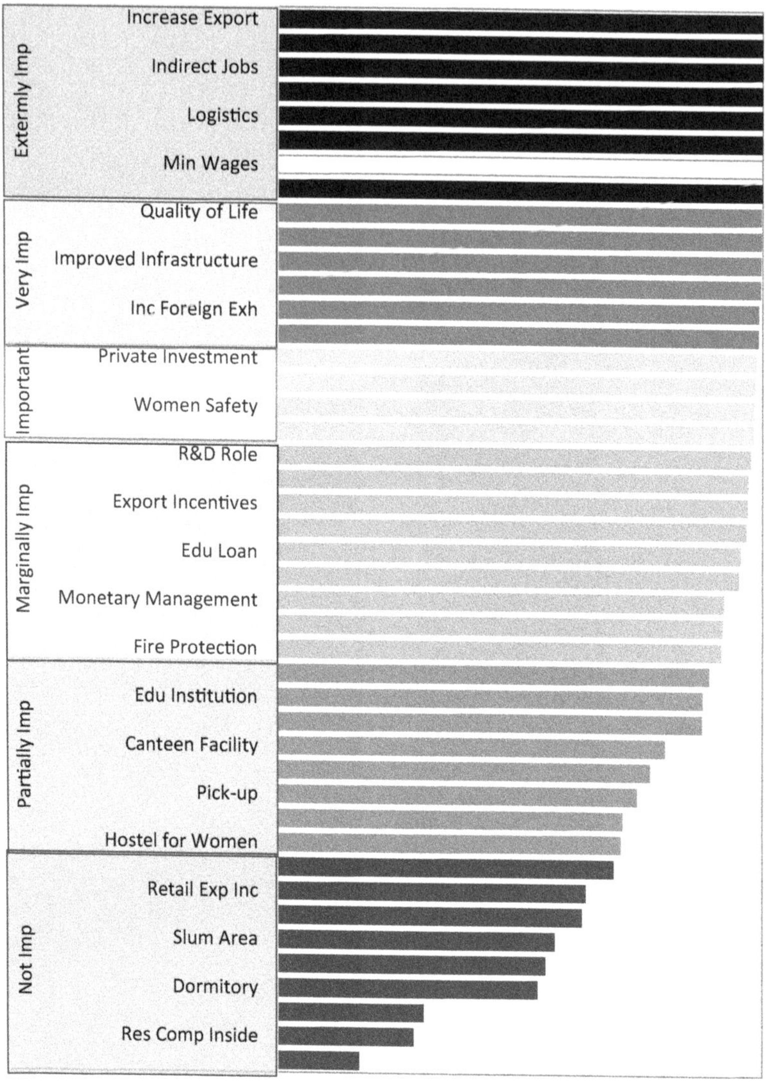

Figure 7.60: Importance of Socio-Economic Factors

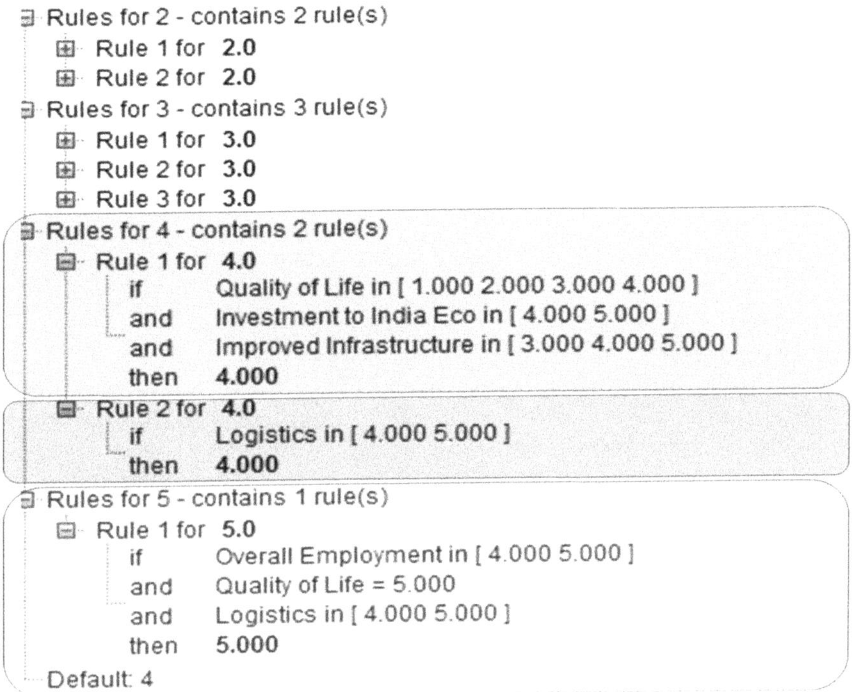

Figure 7.61: Combination of Inputs for Overall Model—Impact of SEZ on Socio-Economic Factors

7.2.6 Final Model

- Figures 7.63 and 7.64 depict the summary of models as explained in this section. The individual models were analysed and as per the statistical results, following factors are important for the socio-economic impact on SEZs;
  1. Economic factors
  2. Social factors
  3. Indirect economic factors
  4. Other local factors
  5. Housing factors

- Thus, it is derived that SEZs have both economic (both direct and indirect economic) and social impact. Overall, SEZs have a positive socio-economic impact.
- Other local factors and housing factors were ranked comparatively with less importance, which may require attention of the authorities.

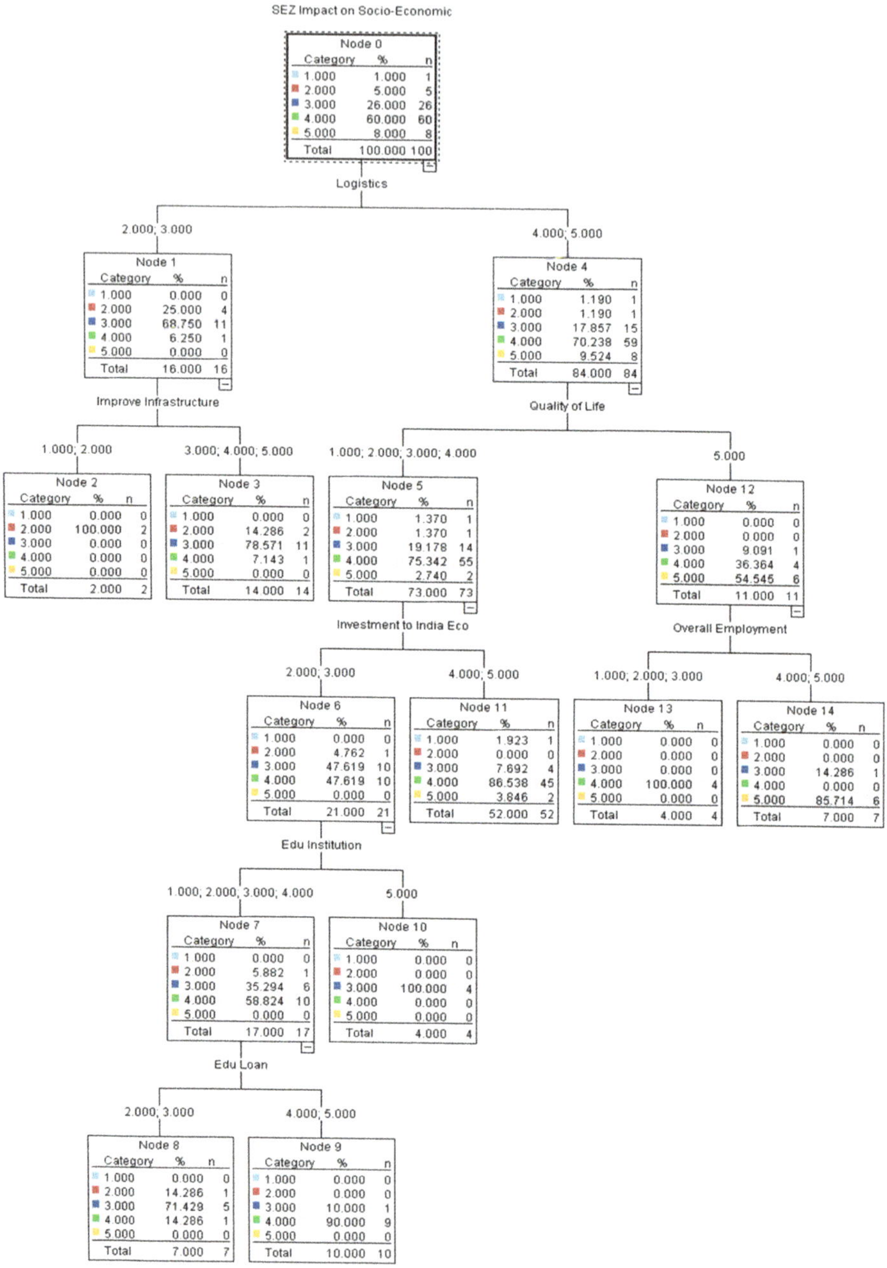

Figure 7.62: Combination of Inputs for Overall Model—Impact of SEZ on Socio-Economic Factors

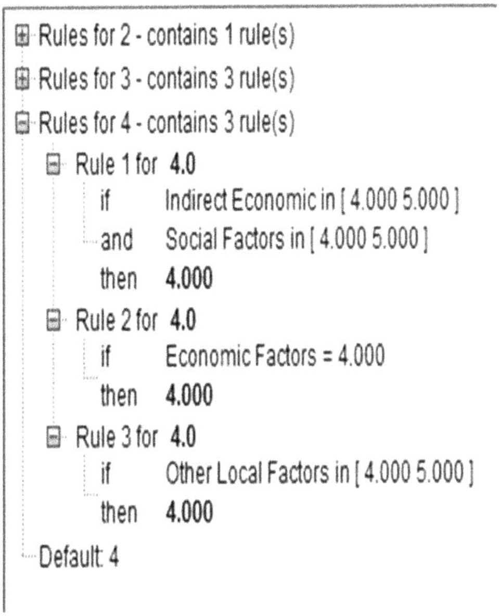

Figure 7.63: Final Model

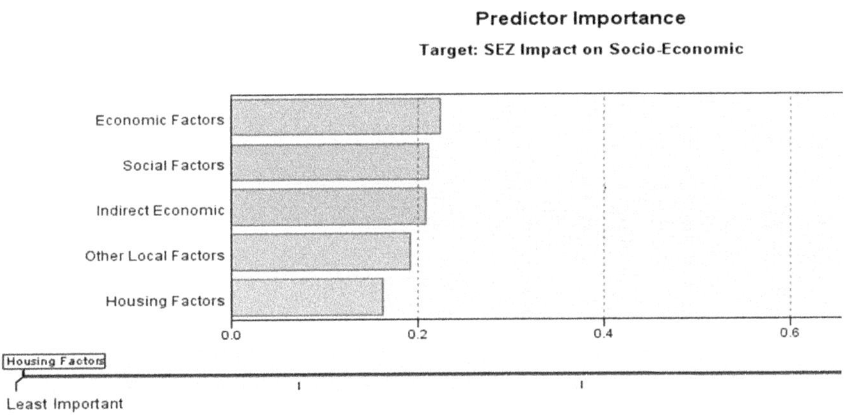

Figure 7.64: Final Model

Segment II Socio-Economic Impact of SEZs in Gujarat: From the Perspective of Developers

7.3 Analysis of Responses from the Developers (Descriptive and Statistical)

7.3.1 Introduction

At the apex of the SEZ's architecture scats, the Development Authority on behalf of the Union Ministry of Commerce, government of India with the mandate of development and administration. The next tier in many of the SEZs comprises of a developer or co-developer, who dons the mantle of the promoter or owner of the SEZ. The developer leases parcels of land to the unit holders for long-term tenures and collects rent from them at the rates notified by the Development Authority. The developer or a related entity could also be a unit holder in the same SEZ, for example, Zydus Infrastructure is the developer and Zydus Cadila (related entity) is one of the unit holders in the Zydus SEZ.

The guidelines issued by the government of India through Instruction No. 65 of 27 October 2010 (Ref no. F.No.D-1/19/2009/SEZ) elaborate on the role of a developer of a SEZ right from the stage of Site Identification to the Development Plan and Physical Infrastructure. The onus of the development of the SEZ both for economic facilities and social infrastructure is laid squarely on the shoulders of the developer. The developer bifurcates the area allotted to the SEZ into the operational part (processing area) for the business activities with highly restricted access and the non-operational part (non-processing area) with relatively open access for creating the social infrastructure necessary for the direct and indirect employees. The emphasis is on creation of facilities such as industrial training centres, ITI's (Industrial Training Institutes), vocational training programmes and other such community development programmes. The guidelines also detail on the physical infrastructure to be provided consisting of external connectivity, water supply, drainage, sewerage, solid waste management, power supply, medical and food facility, housing including low-cost housing. The developer is also required to work with the state government for the regional development, promote MSMEs and provide low-cost housing for the economically weak and low-cost food for dormitory residents.

Thus, in the scheme of socio-economic development and impact of SEZs, the developer holds the key.

7.3.2 Data Collection

For the purpose of field research, a questionnaire (Appendix 2.B) was addressed to the five developers of the six SEZs selected for the study. As mentioned earlier, in the Research Methodology Chapter, the number of developers is only five as two of the selected SEZs, namely the Electronic Park and the Apparel Park have a common developer namely GIDC. The questionnaire was followed up with telephonic interview or personal interview with the CEO of the developer.

The questionnaire addressed to the developers consists of seven sections with different scope of information. Sections one, three and six are specific in nature and individual responses are detailed. Sections two, four, five and seven solicit the opinion of the respondent on socio-economic impact of SEZs and the responses are tabulated to arrive at the modal choice. A brief on the various parts of the questionnaire is sketched below:

1. General Information (Q 1.1–Q 1.6)
2. SEZs—Business model analysis (Q 2.1–Q 2.2)
3. Socio-economic development indicators (Q 3)
4. Social impact (Q 4.1–Q 4.4)
5. Economic impact (Q 5.1–Q 5.3)
6. Corporate responsibility (Q 6.1–Q 6.6)
7. Micro, Small and Medium Size Business (MSME) (Q 7.1–Q 7.4)

The views of each developer on the three specific topics (Sections One, Three and Six) are listed first, followed by summary in tabular form and the consensual views of the developers on the general topics.

Section One: General Information (Q 1.1–Q 1.6)

7.3.3 SEZ Developer 1 (SEZD1)

SEZD1 notified in 2006 (further notification for increased area issued in 2010 and 2011) with land of 1,682.65 hectares is one of the larger multi-products SEZs with 55 units and 6,232 direct employees (total direct and indirect employees 14,400 persons). The ownership pattern consists of joint venture between ONGC (a central government enterprise) and GIDC (a state government undertaking). It has recorded impressive growth in export turnover from $511 million in 2016–2017 to $724 million in 2017–2018 (40 per cent) and to $1,118 million in 2018–2019 (54 per cent).

In respect of the five socio-economic development indicators, SEZD1 has ranked Demographic and other Local Services as "Very Good" and all others namely, Direct Economic, Indirect/wider economic and Housing as "Good" (Table 7.9). In the course of discussions, the CEO, who filled in the questionnaire, reiterated his strong belief in the importance of the demography and provision of local services like health services, social support as the prime movers for the socio-economic development of the SEZ.

Table 7.9: Socio-Economic Development Indicators (Q 3)

Factors	SEZD1	SEZD2	SEZD3	SEZD4	SEZD5
Direct economic (local and non-local employment/skill group and training)	G	VG	P	VG	O
Indirect /wider economic/ expenditure (employees' retail expenditure/ linked suppliers to main development/labour market pressures/wider multiplier effects)	G	VG	A	O	A
Demographic changes in population size (temporary and permanent)/changes in other population characteristics (e.g. family size, income levels, socio-economic groups)	VG	G	VG	O	P
Housing (various housing tenure types—public and private/house prices/homelessness and other housing problems)	G	G	G	P	G
Other Local Services public and private sector educational services/health services/social support/others (e.g. police, fire, recreation, transport/local finances)	VG	VG	O	VG	VG

(G = GOOD; VG = VERY GOOD; P = POOR; O = Outstanding; A = Average; N.R. = No Response)

Table 7.10: Corporate Responsibility (Q 6.2)

Sr. No	Activity	SEZD1	SEZD2	SEZ D3	SEZD4	SEZD5
1	Promotion of education	VG	VG	G	O	NR
2	Promoting gender equality and empowering women	G	VG	VG	VG	NR
3	Health Care Services	VG	VG	VG	VG	NR
4	Ensuring environmental sustainability,	A	VG	O	VG	NR
5	Employment enhancing vocational skills, social business projects.	A	G	G	P	NR
6	Sports/Yoga/Cultural Activities etc.	A	G	A	O	NR
7	Welfare activities for SC/ST/OBC/Minority	A	NR	G	P	NR

(G = GOOD; VG = VERY GOOD; P = POOR; O = Outstanding; A = Average; N.R. = No Response)

SEZD1 has replied in the affirmative regarding applicability of CSR. From the CSR activities listed, the respondent has ranked the "Promotion of Education" and "Health Care Services" as "Very Good"; "Promotion of gender equality and empowering women" as "Good"; the remaining three activities have been ranked "Average" (Table 7.10). The priority is given to education, health followed by women empowerment and others.

For the environmental sustainability issues, "Very Good" ranking has been allotted to "Water contamination", "Air pollution" and "Land degradation" and "Average" to the remaining two issues (Table 7.11).

The respondent agrees that government policies are in place for environmental protection. The respondent disagrees that the infrastructure and other assistance is provided by government for safeguarding the environment (Table 7.12).

On the suggestions regarding new opportunities for utilization of vacant land, SEZD1 ranked the development of residential complex and change from single to multi-product as "Very Good"; the diversion to domestic industries as "Good" and others as "Average" (Table 7.13).

Table 7.11: Environmental Sustainability (Q 6.3)

Sr. No	Factors	SEZD1	SEZD 2	SEZD3	SEZD4	SEZD5
1	Water contamination/ waste water disposal	VG	P	G	P	O
2	Air pollution	VG	P	G	VG	O
3	Land degradation	VG	P	G	P	O
4	Sound pollution	A	P	G	P	O
5	Conservation of Indigenous Fauna	A	A	G	G	O

(G = GOOD; VG = VERY GOOD; P = POOR; O = Outstanding; A = Average N.R. = No Response)

Table 7.12: Government Policies—Environment

Sr. No.	Factors	SEZD1	SEZD2	SEZD3	SEZD4	SEZD5
1	Government policies in place for environment protection	A	A	A	N	A
2	The infrastructure and other assistance is provided by government for safeguarding the environment	DA	A	A	N	DA

(A = AGREE; DA = DISAGREE; NR = NO RESPONSE; N = NEUTRAL; SA = STRONGLY AGREE)

Finally, on the open-ended question regarding methods for evaluation of SEZ opportunities, the respondent opined that there should be monitoring of each SEZ on weekly basis.

7.3.4 SEZ Developer 2 (SEZD2)

SEZD2 notified in 2006 (further notification for increased area issued on 04.09.2017) has a land area of 114 hectares. It's a sector-specific (pharmaceuticals) SEZ with 12 units and 5,689 direct employees. The SEZ is 100 per cent privately owned. The export turnover has increased from $28.86 million in 2016–2017 to

Table 7.13: Vacant Land Utilization

Sr. No	Parameters	SEZD1	SEZD2	SEZD3	SEZD4	SEZD5
1	Develop Residential Complex/malls/other infrastructure, etc.	VG	P	NR	G	NR
2	Divert to Domestic industries	G	A	NR	VG	NR
3	Change from single to Multi-product	VG	VG	G	O	NR
4	Dedicated Service Sector	A	A	G	VG	NR
5	Priority to MSME	A	G	G	O	NR
6	Sectoral broad banding	A	VG	G	VG	NR

(G = GOOD; VG = VERY GOOD; P = POOR; O = Outstanding; A = Average; NR = No Response)

$36.30 million in 2017–2018 (35.3 per cent) and to $44.86 million in 2018–2019 (23.6 per cent).

SEZD2 has ranked Direct Economic, Indirect/wider economic and other Local Services as "Very Good" and others namely, Demographic and Housing as "Good" (Table 7.9).

The CEO who supervised the answers in the questionnaire was of the opinion that the prime driver of the SEZ is economic and other matters follow. For the success of the SEZ, tapping the local services including talent pool and nurturing of the same are important aspects; considering that pharmaceutical manufacture requires skilled manpower; the importance of pharmacy education centres cannot be over-stressed.

CSR is applicable for SEZD2. Four of the seven CSR activities listed have secured "Very Good" ranking showing the importance of these activities. Sports, yoga/cultural activities and employment enhancing vocational skills have been assigned "Good" ranking reflecting the priority for the developer (Table 7.10).

Environment faces a threat from the pharmaceutical industry in that many of the raw materials can contaminate the water and soil. The waste products of the pharmaceuticals industry need to be treated before they are released. As such, it is intriguing that the developer ranks almost all the environmental sustainability issues as "Poor" except for conservation of indigenous fauna which is ranked as "Average" (Table 7.11).

The respondent agrees that government policies are in place for environmental protection and that the infrastructure and other assistance are provided by government for safeguarding the environment (Table 7.12).

SEZD2 assigns "Very Good" ranking for the change from single to multi-product and sectoral broad banding as the new opportunities for utilization of vacant land. Priority to MSME is ranked as "Good" on this score. The proposal to divert to domestic industries and dedicated service sector does not appeal to the developer securing only "Average" ranking. The idea of developing residential complexes for utilizing vacant land is rejected with "Poor" ranking (Table 7.13).

The respondent has opted not to answer the open-ended question regarding methods for evaluation of SEZ opportunities.

7.3.5 SEZ Developer 3 (SEZD3)

SEZD3 notified on 27.06.2006 consists of two sector-specific SEZs namely the Apparel Park with area of 20.41 hectares and the Electronic SEZ with land area of 28 hectares under a single developer. The Apparel Park has 10 units and 1,620 direct employees; while the Electronic SEZ has 12 units and 689 employees. The SEZs are 100 per cent state government enterprises. The exports turnover of Electronic SEZ has increased from $10.55 million in 2017–2018 to $13.42 million in 2018–2019 (27 per cent) and in case of Apparel Park it has increased from $9.13 million in 2017–2018 to $14.39 in 2018–2019 (58 per cent).

Other local services have attracted the highest possible ranking of "Outstanding" showing the importance given to the educational services, health services, police, and fire, in the scheme of things by the developer. SEZD3 has reposed faith in the Demographic by ranking it "Very Good" as a factor that contributes to socio-economic development. Housing has been ranked as "Good", while indirect economic merits ranking of "Average" only (Table 7.9). What is surprising is that the Direct economic as a factor has been ranked "Poor" by the respondent. This implies that the respondent prioritizes social development over the economic development. This is a divergent view from the one generally held by the other developers.

The respondent has not clarified whether CSR is applicable or not. Top ranking of "Outstanding" has been assigned to ensuring environmental sustainability. Gender equality promotion and health care services merit "Very Good". One notch lower ranking of "Good" is allotted to promotion of education, employment-enhancing skills and welfare activities for the vulnerable sections of the society. Not much importance is given to sports/yoga which get "Average" ranking (Table 7.10). This perhaps reflects the less importance given to sports by society in general in India.

The respondent has rated all the environmental sustainability issues as "Good" (Table 7.11). Perhaps no application of mind has been done while responding to this question.

The respondent agrees that government policies are in place for environmental protection and that the infrastructure and other assistance are provided by government for safeguarding the environment (Table 7.12).

SEZD3 has chosen not to assign any ranking to the suggestion that residential complexes be developed to use vacant land. The respondent is not enthused with the proposal to divert to domestic industry for this purpose. However, all other suggestions have merited "Good" ranking suggesting that the developer feels that these could be workable solutions to the vacant land issue in SEZs (Table 7.13).

The respondent did not proffer any response to the open-ended question regarding methods for evaluation of SEZ opportunities.

7.3.6 SEZ Developer 4 (SEZD4)

SEZD4, which began life as a FTZ, changed to an EPZ and finally to a SEZ on 01.11.2000, is one of the larger SEZs with an area of 400 hectares. It houses 254 units and provides direct employment to 27,725 employees as on 31.08.2019. The SEZ is 100 per cent owned by the government of India and is a multi-product SEZ strategically located close to Kandla Port (Deen Dayal Port Trust). The exports turnover has increased from $610.66 million in 2016–2017 to $613.16 in 2017–2018 (4 per cent) and to $1052.92 million in 2018–2019 (56.41 per cent).

Indirect/wider economic/expenditure and Demographic as the factors that contribute to socio-economic development merit the highest ranking of "Outstanding". The respondent in the course of discussions reiterated that the ultimate benefit of SEZ is development of the neighbouring areas and by extension development of the entire state. He was also very upbeat on the demographic dividend. "Very Good" ranking is assigned to Direct economic and to other local services showing their importance for the development of the SEZ. The respondent has however allotted "Poor" rank to housing showing its diminishing importance as per the perception of SEZD4 (Table 7.9).

The respondent has stated that CSR is not applicable; nevertheless, SEZD4 is involved in social activities. The respondent feels that education together with sports deserve top billing of "Outstanding"; followed by gender equality, health care services, and environmental sustainability at "Very Good". SEZD4, however, feels that employment enhancing skills and welfare activities for the vulnerable sections of the society merit "Poor" ranking (Table 7.10).

As an industrial hub, Kandla is beset with the problems associated with water, air and noise pollution. SEZD4 rates water contamination and sound pollution as the top priority areas on environmental sustainability with the top ranking. Following closely behind with "Very Good" ranking is the issue of air pollution. Next is the conservation of indigenous fauna; incidentally, land degradation is assigned minimum marks or "Poor" ranking that may reflect on the plentiful barren land available in Kandla (Table 7.11).

The respondent prefers to take a neutral stance on the statements that government policies are in place for environmental protection and that the infrastructure and other assistance is provided by government for safeguarding the environment (Table 7.12).

SEZD4 believes that of the many options for new opportunities for SEZs to utilize vacant land, priority to MSMEs and change from single to multi-product are the best options with the highest marks. Next are the choices of dedicated service sector, diversion to domestic industry and sectoral broad banding with ranking of "Very Good". Development of residential complexes for use of vacant land merits the least preference with "Good" ranking (Table 7.13).

The respondent suggested that the NFE positive criterion is very narrow in its approach. The overall socio-economic development indicators should be used to identify, analyse and evaluate SEZ opportunities in India. The research team tends to agree with the views of SEZD4 in this respect.

7.3.7 SEZ Developer 5 (SEZD5)

SEZD5 is a multi-product SEZ in the private sector established on 01.11.2000 having an area of 49.99 hectares. The SEZ hosts 150 units and the strength of direct employees is 23,381. The exports turnover has decreased from $2,844.27 million in 2016–2017 to $2,245.23 million in 2017–2018 (–21.06 per cent) and to $940.79 million in 2018–2019 (–58.09 per cent).

SEZD5 has ascribed top billing for Direct economic as the factor that characterizes development in their SEZ. The other factors in decreasing order of importance are other local services (Very Good), housing (Good), Indirect/wider economic/expenditure (Average) and demographic (Poor). In the course of telephonic discussions, the CEO affirmed that the direct economic is the prime mover for socio-economic development and all other factors are secondary (Table 7.9).

The respondent confirms that CSR is not applicable; hence no rating has been given on the CSR activities.

With regard to the environmental sustainability issues, SEZD5 has assigned "Outstanding" ranking to all the parameters with justifications; waste water disposal is ensured, there are no air polluting industries in the SEZ, land degradation is absent, there is no sound pollution and there are no hazardous or toxic industries, hence no loss of indigenous fauna (Table 7.10).

The respondent agrees that government policies are in place for environmental protection; however, he disagrees that the infrastructure and other assistance is provided by government for safeguarding the environment (Table 7.11). SEZD5 has given no ranking on the various options for utilization of vacant land on the ground that this SEZ has no vacant land.

The respondent suggested that the exports, employment, inflow of foreign exchange, ease of doing business should be used to identify, analyse and evaluate SEZ opportunities in India.

The responses of the developers as given above in respect of questions of Section Three and Six are interpreted below:

- Majority of the developers agreed that Direct economic and Other local services are the top indicators followed by Indirect economic, Demographic and Housing.
- Only some of the developers carry out CSR activities; however, almost all responded on the activities to be performed under CSR.
- Health and Education Segment are the preferred areas under CSR as rated by all developers. It shows concern for the quality of living and education of people.
- All developers also agreed that CSR activities should be directed towards women empowerment and promoting gender equality; this is in line with the Millennium Development Goals. Another aspect where developers are on the same page is on the importance of environmental sustainability in and around SEZs.
- The various aspects of environmental sustainability merit different ranking by the developers. It implies that inter se ranking of environmental issues is dependent upon the type of activity in the unit and location of the SEZ.
- Majority of the developers agreed that there are government policies in place for environment protection; some of the developers have shown dissatisfaction over the lack of government initiative in providing proper infrastructure and assistance for safeguarding the environment.

- All developers agreed that the sector-specific SEZs should be converted to multi-product SEZs for utilization of vacant land in SEZs.
- Sectoral Broad banding, priority to MSME and dedicated Service Sector SEZs are ranked next in descending order for utilization of vacant land.

Section Two: SEZs: Business Models (Q 2.1 & 2.2)

7.3.8 Business Model Analysis (Q 2.1 & 2.2)

The first part of business model analysis (Table 7.14) gives ranking by the respondents on the various ownership patterns of SEZs.

Table 7.14: Business Model Analysis—Ownership Pattern

Ownership Pattern	SEZD1	SEZD2	SEZD3	SEZD4	SEZD5	Average
Private	2	5	2	3	NR	3
Zones developed by Foreign Developers	1	4	4	3	NR	3
Joint ventures with local Co as Private FDI	4	4	1	3	NR	3
Zones developed through Government-Government partnership	4	3	3	4	NR	3.5
Government (State/ Central)	5	3	1	4	NR	3.25
Public-Private Partnership (PPP) model	5	3	5	3	NR	4

(1 = Poor; 2 = Average;3 = Good; 4 = Very Good; 5 = Outstanding; NR = No Response)

On basis of simple average of the four responses (SEZD5 has not assigned any ranking), it is observed that the PPP model is ranked the highest "Very Good", followed by zones developed by government/government partnership and government (central/state) with ranking above "Good" but not equivalent to "Very Good". The other ownership models are ranked "Good".

The second part of the business model analysis (Table 7.15) invites ranking from the respondents on the contribution of SEZ units on the parameters as tabulated below:

Table 7.15: Business Model Analysis—SEZ Contribution

Parameter	SEZD1	SEZD2	SEZD3	SEZD4	SEZD5	Average
Employment	5	4	3	5	5	4.4
Bridging of Demand-Supply Gap	4	4	2	2	1	2.6
Socio-economic Development	4	NR	1	4	3	3
Sustainable Development	4	NR	2	3	4	2.6
Corporate Governance	4	NR	4	2	2	3

(1 = Poor; 2 = Average; 3 = Good; 4 = Very Good; 5 = Outstanding: NR= No Response)

The SEZ Contribution on Employment parameter merits top ranking of more than "Very Good". For the parameters on socio-economic development and corporate governance, SEZs' contribution is ranked as "Good". The least contribution is on the parameters of demand-supply gap bridging and on sustainable development of above "Average" but below "Good".

Section Three: Social Impact (Q 4.1–Q 4.4)

7.3.9 Social Impact Analysis (Q 4.1–Q 4.4)

The first question of Part 4 relates to the stance of the SEZ on certain statements as briefed in Table 7.16.

It can be surmized that the SEZs agree on the fact that landless labourers have secured jobs and livelihoods courtesy the SEZs and that the prices of neighbouring land have gone north on the same account. With respect to other statements, there is overwhelming neutral stance by the SEZs.

On the specific issue of impact on land owners due to the appropriation of land, the ranking given by the respondents on the statements is tabled in 7.17.

It would be seen that the average ranking on all the three responses is above "Average" and below or equal to "Good". This implies that the developers affirm that a lot needs to be done in terms of the social security of the ousted including the land owners, who stand deprived of land consequent upon setting up of a SEZ (SEZD5 has not assigned any ranking).

The impact on the local people in terms of visible benefits is measured next. The response of the developers on the selected parameters is in Table 7.18.

Table 7.16: Social Impact

Parameters	SEZD1	SEZD2	SEZD3	SEZD4	SEZD5	Consensus
Misuse of land in SEZs.	A	DA	N	SA	S DA	N
SEZs have supported landless labourers in rural areas towards jobs/livelihood.	A	NR	A	A	NR	A
SEZs have dedicated anti-corruption standards/policies	DA	A	N	DA	A	N
The ousted have been compensated while acquiring land	N	DA	N	A	NR	N
Prices of neighbouring land/ residential and commercial units have shown rise	A	A	A	SA	N	A
Labour conditions and labour laws are favourable from social aspects.	N	A	SA	N	N	N

(A = AGREE; DA = DISAGREE; NR = NO RESPONSE; N = NEUTRAL;
SA = STRONGLY AGREE; SDA = STRONGLY DISAGREE)

Table 7.17: Impact on Land Owners

Question	SEZD1	SEZD2	SEZD3	SEZD4	SEZD5	Average
Whether they have continued with traditional livelihood?	3	3	2	1	NR	2.25
Whether they have secured employment?	4	3	2	3	NR	3
Whether they have access to education and health care services?	3	3	2	3	NR	2.75

(1=Poor; 2=Average; 3= Good; 4 = Very Good; 5=Outstanding; NR=No Response)

Table 7.18: Impact on Local People

Questions	SEZD1	SEZD2	SEZD3	SEZD4	SEZD5	Average
Whether as a result of SEZs they have motorable road to district/taluka HQ?	4	4	3	3	NR	3.5
Whether they have mobile connection facilities?	4	3	2	4	NR	3.25
Whether the developer has taken any step to preserve and promote the local traditional arts/culture?	2	3	2	1	NR	2
Whether they are compelled to migrate to other places?	1	1	3	3	NR	2
Whether any local person has been assisted in setting of unit in SEZ.	1	3	2	1	NR	1.75

(1=Poor; 2=Average; 3=Good; 4 = Very Good; 5 = Outstanding; NR=No Response)

The developers rank the effect of 'motorable road to district/taluka headquarters' as a result of the setting up of SEZs more than "Good", implying that connectivity to the district HQ is largely a result of the presence of SEZs (SEZD5 has not assigned any ranking). On a similar note, the mobile connectivity is ascribed to the SEZs. However, the developers agreed that negligible efforts have been made to preserve the local arts and culture. It is also not likely that any local person has been assisted in setting up of a unit in the SEZ, belying the expectation that the SEZ would help in promoting the entrepreneurial culture in the locals. There is no compulsion on the locals to migrate to other places as a consequence of the SEZs as per the developers.

The final question relates to the opinion of the developers on the factors which are responsible for the slow growth of SEZ in the five-year period 2013–2018 as compared to 2006–2012.

In response SEZD1, SEZD4 and SEZD5 cite the introduction of the Minimum Alternate Tax (MAT) as the factor responsible for the slow-down. SEZD4 affirms that in addition to MAT, the sunset clause, which comes into effect on 01.04.2020 abolishing Income Tax benefits for the SEZ units, is another factor for reducing the pace of growth.

SEZD2 and SEZD3 have preferred to proffer no answer.

It is apparent that MAT and the withdrawal of Income Tax benefits are twin policy assaults on SEZs; these factors have resulted in the loss of sheen of SEZs as instruments of investment, growth and exports promotion.

Section Four: Economic Impact (Q 5.1–Q 5.3)

7.3.10 Economic Impact Analysis (Q 5)

Question 1 of Part 5 pertains to the economic impact of SEZs, measured in five subgroups of Export Promotion, Performance Measures, Geographic concentration indicators, FDI indicators and Foreign Controlled affiliates (FCA). The ranking assigned is tabulated in Table 7.19.

The developers are upbeat on the economic impact of SEZs in the area of exports promotion. The ranking given for growth in exports by volume is close to "Outstanding". It is also perceived that the SEZs ease the import of raw materials and this factor is ranked as "Very Good". The contribution of the factors of value addition in exports and new products and services is above "Good". However, at least one SEZ has recorded the value addition norms and new products and services due to SEZ as "Poor".

On the performance measures, the developers affirm that accretion of new units is close to "Outstanding" while the market share of exports is close to "Very Good".

On the other hand, in respect of the geographic concentration indicators, one SEZ has chosen not to assign any marks and the average marks of the remaining four SEZ developers for all the parameters range from above "Average" to "Good". Thus, in the opinion of the developers, the economic impact of the geographical distribution of export or import markets, services trading partner and bilateral, intra-regional trade is neutral at best.

In a similar vein, the developers believe that the influence of FDI indicators on the economic impact is not significant. The ranking assigned on the two parameters is above "Average" and below "Good".

In respect of the Foreign Controlled Affiliates (FCA), most of the SEZs have allotted the median marks of 3 that relates to "Good". Thus, the developers believe

Table 7.19: Economic Impact- General

Parameter	SEZD1	SEZD2	SEZD3	SEZD4	SEZD5	Average
1.Export Promotion (Trade Openness)						
1.1 Growth in Exports in terms of volume	5	4	4	5	5	4.6
1.2 New products and Services	4	4	5	1	3	3.4
1.3 Ease of Import of Raw Materials	5	3	4	3	5	4
1.4 Export Norms like value addition, etc.	4	5	3	1	5	3.6
2.Trade Performance Indicators						
2.1 Market share of Exports	4	4	3	4	4	3.8
2.2 Accretion of new units	5	5	3	5	5	4.6
3.Geographic concentration Indicators						
3.1 Geographical distribution of export markets	3	3	4	1	NR	2.75
3.2 Geographical distribution of import markets	3	3	3	4	NR	3.25
3.3 Services trading partner (exports/imports)	3	3	4	1	NR	2.75
3.4 Bilateral, Intra and extra regional trade intensity by region and partner country	3	3	4	2	NR	3
4.FDI Indicator						
4.1 FDI financial flows as percentage of GDP	3	3	2	1	4	2.6
4.2 FDI financial flow as percentage of Gross Capital Formation	3	3	2	1	3	2.4

Continued

Table 7.19: *Continued*

Parameter	SEZD1	SEZD2	SEZD3	SEZD4	SEZD5	Average
5.Foreign Controlled Affiliates (FCA)						
5.1 FCAs' share of the home country value added	3	3	3	3	4	3.2
5.2 FCAs' share of the host country value added	3	3	3	3	3	3
5.3 FCAs' share of the home country employment	3	4	2	1	3	2.6
5.4 FCAs' share of the host country employment	3	3	2	4	4	3.2
5.5 FCAs' sales as a percentage of the home country's total exports	3	3	3	3	3	3

(1 = Poor; 2 = Average; 3 = Good; 4 = Very Good; 5 = Outstanding)

that in respect of FCAs' whether it is parameter of value addition in home/host country or employment in home/host country the economic impact is "Good".

The second question of the economic impact is on Likert scale and relates to trade and SEZs. The results are tabulated in Table 7.20.

The developers agree that SEZs have contributed towards technology contribution and that trade policy facilitators like WTO/MFN help SEZs economy. However, the stance of the developers is that the impact of price indicators and trade intensity and specialization indicators on the SEZ economy is neutral.

In the final question of Part 5, the developers are asked open-ended question to spell the economic factors or indicators which will be able to develop the economic growth from SEZs.

In response, SEZD1 lists the Removal of Minimum Alternative Tax (MAT) and Exemption of VAT as the two economic factors for spurring economic growth of SEZs.

SEZD2 has not listed any factors.

SEZD3 affirms that Labour and Technologies are the two economic indicators for economic growth from SEZs.

Table 7.20: Economic Impact—Trade and SEZs

Averments	SEZD1	SEZD2	SEZD3	SEZD4	SEZD5	Consensus
SEZs have contributed towards Tech up gradation	A	A	SA	DA	A	A
Trade policy facilitators like WTO/MFN help SEZs economy	N	A	A	SDA	A	A
Impact of Price indicators like Terms of trade, Real effective exchange rate affected economy of SEZs	N	N	A	SA	N	N
Trade intensity and specialization indicators like export specialization and net trade specialization indices affect SEZs	A	N	N	A	N	N

(A = AGREE; DA = DISAGREE; NR = NO RESPONSE; N = NEUTRAL;
SA = STRONGLY AGREE; SDA = STRONGLY DISAGREE)

SEZD4 reiterates that Abolition of MAT, Introduction/continuation of Income Tax exemption in some form, grant of incentives distinct from those already available under FTAs are the factors that will spur the economic growth of SEZs.

SEZD5 believes that improvement in SEZ Policy is necessary to develop the economic growth of SEZs.

Section Five: Micro-, Small- and Medium-Size Business (Q 7.1–Q 7.3)

7.3.11 Promotion of MSME in SEZs

Part Seven of the questionnaire relates to promotion of MSME in SEZs. The results are tabulated in Table 7.21.

Table 7.21: Promotion of MSME in SEZs

Question	SEZD1	SEZD2	SEZD3	SEZD4	SEZD5	Average
How far SEZs help in government initiatives (Make in India etc.)	4	3	NR	3	5	3.75
How far MSME segment benefitted from SEZ?	3	3	NR	1	NR	2.33
Promotional measures can be adopted by the Government						
Special MSME SEZs	1	2	3	2	NR	2
Special provisions for entry into existing SEZs	3	3	4	3	NR	3.25
Relaxed norms for supply to/from MSME units	1	4	3	4	NR	3
Incentives based on performance of MSME units in SEZs	4	4	4	2	NR	3.5
Clustering of small and large enterprises	3	3	3	5	NR	3.5

(1 = Poor; 2 = Average; 3 = Good; 4 = Very Good; 5 = Outstanding; NR = No Response)

The consensus view of the developers with regard to the role of SEZs in government initiatives like Make in India and start-up is ranked closer to "Very Good".

The benefit to MSME segment business and vendors from SEZs is rated just above "Average"; implying that no real benefits have percolated to MSMEs from SEZs.

Asked to rank the promotional measures, which could be adopted by the government for MSMEs in SEZs, the choice was for clustering of small and large enterprises and for performance-based incentives for MSMEs in SEZs; both these suggested measures were ranked more than "Good". The developers were not so enthused on the measures like relaxation in norms for supply by MSMEs and special provisions for entry of MSMEs into SEZs; these secured "Good" rank. As regards the suggestion of special SEZs for MSMEs, the ranking was "Average" and at least one developer ranked it as "Poor" idea.

Other Suggestions: Only SEZD4 has offered suggestions on the following lines. SEZ Act 2005 and Rules 2006 are tuned to SEZs dealing in products. The law does not adequately address the peculiarities of a service-based SEZ like GIFT SEZ.

The NFE criterion is very narrow. More broad-based parameters, such as value addition, innovation, patents filed, social indicators like growth in household incomes, increase in women's participation in the economy and economic indicators such as growth of per capita incomes, addition to infrastructure, transport facilities need to be incorporated and the benefits accrued due to setting up and functioning of a SEZ can be objectively rated as a weighted average of the above-mentioned factors and other parameters that may be considered relevant.

Already FTAs and other schemes give benefit of duty-free imports. The only charm of situating a unit in a SEZ is the Direct Tax (Income Tax) benefit. Therefore, the Direct Tax exemption beyond 31.03.2020 needs to be restored in some form for the SEZ scheme to remain lucrative.

The researchers by and large agree with the suggestions made by SEZD4.

Part II Case Study

7.4 Case Study: Cross Cases Contrast

One unit each that is engaged in manufacturing with good turnover and has generated substantial employment was identified by the researcher from each sample SEZ. A set of questionnaire (Appendix 2.C) was circulated to the selected units (six in all). The questionnaire was followed by personal and telephonic interview. The questions are grouped under three headings as below:

1. Organizational Changes and SEZs (Q 1.1–Q 1.4)
2. Opportunity Identification (Q 2.1–Q 2.6)
3. Strategic Reforms (Q 3.1–Q 3.6)

The first part covers the responses by each of the units, followed by cross case study analysis and interpretation thereof.

7.4.1 Unit A

Unit A established in 2011 is a leading Liquid Handling Equipment (LHE) manufacturer. The process is ISO 17025 certified; the products basket includes pipettes, bottle top dispensers and other glass products. The products are used in the wellness industry, laboratories and FMCG (Fast Moving Consumer Goods).

The firm believes in the application of all the management principles listed in the questionnaire. Given the high accuracy needed in the measuring instruments like pipettes, cutting-edge technology is used in the manufacturing process. Importance is given to Zero Defects (Nil Rejection) in the manufacturing process. Therefore, innovation is encouraged and the employees strive to reduce any kind of waste. The managers at the manufacturing sites have a good idea and understanding of how corporate strategy is formed. They do know the importance of maintaining quality and delivery schedule in the manufacturing process; their site vision and strategy broadly fits with the corporate mission and statement.

The individuals will need to be organized, sequential, planned and detailed-oriented in their style of working. The firm has a Research and Development wing and it believes that Five S and Zero Defect will help increase employee morale and working efficiency.

When it comes to identification of opportunities for SEZs that hold promise, the firm has no hesitation in choosing pharmaceuticals, electronics and textiles industry. It is affirmed that location is the key to the success of the SEZ; government policies, laws and regulations, stability and consistency of the government and management and service are equally important factors. Other factors like macroeconomics, industrial investment support, investment cost and labour are rated Very Good. One reason for this ranking could be the relative high logistics cost for the storage and movement of the products; thus, location proximal to Port/Highway/Railhead is of prime importance.

The role of new digital technology in the promotion of SEZs is manifest in improved performance and flexibility, mass customization, increasing productivity and reorganization of the supply chain.

Research and Development will derive maximum benefit from the new technologies. The impact of new technologies will also be high for Administration and HR, Sales and Marketing and for the Manufacturing Department. The new technology with huge scope is Artificial Intelligence (AI). The benefits for the unit include reduction in costs, quality, innovation, employment structure, customer structure through use of the new technology.

For building a competitive advantage over SEZs located outside the country, a stimulus package is must to revive the SEZ units. The respondent also states the need for reform in government policies and procedures. The strategic resources most needed are government and institutional support, infrastructure and location. Other factors rank lower.

Employment generation, exports promotion, and filling the demand-supply gap are the major contributions of SEZ units. Finally, the respondent agrees with the proposition that HR is the weak spot in corporate transformation. The firm disagrees with the suggestion that people, talent and future of work are part of the new approaches to strategic management. The respondent is neutral on the other listed factors.

The unit has not offered any suggestions.

7.4.2 Unit B

The parent Company of Unit B was established in 1980 and has manufacturing facilities spread over eight different locations in India. Unit B was established in 2009 and accounts for a major part of exports of the company. The products include both formulations and API (Active Pharmaceutical Ingredient); products like drugs related to neurology, psychiatry and cardiovascular treatment are exported to the highly regulated markets of Europe and USA. The firm has a robust R&D wing.

The firm acknowledges application of all the management principles listed in the questionnaire. The firm believes in an open culture rather than Command and Control type of leadership. Accordingly, it has an open communication culture and innovation is promoted. The management empowers employees to improve processes and there is inter-departmental cooperation. As a multi-locational company, the priority is that the head of unit, site leader have perfect understanding of the formation of corporate strategy and the vision and strategy of managers at the manufacturing units mirror that of the corporate level.

The management leaves it to the employees to choose the work style that is best suited at the operational level. All the four styles are looked upon as not mutually exclusive. Similarly, implementation of all the listed quality programs, whether it is Five S, TQM (Total Quality Management), Six Sigma or Zero Defect can all either singly or severally help in increasing employee morale and working efficiency.

In the opinion of the management, the most promising industry sectors for SEZs are pharmaceuticals followed by IT/ITeS and Financial Services. Petro, crude is ranked next, with textiles at the bottom of the pack. The firm recognizes that the most important parameters for SEZ opportunities are availability of skilled labour, industrial investment support and location. Other factors like government policies, laws and regulations, investment and stability/consistency of the government are ranked lower. This implies that the output of the firm depends on the skills of the employees.

Unit B ranks mass customization as the main outcome of new digital technology. The next rank is allotted to increased productivity followed by improved performance and flexibility. Massive re-organization of supply chain as an outcome of digital technology secures minimum marks.

New technology is perceived to be useful in Research and Development, Manufacturing Department, HR and Finance. The new technologies which have scope are Artificial Intelligence (AI), Big Data Analytics, 3D Printing and Robots. By redesigning the value chain and use of new technologies, there is increase in flexibility, quality and innovation structure. The new technologies should also result in lower costs and improved procurement and supplier structure.

For building a competitive advantage over SEZs located outside the country, rather than the need for reform in government policies in the procedures and a stimulus package; the procedures mandated by the government need to be simplified and synchronized. Infrastructure ranks as the top requirement as a strategic resource. The location of the unit and market also matter.

The contribution of SEZ units includes employment generation, exports promotion, demand-supply and positive socio-economic impact. Finally, roadmap for building corporate innovative capabilities, internet of things and people hold the key for new approaches to strategic management. The respondent is not upbeat on e-commerce strategy.

The unit has not proffered any suggestions.

7.4.3 Unit C

Plastic recycling is the forte of Unit C. Established in 1997, it is a major player in the import of LDPE (Low Density Polyethylene), HDPE (High Density Polyethylene) for manufacture of plastic agglomerates, PET bottles agglomerates and other related products.

The firm believes in the application of all the listed management principles except for the engagement with external stakeholders. The firm agrees with the proposition that there is more competition and less cooperation between the departments; this could be a result of the stratifications that have occurred over the years in the firm's life. The view of the firm on communication culture is neutral again suggesting that working in silos is prevalent in the firm. However, the management feels that the employees are empowered to innovate, improve the processes and reduce any kind of waste. Command and control is the preferred leadership style. The firm agrees that the head of unit, site leader have a good understanding of how the corporate strategy is formed and the manufacturing unit managers know best the criteria for manufacturing jobs to increase the efficiency.

Work style that defines the firm is organized, sequential, planned and detail-oriented. TQM (Total Quality Management) is the programme of choice and implementation of the same is bound to help increase employee morale and working efficiency.

The most promising sectors for SEZs are pharmaceuticals, financial services, IT/ITeS and textiles. Government policies is ranked as the parameter of utmost importance for identification of SEZ opportunities. Other important factors are location advantage, investment cost, laws and regulations, macroeconomics of the country and industrial investment support. The remaining factors are not so important. The choice of factors could be explained by the fact that plastic agglomerates are low-value, high-volume cargo and, therefore, location is important from logistics point of view. Government policies are important as the duty on import of raw materials dictates the economics of the manufacture and marketing of the product. Similarly, restrictions imposed by government on the use of plastic due to environmental concerns impacts the demand for the product.

Improved performance and flexibility, through the use of new digital technologies figure as important tools for the promotion of SEZs. Other outcomes of the new technologies include increased productivity, mass customization and reorganization of the supply chain.

Marketing and Sales Department, Administration and HR Department, Finance Department and Corporate Planning Department will derive benefit from the new technologies. The three new technologies that have scope are Block-chain technology, Internet of Things (IoT) and Robots. The use of new technologies will benefit the unit in multiple ways ranging from increase of flexibility, service level and quality to reduction of costs and improvement in the procurement and supplier structure. It will also help in the sourcing by region and employment structure.

Not only a change in government policies in respect of procedures, but a stimulus package is also necessary for the SEZ units to defend or build competitive advantage over other SEZs located outside the country. The respondent has marked all the boxes of strategic resources needed.

SEZs contribute to dynamic economics on all parameters like employment, demand-supply, promotion of exports, socio-economic impact and so on. The net operating costs reduction is achieved by decreasing the wastage and increasing the quality level.

The unit strongly agrees with the proposition that the Internet of Things (IoT) strategy is the best. It also agrees that technologies that impact everyone, a roadmap for building corporate innovative capabilities and people, talent and future of work are the technologies to look out for. The respondent is not so upbeat on e-commerce strategy.

The unit did not offer any suggestions.

7.4.4 Unit D

Unit D is into the manufacture of agro chemicals, speciality and performance chemicals. The firm set up the first unit in 2009; second unit in 2016 and the third unit in the same SEZ in 2018. For the second and third units, it has Zero Liquid Discharge (ZLD) through state-of-the-art technology; this is indeed a remarkable achievement. The firm has ISO 9001, ISO 14001 certifications for its manufacturing facilities. Popular fungicides like Mancozeb, Zineb and Cynoxamil figure in the products basket. The production process is environment-friendly in that no charcoal is used.

All the management principles listed in the questionnaire are applied by the firm. The firm has a progressive culture of working and communication. It strongly agrees with the proposition that employees are empowered to improve the processes and to adapt innovative methods at different levels. The communication flow is transparent and there is less use of official channels for communication. However, the firm also believes that command and control is the most effective leadership rather than open culture. The firm has a clear vision, mission and strategy which are shared with the employees. In the manufacturing units, the managers have a site vision which is closely aligned with the corporate mission statement. The employees are dedicated and strive to reduce any kind of waste, whether it is waste of time or of production space. The emphasis is on maintaining and improving quality of the products.

The individuals will need to be logical, analytical, linear and data-oriented. The firm uses PLC (Programmable Logic Control) and DCS (Distributed Control Systems) in its operations. Implementation of all the listed quality programmes namely Five S, TQM (Total Quality Management), Six Sigma and Zero Defect would help increase employee morale and working efficiency.

Pharmaceutical industry holds promise if opportunities for SEZs were to be identified. The key parameters for identification, analysis and evaluation of SEZ opportunities are government policies, laws and regulations and stability and consistency of the government. The rationale for this choice could be the highly regulated environment for the manufacture, storage and marketing of the agro chemicals, given that most of them are poisonous by nature.

The major outcome of the use of new digital technology in the promotion of SEZs is the increased productivity. The impact of this technology is minimal for improved performance and flexibility, mass customization and reorganization of the supply chain.

The departments that will benefit from the new technologies are Manufacturing and Sales Department. Only Artificial Intelligence (AI) is selected from the list of new technologies that has scope in SEZ. The use of AI will result in increased service level, reduce costs and improve procurement and supplier structure.

Change in government policies in respect of procedures is necessary for the SEZ units to defend or build competitive advantage over other SEZs located outside India. Government and Institutional Support and Market figure as the strategic resources needed.

The SEZ contribution to economic dynamics lies largely in exports leading to foreign exchange earnings. By exercising control on fixed costs, the unit reduces net operating costs and generates more revenue. Finally, a roadmap for building corporate innovative capabilities, people, talent and future of work, Internet of Things (IoT) are the new approaches to strategic management. The respondent disagrees with the proposition that there is need for new organization structure and that HR is the weak spot in corporate transformation.

No specific suggestions were made by the unit.

7.4.5 Unit E

Unit E established in 2006 is a leading manufacturer of automobile lubricants. The products basket includes brake fluids, lubricating oils and greases, coolants, antifreeze and other related products. The main raw material is glycol which is imported.

The firm believes in the application of all the management principles listed in the questionnaire. Given the comparatively low employee strength, the business process is system-driven, implying that there is little human intervention. Nevertheless, innovation is encouraged and the employees strive to reduce any kind of waste. The managers at the manufacturing sites have just a general idea and understanding of how corporate strategy is formed. They do know however the importance of maintaining quality and delivery schedule in the manufacturing process. Their site vision and strategy broadly fit with the corporate mission and statement.

The individuals will need to be organized, sequential, planned and detailed-oriented in their style of working. The firm has a Research and Development wing and it believes that TQM (Total Quality Management) will help increase employee morale and working efficiency.

When it comes to identification of opportunities for SEZs that hold promise, the firm has no hesitation in choosing Chemicals and Pharmaceutical industry. It is affirmed that location is the key to the success of the SEZ and that the infrastructure needs improvement. All other factors are rated Very Good; except for the investment cost and country macroeconomics, which merit only Good ranking. One reason for this ranking could be the relative high logistics cost for the storage and movement of the liquid product; thus, location proximal to Port/Highway/Railhead is very important.

The role of new digital technology in the promotion of SEZs is manifest in improved performance and flexibility as well as in mass customization. However, the role is limited for increasing productivity and reorganization of the supply chain.

Research and Development will derive maximum benefit from the new technologies. The impact of new technologies will also be high for corporate functions, Finance and the Manufacturing Department. It will be above average on HR and Sales. The new technologies which have scope are Artificial Intelligence (AI), big data analytics, 3D Printing and Internet of Things. Augmented Reality and Robots have little scope; while Drones and Virtual Reality are ruled out as new technologies required. Reduction in costs is the prime mover for use of new technologies for the benefit of the unit.

The changes effected by the government in 2011 by bringing in MAT and the sunset clause for Income Tax has killed the SEZ policy. Hence for building a competitive advantage over SEZs located outside the country, a stimulus package is must to revive the SEZ units. The strategic resource that is the need of the day is government and institutional support. Other factors are not significant.

Employment generation, exports promotion, positive socio-economic impact and filling the demand-supply gap are the major contributions of SEZ units. Finally, e-commerce, a roadmap for building corporate innovative capabilities and people hold the key for new approaches to strategic management. The respondent is neutral on the need for new organization structure and Internet of Things.

The unit has not offered any suggestions.

7.4.6 Unit F

Unit F established in 2014 is a star exporter of textiles. It manufactures a wide array of products ranging from bedcovers to bottoms. The firm acknowledges application of all the management principles listed save for the engagement with external stakeholders. Engaged in a highly competitive field, innovation at different levels of operations and process improvement through participation by employees are critical to the success of the firm. It follows that this model requires transparent information flow and an open communication culture. Manufacturing and manufacturing processes are at the heart of the firm's mission, vision and goals. Naturally, the managers at the manufacturing sites have the vision and strategy that fits with the corporate mission and statement.

The management believes that the work style should be organized, sequential and planned; it should be supportive, emotionally oriented at the same time. TQM (Total Quality Management) is selected as the programme of choice for increasing employee morale and working efficiency.

In the opinion of the management, the most promising industry sectors for SEZs are IT/ITeS, gems and jewellery and pharmaceuticals. The firm recognizes that the most important parameters for SEZ opportunities are government policies and laws and regulations. Other factors considered important for the success of SEZs are investment, skilled labour and stability/consistency of the government. This implies that the firm is compliant with government rules and regulations and/or that the cost of non-compliance is too high.

F ranks increased productivity as the main outcome of new digital technology. The next rank is allotted to improved performance and flexibility. Mass customization as an outcome of digital technology secures minimum marks.

New technology is perceived to be useful in Research and Development, Manufacturing Department, HR and Sales. The new technologies which have scope are Artificial Intelligence (AI), Drones, 3D Printing and Robots. By redesigning the value chain and use of new technologies, there is increase in flexibility, quality and service level.

For building a competitive advantage over SEZs located outside the country, the most important reform needed is change in government policies in the procedures. Market ranks as the top requirement as a strategic resource. The location of the unit in India and agglomeration with local supplier hardly matters.

Employment generation, exports promotion and positive socio-economic impact are the major contributions of SEZ units. Finally, e-commerce, Internet of Things and people hold the key for new approaches to strategic management. There is no need for new organization structure. The unit has not proffered any suggestions.

7.4.7 Cross Cases Contrast Analysis

With the help of tables, the choices made/options exercised and the views expressed by the six units are juxtaposed to build a cross cases contrast. The consensual position is derived, this enables the researcher to draw meaningful conclusions and make suggestions that should help the stakeholders involved.

Section One: Organization Change and SEZs

7.4.7.1 Organization Culture: SEZs (Q 1.1–Q 1.2.12) Table 7.22 clubs the responses of the six units in respect of organization change, application of management principles and statements related to Management Commitments and Company (Q 1.1–Q 1.2.12).

- The units unanimously agreed on the need to apply management principles to provide direct and indirect benefits on corporate level in matters of regulations and risk management. On the matter of engagement with external stakeholders four units accepted and two units denied the application of management principles.
- The units definitely agree with the proposition that management empowers employees to improve processes and reduce failure rates. One reason for this could be that all the units are manufacturing units and process improvement translates into visible gains.
- There is more cooperation than competition between the departments inter se as per the opinion of five units. One unit has, however, taken a contrary stand in this regard, which may need further investigation. Only two units agree that communication with employees is through official channels.
- Most of the Units have opted for open and transparent communication culture among the departments and different management levels instead of formal communication mode.
- On the other statements, regarding communication to the employees of the mission, vision and goals and on adapting innovation and waste reduction, the units have responded positively.
- Preference for command-and-control type of leadership has been made by four units, one unit has disagreed while the other has indicated neutral stance.
- Statements on the unit heads having good understanding of corporate strategy and managers knowing the important criteria for manufacturing jobs have also elicited positive responses.
- That the managers of the manufacturing units have a site vision that aligns with the corporate mission statement is agreed upon by the units.

Table 7.22: Company Culture—SEZ Units (Q 1.1–Q 1.2.12)

Parameters	UNIT A	UNIT B	UNIT C	UNIT D	UNIT E	UNIT F
Application of Management principles pertaining to Corporate Policies, regulatory guidelines, consistency on risk assessment and for providing of direct and indirect economic benefits.	Yes	Yes	Yes	Yes	Yes	Yes
Application of Management principles pertaining to engagement with external stakeholders.	Yes	Yes	No	Yes	Yes	No
Management empowers employees to improve the processes and reduce failure rate.	SA	A	SA	SA	A	A
There is more competition and less cooperation between departments.	DA	DA	A	DA	DA	DA
Official channels are used for communicating.	N	A	N	DA	N	A
Company has an open communication culture. Transparent culture of flow of information between the departments and different levels of management.	SA	A	N	SA	A	A
There is adaption of innovation at different levels.	SA	A	A	SA	A	A
Our employees strive to reduce any kind of waste. (waste of time, waste of production space, etc.)	SA	A	A	SA	A	A

Continued

Table 7.22: *Continued*

Parameters	UNIT A	UNIT B	UNIT C	UNIT D	UNIT E	UNIT F
Command and control is seen as the most effective leadership style rather than open culture.	A	DA	A	SA	N	A
Our vision, mission and strategy is broadly communicated and followed by our employees.	A	A	A	SA	A	A
Goal and objectives of the manufacturing units are closely linked with corporate objectives.	A	A	N	SA	A	A
Head of unit, site leader, etc. have a good understanding of how the Corporate/Divisional strategy is formed.	A	SA	A	SA	N	A
Managers of manufacturing unit know the most important criteria for manufacturing jobs. (low costs, delivery, quality, etc.)	A	A	A	SA	A	A
Managers and staff of the manufacturing unit have a site vision and strategy that is closely related to the corporate mission statement.	A	SA	NR	SA	A	A

(A = AGREE; SA = STRONGLY AGREE; NR = NO RESPONSE; N = NEUTRAL; DA = DISAGREE; SDA = STRONGLY DISAGREE)

Table 7.23: Adaption of Work Style (Q 1.3)

Method	Unit A	Unit B	Unit C	Unit D	Unit E	Unit F
Logical, analytical, linear and data-oriented	NS	✓	NS	✓	NS	NS
Organized, sequential, planned and detailed-oriented	✓	✓	✓	NS	✓	✓
Supportive, expressive, and emotionally oriented	NS	✓	NS	NS	NS	✓
Big-picture, integrative, and ideation-oriented	NS	✓	NS	NS	NS	NS

(✓ = SELECTED; NS= NOT SELECTED)

7.4.7.2 Work Style (Q 1.3) The responses of the units in the matter of adaption of working styles are tabulated at Table 7.23 (Q 1.3).

- All the units with the exception of Unit D have selected the working style titled as organized, sequential, planned and detailed-oriented work style.
- Unit D on the other hand has opted for the style titled logical, analytical, linear and data-oriented style of work.
- Unit F has a mixed working style of organized, sequential, planned and detailed-oriented work style, and supportive, expressive and emotionally oriented work style. This is possibly desirable in context of the unit's activity.
- Unit B has opted for all the styles, this could imply that its working style is work in progress.

7.4.7.3 Quality Programmes (Q 1.4) The responses of the units in respect of adaption of Quality Management Programmes are tabulated in Table 7.24 (Q 1.3).

- On given a choice among four reputed quality programs, two units namely B and D have opted to choose all the four programmes listed; these responses could be probably discounted.
- TQM is the programme of choice opted by all units except Unit A. Unit A has in addition to Five S selected Zero defect as the programme of choice. The units have apparently made pragmatic choice.

Table 7.24: Quality Programmes in SEZ Units (Q 1.4)

Methods	Unit A	Unit B	Unit C	Unit D	Unit E	Unit F
Five S	✓	✓	NS	✓	NS	NS
TQM	NS	✓	✓	✓	✓	✓
Six Sigma	NS	✓	NS	✓	NS	NS
Zero defect	✓	✓	NS	✓	NS	NS
Others (Pls specify)	NS	NS	NS	NS	NS	NS

(✓ = SELECTED; NS = NOT SELECTED)

- The conclusion is that on discounting the choices made by Units B and D, the concept of Six Sigma is yet to be accepted as a quality tool.

Section Two: Opportunity Identification (Q 2.1–Q 2.6)

7.4.7.4 **Promising Sectors in SEZs (Q 2.1)** The units were asked to select the most promising sectors for setting up SEZs. The unit responses are given in Table 7.25 (Q 2.1).

- All the units are unanimous that pharmaceuticals sector is the sector of choice and the most promising sector for SEZs.
- IT/ITeS and textiles have appeal in at least half of the units as promising sectors.

Table 7.25: Top Promising Sectors (Q 2.1)

Sectors	Unit A	Unit B	Unit C	Unit D	Unit E	Unit F
IT/ITeS	NS	✓	✓	NS	NS	✓
Textiles	✓	✓	✓	NS	NS	NS
Gems & Jewellery	NS	✓	NS	NS	NS	✓
Electronic	✓	✓	NS	NS	NS	NS
Pharmaceutical	✓	✓	✓	✓	✓	✓
Financial Services	NS	NS	✓	NS	NS	NS
Petro, Crude etc.	NS	✓	NS	NS	NS	NS
Others (Please specify)	NS	NS	NS	NS	✓	NS

(✓ = SELECTED; NS = NOT SELECTED)

- If we discount the choice of Unit B, who selected all the sectors listed; Electronics, Gems and Jewellery and Financial Services has been picked by one unit each; none of the units other than B has chosen Petro, crude and so on. One unit has selected in Others category the industry of chemicals.
- The authorities need to focus on development of the selected fields especially pharmaceuticals, IT/ITeS and textiles, which are viewed as having huge opportunity and potential.

7.4.7.5 **Parameters for SEZs Opportunity (Q 2.2)** The units were asked to rank various factors/parameters in order of importance for the evaluation of SEZ opportunities. The results of the ranking are tabulated in Table 7.26 (Q 2.2).

- Government policies emerge as the top determining factor to evaluate SEZ opportunities. This shows that the units view regulatory environment and a friendly policy environment as the most important parameter. The parameter of laws and regulations is perceived to be almost equally important.

Table 7.26: Parameters for SEZ Opportunities (Q 2.2)

Parameters	Unit A	Unit B	Unit C	Unit D	Unit E	Unit F
Location advantage	5	4	4	NR	5	3
Macroeconomics of the country	4	3	4	NR	3	1
Industrial investment support	4	4	4	NR	4	4
Investment cost	4	3	4	NR	3	4
Skilled labour	4	4	3	NR	4	4
Management and service	5	3	3	NR	4	3
Government policies	5	3	5	4	4	5
Laws and regulations	5	3	4	4	4	5
Stability and consistency of the government	5	3	2	4	4	4
Others (Pls. specify)	NR	NR	NR	NR	✓	NR

(1 = POOR, 2 = AVERAGE, 3 = GOOD, 4 = VERY GOOD, 5 = OUTSTANDING, NR = NO RESPONSE: ✓=New Parameter)

- Close behind is the parameter of location advantage, which can be explained by the fact that infrastructure development is uneven in India. Per unit road transportation costs remain high, hence it makes sense to choose location close to supply sources and the market for the products.
- Stability and consistency of the government merits importance as a parameter for evaluation of opportunity.
- Unit E has suggested a new parameter "Infrastructure should be improved for SEZ".

7.4.7.6 Digital Technologies and SEZs (Q 2.3) The units were asked to rank the advantages of new digital technologies and the result of the ranking is reproduced at Table 7.27 (Q 2.3).

- The units unanimously agree on the result of "Increased Productivity" as the advantage of new technology.
- However, not all units view that new technology will result in "Improved performance and flexibility".
- Mass customization is also counted as an advantage of the new technologies.

7.4.7.7 Scope of New Technologies in SEZs (Q 2.4) The units were requested to choose new technologies having scope in their units. Two units have in addition to choosing ranked the new technologies also. The result of the ranking allotted is given in Table 7.28 (Q 2.4)

- Artificial Intelligence (AI) is selected by most units and has top ranking in the list of effective technology in SEZs.

Table 7.27: Ranking of Role of New Digital Technologies in Promotion of SEZs (Q 2.3)

Parameters	Unit A	Unit B	Unit C	Unit D	Unit E	Unit F
Improved performance and flexibility	4	2	4	2	4	4
Increased productivity	4	3	3	4	3	5
A massive reorganization of the supply chain	4	1	3	2	3	3
Mass Customization	4	4	3	2	4	2

(1 = POOR, 2 = AVERAGE, 3 = GOOD, 4 = VERY GOOD, 5 = OUTSTANDING)

Table 7.28: Scope of New Technologies in SEZs (Q 2.4)

New Tech	Unit A	Unit B	Unit C	Unit D	Unit E	Unit F
Block-chain Technology	NS	NS	✓	2	NS	NS
Artificial Intelligence (AI)	NS	✓	NS	4	4	✓
Big Data analytics	✓	✓	NS	2	3	NS
Augmented Reality (AR)	NS	NS	NS	2	2	NS
Drones	NS	NS	NS	2	1	✓
Internet of Things (IoT)	NS	NS	✓	2	3	NS
Virtual Reality (VR)	NS	NS	NS	2	1	NS
3D Printing	NS	✓	NS	2	3	✓
Robots	NS	✓	✓	2	2	✓

(1 = POOR, 2 = AVERAGE, 3 = GOOD, 4 = VERY GOOD, 5 = OUTSTANDING: ✓ = SELECTED; NS= NOT SELECTED)

- Other technologies that figure in the choices made are Big Data Analytics and Robots.
- There is no unanimity on other technologies like Block chain, 3D Printing, Internet of Things (IoT).
- The units are not enthused on the scope of Augmented Reality (AR) and Virtual Reality (VR).

7.4.7.8 **Functional Level of Application of New Technologies (Q 2.5)** Table 7.29 gives summary of responses given by six units in respect of which level of function of organization, the new technologies for manufacturing and service sectors in SEZs have greater scope (Q 2.5).

- Manufacturing and Administration and HR departments are perceived as the major beneficiaries of new technologies.
- The new technologies also help Research and Development and Sales and Marketing Departments.
- There is no unanimity on the role of new technologies at Corporate Level and Finance Department.

Table 7.29: Function Level of Organization—New Technologies Will Be Useful (Q 2.5)

Features	Unit A	Unit B	Unit C	Unit D	Unit E	Unit F
Corporate Level	NS	NS	✓	NS	4	NS
Research and Development	✓	✓	NS	NS	5	✓
Manufacturing Department	✓	✓	NS	✓	4	✓
Administration and HR Department	✓	✓	✓	NS	3	✓
Sales and Marketing Department	✓	NS	✓	✓	3	✓
Finance Department	NS	✓	✓	NS	4	NS

(✓ = SELECTED; NS= NOT SELECTED: 1 = POOR, 2 = AVERAGE, 3 = GOOD, 4 = VERY GOOD, 5 = OUTSTANDING)

7.4.7.9 **Value Chain and Proposition (Q 2.6)** Table 7.30 gives summary of responses given by six units in respect of redesigning value chain and proposition using new technologies in their units (Q 2.6).

- The units unanimously agree that reduction in costs is the major benefit that accrues from the application of new technologies.
- Increase in quality aspects and improvement in procurement and supplier structure is counted as the other benefits of new technology application.
- Half or less than half of the units opine that the new technology will be advantageous for flexibility, increasing service level and improving innovation structure and employment structure.

Section Three: Strategic Reforms (Q 3.1–Q 3.6)

7.4.7.10 **Competitive Advantage over Other SEZs Outside India (Q 3.1)** Table 7.31 gives summary of responses given by six units in respect of

Table 7.30: Redesigning Value Chain & Use of New Technologies (Q 2.6)

Parameters	Unit A	Unit B	Unit C	Unit D	Unit E	Unit F
Increase of Flexibility	NS	✓	✓	NS	NS	✓
Increase Quality	✓	✓	✓	NS	NS	✓
Increase service level	NS	NS	✓	✓	NS	✓
Reduction of costs	✓	✓	✓	✓	✓	✓
Improved procurement and supplier structure	✓	✓	✓	✓	NS	✓
Sourcing by region	NS	NS	✓	NS	NS	NS
Innovation structure	✓	✓	NS	NS	NS	✓
Customer structure	✓	NS	NS	NS	NS	NS
Employment structure	✓	NS	✓	NS	NS	NS

(✓ = SELECTED; NS= NOT SELECTED)

competitive redesigning value chain and proposition using new technologies in their units (Q 3.1).

- Most units opined that change in government policies in respect of procedures is necessary to have competitive advantages over other SEZs located outside India.
- As regards stimulus package, the response was mixed with about half of the units affirming the need for stimulus package.
- In any other points, Unit B requested for "synchronization and simplification of procedures", while Unit E stated that "SEZ Policy was killed in 2011".

7.4.7.11 **Strategic Resources and Competencies (Q 3.2)** Table 7.32 gives summary of responses given by six units in respect of strategic resources and

Table 7.31: Competetive Advantages Over Other SEZs Outside India (Q 3.1)

Resources	Unit A	Unit B	Unit C	Unit D	Unit E	Unit F
Location	5	2	✓	NS	NS	1
Agglomeration with local suppliers	4	5	✓	NS	NS	1
Govt. and Institutional support	5	4	✓	4	✓	3
Factors of production	4	5	✓	NS	NS	3
Infrastructure	5	1	✓	NS	NS	2
Market	4	3	✓	4	NS	5

(NR = NO RESPONSE)

Table 7.32: Strategic Resources and Competencies (Q 3.2)

Drivers	Unit A	Unit B	Unit C	Unit D	Unit E	Unit F
A change in government policies required in respect of procedures?	Yes	No	Yes	Yes	NR	Yes
A stimulus package is required?	Yes	No	Yes	NR	Yes	No
Any other	NR	Yes	NR	NR	Yes	NR

(✓ = SELECTED; NS = NOT SELECTED: 1 = POOR, 2 = AVERAGE, 3 = GOOD, 4 = VERY GOOD, 5 = OUTSTANDING)

competencies required in their units. While four units have ranked the parameters, two units have selected the parameters without assigning any values (Q 3.2).

- Government and Institutional Support is the one resource that all units agree upon as the most important one. Market is next in importance for most of the units.
- There is no unanimity on other resources like infrastructure, location, agglomeration and factors of production.

7.4.7.12 **SEZs and Dynamic Economics (Q 3.3)** Table 7.33 gives summary of responses given by six units in respect of contribution of SEZ units towards dynamic economics (Q 3.3).

- SEZ units are perceived as foreign exchange earners; this is obvious as the production thereof is largely for exports.

Table 7.33: SEZ Units—Contribution to Dynamic Economic (Q 3.3)

Drivers	Unit A	Unit B	Unit C	Unit D	Unit E	Unit F
Employment	✓	✓	✓	NS	✓	✓
Demand-supply	✓	✓	✓	NS	✓	NS
Socio-economic impact	NS	✓	✓	NS	✓	✓
Sustainability	NS	✓	✓	NS	NS	NS
Foreign exchange earner	✓	✓	✓	✓	✓	✓

(✓ = SELECTED; NO ✓ OR BLANK = NOT SELECTED)

- The other main contribution as perceived by the units is generation of employment. Majority of the units agreed that the units have positive socio-economic impact and contribute to the reduction of demand-supply gap.

7.4.7.13 **New Approaches to Strategic Management (Q 3.5)** Table 7.34 gives summary of responses given by six units in respect of new approaches to strategic management (Q 3.5)

Table 7.34: New Approaches to Strategic Management (Q 3.5)

Approach	Unit A	Unit B	Unit C	Unit D	Unit E	Unit F
Internet of Things (IoT)	N	A	SA	A	N	A
Technologies that will impact everyone	N	A	A	A	A	A
E-Commerce	N	N	N	DA	A	A
People, Talent and future of work	SDA	A	A	A	A	A
Need for New Organization Structure	N	N	A	DA	N	DA
HR—the weak spot in corporate transformation	A	N	N	DA	A	A
Roadmap for building corporate innovative capabilities	N	DA	A	DA	A	A

(A = AGREE; SA = STRONGLY AGREE; NR = NO RESPONSE; N = NEUTRAL; DA = DISAGREE; SDA = STRONGLY DISAGREE)

There is no unanimity among the units on the best approach to strategic management. Some approaches which have secured agreement from more than 50 per cent of the units are:

1. Technologies that will impact everyone,
2. People, talent and future of work,
3. Internet of Things (IoT),
4. Roadmap for building corporate innovative capabilities.

Part III Validation

7.5 Validation of Research Proposal Framework

7.5.1 Validation of Socio-Economic Indicators

The researchers chose the following Six Variables ("Methods of Environmental Impact Assessment" edited by Peter Morris and Riki Therivel):

1. Direct economic
2. Indirect/wider economic/expenditure
3. Demographic
4. Housing
5. Other local services
6. Socio-cultural

Assigning values to these indicators would help researcher in seeking answers to the following research questions:

1) Whether SEZs in Gujarat are effective on the development front in the context of social and economic aspects?
2) Impact assessment of Gujarat SEZs by reckoning metrics based on Direct Economic Impact, Indirect/wider Economic Impact and Social Impact.

Quantitative or qualitative values were assigned to build the socio-economic index. The values could be assigned by considering a subset of factors for each variable as given in Chapter 2, Table 2.3 under 2.8.6.1 Socio-Economic Variables.

These indicators were applied across six units with representation from both multi-product and sector-specific SEZ category for the purpose of comparison; it was necessary to have a quality check to test the indicator and conduct an exercise for validation of the indicators.

Each of the six units selected for the validation process were provided the structured questionnaire designed (Appendix 2.D) to elicit response on the variables, whether any other variable could be included and the inter-se ranking in terms of weight of the variables.

The first query to the participants was:

I. **Question No 1** ***If the variables listed are adequate components of the socio-economic index?***

All the six units responded positively that the six variables listed are adequate components of the socio-economic index. Unit C added that the factors are comprehensive indicators to derive the meaningful conclusion. Unit E endorsed that they seem to cover everything.

II. Question No 2 ***proposed that variables no. 1 (Direct Economic) and 2 (Indirect/wider economic/expenditure) are the driving factors and should be allotted heavy weights in contrast to the other variables which should be allotted light weights. The units were asked whether they agree with the proposal.***

Units A, C and D agreed with the proposition. Unit B agreed that variable 1 and 2 are important but disagreed that the other variables can be assigned light weights, as variable no. 5 (other local services) and variable no. 6 (socio-cultural) are equally important as 1 and 2. Unit E was of the opinion that along with variable nos. 1 and 2, equally heavy weights should be considered for variable no. 4 (housing) and no. 5. Unit F also agreed that variable nos. 1 and 2 should have heavy weights which should be twice as that of other variables.

Thus, the overwhelming opinion was that variable nos. 1 and 2 should have heavy weights. However, the units did not agree that all other variables should be assigned light weights; the ratio is in favour of assigning next heavier weight after the weight assigned to 1 and 2 to variable no. 5, followed by 4 and 6. The lightest weight would be assigned to variable no. 3 (Demographic).

III. Question no. 3 ***is related to previous question no.2 and queries whether assigning equal weights to the six variables is justified or what should be the weights to be assigned to each variable in the opinion of the respondents.***

Unit A has quantified the weights to be given to each variable as follows:

Variables: 1–30%; 2–30%; 3–10%; 4–10%; 5–15% and 6–5%.

The weights assigned by Unit A are in sync with answer to question no. 2.

Unit B reiterated the answer to no. 2, that together with variables nos. 1 and 2, variable no. 5 was also important as it pertains to infrastructure facilities. Therefore, the six variables should not be assigned equal weights.

Units C and D replied positively to the proposition that all the variables should be assigned equal weights. This is not in sync with the answers given by them to question 2 wherein they agreed that variables nos. 1 and 2 should be assigned heavy weights.

Unit E reaffirmed that all variables should not have equal weights and that the weights should be graded as 1 and 2 most important, next 4 and 5 and finally 3 and 6.

Unit F denied that all the variables should be assigned equal weights. The answer was in synchronization with the answer to question 2.

Considering both the replies to question 2 and 3, it is surmised that the weights which may be assigned to the variables as per the submissions made by the six units are 1–30%; 2–30%; 3–5%; 4–10%; 5–15% and 6–10%.

IV. The next question no. 4 ***seeks opinion of the units on the threshold level used for classifying answers in the main questionnaire as 1: Poor, 2: Average, 3: Good, 4: Very Good and 5: Outstanding.***

All the respondents submitted that the scale is fine and have allotted varying degrees as follows:

Unit A: OK	Unit B: Good	Unit C: Outstanding
Unit D: Very Good	Unit E: Good	Unit F: Perfect

V. Question no. 5 ***seeks opinion whether the proposed socio-economic index to be built on the six variables measures what it should measure.***

The respondents replied as follows:

Unit A: Yes	Unit B: No Comments	Unit C: No comments
Unit D: Yes	Unit E: Can't say	Unit F: Yes

As 50 per cent of the respondents replied in the affirmative and there is no negation, we could consider that the socio-economic index is the appropriate measure.

VI. Question no. 6 ***elicits opinion of the respondents as to whether there is any other variable which is left out and needs to be considered within the index.***

Most of the units have replied that the variables used to construct the proposed socio-economic index are perfect and no variable is left out. Unit A opined that it is perfect, Unit B said all are covered and Unit C remarked that the parameters are adequate to address the issues. Unit D has replied with a Yes; but they have not specified any other variable which is left out. Unit E affirmed that most are covered, but they have also not mentioned any other variable to be covered. Unit F has replied that there is no variable left out. Thus, the majority opinion is that there is no variable which is left out and needs to be considered within the index.

VII. **The next question no. 7 is *open-ended and asks the units to name the variable which relates most to their SEZ and which variables are more related to the SEZs in Gujarat.***

Though the question is in two parts, all the units have given a single response, therefore it may be derived that the variables considered important for their units are also equally important for the SEZs in Gujarat. Units A and Unit F have singled out variable nos. 1 and 2 as the most important variables. Units B and E stated that variables nos. 1, 2 and 5 are the most important variables. Unit C affirmed that variable no. 2 is the most important. Unit D has replied with a Yes, even though this is an open-ended question, thus this response may be discounted.

The ranking of variables is summarized in Table 7.35.

Thus, the most important variables would be 1, 2 and 5.

VIII. **The final question *seeks suggestions from the units on how the index can be improved further*.**

Units B, D and F have replied with blank lines or that there is no suggestion/comment from their end. Unit A affirmed that most are covered and offered no suggestion. Unit C stated that all parameters detailed are adequate to derive a meaningful index. Unit E commented that the index evolves with time and experience and also the situational changes.

Table 7.35: Ranking of Variables

Rank	Variable	Weighment
I	Direct economic	Heavier
II	Indirect/wider economic/expenditure	Heavier
III	Other local services	Heavier
IV	Housing	Less heavy
V	Socio-cultural	Less heavy
VI	Demographic	Least heavy

7.6 Synopsis

The research was conducted in three parts. The first part consisted in soliciting replies from 492 SEZ units from six SEZs in a comprehensive questionnaire having questions in nine categories as follows: (1) General Information (2) Direct Economic (3) Indirect Economic (4) Demographic (5) Housing (6) Other Local Services (7) Social Impact (8) Socio-economic Impact and (9) Type of Drivers—Impact on SEZs.

One hundred and one respondents submitted complete replies. The data size consists of 176 columns (including serial number) and 101 rows (data).

Statistical Analysis: At first, the Cronbach's alpha method is used to test the reliability and internal consistency of items used for obtaining responses from the units. The results show that Cronbach's alpha is 0.8728, which means the questionnaire of 49 items measures the same construct. The item-adjusted total correlation and squared multiple coefficient are consistently high and the Cronbach's alpha values do not differ significantly. In all, there is overwhelming evidence that the questions measure the same construct.

Once the reliability and internal consistency is established, the statistical analysis of the responses is done on a sequential basis.

General Information: The first response in general information pertains to the location of the unit in Gujarat. The location of the six selected SEZs with the number of units in each SEZ is depicted pictorially in a sized bubble. Only eight districts in the state house SEZs; there are no SEZs in 25 districts. Most SEZs were commissioned post the SEZs Act 2005 and SEZs rules 2006. In fact, large number of SEZs date from 2008 onwards; from 2013, the pace slackened due to the withdrawal of MAT and DDT. The ownership is overwhelmingly Indian; foreign investment and ownership is limited to some units located in PHARMEZ and Electronic Park, Gandhinagar, showing there is a need to attract foreign investment on a larger scale.

The revenue was plotted for three years 2016–2018 with the composition of the employees (male/female). The employees in the selected SEZs are predominantly male, with the exception of Ahmedabad Apparel Park, which has a substantial women workforce. There is consistent increase in revenue year-on-year basis in all SEZs except Sachin SEZ, Surat, which may be explained by the global decline in demand for diamonds. On working the variance analysis in revenue growth and plotting the same for three years sectors, it emerges that on hierarchical basis the top-line growth is more in pharmaceuticals, apparel and chemical and petrochemicals.

Direct Economic: SEZ-wise data of all three classes of employees namely permanent, contractual and daily wages is plotted skill-wise (skilled, semi-skilled and unskilled). The relationship is further established by using Pearson Chi-Square test with the H1 hypothesis "there is significant relationship between Job type and Skill type". The P value is found to be 0 for both Pearson Chi-Square test and Likelihood Ratio Chi-Square; thus, the H1 hypothesis is correct.

The industry-wise activity-wise data of employment is plotted and it is clear that the manufacturing industries have more employment in all skill category as compared to the employment in trading, service and combined industry. There are more skilled employees in permanent category, while there are more unskilled employees in contractual and daily wages category. Sachin SEZ has maximum number of employees (permanent and contractual) both in the skilled and semi-skilled category; Sachin SEZ is followed by Apparel Park, Ahmedabad.

The employment pattern based on the gender and industry is plotted in a pie chart. Employment is dependent upon the type of activity, that is, manufacturing/trading/services/combined as well as nature of industries. Heavy Industries employ more men, while light industries like textiles and apparel have women in almost equal numbers.

By plotting the employment pattern of locals in all three nature of employment and skill categories in the six SEZs in a bar diagram, it is deduced that priority is given to the local residents across all categories. This gives a fillip to local economic development and a boost to social parameters.

The responses regarding training and skill improvement for employees is determined through correspondence analysis on symmetric basis. The results show that the focus is on development of high skills through training. HR factors are plotted on a scale from Not Important to Very Important.

The impact of government policy on SEZ growth in different areas is shown by three-dimensional boxes in descending order, it is observed that the maximum impact is by labour-related policies, followed by facility for R&D and job work from DTA. It is also seen that the standard deviation across SEZs is low, suggesting uniformity in responses.

On plotting the various components of economic impact of SEZs in an asymmetric pie diagram, it is found that the maximum benefit accrued from SEZ operation is in increase of exports. Ease in business process, infrastructure development and enhanced standard of living are other substantial benefits perceived due to SEZs.

To determine the most important factor for Human Capital Development, a Decision Tree based on CHAID (Chi Square Automatic Interactive Detection) algorithm is run. In the model the Revenue Growth performance is taken as the output variable while the parameters are taken as inputs. A direct linkage between Organisational Culture and Performance is clearly established. The next two important factors are R&D activities and unit activity type. These factors are plotted in predictor type chart as the factors for predicting revenue growth. These findings are further validated through logistic regression method. It is seen irrespective of the unit size and similar firms in the same SEZ, invariably the Human Capital Development and Revenue growth depend upon organizational culture, followed by R&D activity and unit activity type.

The responses on the impact of SEZ on local economy are plotted on a pie chart. The total number of responses saying High or Moderate total around 90 per cent, which affirms that one objective of the SEZ, that is, boost to the local economy is met.

Indirect Economic: Based on the responses from the units, the impact of various Human Capital Factors on indirect economic is depicted in bar chart for ayes and nays. About 90 per cent of the respondents agreed on the importance of the factors and the factors in hierarchy of importance are level of competitiveness, linkage to local supplier, labour mobility and international quality standards.

The benefits accruing to a unit in SEZ on account of proximity to other units in the SEZ is captured on a bar diagram. Benefits are maximized in area of formal and informal networking followed by policies and strategies. Product development and process/quality control are areas where not much benefit is perceived given the heterogeneity in products and processes.

In order to work out the multiplier effects, the five parameters of indirect economic are cross mapped on x and y axis. The correlation is found to be moderate between "SEZ leads to multiplier effects" and "SEZs contribute to indirect jobs". It is weak between "SEZ leads to multiplier effects" and "Labour issues" as well as with "retail expenditure". There is no correlation between "SEZ leads to multiplier effects" and "Role of R&D in your unit is very important".

The linkage of the unit with Domestic Tariff Area (DTA) is mapped on dot plot. Almost half of the respondents get up to 40–60 per cent of job work from DTA and a quarter of the respondents get almost 60–80 per cent work from DTA.

The frequency of competition among units inter se is graphically mapped and results in a bell curve. About half the participants opted for low competition, while 30 per cent affirmed that the competition was moderate.

Demographic: The average age of SEZ workers is depicted in a bar diagram. More than half the SEZ workers are in the 25–35 years age group; while another third are from 35–45 years age group.

The average no. of dependants of workers is plotted on a pie chart. Almost 57 per cent of the workers have two to four dependants showing that most families are nuclear in nature while 20 per cent of the workers have four to six dependants implying that the parents also reside with the workers. Fewer number of dependants also point to less claimants to the cake and therefore better outcomes with regard to education, health and quality of life.

The answers provided by the respondents on single wage earner in the family was plotted on a bar diagram. It reveals bell curve formation with about 46 per cent at the peak moderate response.

The data of dwelling place of the workers in terms of proximity from work place is plotted on a dot plot chart. Most of the employees have dwelling place within range of 5 to 10 kilometres from the unit; a negligible number of workers live in the SEZ premises exhibiting the need to build dormitories and low-cost residential units for workers in the non-processing area of SEZ.

It is observed that almost 60 per cent of the permanent workers reside in the vicinity of the unit while around 40 per cent of the temporary workers live nearby. Thus, SEZs are beneficial for the local economy.

The income level of the nearby families is found to be higher as two-thirds of the families belong to Upper Middle Income category while one-third belong to Higher income category.

Housing: A Chi-square and likelihood ratio chi-square analysis is run for housing-related social factors. There is agreement on the proposition that "Housing areas near SEZs are becoming cosmopolitan" and "Renting near SEZ is difficult". However, the proposition that "There are residential complexes inside SEZs" and "Hostel facilities for women" evoked negative responses. This data is also plotted diagrammatically in colour-coded boxes.

Other Local Services: The importance of social factors is determined by coefficient of variance analysis by plotting the average score and standard deviation. The most important factors are life security, women's safety and canteen facility while the "good to have" facilities are medical room and pick and drop. The desirable facilities include educational loans and social schemes; while the fourth quadrant representing relatively unimportant facilities houses educational facilities and gymnasium.

Social Impact: The responses regarding women as family head, but still facing domestic violence is mapped. A quarter of the working women are believed to be family head by virtue of being sole member of the family with an income; interestingly, it is believed that at least a quarter of such women are victims of domestic violence.

On mapping the male–female ratio across different job skills and job profiles, it emerges that female workers are present across job profiles almost in the same proportion as their overall strength; the units affirmed that they would prefer women workers, but then the jobs offered to women are purely dependant on the nature of jobs.

As regards compliances, most units agree to have the labour audits done regularly, almost 93 per cent on annual basis. The units comply with the labour laws at different intervals.

The marital status of women employees reveals that one-third of the women are unmarried, around 63 per cent are married and the balance 4 per cent comprises of divorced, widowed or single mother.

The employee absenteeism data reveals formation of a bell curve with more than half of the employees recording two days of absence in a month. At the most, on an average, the maximum absenteeism is for three days in a month.

About half of the units agree that they conduct women-centric camps on topics like sexual harassment, education, women's rights. More than two-thirds of the units disagree with the idea that there should be menstrual hygiene camps, reinforcing the notion that women hygiene issues tend to be put on the backburner.

The social objectives are then mapped on a correspondence analysis into four quadrants. The largest blob consists of respondents who strongly agree that SEZs contribute to social objectives and protect minimum wages. They disagree that SEZs around urban areas have increased the regional inequalities. SEZs are neutral on promotion of marginalized community and tackling of social problems like crime. Units agree that SEZs promote women employment and that they improve the lifestyle of employees.

On the different facets of women protection, the consensus is that the transport facility and legal mechanism to protect women has overwhelming importance. Next is maternity leave and crèche facility provision.

Socio-economic Impact: That SEZs have a socio-economic impact gets approval from about 68 per cent of the respondents; in fact, 8 per cent agree strongly. Around 26 per cent opted for neutral option while 6 per cent disagreed with the proposition.

Economic Drivers: The majority agreed that the economic drivers have a positive impact. About a quarter remain neutral while a small number (5 per cent) disagreed with the proposition.

The conceptual, analytical and technical skills are mapped across manufacturing, service and trading industry. High importance is given by service industry (particularly IT/ITeS) to these skills. On the other hand, manufacturing and trading are labour-intensive and require more of semi-skilled and unskilled workers.

Drivers: An association map is drawn between the ratings and SEZ parameters. The drivers having impact are infrastructure facility inside SEZs, single-window mechanism and exports. Most respondents also agreed that economic drivers like monetary management are useful. The units strongly disagree that SEZ policies has acted as a driver for investment. They are neutral on FDI and private local investment.

The restoration of exemption from MAT and DDT has to be considered for early revival of SEZs.

Models building:

Models were then built on the relationship of one dependant variable with other independent variables to determine which models contribute towards socio-economic impact. Models based on (1) Economic Impact, (2) Indirect Economic Impact, (3) Housing Impact, (4) Other Local Services Impact, (5) Social Impact and (6) Type of Drivers—Impact on SEZs.

The method used is Likelihood Ratio, since the data is non-numerical in nature. The likelihood ratio is used to determine whether one model fits the data better than the other. Hence the parameter/group of parameters missing in the other model, if added to the model, increase the likelihood. Such parameter/group of parameters are defined to be important in influencing the outcome of the variance model.

Decision Tree analysis with entropy method and information gain: Entropy is a measure of disorder, ideal values would range from 0 to 1; could be more than 1, but that will mean greater disorder or uncertainty, and therefore contrary to the statistical goals. By getting additional information (information gain), the value of entropy is reduced around the target variable. Decision tree places all the options on the table, enables analysis of the consequences of a decision and provides the framework for determining the values of the outcomes and the probabilities thereof, thus, assists in taking the best decision.

Economic impact was analysed by the Likelihood Ratio method and the parameters that emerged important are increase in exports, employment and foreign exchange and improvement in infrastructure and demographic pattern. Ease of Business had marginal importance while improved living standards and capital-intensive projects were ranked unimportant.

The combination of inputs for higher SEZ impact on local economy was worked out using entropy method and Decision Tree analysis. From the mathematical models, it emerges that the following factors namely increase in exports, employment and foreign exchange and improvement in infrastructure, demography and ease of business, boosted the local economy.

Indirect Economic Impact: By using the Likelihood Ratio, the four features emerge important namely role of R&D, labour issues, indirect or induced jobs and retail expenditure. The features of competition within the zone and connected DTA suppliers are found to be less important or unimportant.

Next, the combination of inputs for higher SEZ indirect economic impact is derived using mathematical equations—entropy method and Decision Tree analysis. Similar results are obtained showing importance of labour issues, retail expenditure, R& D and indirect jobs.

Housing Impact: was analysed by the Likelihood Ratio method and the parameters that emerged important are non-processing area for housing purpose, dedicated hostel for women and separate dormitory for employees. Residence within the zone had marginal importance while renting house near SEZs and slum area near SEZs were ranked unimportant.

The combination of inputs for higher SEZ impact on housing was worked out using entropy method and Decision Tree analysis. The mathematical model supplements the results as obtained by likelihood ratio.

Other Local Services: By using the Likelihood Ratio, the seven features that emerge important are health insurance, pick-and-drop facility, fire protection, in-house loan, dedicated medical room, women's safety measures and education loan. Canteen facility has marginal importance. The features of gymnasium and education institution facility are found to be less important or unimportant.

Next, the combination of inputs for other local services is derived using mathematical equations—entropy method and Decision Tree analysis. The mathematical model supplements the results as obtained through Likelihood Ratio.

Social Impact: was analysed by the Likelihood Ratio method and the seven features that emerged important are protection of minimum wages, working hours and gender equality; SEZs role in tackling social problems; promotion of marginalized community women; reduction of community stress; impact on quality of life; women employment and empowerment and regional inequalities.

The combination of inputs for higher SEZ impact on Social Impact was worked out using entropy method and Decision Tree analysis and the results as obtained by mathematical model (likelihood ratio) is supplemented.

Type of Drivers—Impact on SEZ: The statistically important drivers impacting SEZs are ranked as follows: Investment and contribution to Indian Economy, logistics facilities, Export Incentive Scheme, improved infrastructure facility, single window mechanism, Foreign Direct Investment, Private Investment and Inflation and Capacity utilization. Monetary management is unimportant.

The combination for important drivers impacting SEZs using entropy method and Decision Tree analysis was worked out; the results obtained supplement the results through mathematical models.

Finally, the overall model summary is constructed by showing various key features for SEZ socio-economic impact; with a multi-layer perceptron and stopping rule of error cannot be further reduced. The following features are important: Economic Factors; Social Factors; Indirect Economic; Other local factors; Housing factors. It is therefore derived that SEZs have both economic (direct and indirect) as well as social impact.

SEZ developers have a vantage position and partly hold the key to socio-economic impact of SEZs. The developers for the study were selected through a rigorous process to include multi-product and sector-specific SEZs. Care was also taken to include SEZs under government and private ownership and through the government–government partnership model.

The consensus on the ownership model is that the Public-Private Partnership (PPP) model is the preferred one. This is understandable considering the heavy investments in the infrastructure of a SEZ; the participation of government would make things easier especially in the matter of land acquisition. It is agreed that employment generation is the biggest contribution of SEZ units and therefore SEZs should be encouraged on this account.

The crux of the questionnaire is on the factors as assessed by the developers which contribute to the socio-economic development. Stress is given by the developers to the economic factors namely direct economic and indirect economic followed by other local services like public and private sector education, and so on. Next follows demographic as a game-changer and housing brings up the rear. Hence the research finding arrived at earlier that economic parameters are paramount as compared to social ones gets validated.

On the social indicators front, the developers believe that benefits like motorable road to the taluka/district HQ and mobile connectivity result from SEZs. They also hold the belief that no migration out takes place as a result of SEZs and the ousted benefit through jobs in the SEZs. The withdrawal of IT benefits from 1.4.2020 and imposition of MAT are held to be responsible for the slowdown in SEZs growth in the five-year period from 2013 to 2018 as compared to the block of earlier five years.

Export promotion ranks foremost among the economic impact factors for SEZs. An important measure for the development of SEZs is the accretion of new units.

The developers have differing views on the priority to be allocated to the various CSR activities. Incidentally, most developers consider women empowerment and gender equality as one of the important CSR activity. The response of the developers regarding pollution and environmental sustainability differs; probably the developers view these issues from their perspective. Most developers are on the same page with regard to utilization of vacant land; change to multi-product will create new opportunity for using the vacant land is high on priority. The development of vacant land into residential complexes has a low priority.

The developers do not hold much brief for the MSMEs in SEZs. However, they hold the belief that clustering of small and large enterprises will promote and protect the interest of MSMEs.

The next part deals with the case study and cross contrast of six units of six SEZs. Each of the units is different in design, products and organizational culture. Naturally, the choice of strategy varies in each case. Nevertheless, a few points that are in common enable us to draw some conclusions that are important to our research.

All the units say that they believe in the application of management principles; a couple of units have reservation on the part of engaging with external stakeholders. Most units perceive that the communication style followed is open and management empowers employees to improve the processes. The units believe that their employees practice innovation and strive to reduce any kind of waste. By and large, the units agree that the goal and objectives of the manufacturing units are closely linked with corporate objectives. The vision and strategy is broadly communicated and followed by the employees.

The preferred work styles are organized, sequential, planned and detailed-oriented and logical, analytical, linear and data-oriented. None of the units are comfortable with emotionally oriented or ideation-oriented work styles.

Most units choose TQM (Total Quality Management) as the quality programme to be implemented to increase employee and working efficiency.

There is unanimity in the choice of pharmaceuticals as the most promising sector for SEZs. However, the choice of parameters to be used to identify, analyse and evaluate SEZs opportunities, reveal divergence of views. Nevertheless, most of the units agree that government policies and laws and regulations play a big role in the evaluation process.

There is consensus that the new digital technologies help in increased productivity. Some perceive that the benefit is also in mass customization.

Most units assert that Manufacturing, Administration and HR are the functions in the organization that will derive the maximum benefit from new technologies. Artificial Intelligence (AI) is one technology that figures in all the responses as the new technology of choice. The units will be benefited in multifarious ways through new technologies; most agreed that reduction of costs and increase in quality will be the desired outcomes.

Change in government policies regarding procedures is reiterated by most units in order to have a level playing field with foreign SEZ units. Only a few units felt the need for a stimulus package.

The most needed strategic resource is government and institutional support. All agreed that SEZ units contribute to the exports from the country. Most counted employment, socio-economic impact and demand-supply as other contributions from the units.

There was no consensus in the choice of new approaches to strategic management; most units chose technologies that will impact everyone. Some agreed that people, talent and future of work hold the key to new approaches.

The final part of the study deals with the validation of questionnaire from six units of different SEZs. It is validated that the six variables, namely (1) Direct Economic; (2) Indirect/wider economic; (3) Demographic; (4) Housing; (5) Other local services and (6) Socio-cultural are adequate to build the socio-economic index. The weights to be assigned to the variables differ with variable nos. 1, 2 and 5 assigned heavier weights, while 4 and 6 less heavy weights and 3 the lightest weight. The variables are comprehensive and there is no variable left out for constructing the index.

This research study is therefore comprehensive and covers rigorously the various aspects of socio-economic as well as key drivers for overall development of SEZs. The responses received in four different questionnaires (Appendix 2.A, 2.B, 2.C & 2.D) from HR managers, Unit's CEOs, developers constitute a valuable storehouse of data. This data has been scientifically analysed and findings derived to meet the objectives of the study and the statement of the problem as mentioned in Chapter 2 (2.2 and 2.3).

The conclusions and suggestions are covered in latter chapters (Chapter 8).

8 Conclusion and Recommendation

A body of research attains significance and gains useful application when it affords resolutions of constraints and bottlenecks or offers improved models of performance for application. Economic research in particular affords scope for inferences based on real-time data and the researcher is in a pivotal position to give suggestions and recommendations as per his/her understanding of the research problem.

This chapter outlines the major findings and the outcome of the research. The scope covers the functioning of SEZs in Gujarat; assessment of direct economic benefits like FDI, employment, exports growth; assessment on similar lines of indirect economic benefits like induced employment; identification of the drivers for SEZ development and the importance of socio-economic factors for the holistic growth of SEZs.

Recommendations are addressed to SEZs units and stakeholders, academia and industry, state and central government departments, in addition to detailing the conclusions arrived at during the various phases of the research work.

8.1 Major Findings and Outcome

Though the findings are covered both in detailed and summary form in the previous chapter, the major findings are restated in the context of the research objectives and the research problem. The basic objective of the study as stated earlier is to examine the contribution of Gujarat SEZs in socio-economic development and to answer the following questions:

1) Whether SEZs in Gujarat are effective on the development front in the context of social and economic aspects?
2) Impact assessment of Gujarat SEZs by reckoning metrics based on Direct Economic Impact, Indirect/wider Economic Impact and Social Impact (i.e. socio-economic impact)
3) How vacant land in SEZ can be optimally utilized in Gujarat to fulfil the export promotion, employment generation and overall socio-economic development?

The study was undertaken with the premise that there is at least one significant independent variable or input variables such as Direct Economic, Indirect Economic, Demographic, Housing, Social Services, Socio-Cultural factors affecting socio-economic growth of SEZs (Special Economic Zones) in the state of Gujarat.

Data collected through field research was systematically compiled, grouped and tested through standard statistical techniques. The results indicate that the hypothesis is validated and there is in fact more than one significant input variable that affects socio-economic growth of Gujarat SEZs. The final model with predictor importance lists the factors on a scale from most important to less important as follows:

- Economic factors
- Social factors
- Indirect economic
- Other local factors
- Housing

SEZs in Gujarat therefore are effective on the development front in the context of both economic (direct and indirect) as well as social aspects.

As regards socio-economic impact with metrics, 22 socio-economic factors as determined through a rigorous process of statistical tests were assessed. Table 8.1 lists the final assessment ranking in order of descending importance of these 22 factors in six classes.

This classification would be very useful to decision makers for framing policies and monitoring implementation for the growth of SEZs and increasing their

Table 8.1: Key Factors—Socio-Economic Impact in SEZs

Extremely Important	**Very Important**
• Export growth • Indirect Jobs • Logistics • Minimum wages	• Quality of life • Improved infrastructure • Increase in foreign exchange
Important	**Marginally Important**
• Private Investments • Women's safety	• R&D Role • Export incentive • Education loan • Monetary management • Fire Protection
Partially Important	**Not important**
• Educational Institutions • Canteen facility • Pick-up facility • Hostel for women	• Increase in retail expenditure • Slum area near SEZs • Dormitory facility • Residential complex inside SEZs

socio-economic impact for the benefit of the state and the national economy and society.

Before attempting to present the optimal uses of vacant land in SEZs as derived through this research study, it is important to understand the underlying factors responsible for vacant land in SEZs. From research findings, it is apparent that one major factor for the substantial area of notified SEZ land lying vacant is the withdrawal of incentives like exemption from MAT and DDT. The allure of SEZs is no longer there; thus, relevant policy changes need to be reviewed.

Research findings point to some of the optimal uses of vacant land in line with the SEZ objectives of export promotion, employment generation, investment and infrastructure development as follows:

- **Conversion of sector-specific to multi-product SEZs:** Sector-specific SEZs need to be converted to multi-product SEZs. Units dealing in IT/ITeS services may be established across SEZs, even in SEZs that have largely manufacturing activities.
- **Services and Trading Activities:** SEZ units dealing with trading and warehousing activities can be set up in the existing manufacturing SEZs; this is relevant for Gujarat considering its numerous sea ports and excellent connectivity. On similar lines, service SEZs promoting the 12 services

identified as champion services and SEZs that cater to the MSME segment could help in utilization of vacant land.
- **Broad Banding:** Scope of broad banding may be amended in the policy, considering the activities of the units in the changing business scenario.

8.2 Research Conclusion

General: The 20 operational SEZs are located in 8 of the 33 districts of Gujarat; hence, there is a strong case for establishment of SEZs in the other 25 districts. It is only after the enactment of the SEZs Act 2005 and SEZs rules 2006, that most of the SEZs were commissioned. Hence it is proved that legal framework and rules are necessary to inspire confidence among investors. Policy changes dampen the sentiment; once MAT and DDT was withdrawn in 2013, the pace of opening of new SEZs was arrested. The expectation that SEZs would attract FDI in a big way was belied; only some units in PHARMEZ and Electronic Park, Gandhinagar, have foreign investment; the need to attract FDI in SEZs in a big way remains unfulfilled.

SEZ employment pattern shows ratio skewed towards males across all industries, except in apparels where male/female ratio is close to unity. Analysis of top line in rupee terms for the triennial 2016–2018 reveals consistent growth both overall and in all sectors, except in Diamonds—Sachin (Surat). Within growing sectors, at the apex of the growth pyramid is the pharmaceuticals sector followed by apparel sector SEZs.

A brief of the factors in the final predictor model is outlined below:

Economic Impact: The maximum economic impact of SEZ derived through different processes is increase in exports. This may be considered an expected outcome since goods and services produced in SEZs are exported by default. Nevertheless, this outcome indicates that the chief focus of SEZ-related policies should be increase in exports. The impact of SEZs can be seen in employment too. SEZ employees can be classified by (1) Job tenure (permanent, contractual and daily wages), (2) Skill sets (skilled, semi-skilled and unskilled) (3) Sector (manufacturing, trade and service) and (4) Local and non-local. Based on this classification, it is concluded that:

- Manufacturing sector has more jobs of all tenure types.
- More permanent employees are skilled.
- The trade and service industry employs larger number of skilled employees rather than semi-skilled or unskilled.

- Wages are a factor of skills, that is, generally higher the skills, more the wages.
- Wages in SEZs are generally higher than the wages prevailing in DTA.
- SEZ units prefer to employ local workers. Non-local workers are employed mostly for specialized skill jobs or where local talent is not available.

Social Impact: The deliverables include minimum wages protection, regulation of working hours, gender equality (equal wages for equal work) resulting in women empowerment and quality of life.

Some women-specific measures taken are conducting of women-centric camps on topics like sexual harassment and women's rights. However, much more remains to be done to get more women in the workforce by providing facilities like transport pick and drop, women hostels, crèche facility, maternity benefits, and so on.

Indirect economic: The multiplier effect of SEZs is manifest in the increase of indirect or induced jobs, thus boosting the local economy. On an average, half the job work of SEZ units is outsourced to local units in DTA (non SEZ units). There is reason to believe that the R&D activities in the SEZ benefit the economy in an indirect manner.

Other local factors: Some of the important local factors are women's safety measures, pick and drop facility, medical room and canteen facility. There is ample scope for further action and measures in the realm of women empowerment, continuing education and training and other such schemes which usher in better quality of life to the community.

Housing Impact: While the housing aspect was not viewed as a priority area, nevertheless, the need for utilization of non-processing area for housing purpose, hostel dedicated for women employees and separate dormitory for employees are some of the initiatives that are acknowledged as necessary by the stakeholders.

Through this research study, the drivers that impact SEZs could be established and they are listed below in order of importance:

1. Investment to India's economy
2. Logistics facilities
3. Export Incentives
4. Improved infrastructure facility
5. Single Window Mechanism
6. Foreign Direct Investment (FDI)
7. Private Investments
8. Inflation and Capacity Utilization

Government policy is acknowledged to have huge influence on SEZ growth in different areas particularly in areas linked with labour laws and policies, facility for R&D and job work from DTA.

Hence the researcher could attain the objectives with which the study was initiated. SEZs do have huge socio-economic impact and emerge as useful tools to promote exports growth, generate employment, and improve investment and infrastructure.

A few suggestions and recommendations are outlined in the next section of this chapter.

8.3 Research Recommendation

The research recommendations flow from this exhaustive research work. It is attempted to capture and encapsulate the results of the detailed interactions with the various stakeholders in the course of this research work. All the stakeholders whether they belong to the units, developers, authority or others are confident that SEZs can have a bigger socio-economic impact and emerge as role model for the economic and social development.

For convenience, the recommendations are grouped as those relevant to SEZs units, developers (stakeholders), government (central and state), academia and from management perspective, in three categories:

1. Administrative
2. Fiscal
3. Non-fiscal

8.3.1 Relevant to Units in SEZs

I. Administrative

- Units may boost revenue generation by way of enhancing existing product mix and by carrying out broad-banding activities in related segment and services.
- SEZs units may give preference to local residents for employment in all skill groups under permanent and temporary (contractual and daily wages) category. This will help in developing the local economy and also protect the interest of local residents. It will also promote social harmony, protect local culture and reduce social evils and conflicts.

- Facilities like canteen and transportation for employees and dedicated transport for women employees may be provided by the units/SEZ developers.
- To promote local entrepreneurs in the setting up of units in SEZs, by developing the entrepreneurship skills of local people. This measure will go a long way in preserving the local traditional arts/culture thus contributing to the socio-cultural aspect.
- Units/SEZs to have dedicated R&D facility. Quality development programmes to be conducted on regular basis.

II. Fiscal

- To introduce incentives scheme for skill upgradation.
- Employees may be recognized for outstanding contribution through schemes like "best employee of the month".
- Reward mechanism for timely completion of tasks.
- Protection of monetary benefits for work beyond normal working hours.

III. Non-Fiscal

- Units to conduct government promoted and recognized programmes for skill development, training and workshops to upgrade the skills for all type of employee categories.

8.3.2 Relevant to SEZs Developers (Stakeholders)

I. Administrative

- **Infrastructure Measures:** Developer may provide infrastructure facilities like building for educational institutions, hospitals, health clinic, recreation centres and residential complex for employees. Dormitory and womens hostels may also be provided for better working life of employees. Establishment of fire station, Group Health Insurance Schemes for all types of workers, transportation services for pick up/drop, medical room-OPD facility, educational scheme, women safety measures, common canteen facility, conference rooms, gymnasium, recreation centres are some of the measures needed so that social objectives can be achieved. These measures will improve indirect economy and contribute overall to the socio-development of local community area by the SEZs.

- **Environment:** Developer may ensure compliance with government norms on environmental protection. Developer may set up proper mechanism/ infrastructure to monitor environmental aspects.
- **CSR activities:**
  1. Dedicated budget for CSR activities.
  2. Promotion of government programmes on skill development. Education institute for skill development to be established in each SEZ for upgrading skills of employees.
  3. Promotion of sports/yoga activities under Fit India programme.
  4. Social business projects and cultural activities should be promoted to preserve the local arts and culture.
  5. Dedicated social activities with involvement of members from marginalized community.

II. Fiscal

- SEZs developers may consider listing on National/International Exchanges. This will enable them generate additional revenue for SEZs activities.
- Developers may introduce competitive rebate scheme for timely setting up of units.
- Mechanism for rebate on advance/one time service charges to the units.

III. Non-Fiscal

- Establishment of common R&D centre depending upon the type of industry/product design. Such a common centre will benefit all the units in the SEZ. One outcome could be the designing of innovative or niche products. This would help the units to diversify export markets/segments.
- Convention centre, common meeting room and other infrastructure may be set up.

8.3.3 Relevant to Central/Gujarat/Other State Governments

8.3.3.1 Central Government

I. Administrative

- **SEZs Business Model**: Public-Private Partnership (PPP) business model may be encouraged as the preferred business model for establishing the new SEZs. This model will ease in getting the investments and technology transfer.

- **Administrative Measures**:
  1. Role of Administrative Machinery in SEZs needs review and restructuring.
  2. One strategy could be establishment of office of CHIEF TRADE COMMISSIONER OF INDIA functioning with autonomy. This office can be a catalyst for all investments and business proposals related to exports promotion.
  3. Similar review of role of various Exports Promotion Councils and trade bodies.
  4. Mechanism may be evolved for prompt resolution of SEZ-related issues between two states inter se or between a state and the centre.

- **Digital Reforms**:

Government could usher in reforms through digital platform:

1. "One form one portal": Building of Integrated foreign trade system with single interface for exports or investment covering the whole gamut including trade and investment-related policies and various forms.
2. Creating a dedicated data base of vendors of SEZs supplies.
3. Vacancy, job notification using digital platform. Flowchart of vacancy board is shown in Figure 8.1.

- **Policy reforms/measures**
- FTA/PTA/Bilateral Agreements
  1. Dissemination of information pertaining to bilateral agreements, Free Trade Agreements with various nations, negotiation and progress thereof.
  2. BRICS, BIMSTEC, SAARC initiatives; Group of US, Japan and Australia towards Inclusiveness of Asia Pacific Region nations; Act East Policies (2014); these measures will go a long way in furthering socio-economic growth.
  3. Promotion of investments in other nations to help ramp-up value chain of SEZs segments.
  4. New services FTA may be considered to promote service sector SEZs.

- SUSTAINABLE SEZs (SSEZs)**:** Government may introduce a Sustainable India SEZs Investment plan aimed at digital and "green" public infrastructure. Suitable environmental policies and measures are necessary towards attaining UN's SDG 2030 objectives.

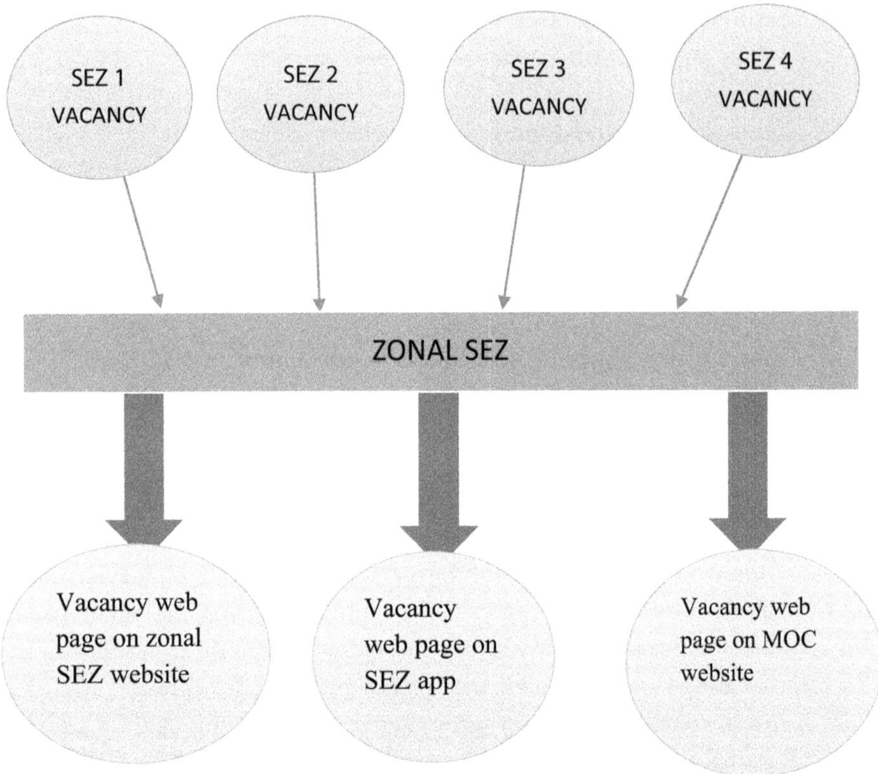

Figure 8.1: Flowchart of Vacancies in State SEZs

- Micro, Small and Medium Enterprises (MSME segment):
- Mission: SEZs may be considered as integral component of country's economic progress; SEZ objectives may be aligned with various government's initiatives, programmes and schemes like Make in India and Start-up/Stand-up schemes for the promotion of the MSME/SME segment.
- Procurement of goods and services by SEZs: Minimum 40 per cent of procurement of goods and services from MSME sector and other vendors belonging to marginalized society like women, SC/ST/OBC, disabled, Ex-servicemen, all situated in domestic area (DTA). This will promote the local domestic industry and address social issues.
- Dedicated SEZs for MSME Category:
  1. MSME clusters could be established in association with state government for exports, for example, Kolhapuri chappals cluster at Kolhapur, Maharashtra; garments cluster at Nagpur, Maharashtra; silver

ornaments cluster at Hupari, District Kolhapur; dry food-processing cluster at Bhavnagar, Gujarat.
2. Setting dedicated MSME centre in every SEZs to cater to the need of SEZs units for their domestic supplies and services from MSME.

- Special SEZs for women/marginalized society:
  The concept of SEZs exclusively for entrepreneurs belonging to the weaker section of society like women or members of marginalized communities (SC/ST/OBC/Disabled/Ex-servicemen) needs to be explored. Such a move will go a long way in women empowerment and push the development of the vulnerable section of society.
- Stimulus Package: In addition to reform of policies and procedures, government may consider a stimulus package for the SEZs units; this is needed to enable the units to have a competitive edge over SEZs outside India, particularly those in the neighbouring countries like Myanmar, Nepal, Pakistan and Sri Lanka.
- Labour Laws: Government may consider amending existing labour laws to make them more industry-friendly.
- Technology Upgradation scheme: A dedicated fund for technology transfer/upgradation in the form of long-term loan at a low rate of interest may be set up; the units could develop State of Art Technology by drawing from such fund.

Operational Measures

- Permission for job work for DTA—Policy may be modified to allow SEZ units to carry out job work with upper cap from domestic area (DTA) to SEZs. This will help in retention of employment and utilization of capacity especially when export orders are less. Concessional rate of duty equivalent to the lowest rate of FTA on DTA sales by SEZ units can give more potential for manpower generation.
- Net Foreign Exchange (NFE) Criterion: NFE criterion is very narrow. More broad-based parameters, such as value addition, innovation, patents filed, social indicators like growth in household incomes, increase in women's participation in the economy and economic indicators such as growth of per capita income, addition to infrastructure, and transport facilities need to be incorporated. Thus, the benefits accrued due to setting up and functioning of a SEZ can be objectively rated as a weighted average of

the above-mentioned factors and other parameters that may be considered relevant.

- Monitoring of each SEZ on quarterly basis instead of present annual system. This should enable the government/authorities to promptly raise red flag and take timely remedial action.

II. Fiscal

- **Ranking of Parameters for Fiscal Incentives**

The government may consider the introduction of four-tier structure of incentives for investors as below:

Tier I—Based on job and investment committed.
Tier II—Based on exports potential.
Tier III—Based on technological up-gradation and HR practices.
Tier IV—Based on minimum mandatory exports with minimum guaranteed procurement of raw material say 40 per cent, and so on from DTA including MSME/SME to protect the domestic segment.

- MAT/DDT: In order that investors regain confidence in SEZs in India, it is necessary to restore the benefits of Minimum Alternative Tax (MAT) and Dividend Distribution Tax (DDT) which have been withdrawn. The Sunset Clause also needs to be withdrawn. Otherwise, introduction/continuation of income tax exemption in some form, grant of incentives distinct from the ones already available under FTAs may be considered to be reinstated.
- National mission to give impetus to economy may include SEZs as one of the tools. Scheme on Capital Incentives for projects (SEZs) finance may be put in place.
- Terms of trade and Real Effective Exchange Rate affect SEZs in a big way. Hence, monetary policies may be geared to protect to the extent possible.
- Formation of Independent SEZ Investment Company Limited (proposed) may be considered.
- Reduction in Charges:
  1. Insurance Premium: Reduction in premium rates for various products of ECGC, which will ease the burden of exporters.
  2. Port Charges/Wharfage Charges/Terminal Handling Charges (THC): There is a need to rationalize these charges maybe for a specific period to reduce the costs for the exporter.

3. Warehousing Costs: The turnaround time at ports/airports is too long resulting in high warehousing costs; this makes exports uncompetitive. Measures for quicker turnaround need to be taken.

III. Non-Fiscal

- Ease of Doing Business: SEZs should take the lead in creating a trade and investor-friendly environment, so that investors particularly overseas investors are attracted by some of the following measures/change in policies and procedures:
- Single Window Mechanism—with the help of technology
- Online Trading and Services
- One-Stop Shop concept
- Investor's protection policy
- Zero tolerance policy on corruption
- Policies on green operation for reduction of e-waste and recycling waste
- Subsidized electricity and land lease charges
- Visa assistance, value-added services, time-bound services
- Recognition of fund structure (e.g. LLP and Trust)
- Formation of autonomous Cluster Fund
- Building training and product development centres within SEZs

Setting of special SEZs courts/tribunals/arbitration for dispute settlement

- Soft skills development: Importance of skill development through:

1. Skill development workshops/program
2. International skill development institutes in non-processing area of SEZs
3. Revival of Industrial Training Institute (ITI)

8.3.3.2 Gujarat State Government

I. Administrative

- New SEZs: Establishment of new SEZs to cover the 25 districts that do not have a single SEZ to reduce regional disparity and to take benefit of the infrastructure, logistics, availability of local skilled manpower and proximity to the ports/airports/rail terminals.

- Dedicated provision and budget to be enhanced and utilized under TIES (trade infrastructure for export scheme) scheme for overall development of trade, infrastructure, exports-related activity and so on.
- Need for administrative reforms for expansion of existing SEZs and new SEZs. The four major areas of action in order of priority are as follows:

1. Institutional and regulatory
2. Infrastructure
3. Non-fiscal intervention
4. Fiscal intervention

8.3.3.3 Other State Governments

State governments need to identify, analyze and evaluate SEZ opportunities by reckoning the parameters:

- Location advantage
- Cluster formation/common R&D facilities, training and skill development centres
- Availability of skilled labour
- Formation of state SEZs (exports) cell

Every state/UT needs to have a dedicated Exports Cell headed by full-time Export Commissioner, who will be responsible for promotion and monitoring of exports from the state, including exports from SEZs. He shall also monitor export-related activities like:

- Research and Development.
- Business Matchmaking Services/Market Intelligence.
- Advertising and public relations.
- Trade fairs and conferences, liaison with embassies and council offices.
- Process/procedures streamlining in export.
- Roles of concerned authorities, implementation of online processes, committees need to be redefined for quick and prompt action.
- Seamless integration of the EDI system.
- Social Enterprises Zones (SoEZ): "Social enterprise" or "Social venture" zones could be developed to assist in the economic development or redevelopment of localities beset with low employment, social problems and limited investment.
- Utilization of Vacant Land in SEZs.

In respect of the vacant land in notified SEZs, some of the measures that could be undertaken to address this issue in Gujarat and other states would be as follows:

- FDI Policy changes: Policies related to FDI may be re-framed to encourage foreign investment in SEZs. This is the route followed successfully by many countries to get the benefit of employment generation and export promotion.
- Marketing Plan: In order to attract firms to set up units in the vacant land in SEZs, it may be necessary to introduce marketing schemes like special discount offer period, dynamic or product-wise, area-wise rates for lease charges. In case of Gujarat, other SEZs may link and get the benefits of Financial Services from IFSC Gift city.
- State industrial policy/SEZ Act**:** States may formulate industry-friendly policies and incentives/subsidy schemes particularly for light industry like textiles, gems and jewellery where women are employed in large number; this will support woman empowerment and gender equality. State SEZs Acts may be amended in line with latest SEZs policies.
- Stimulus Package/Financial Incentives: Special Incentives for developers for promoting infrastructure activities in non-processing areas of SEZs to fulfill social objectives. These measures will help in increase of investment in SEZ and generation of employment while filling the vacant SEZ land.

The researcher built six models and final model analysis predictor-wise for overall socio-economic impact in SEZs. On the basis of the models, a profit and loss statement covering all key elements and drivers for overall socio-economic development in SEZs is prepared. The P&L statement is shown in Table 8.2.

8.3.4 Relevant to Students/Academia/Research Institutions

- The importance of SEZs in the economic development cannot be over emphasized. This research seeks to spur interest for further research in this direction. The academia could review and study in depth the different facets of SEZ operations in the context of their objectives of exports promotion, employment generation, investments and infrastructural development. From this study it emerges that the units do not lay much store in incentives. This is a finding contrary to expectation. Academia could pursue on this line; a benchmarking exercise of the incentives offered by the neighbouring and competitor economies for SEZs. The results would be helpful in policy making.

Table 8.2: Socio-Economic Development in SEZs—Profit and Loss Statement

Sr. No	Models	Key Element
01	**ECONOMIC FACTORS**	• Increase Export • Overall Employment • Increase Foreign exchange • Improve Infrastructure • Improve Demographic pattern • Ease of doing business
	+/-	
02	**SOCIAL FACTORS**	• Minimum Wages • Tackling Social Problems • Promote Marginalized Community • Reduced Community stress • Quality of Life • Women Empowerment • Regional Inequalities
	+/-	
03	**INDIRECT ECONOMIC FACTORS**	• Role of R&D • Labour Issues/Laws • Indirect and induced jobs • Increase in retail expenditure
	=	
	COMBINED SOCIO-ECONOMIC IMPACT	**ADDITIONAL GDP GROWTH**
	+/–	
	Net Cost of/Revenue from zones	• Investments • Income from Zone • Less Subsidies etc. • Operating Costs
	=	
	Financial Viability of Zone	• Stimulus Package • Payback Time of Zone Investment
	+/–	

Table 8.2: *Continued*

Sr. No	Models	Key Element
04	**OTHER LOCAL FACTORS**	• Health Insurance • Pick-Up/Drop Facility • Fire Protection • In-House loan • Medical Room • Women Safety • Education loan
	+/-	
05	**HOUSING FACTORS**	• Non-Processing Area for Housing • Hostel for women • Dormitory • Residential Complex Inside SEZs
	=	
	OVERALL SOCIO-ECONOMIC IMPACT	• Long Term SEZ Transformation • Impetus to Economy • Creation of Manufacturing hub • Job Creation • Improve social/quality of life

- This study will be helpful to validate and to carry out further studies on social drivers and economic drivers independently.
- The study does not involve use of time series data. Academia could compile time series data to study the direct and indirect socio-economic impact of SEZs on the local community.

8.3.5 Managerial Implications

- The production of goods and services in the SEZs caters to the global market and therefore it is necessary to improve processes to produce quality products and services with minimum rejects and competitive cost. Thus, employee empowerment, promotion of workers participation in management, adoption of innovative ideas of employees, implementation of quality programmes, open and transparent communication culture (two-way communication) need to be adapted by the SEZ units.

- In order to obtain high per capita income, stress needs to be given to training and development of the workforce at all levels. The adoption of best HR practices will help in corporate transformation.
- Promotion of Digital Platform: New digital technologies and e-commerce may be embraced for backward and forward supply linkage chain. New technologies like Block Chain Technology may be married to AI and Big Data Analytics for optimal results. Units could adopt Internet of Things (IoT) platform.

9

Research Limitations and Scope for Future Research

The research findings are the result of a regimen of thorough statistical analysis. Ways and measures for improving the socio-economic impact of SEZs in Gujarat and in India in particular are spelt out through model building. The drivers for overall growth of SEZs are identified in order of importance.

Nonetheless, like all research findings, limitations and concerns due to various factors are unavoidable. This chapter details the limitations and gives recommendations for future research.

9.1 Research Limitations

Some of the limitations and concerns are detailed as follows:

- Secondary data for the research study were primarily based on desk-based research from publicly available information sources like company annual reports, academic journals and websites; hence the research findings are subject to the accuracy of such data.
- For the purpose of field research and collection and testing of primary data, responses to the research questions were solicited from units within

six SEZs (three SEZs each, from multiple and sector-specific category). The selection is based on the age of SEZs, activity, cluster-based industries involved in manufacturing and having reasonable units and employees within these sample SEZs.

- Notwithstanding the above, all the 20 operational SEZs in Gujarat have similar nature of operations and therefore have the same issues, same concerns; the IFSC at GIFT, Gandhinagar, is an exception having unique nature of operations. Therefore, the generalization of research findings is based on outsized likenesses among SEZs, rather than the small differences that exist.
- Data available in the public domain is rather limited, and some units in the SEZs take cover of "confidentiality" for not furnishing the information. Nevertheless, information/answers to all the questions in the questionnaire were provided by most of the respondents. A few units skipped some of the questions. Some of the interviewees declined to answer or provide detailed desired information on flimsy grounds. Such gaps were filled by collecting data and information from various public resources such as units, websites, articles and informal interviews.
- As the researcher is part of the authority (Joint Development Commissioner, Ministry of Commerce, Government of India), breaking the ice was a herculean task. The respondents had to be convinced that the data collection exercise was not for monitoring or other activity by the government, but only for academic purpose.
- Six variables were considered to study the impact on socio-economic development, namely, (a) Direct Economic, (b) Indirect/Wider economic/ expenditure, (c) Demographic, (d) Housing, (e) Other local services and (f) Socio-Cultural. These six variables were validated and found to be adequate to build the socio-economic index giving heavier weight to (a), (b) and (e) followed by (d), (f) and least weight to (c). The hierarchy of variables as arrived from the model built and validation thereof is representative of the socio-economic impact of SEZs in Gujarat and should hold good for other states in India.

9.2 Scope for Future Research

This is an empirical study and would be helpful to policy makers in decision making for sustainable growth of SEZs in Gujarat. The study points out the way to the authorities to renew and fulfill SEZs objectives mainly on the front of employment generation and growth of exports and investments.

However, it is desirable to undertake more such empirical studies for a detailed analysis to understand the policy implications.

- Study on SEZ policies and practices in China and other neighbouring countries in the realm of export promotion, emerging areas and re-engineering of existing SEZs in these sectors
- Further, study on SMEs should be conducted with the objective of increasing their involvement with SEZs
- Keeping in view of other emerging global challenges like sustainable goals agenda 2030, the in-depth analysis in terms of the functioning of SEZs requires further research and analysis to be carried out in other areas like Sustainable Development of SEZs, socio-legal, socio-cultural and socio-environmental impact on SEZs in the state of Gujarat as well as in other regions.
- Research can be conducted in different regions outside Gujarat at different time and analysis of data can be done through other statistical techniques.
- Further, the suggested model may be tested across the different sectors, products and services.

Bibliography

Abeywardene, J., De Alwis, R., Jayasena, A., & Jayaweera, S. (1994). Export processing zones in Sri Lanka: Economic impact and social issues (No. 993051693402676). International Labour Organization.

Abreu, S. (2014). The struggle against SEZ in Goa. *Goa 2011: Reviewing and Recovering Fifty Years.*

Agarwal, S., & Levien, M. (2019). Dalits and dispossession: A comparison. *Journal of Contemporary Asia, 50*, 1–27.

Aggarwal, A. (2007). Impact of special economic zones on employment, poverty and human development (No. 194). Working Paper.

Aggarwal, A. (2010a). Economic impacts of SEZs: Theoretical approaches and analysis of newly notified SEZs in India.

Aggarwal, A. (2010b). SEZ-led growth in Taiwan, Korea, and India implementing a successful strategy.

Alkon, M. (2018). Do special economic zones induce developmental spillovers? Evidence from India's states. *World Development, 107*, 396–409.

Anita, N. (2016). Impact of special economic zones on Indian economy. *International Journal of Social Science and Humanities Research, 4*(1), 565–573.

Anuradha, N., & Mahendra, B. (2010). Mangalore SEZ- towards greater economic activity and development of the region. *Institute of Town Planners India Journal, 7*(1), 50–64.

Anwar, M. A. (2014). New modes of industrial manufacturing: India's experience with special economic zones. *Bulletin of Geography. Socio-economic Series, 24*(24), 7–25.

An, T. S., & Kritchanchai, D. (2018, December). Hospital capacity planning for special economic zone in Thailand: A case study in Kanchanaburi province. In 2018 IEEE International

Conference on Industrial Engineering and Engineering Management (IEEM) (pp. 1593–1597). IEEE.

Atta Ramachandrabh. (2003). SEZs and the environment. Economic and Political Weekly, May 17, 2003.

Azhar, A., & Adil, S. (2019). The effects of agglomeration on socio-economic outcomes: A district level panel study of Punjab. *The Pakistan Development Review, 58*(2), 159–176.

Bhattacharya, D. (1998). Export processing zones in Bangladesh: Economic impact and social issues (No. 80). International Labour Organization.

Bhattacharya, D., & Rahman, M. (1999). Female employment under export-propelled industrialization: Prospects for internalizing global opportunities in Bangladesh's apparel sector (No. 10). UNRISD Occasional Paper.

Bhatnagar, V. K., & Shrivastava, S. K. (2009) Special Economic Zones (SEZs)—A study of Tata Motors and Reliance Industries Limited. *Research Link, National Journal, VIII*(5), 64.

Birajdar Shirmant. (2011). A study on special economic zone and their implication on sustainable development. *Indian Streams Research Journal*, I(X), 116–119.

Chakraborty, J., & Basu, P. (2019). Linking industrial hazards and social inequalities: Environmental injustice in Gujarat, India. *International Journal of Environmental Research and Public Health, 16*(1), 42.

Chakraborty, T., Gundimeda, H., & Kathuria, V. (2017). Have the special economic zones succeeded in attracting FDI?—Analysis for India. *Theoretical Economics Letters, 7*(03), 623.

Chandrachud, S., & Gajalakshmi, D. N. (2013, March). The current status of SEZ, India. *IOSR Journal of Business and Management (IOSR-JBM), 9*(5), 18–27.

Chen, X. (1987). Magic and myth of migration: A case study of a special economic zone in China. *Asia-Pacific Population Journal, 2*(3), 57–76.

Cheesman, A. (2012). *Special economic zones & development: Geography and linkages in the Indian EOU scheme*. Development Planning Unit, University College London.

Choudhury, K. R. (2010). Review paper special economic zones in China. *SIES Journal of Management, 7*(1), 114–120.

Cirera, X., & Lakshman, R. W. (2017). The impact of export processing zones on employment, wages and labour conditions in developing countries: Systematic review. *Journal of Development Effectiveness, 9*(3), 344–360.

Comptroller & Auditor General of India. (2014). *CAG performance audit report on special economic zones*. Department of Revenue-Indirect Taxes, New Delhi.

Crane, B., Albrecht, C., Duffin, K. M., & Albrecht, C. (2018). China's special economic zones: An analysis of policy to reduce regional disparities. *Regional Studies, Regional Science, 5*(1), 98–107.

Curran, S., Cook, J., Hampton, K., Clark, C., Yorgey, G., & Anderson, C. L. (2009). The Impacts of Special Economic Zones, Evans School Policy Analysis and Research (EPAR).

Damborsky, M., Wokoun, R., Krejcova, N., & Kaderabkova, B. (2012). Industrial zones–an effective tool of regional development support in transitive economy? Case study: The Czech Republic.

Daniel, D., Dail, F., & Syed, A. (1997). An empirical study of human resourcemanagement policies and practices in foreign-invested enterprises in China: The case of ShenzenSpecial

Economic Zone. *The International Journal of Human Resource Management*, *8*(5), 595–613.

Das, C. (2017). Special economic zone and its impact on LDC (Less Develop Country) economy: A brief review of India.

Davies, R. B., Edwards, T. H., & Mazhikeyev, A. (2018). The impact of special economic zones on electricity intensity of firms. *The Energy Journal*, *39*(Special Issue 1), 5–23.

Davies, R. B., & Mazhikeyev, A. (2019). The impact of special economic zones on exporting behaviour. *Review of Economic Analysis*. *11*(2019), 145–174.

Deepak, S. (2012). Special economic zones in India: Investment, trade, employment generation and impact assessment.

Degtyareva, I., Shalina, O., & Tokareva, G. (2019, January). Use of the mechanism of the priority social and economic development areas in order to accelerate the industrialization of Russian regions. In *2nd International scientific conference on new industrialization: Global, national, regional dimension (SICNI 2018)*. Atlantis Press. Netherlands.

Deni, S., Husain, T., & Abbas, D. (2019). Socio-cultural public response on Morotai Island as special economic zone (KEK) in Indonesia.

Dennis, A. R. (1987). Export processing zones and economic development in Asia: A review and reassessment of a means of promoting growth and jobs. *American Journal of economics and Sociology*, *46*(1), 89–106.

Devadas, V., & Gupta, V. (2011). Planning for special economic zone: A regional perspective. *Institute of Town Planners, India Journal*, *8*(2), 53–58.

Ding, D., Fields, D., & Akhtar, S. (1997). An empirical study of human resource management policies and practices in foreign-invested enterprises in China: The case of Shenzen Special Economic Zone. *International Journal of Human Resource Management*, *8*(5), 595–613.

Druzhinin, A. (2019). The sea factor in the spatial and socio-economic dynamics of today's Russia. *QuaestionesGeographicae*, *38*(2), 91–100.

Ebenstein, A. (2012). Winners and losers of multinational firm entry into developing countries: Evidence from the special economic zones of the People's Republic of China. *Asian Development Review*, *29*(1), 29–56.

Esmaeilpour, M., & Ebrahimi, M. (2015). A study on the impacts of Pars Special Economic Energy Zone on the development process of Kangan city. *European Online Journal of Natural and Social Sciences: Proceedings*, *4*(1(s)), 741.

Frazier, M. (2018). Emergence of a New Hanseatic League: How special economic zones will reshape global governance. *Chapman Law Review*, *21*, 333.

Gopalakrishnan, S. (2007). Negative aspects of special economic zones in China. *Economic and Political Weekly*, *42*, 1492–1494.

Guang, T., Wang, C. H., Yongan, W., Yu, L., & Qishui, C. (2018). Population strategy and economic development in Shantou.

Gupta, K. L. (2016). Study on economic and legal aspects of special economic zones set up in Gujarat under the special economic zones act 2005.

Hakami, M. S. (2012). A study of special economic zones problems and prospects with special reference to Raigad and Pune district.

Huq, I. A. (2008). Twisting the Dragon's tale: India's path to successful SEZs? The answer may lie in China. NUJS Law Review.

Hyun, Y., & Ravi, S. (2017). Evaluating the effect of place-based development policies: Evidence from Indian SEZs.Working Paper.

IBEF – India Brand Equity Foundation. (2012). SEZs' role in Indian manufacturing growth.

Jarosiński, A. K. (2016). The impact of special economic zones on the level of socio-economic changes of polish regions. *Warsaw Forum of Economic Sociology*, *7*, No. *2* (14), 115–137. SzkołaGłównaHandlowa.

Javed, S. H. (2012). Establishing special economic zones in Pakistan: Learning from China's experience.

Jenkins, R., Kennedy, L., Mukhopadhyay, P., & Pradhan, K. C. (2015). Special economic zones in India: Interrogating the nexus of land, development and urbanization. *Environment and Urbanization ASIA*, *6*(1), 1–17.

Jensen, C., & Winiarczyk, M. (2014). Special economic zones–20 years later. Case Research Paper (467).

Kadam, R. N. (2012). A Big Bang of special economic zones (SEZs) on Indian economy: Issues and facts, vol. 2.

Kam, W. P., Wahyuni, S., & Kee, N. K. (2009). Benchmarking survey of establishments in Batam, Bintan and Karimun Special Economic Zone (BBK SEZ). *Survey Report. Asia Competitiveness Institute.*

Khan, K., & Anwar, S. (2017, December). Special economic zones (SEZs) and CPEC: Background, challenges and strategies. In *33rd AGM and conference on redefining prosperity paths in changing global economy: Opportunities and challenge for Pakistan. Islamabad: Pakistan Institute for Development Economics. Accessed February* (Vol. 12, p. 2019).

Khan, N., & Varshney, P. K. (2012). Future prospects of special economic zones in India.

Kinyondo, A., Newman, C., & Tarp, F. (2016). The role and effectiveness of Special Economic Zones in Tanzania (No. 2016/122). WIDER Working Paper.

Kumar, D. U. (2018). Impact of SEZ on inequality: A study of Sri City SEZ in Andhra Pradesh, India. *International Journal of Pure and Applied Mathematics*, *119*(18), 3067–3080.

Kumar, R. S. K. (2008). SEZs in India: Concept, objectives and strategies.

Kumar, V., & Singh, A. (2011, July). Employment and export. *International Referred Research Journal*, *11*(22), 80–81.

Kumari, N., & Dhanju, K. (2017). Export performance and efficiency of special economic zone in Haryana, CASIRJ.

Kumari, B., Tayyab, M., & Rahman, A. (2018). Role of Special Economic Zone (SEZs) in creation of employment, investment and export in India.

Lakshmanan, L. (2009). Evolution of special economic zones and some issues: The Indian experience. RBI.

Leong, A., & Pratap, S. (2011). China's capitalist development and its implications for labour with special reference to the Shenzhen SEZ. Hong Kong: Asia Monitor Resource Centre. www.amrc.org.hk/sites/default/files/SEZ%20and% 20China's% 20Capitalist% 20Development.Pdf.

Luthuli, M. N., & Houghton, J. (2015). Indirect economic impact of special economic zones: An exploration of DubeTrade Port, KZN, in relation to its local stakeholders. Economies of Regions Learning Network.

Madani, D. (1999, Aug). A review of the role and impact of export processing zones.

Maharashtra Economic Development Council (MEDC). (2008, Aug 23). SEZs in India: Major leap forward 5. Maharashtra Economic Development Council (MEDC). PricewaterhouseCoopers (PwC).

Mane, A. B., & Salve, P. S. (2018). Aspects and pitfalls of SEZ on rural economy of Maharashtra.

Menon, S. N., & Mitra, S. K. (2009). Special economic zones: The rationale. *Occasional Paper, 16.*

Moberg, L. (2018). The political economy of special economic zones: Lessons for the United States. *Chapman Law Review, 21*, 407.

More, J. B. (2015). Impact of special economic zone in India. *IRACST—International Journal of Commerce, Business and Management (IJCBM), 4*(1), 873–879.

Mukherjee, A., Deb, S., Deora, S., Goyal, T. M., & Bhardwaj, B. (2015). *Diversifying India's services exports through SEZs: Status, issues and the way forward* (No. 312). Working Paper.

Nair, K. C., Bihari, V., Pangtey, B. S., Pathak, M. K., Fareed, M., Mathur, N., & Srivastava, A. K. (2011). Respiratory health problems associated to infrastructural development among residents living near Special Economic Zone in India. *Clean Technologies and Environmental Policy, 13*(5), 697–702.

Nallathiga, R. (2007). Promoting industrial and regional economic development through special economic zones: The case of NMSEZ. *The Asian Economic Review, 49*(1), 109–124.

Nekolová, J., & Novosák, J. (2014). Location of economic activities in the Ostrava metropolitan area (Czech Republic): Focused on brownfield redevelopment.

Newman, C., & Page, J. M. (2017). *Industrial clusters: The case for special economic zones in Africa* (No. 2017/15). WIDER Working Paper.

Nidheesh, K. B. (2008). Project affected people's views on working of special economic zones in India.

Omar, K., & Stoever, W. (2008). The role of technology and human capital in the EPZ life-cycle. *Transnational Corporations, 17*(1), 135.

Palit, A. (2009). Growth of special economic zones (SEZs) in India: Issues and perspectives. *Journal of Infrastructure Development, 1*(2), 133–152.

Pandit, N. (2014). Special economic zones (SEZS) in India and Gujarat: A policy and performance perspective. *IRJBM–(www. irjbm. org) July-2014-Volume No–VII pages*, 36–49.

Parmar, B. D., & Bhaiya, S. R. (2015). Millennium development goals and re-examine the economic development with special reference to Gujarat. *International Journal for Innovative Research in Multidisciplinary Field, 1*(1), 1–11.

Partha, M. (2009). The promised land of SEZs. *Occasional Paper* (17).

Partha, M., & Pradhan, K. C. (2009). Location of SEZs and policy benefits: What does the data say? *Occasional Paper* (18).

Parwez, S. (2015). Modified labour welfare measures for special economic zone & implications. *The Indian Journal of Industrial Relations, 50*(3), 386–396.

Parwez, S. (2016). A study on special economic zone implicated land acquisition and utilisation. *International Journal of Development and Conflict, 6*(2), 136–153.

Parwez, S. (2018). Enterprising SEZ enclaves and economic development in India.

Paul, S., & Sarma, V. J. (2013). The livelihood effects of industrialization on displaced households: Evidence from Falta Special Economic Zone, West Bengal. ZEW-Centre for European Economic Research Discussion Paper (13–083).

Phyrum, K., Sothy, V., & Horn, K. S. (2007). Social and economic impacts of GMS Southern Economic Corridor on Cambodia. Research and Learning Resource Centre of the Mekong Institute.

Prajapati, H. K. (2016). An empirical study on problems of Sezin India.

Raheem, A. A. (2011). Impact of special economic zone (SEZ) on human development and poverty reduction: An Indian experience. *International Journal of Multidisciplinary Research*, 1(7)., 177–188.

Rao, S. P., & Dr. Usha, P. (2018). Economic empowerment: The changing approach of economic role of women in India.

Razzaque, M. A., Khondker, B. H., & Eusuf, A. (2018). Promoting inclusive growth in Bangladesh through special economic zones.

Remedio, E. M. (1996). Export processing zones in the Philippines: A review of employment, working conditions and labour relations (No. 77). Geneva: International Labour Office.

Rickne, J. (2010). Gender, wages and social security in China's industrial sector (No. 2010: 8). Working Paper.

Romer, P. M. (1993). Two strategies for economic development: Using ideas and producing ideas. Proceedings of the World Bank annual conference on development economics. Washington, DC: World Bank.

Rustidja, E. S., Purnamawati, A., & Setiawati, R. (2017). Investment promotion for community economic development of special economic zone: Study of SEZ Mandalika and Bitung in Indonesia. *European Journal of Economics and Business Studies*, *3*(2), 138–147.

Rzepka, A., & Bujak, M. (2015). The cross-sectional analysis of special economic zones in the age of globalisation. The Krakowska special economic zone (Kraków Technology Park (Ktp))–A case study. *International Journal of Research*, *32*, 32–40.

Sahoo, P. (2015). Time to review the Special Economic Zones Act. *Economic & Political Weekly*, *50*(14), 23.

Sampat, P. (2010). Special economic zones in India: Reconfiguring displacement in a neoliberal order? *City & Society*, *22*(2), 166–182.

Shah, A., Nandani, D., & Joshi, H. (2012). Marginalisation or mainstreaming? Evidence from special economic zones in Gujarat. Gujarat Institute of Development Research.

Sharma, N. K. (2009). Special economic zones: Socio-economic implications. *Economic and Political Weekly*, *44*(20), 18–21.

Shrivastava, A., & Panga, M. (2017). A study on export performance of India with reference to special economic zones. *International Journal of Management*, *VII*, 42–48.

Singala, S., Atmavilas, Y., & Singh, E. (2011, March). Special economic zones in India: Policies, performance and problems. *ASCI Journal of Management*, *40*, 21–59.

Singh, J. (2009). *Labour law and special economic zones in India*. Centre for the Study of Law and Governance, Jawaharlal Nehru University.

Singh, T. D., & Sanjeev, D. (2019). Case study: Assessment of SEZ location impact on business development in Madhya Pradesh, India. *Advances in Management, 12*(2), 23–28.

Sivaramakrishnan, K. C. (2009). Special economic zones: Issues of urban growth and management. *Occasional Paper* (19).

Smith, C. (2003). Living at work: Management control and the dormitory labour system in China. *Asia Pacific Journal of Management, 20*(3), 333–358.

Steenburgen, V., & Javorcik, B. (2017). Analysing the impact of the Kigali special economic zone on firm behaviour. International Growth Centre Policy Working Paper.

Tantri, M. L. (2011). *Special economic zones in India: Are these Enclaves efficient?* Institute for Social and Economic Change.

Tantri, M. L. (2013). *India's SEZ policy: A retrospective analysis.* Institute for Social and Economic Change.

Thabchumpon, N., Middleton, C., & Aung, Z. (2012, July). Development, democracy, and human security in Myanmar: A case study of the Dawei special economic zone. In *International conference on International relations and development (ICIRD)*, Chiangmai University (pp. 26–27).

Walsh, J. (2015, May). The special economic zones of the greater Mekong sub region: Land ownership and social transformation. In *An international academic conference.*

Wei, I. G. (1999). The dynamics of export-processing zones. United Nations Conference on Trade and Development (UNCTAD). Geneva: UNCTAD Discussion Papers.

Wrobel, R. (2014). Ten years of Kaesong Industrial Complex: A brief history of the last economic cooperation project of the Korean peninsula. *Economic and Environmental Studies, 14*(2), 125–148.

Zhiqiqng, L. (2002, Sep). Foreign direct investmentand technology spillover: Evidence from China. *Department of Economics Journal of Comparative Economics, 30*(3), 579–602.

Books

Aggarwal, A. (2012). *Social and economic impact of SEZs in India* (1st ed.). New Delhi: Oxford University Press.

Asher, M. (2014). Gujarat and Punjab, The Entrepreneur's Paradise and the Land of the Farmer.

Power, Policy and Protest, The Politics of India's Special Economic Zones (2014). Oxford University Press, pp. 137–169.

Websites

SEZ in India: http://sezindia.nic.in/

SEEPZ Special Economic Zone: www.seepz.com

Kandla Special Economic Zone: http://www.kasez.com

SEZ Act, 2005: http://www.sezindia.nic.in/SEZ%20Act,%202005.pdf

SEZ Rule, 2006: http://sezindia.nic.in/sez-rules2006.pdf

SEZ Fact Sheet, retrieved from http://www.sezindia.nic.in/about-fsheet.asp

Index

C

E

F

G

H

I

J

M

N

O

S

T

www.ingramcontent.com/pod-product-compliance
Ingram Content Group UK Ltd.
Pitfield, Milton Keynes, MK11 3LW, UK
UKHW021834100926
8556IPUK00004B/344

9 781433 184376